Jewish History

Jewish History

4,000 Years of Accomplishment, Agony, and Survival

Ralph Shapiro

VANTAGE PRESS
New York

FIRST EDITION

All rights reserved, including the right of
reproduction in whole or in part in any form.

Copyright © 2002 by Ralph Shapiro

Published by Vantage Press, Inc.
516 West 34th Street, New York, New York 10001

Manufactured in the United States of America
ISBN: 0-533-13803-5

Library of Congress Catalog Card No.: 00-91275

0 9 8 7 6 5 4 3 2 1

Contents

Prologue   1

Part I: Biblical History
Preface to Part I   5
  1. Torah Period History   7
  2. The Jewish Kingdoms   43
  3. Creation of Rabbinical Judaism   71
  4. The Second Jewish Commonwealth   75
  5. Roman Domination   83
  6. The Development of the Talmud   95
  7. The Muslim World   102

Part II: A History of the Jewish People in Europe
Preface to Part II   109
  1. Initial Jewish Migration to Europe   111
  2. The Medieval Period   113
  3. The Golden Age in Spain   117
  4. Four Centuries of Terror   120
  5. Expulsion and Migration   124
  6. Religious Degeneration   128
  7. Oppression in Poland   132
  8. Oppression in Russia   134
  9. The Age of Jewish Enlightenment   136
10. European Political Liberalism   144
11. Renewed Anti-Semitism   149
12. Birth of Zionism   153
13. Life in the Twentieth Century   156
14. World War I   158
15. Period Between the Two World Wars   163
16. World War II History   169
17. Post World War II History   170
18. Contemporary History   179

Part III: A History of the Jewish People in the United States

Preface to Part III	185
1. Jews Arrive in America	187
2. Jewish Immigration From Germany	191
3. Jewish Immigration From Eastern Europe	193
4. Contributing to the Development of the United States	195
5. Religious Development	214
6. National Communal Organizations	221
7. Zionism in the United States	229
8. Support of the Creation of the State of Israel	233
9. Political Support to the Soviet Jews	237
10. Bigotry Against Jews in the U.S.	242
11. Anti-Semitism in the U.S.	248
12. Contemporary History	252

Part IV: Holocaust History

Preface to Part IV	257
Introduction	259
1. Beginning of the Evil	261
2. Degradation of Jewish Life	264
3. "Final Solution" Planning	272
4. The Final Solution in Action	277
5. Jewish Resistance	288
6. Countries That Resisted Hitler's "Final Solution"	291
7. Vatican's Attitude Toward the Holocaust	293
8. Gentiles Who Saved Jews During the Holocaust	294
9. Grim Statistics	298
10. Liberation	299
11. Survival	306
12. Rehabilitation	310
13. Resettlement	312
14. Nazis Brought to Justice: Nuremberg Trial	315
15. The American Response	320
16. Criticism of the American Response	327
17. Holocaust Deniers	330

Part V: A History of the State of Israel

Preface to Part V	335
Introduction	337
1. Early History	342
2. Israeli Political Scene	349
3. How They Lived	354
4. Two Decades of Disappointments	360
5. World War II Years	365
6. Birth of the State of Israel	368
7. The War of Independence	376
8. Highlights of the First Fifty Years	385
9. Gentile Friends of Israel	410

Part VI: Survival of the Jewish People

Preface to Part VI	417
1. Historical Challenges to Survival	418
2. Road to Survival	424
3. Interdenominational Conflict Challenges	433
4. State of Israel: Vital Haven	434
5. Recent Survivability Evidence	435
6. Jewish Population History	437
7. Hope for the Future	440
Index	441

Jewish History

Prologue

The extremely long history of the Jewish people has been full of accomplishments that left legacies to the Jewish people and to the world in general. In the biblical period, the Torah provided the foundation of Judaism. The "One God" concept captivated the people who looked for a **higher-being** that affected and influenced the lives of everyone. It originally attracted many people to Judaism and later became the basis for Christianity and Muhammadanism. The remarkable biblical Ten Commandments given to Moses serve as the moral and ethical guidelines for most people today. Many of the biblical laws serve as the basis for civil and criminal laws in practice today. The Jewish people's fight for religious freedom and independence that was led by the Maccabees in the second century B.C.E. was the first demonstration of a people's determination to fight for a just cause, enabling poorly armed people to overcome strong, tyrannical rulers. In modern history, Jews have been involved in most movements to liberate and improve Western society.

The history of the Jewish people is short of glory and full of tragedies. Considering all the agony that the Jewish people suffered during their four thousand-year history, including two thousand years in exile, that Judaism was able to survive is "stranger than fiction."

My objective was to create easy-to-read, informative narratives covering this complex and exciting four thousand-year history from a Jewish perspective that would appeal to both Jews and non-Jews who have an interest in biblical, European, American, and Israeli history. I especially wanted to apply this approach in presenting the comprehensive Holocaust history so that younger readers would fully grasp the impact of this tragedy for the Jewish people and remember it.

Part I

Biblical History

A Jewish Perspective

Preface to Part I

Jewish biblical history covers the two thousand years, from Abraham, the father of the Jewish people to the second century of the Common Era, when the Jewish people were expelled from their Holy Land. In addition, two post-biblical period subjects that were influential in perpetuating Judaism have been included. One is a brief summary of the development and content of the Talmud, which has been the prime educational tool for the Jewish people for the past fifteen hundred years. The other explains how Muslim rule over the Mediterranean area countries stimulated the bonding of the dispersed Jewish people.

Except for meager corroborative archeological findings, the only source of the earliest history of the Jewish people is the first five books of the Bible, called the *Torah* in Hebrew. Because the Torah was fundamentally written as a religious document, any attempt to use it as a source of history has to be subjective. There is no uniform view among Jewish theologians regarding whether today's version of the Torah is literally God's spoken word to Moses (revelation at Sinai) or whether it is an adaptation of the original writing by Moses. Traditionalists accept the Moses authorship of the Torah; modernists do not. My approach was to treat events presented in the Torah as historical events, adding some commentaries by noted Jewish theologians to provide a more modern Jewish perspective on these events. The explanations of Torah narrative connections to current traditional Jewish customs and religious practices provide an informative perspective on this portion of biblical history.

There is no disagreement among Jewish theologians of all denominations about the Bible's message—there is a Covenant between the Jewish people and God, and the Jewish people should continue to adhere to the moral, ethical, and judicial code that Moses prescribed in the Bible for the ancient Hebrews. This Mosaic heritage has become the behavioral standard for western civilization, generally referred to as the Judeo-Christian Code of Ethics, with the Ten Commandments as the foundation. The legacies of the major biblical figures will enlighten the reader regarding the Jewish cultural heritage and the Judaic contributions to western society.

This volume starts with brief discussions of the Torah stories of creation, the Garden of Eden, and Noah and the flood that are accompanied with "modern" interpretations offered by leading rabbis many centuries ago. Essentially all the historical events included in the first five books of the Bible are then discussed. Events that took place then have a remarkable impact on current events between Arabs and Jews relating to the establishment of a Palestinian State. The Torah period is followed by the history of the United Jewish Kingdom under the well-known Kings Saul, David, and Solomon and the lesser-known history of the divided kingdoms of Israel and Judah, derived from the biblical books that cover these periods. A section is devoted to the history of the Hebrew Prophets who lived during the latter period. Many of their illustrious quotations are included, providing ready access to the Prophets' profound messages that have endured throughout the ages.

The history continues with the story of the Sage Ezra, who created rabbinical Judaism that replaced the archaic biblical sacrificial system for honoring God, a major step that sustained the Jews as a "people" without a nation. It is followed by the heroism of the Maccabees. They fought the Greeks to win independence and develop a prosperous Jewish nation that fostered the Jewish Diaspora, only to lose its moral purpose and then its independence. The next major sections deal with the development of Christianity and the relationship between Christians and Jews that had lasting consequences to the Jewish people. The biblical history concludes with the Roman destruction of the second Holy Temple in Jerusalem, the Roman expulsion of the Jewish people from Palestine, and the story of the rabbis who took the crucial steps that sustained Judaism during this critical period and long after.

1
Torah Period History

The Torah (meaning to direct or guide; also called the Pentateuch) consisting of the Five Books of Moses, represents the only source of history covering the three Hebrew Patriarchs, Moses, the Exodus from Egypt, and the forty-year wandering in the desert. The Torah is fundamentally a religious document that provides the Judaic moral guide and the basis for the Judaic religious practices. As a cultural-historical document, it differs from historical documents of other cultures of the biblical period in one curious respect. The Torah narratives and those in the follow-up biblical books contain character flaws associated with the major Jewish biblical figures, whereas the historical documents of other cultures are devoid of any negatives when describing their rulers. The venerated Jewish personalities are presented as having normal human frailties.

Before Hebrew History Began

The Creation Story—The opening chapter of the Book of Genesis describes how God created the world including the earth, the animals, and man and woman in six days, and rested on the seventh day. Man was given dominion over all the animals and other creatures.

Descriptions of the world's creation are found in Greek, Roman, and Babylonian literature. There is a major difference between the biblical story of creation and these other versions. The biblical version teaches there is one almighty and good God who created the world—the fundamental principle of Judaism. The other versions describe mainly a world of chaos from which a series of sun, moon, and star gods emerged.

Some rabbis and other Jewish scholars maintain that the biblical creation narrative is consistent with the scientific theory that the world's creation was an evolutionary process. In their view, the current knowledge of evolution actually confirms the Book of Genesis's religious teaching, which describes an orderly development of the universe. They join the renowned medieval Rabbis Rashi and Maimonides who considered the seven-day duration of the creation process described in Genesis to be an allegorical representation of a lengthier evolution process. The Bible describes an orderly evolutionary development of the world—there was a period of darkness followed by light; lifeless matter progressed to vegetable, animal, and man. This Judaic interpretation of the world's evolution differs from the purely scientific view by attributing the world's evolution as being planned and directed by God, whereas the scientific view has no explanation as to how evolution started. Other biblical "creation story" teachings are that man was the primary goal of God's creation and man is closer to God than the other forms of life, being endowed with the capability to know God.

The biblical description of the world's creation continues with "And there was evening and there was morning, one day." Since evening precedes morning in this Godly description of a day, it became the basis for a day in the Jewish calendar starting after sunset of the previous day.

Garden of Eden—The development of mankind is presented in the story of the Garden of Eden that follows the story of the creation of the world. Adam and Eve lived in Eden, the paradise, where life was easy. No work was required, no clothing was necessary, and food was there for the taking except for fruit from the Tree of Knowledge, which God forbade them to eat. After Adam and Eve disobeyed God and ate from the Tree of Knowledge, God forced Adam and Eve to leave the Garden of Eden and sentenced them to live the way mankind lives today—work to obtain food, wear clothing, raise families, and women suffer the pains of childbirth.

The Garden of Eden story offers several messages from a traditional Judaic viewpoint. God tested Adam and Eve to see if they would obey Him. God gave man the freedom of choice to select between good and evil, and God included the evil behavior part of the story so that man would know the difference between good and evil. Having large families is a blessing—it is God's will for mankind.

In a nontraditional Judaic interpretation, the biblical Garden of Eden is an allegorical story intended to describe the growing up of mankind and to convey several Judaic moral and ethical messages. The story prescribes a moral and social relationship between the sexes, advocates monogamous marriage, introduces the concept of sinful behavior and its consequences, and advocates a more severe penalty to the perpetrator of a sin than to those taken in by the sin. Celibacy is described as unnatural and teaches that marriage is the proper relationship between man and woman in an equal partnership. The biblical Tree of Knowledge is a metaphor representing one's conscience that can distinguish between good and evil. The tree of life, denied to Adam after he sinned, represents immortality that was denied to humanity. These lessons apply to all humanity, not just to the Jewish people.

The Biblical Flood—The biblical story of Noah describes a rain lasting forty days, which turned into a flood that lasted one hundred and ten days. Similar flood stories have been found in historical records of other Middle Eastern civilizations. The major difference is that the other flood stories do not convey ethical values as the biblical version does. The rabbis interpreted the biblical flood story to contain several ethical messages.

- Sin is a serious matter; there is a moral and ethical difference between right and wrong.
- Man was endowed with the ability to know right from wrong and with the free will to choose.
- The basis of human society is justice; any society that is devoid of justice deserves to perish.

The credence of the occurrence of a major flood has been strengthened by the archeological evidence of a major flood in Mesopotamia dating back to 4000 B.C.E. Other major floods of lengthy duration, dating back six thousand years, have been discovered in Asia Minor.

Where Hebrew History Began

Fertile Crescent—The early history of the Hebrews took place in an area of the Middle East known as the "Fertile Crescent." This area, relatively flat and fertile with adequate water, was home to both a pastoral and a highly cultivated urban society. It is located in the midst of surrounding desert and mountainous areas. It stretches from the Persian Gulf, through Syria and Israel, to the upper Nile area of Egypt.

Abraham grew up in the city of Ur, in northeastern Babylonia (also called Mesopotamia, now Iraq). He first lived with his family in Haran, which was in western Babylonia (now Syria). Abraham moved to Canaan (now Israel) but went to Egypt in periods of drought in Canaan. Jacob and his family migrated to Upper Egypt, which is the southwestern part of the crescent. It is the area where Moses lived, and it is the location of the biblical Exodus story.

Mesopotamia—The most fertile area within the Fertile Crescent was Mesopotamia (Greek for "*between the two rivers*"), which lay between the Tigris and Euphrates rivers. This area was the home of three highly developed civilizations, the Sumerians, Akkadians, and Babylonians. There were many city-state political areas ruled by kings, and dominated by different cultures at various times. These societies were very advanced, supporting all forms of commerce and capable of building complex and large structures. Archeologists have found remnants of buildings with construction techniques similar to the biblical Tower of Babylon.

These civilizations acquired sophisticated capabilities in arts and crafts and developed one of the earliest writing techniques, known as cuneiform, which is a complex word/expression vocabulary and numbering system. The Sumerians left the earliest detailed records of a civilization that has been discovered to date, going back 6,000 years. This coincides closely with the start of the Jewish calendar that was established by the sages during the rabbinical period, approximately 200 B.C.E. The start of the Hebrew calendar represented their estimate of the start of civilization.

Social groups in that period had various religions centered on ornate temples, with beliefs in multiple gods related to the air, sun, and sky. Sacrifices to the gods were common, including human sacrifice. Some religious groups engaged in immoral acts as a part of their religious rituals.

Canaan—The area first settled by the early Hebrews was the western, more fertile part of the present day Israel, called Canaan. However, the nearby deserts affected the climate so that the area had periodic dry spells—the reason for the Patriarchs to leave Canaan, as described in the Bible. Canaan was important to the larger neighboring countries because it contained the international trade highway that connected Egypt to Mesopotamia. Because of this importance, Egypt and the Mesopotamia periodically fought for control of Canaan.

The Patriarchs (ca. 1800–1600 B.C.E.)

The Patriarchs (founders) of the Hebrews are Abraham, his son Isaac, and his grandson Jacob. We know of them only from the Bible stories and from the Talmud's rabbinical stories that embellished upon the biblical Patriarch narratives. Abraham, the *"father of the Jewish people,"* established the concept of *"one God"* at a time when all societies worshiped multiple gods or idols. This monotheism concept became the foundation of the Hebrew religion and, later, Christianity and Muhammadanism.

In a biblical story involving his nephew Lot, Abraham is referred to as *"Abram the Ivree."* Ivree became translated as *"Hebrew."* This is the first known use of the name Hebrew for Abraham and his descendants. Abraham made many converts to the fundamental Hebrew faith, which was the belief in one God and adherence to ethical and moral values. These converts were Semites, a class of Caucasians that originated in Arabia and migrated to Sumer and Canaan. Based on this biblical history, historians include Hebrews in the *Semitic* group of people.

Abraham—The Bible and Talmud tell of Abraham growing up in the Chaldean city of Ur, where he was exposed to the Babylonian lifestyle. Abraham became upset by the pagan form of religion practiced in Ur and was unhappy with the Babylonian immoral behavior and lack of purpose. God instructed Abraham to leave his country and family to live in a land not tarnished by evil. God promised to bless Abraham, from whom a great nation will follow, and bless everyone that followed Abraham's good ways. In turn, Abraham set out to be a blessing to humanity by his godly lifestyle and by turning others toward his God.

To escape from the Babylonian social and religious environment, Abraham became a shepherd, migrating throughout Canaan to find pastures for his flock. Occasionally he ventured into Egypt to escape the droughts that were common to lower Canaan. In these wanderings, Abraham apparently persuaded many of the mostly nomadic people living in Canaan to accept his view about there being one God for all people. Abraham's message to them was ***God is good and just,*** and to live in God's image, ***people need to be good and just.***

As expected for one of its most important personalities, the Bible generally extols Abraham's character, presenting him as a noble and virtuous character who stood for justice and practiced loving kindness and truth to his fellow man. Oddly, two incidents are described in the Bible that blemishes Abraham's character. This negative image of its "hero" is most unusual for a religious book or for an ancient history book. In one story, Pharaoh's soldiers captured Abraham and Sarah. Abraham did not attempt to protect Sarah from Pharaoh's advances but instructed his wife to lie to Pharaoh in order to save his own life. A similar pattern of lying is described in another incident when Canaanite King Abimelech confronted

Abraham and Sarah and took Sarah into his harem. The purpose of these stories was to convey a message that was as appropriate then as it is today. **"Even the noblest are not always without sin."**

The Covenant With God—Abraham was ninety years old when he entered into a Covenant with God. God's role in the Covenant was to ensure that Abraham's family would multiply and become a great nation. God also promised the land of Canaan as an everlasting possession to Abraham and his descendants. This is the basis of the Jewish claim to Palestine as the Land of Israel. To fulfill the Covenant, Abraham and his descendants were to work towards bringing all the peoples of the world to be under the one God. Abraham agreed to accept the rite of circumcision (*bris*) of all Hebrew males as the sign of the Covenant. This is so important a ritual in Judaism that, except in the case of illness, it is performed on the prescribed eighth day after birth regardless of whether it falls on a religious holiday. The Torah and rabbinical commentaries in the Talmud fail to explain why the ritual is conducted eight days after birth. However, modern medical science has provided an understanding of the merit to its timing. It takes eight days for the blood factor that coagulates and clots blood to mature; the *bris* timing turned out to be for the infant's safety.

As part of the Covenant with Abraham, God changed Abraham's original name, Abram, to Abraham. Abraham means *"father of a multitude of nations,"*—emphasizing Abraham's role of bringing all the peoples of the world to worship God. It became a Jewish tradition to take names that have a philosophical meaning.

To fulfill his promise that Abraham's seed will grow, God indicated that Abraham's wife Sarah, despite her old age, would bear a son, to be called Isaac, and the Covenant with Abraham would be extended to Isaac. God changed Sarah's original name, Sarai, to Sarah, meaning *"princess,"* and blessed Sarah with the promise that she will be the mother of a great nation.

Sodom and Gomorrah—God instructed Abraham to leave his home in Babylon to live in the land of Canaan. Abraham took his nephew Lot with him. For years, they traveled together as shepherds successfully raising their own flocks. When a conflict arose between the two over scarce water, they separated. Lot decided to remain in Sodom, which is near the Dead Sea in Israel; the area normally had rich pastures. Abraham chose to get far away from the city of Sodom, which had a corrupt lifestyle, and went to the unblemished western Canaan area.

Years later, Abraham learned of God's intention to destroy all the people in the wicked cities of Sodom and Gomorrah, whether they were good or bad. Abraham argued with God for justice. He argued that *"the good people should be spared according to God's own rules of justice."* This story brought out Abraham's noble character. Abraham undertook to argue with God for the sake of justice for people he did not know, because he felt anguish over good people being killed without just cause. God was willing to spare the good people in Sodom and Gomorrah but none could be found. God destroyed the two cities with "fire and brimstone."

God spared Lot and his daughters as a favor to Abraham. Lot's wife was also to be spared, but she did not heed God's warning not to look back, and she perished, turning into a pillar of salt. No physical trace of Sodom and Gomorrah has been found to date. However, geologists speculate that these two cities were buried under the shallow portion of the Dead Sea after an earthquake. Archeologists have determined that a volcanic eruption occurred in Abraham's time frame, probably the source of the fire and brimstone quoted in the Bible. Interestingly, there are large salt rocks shaped like pillars in evidence in the hills above the Dead Sea that resemble the salt pillar that Lot's wife turned into as described in the Bible.

Abraham's Son Ishmael, Forebearer of the Muslims—God told Abraham that his yet-to-be-born son Isaac would carry on the promise of the Covenant. In this conversation, Abraham expressed concern over his thirteen-year-old son Ishmael, born to Sarah's handmaid Hagar, who seemed to be left out of God's Covenant promises. God comforted Abraham with the promise that Ishmael would have twelve sons who would carry on to make Ishmael the forebearer of a great nation. The Bible later lists the twelve sons by name; these names are similar to names of extinct small countries found in Middle Eastern historical data. Based on these biblical statements, Muhammad, the founder of the Islamic religion, connected Arab lineage to Ishmael and his father Abraham.

The Sacrifice of Isaac—One of the most famous Bible stories is that of God testing Abraham's willingness to proceed with God's instructions to sacrifice his son Isaac. Abraham apparently was willing to slay his son Isaac even though God previously destined Isaac to be the one to inherit the Covenant with Abraham. God called off the slaying at the last moment, after Abraham demonstrated his complete obedience to God. This message of complete submission to God served as an example of martyrdom that was exhibited by many Jews later in history.

This *Akeda* ("binding") story was a message to the early Hebrews that God was opposed to sacrificing humans in his honor, which was why God stopped the sacrifice of Isaac. For a god to intercede to stop the sacrifice of a child was unusual for that period. Religious rituals involving the sacrifice of children was common among the Semitic peoples, Egyptians, and other Middle East peoples. The *Akeda* story was a message to guide the behavior of future Hebrews—they should not indulge in child sacrifice, and they should fight to have other people end that savage practice. Centuries later, the Hebrew Prophets took on this battle to end child sacrifice when forms of idolatry started to reappear among the Jewish people.

Many rabbis have analyzed the choice of words and details in this provocative *Akeda* story. Their conclusions vary:

- God never intended for Isaac to be sacrificed.
- Abraham was testing God to see if God was just.
- Isaac was not a small youth; he carried the firewood on his back to the Akeda site.
- Sarah pleaded with God to stop the sacrifice of her favorite son.
- Sarah was angry with Abraham over this incident and left him; Sarah is not included in the concluding remarks of the Akeda story that describes Abraham dwelling in Beersheba. The next chapter tells of Sarah dying in Hebron and of Abraham coming to mourn her.

Mount Moriah: Holy to Jews—Jewish tradition identifies Mount Moriah in Jerusalem as the place where Abraham took Isaac to be sacrificed. The Bible indicates that King David brought the Ark of the Covenant to Mount Moriah and King Solomon built the first Hebrew Holy Temple over that site to venerate the site. The Temple was the center of religious activity before it was destroyed by the Babylonians four hundred years later. Mount Moriah, which remained holy even without a temple, became the site of a replacement Holy Temple seventy years later. The Romans destroyed the second Holy Temple in 70 C.E., and all that remains today is a retaining wall of the mount on which the temple stood.

After the Temple was destroyed, the remaining wall became the focus of Jewish prayer and aspiration. For the next two thousand years, when the dispersed Jewish people were oppressed and full of despair, the Wall was there to signify that God had not forsaken his people and that the ultimate redemption that they prayed for would come. The Jewish people originally called it *"Kotel Ha-ma'arivi"* (the "Western Wall"). Because Jews praying at the site offered mournful prayers for God's help, it became known in the English-speaking world as the "Wailing Wall." With the Western Wall accessible to the Jewish people again, its name has reverted to simply, the *"Kotel"* ("wall").

There were several periods when Jews were not allowed access to the Kotel. After the Bar Kochba rebellion in the second century, the Romans and, later, Christian rulers did not permit Jews to enter Jerusalem. Most Muslim rulers who followed the early Palestinian Christian rule permitted Jews to live in Jerusalem with unlimited access to the Kotel. However, several intolerant Muslim rulers only permitted access to the Kotel on Tisha B'Av (the ninth day of the Hebrew calendar month of Av), which is the day commemorating the destruction of both Holy Temples. The situation turned drastically with the First Crusade. The Crusaders slaughtered the entire Jewish population in Jerusalem along with thousands of Arabs in 1099. Jews were able to return to Jerusalem and allowed access to the Western Wall only after the Arabs took back control of Palestine in 1187. Access to the Wall was lost during the period between the War of Independence in 1948 and the Six-Day War in 1967, when Jordan controlled the old section of Jerusalem where the Kotel is located. Jews in Israel and around the world were overjoyed when the state of Israel took control of the old section of Jerusalem and the Kotel was again accessible to the Jewish people.

Mount Moriah: Holy to Muslims—The Muslim interest in Mount Moriah derives from Muhammad's belief that Abraham was the Patriarch of the Arab people as well as to the Hebrews. Muhammad accepted the Hebrew Bible as being holy to Muslims because of this relationship.

In 690 C.E., Caliph Abd al-Malik built the Dome of the Rock on Mount Moriah as a magnificent Arab monument. It was to compete with the other glorious Arab monuments around the world built for the admiration of the new Muslim people. The Dome of the Rock was built over a large rock found on Mount Moriah, which had no theological significance at that time. Years later, the Muslim legend was developed that told of Muhammad leaving Mecca mounted on a winged horse, flying to Mount Moriah, and then flying to heaven from that rock on Mount Moriah. From then on, the Dome of the Rock became an Islamic spiritual center. After being desecrated with crosses by the Crusaders, damaged by an earthquake, and experiencing deterioration with age, the gold dome and the interior were refurbished before achieving its present magnificence.

The Al-Aqsa Mosque, located at the other end of the Temple Mount, was built by the first Arab ruler of Palestine to give the Muslims a house of prayer in Jerusalem. It was located on the Temple Mount in order to be away from the churches and other Christian buildings throughout Jerusalem. It was desecrated and occupied for a hundred years by the Crusaders. The Crusaders, who held the rank of "knight," converted the Mosque to living quarters, which gave rise to their name, *"Templar Knights."* It was restored as a Mosque when the Arabs retook Jerusalem. After years of decay, it underwent restoration in the seventeenth century and became the major Muslim holy institution in Palestine.

Mount Moriah, A Political Issue—For fifteen hundred years, when the Muslims were in control of Mount Moriah, the Arab rulers determined Jewish access rights to the Mount and to the Mount's Western Wall which was holy to the Jewish people. Having no political stature anywhere in the world, the Jewish people had no opportunity to protest the denial of their access. This situation changed when the state of Israel defeated Jordan in the 1967 Six-Day War and the Israelis took control of Jerusalem and Mount Moriah and the Western Wall. The Arabs became the ones whose access rights to their religious buildings on the Mount were in jeopardy. Ultra-Orthodox Jews who would not recognize the state of Israel until the Holy Temple was rebuilt urged the victorious Israeli government to destroy the Dome of the Rock and the Al-Aqsa Mosque to make room for a rebuilt Holy Temple. They justified their request to destroy religious buildings on the past behavior of the Muslims and Christians, indicating that when the Jordanians took control of Jerusalem in 1948, the Arabs desecrated and destroyed Jewish religious buildings and cemeteries in the old Jewish quarter of Jerusalem. They referred to the desecration of the two Muslim holy places on Mount Moriah when the Christian Crusaders occupied Jerusalem and to the Arab desecration of churches in Jerusalem after the Arabs won back control of Jerusalem during the Crusade period. The Israeli government quickly turned down this proposition to destroy the Muslim holy buildings on the Mount.

In recent years, secular archeologists have been interested in digging under Mount Moriah in search of remnants of the original Temple buried twenty feet under the debris that accumulated on top of the Mount before the Arabs built their holy edifices. This is one area where there is agreement between the Muslims and the Orthodox Jews. They both oppose this archeological exploration as being sacrilegious.

Abraham's Legacy to Western Civilization—Abraham's concept that there is *one God* represents the basis of the three major religions of the Western world, Judaism, Christianity, and Islam.

Abraham had this universal view of God:

- God created the world.
- He is the God of all the people of the world.
- People must have faith in God, believing in his goodness and justness and accepting his decisions.

Abraham's Legacy to Judaism—Abraham left this special legacy to the Jewish people through his Covenant with God:

- To continue to receive God's blessing, the Jewish people must live righteously, with justice for all.
- It is the duty of all Jews to transmit the Jewish heritage to their children.
- All males are to receive the rite of circumcision as an eternal symbol of the devotion of the children of Israel to the God of Abraham. The circumcision is the sign of the Covenant between God and the Jewish people—it has been the fundamental element of the Jewish faith through the ages.
- It is the obligation of the Jewish people to teach the message of God's way to the rest of the world.

The Legacy of Sarah's Burial—The Bible tells of Sarah dying in Hebron and Abraham coming to mourn and bury her. Abraham preferred to bury Sarah rather than cremate her, as was the common custom in that period. He also had a reverential concern for having a proper burial for her and finding a satisfactory burial place. These gave rise to four Judaic practices associated with the death of a family member: taking proper care of the dead body; providing a respectful funeral; burying the dead in a sacred cemetery; and observing a mourning period.

Cave of Machpelah: Holy to Jews and Muslims—Abraham sought a place to bury his wife Sarah, who died in Hebron. He selected and bought a cave in Machpelah, near Hebron, that would serve as a family burial ground. Abraham buried Sarah in this "Cave of Machpelah," which became the burial vault for the three Patriarchs and their wives. It became a Jewish holy place, second in importance to the Kotel, where pious Jews went to pray close to the founders of the Jewish people.

Muhammad taught his followers that Abraham was also the Patriarch of the Arab people through Abraham's son Ishmael. As the Muslim religious practice grew, they learned to venerate the Cave of Machpelah, where Abraham was buried, and built a mosque over the Cave in the eighth century. The Muslims allowed Jews to pray in the Cave until 1267, when access was denied to Jews except for a privileged few. This condition lasted for the next seven hundred-year period until after the Six-Day War.

Jacob—Abraham was the father of the Hebrew religion. His grandson Jacob was the father of the twelve tribes of Israel, the source of the Jewish people.

Rebekah, the wife of Abraham's son Isaac bore twins. Esau was the firstborn and Jacob was the younger one. Jacob was determined to receive the firstborn birthright benefit that was traditional in that period. As a youngster, he bought the birthright from his older brother. Later, at his father's deathbed, he conspired with his mother to receive his father's blessing to carry on the mission of Abraham, which was to go to Esau, the first born. His mother preferred Jacob for the birthright role because she felt Esau, being a hunter, did not have the required sensitivity and understanding to carry on God's mission. This stolen birthright blessing and the earlier birthright sale infuriated Esau, who threatened to kill Jacob. Jacob had to flee for his safety.

Jacob is portrayed in the Bible as a person who learned to be humble and respectful to people after his harsh and sometimes sinful experiences earlier in his life. He personified the rabbinical statement that "a repentant sinner comes nearer to God than one that never stumbled or sinned." He is described as a believer in God's capability to affect his life, as indicated in the "Jacob's dream and ladder to heaven" biblical narrative. In the dream, as he prepared to go to sleep, Jacob prayed for Divine protection—attributed in the Talmud as having instituted Judaism's daily Evening Prayer service.

Jacob's Wives—Isaac told his son Jacob to find a wife among his father's people rather than in Canaan. Jacob sought out his uncle Laban, who lived in Haran, where Abraham had lived. He ended up with Laban's two daughters as his wives. Jacob had wanted the younger daughter, Rachel, for his wife and agreed to work for Laban for seven years before Rachel could become his wife. Just as Jacob tricked his father Isaac for the firstborn birthright blessing, Laban tricked Jacob, giving him the firstborn daughter, Leah, instead of Rachel. Jacob had to work for Laban seven more years before Rachel could become his bride.

Rachel's Tomb—Rachel gave birth to Joseph and died after giving birth to Benjamin while the family was passing through Bethlehem. Jacob placed a tombstone there. The Jewish tradition of placing a tombstone on the grave is thought to go back to this event. Jews now venerate Rachel's tomb in Bethlehem as a holy place.

Jacob Becomes Israel—When Jacob finally returned to his homeland, he feared for his safety when he would meet his brother Esau, even though twenty years elapsed since he last saw him. Jacob prayed for forgiveness and for protection from Esau. In what has been viewed by rabbis to be either a prophetic vision or symbolic of Jacob's inner struggle of right versus wrong in his dealings with his brother, the Bible tells of a meeting between Jacob and God's messenger. It describes Jacob wrestling with God's messenger until Jacob received the blessing he was after. Because Jacob had the courage to fight God's messenger and prevailed, the messenger told Jacob that he should be called Israel (*"wrestling with God"*).

The biblical narrative of Jacob wrestling with God's messenger ended with Jacob hurting his thigh. The story included the injunction not to eat the "sinew of the thigh-vein" (*sciatic nerve*). This became a required step in preparing an animal to be kosher; the sciatic nerve, arteries, and tendons must first be removed. Because of the difficulty in removing the sciatic nerve from a cow, the rear quarters of a cow are not considered acceptable as kosher food.

Jacob's Sons and Grandsons: The Twelve Tribes of Israel—Jacob had twelve sons in total, six by Leah, two by Rachel, and two each by the handmaiden of each wife. Joseph was the elder son and Benjamin was the younger son by his favorite wife, Rachel.

During the Exodus, the Hebrews were organized in tribes according to the children's names. This stemmed from the blessing Jacob gave each child when on his deathbed. He characterized each son's behavior, foretold what fate was in store for their descendants, and where each tribe would be located when they got back to the Promised Land. The future role of the tribe of Judah was the brightest. Judah would lead the battle to conquer the Canaan and would be the king over the other tribes. (King David was from the tribe of Judah.) Because of the cruel behavior in avenging the dishonoring of his sister Dinah, the Levi tribe was to be scattered throughout Israel, and was dropped from the tribal count. After the exodus from Egypt, the Levi tribe became assistants to the priests and did not have a specific geographic location in Israel. Jacob gave his favorite son, Joseph, special treatment, accepting as his own sons the two sons of Joseph, who were born and raised in Egypt, Ephraim and Manasseh. He blessed their future because they were willing to give up their aristocratic Egyptian position and identify themselves with their simple, nomadic Jewish family, alien to

Egypt. (Jacob's blessing, "God make thee as Ehpraim and Manasseh" is the standard Conservative and Orthodox blessing offered to boys.) Ehpraim and Manasseh replaced Joseph in the tribal count, accounting for the twelve tribes of Israel. Archeological evidence has been found confirming the existence of the twelve tribes in essentially the locations described in the Bible.

Jacob's Daughter—Jacob's daughter, Dinah, is the subject of the one tale in the Bible that departs from the peaceful narratives of the Patriarchs' lives. The son of a local chieftain had dishonored Dinah. In cruel revenge, two of Dinah's brothers, Levi and Simeon, indiscriminately slaughtered all the men in the chieftain's city instead of attacking the person that was responsible for the attack on Dinah. It was particularly heinous because the brothers had entered a peaceful arrangement with the victims that set them up for the slaughter. Jacob later chastised Levi and Simeon for their sinful behavior when he blessed all his sons just before he died.

Jacob's Last Years—Jacob spent his last twelve years in Egypt under the protection of his son Joseph who had achieved a high position in the Pharaoh's organization. Jacob requested that he be buried in the Cave of Machpelah with his parents and grandparents. The rabbis interpreted this request as encouragement to Jacob's descendants to ultimately go back to the Promised Land. In the Middle Ages when living in Palestine was a hardship and traveling to Palestine was a risk, some rabbis and wealthy pious Jews struggled to get to Palestine in order to live out their last years in the Jewish homeland; some arranged to be buried there on sacred ground.

Joseph and His Brothers—Joseph was his father's favorite. At seventeen, although younger than his brothers, he ordered his brothers around. He wore a multicolored garment that, in those days, was a symbol of authority to the Semitic tribes. Joseph, the *dreamer,* told his brothers that he had visions of his brothers bowing down to him. These actions caused his brothers to be both envious and bitter. It led to Joseph's brothers putting him into a pit from which he was discovered by passing merchants who sold him to nomad Ishmaelites. They took Joseph to Egypt and sold him to an Egyptian army officer. Joseph's family lost contact with him until Joseph brought his family to Egypt years later.

Joseph the Vizier—The Bible describes how Joseph went through two turbulent years in Egyptian captivity until he got an opportunity to interpret Pharaoh's dreams. He warned Pharaoh to store grain during the seven years of plenty in order to protect against a seven-year drought that was to come. In appreciation of this sage advice that Pharaoh attributed to Joseph's God, Pharaoh appointed Joseph as the grand vizier, the highest government position. It was in this capacity that Joseph was able to authorize his family's right to live in Egypt.

The Bible describes Pharaoh having Joseph ride in the chariot behind him, the position of second in command. This biblical description of how Joseph was elevated to the viceroy position exactly matches a description of such a ceremony depicted in an Egyptian mural. The chariot position-of-stature described in the Bible indicates that the Bible's author had an accurate knowledge of the Egyptian customs of the patriarchal period. This knowledge is in evidence in many other biblical narratives of the lives of the Hebrews in Egypt.

Joseph's Historical Role—Joseph's role in Jewish history was to bring Jacob's family to Egypt, which led to the Hebrews' four-hundred-year stay in Egypt before the Exodus led by Moses. Before Joseph died, he asked to be buried in the land of his father and was embalmed in order to preserve his body for a future burial in Canaan. Moses took Joseph's corpse with him during the long Exodus wandering, and Joshua buried Joseph in the city of Shechem after the Hebrews entered Canaan at the end of the Exodus. Shechem was where Joseph's father, Jacob, bought the first plot of land in Canaan as Jewish property.

Migration to Egypt (ca. 1600 B.C.E.)

The Bible covers the periods when Joseph lived in Egypt and when the exodus from Egypt occurred; the approximate three hundred years in between are omitted. Egyptian historical records are normally very detailed and chronologically complete. However, the period when the Hebrews were in Egypt is also omitted from Egyptian historical data. This is attributed to the uniqueness of this period. From 1750 to 1560 B.C.E., Egypt was ruled by the Hyksos who were not Egyptian. The Hyksos used a new military capability in battle against the Egyptians, horses and horse-drawn chariots, which enabled them to defeat the more numerous Egyptians. After the Egyptians wrested control back from the Hyksos, the Egyptians apparently eliminated all Egyptian records of the Hyksos period; the Egyptians considered the Hyksos as hated foreigners. With the absence of true historical data, confirmation of the Hebrew presence in Egypt rests on some sparse Egyptian archeological findings and on inferences based on the knowledge of history during that time period obtained from non-Egyptian sources.

Corroboration of Biblical Events—There are many historical conditions that support the authenticity of the relationships and events described in the Bible.

Egyptians were farmers who frowned on cattle raising; they had no use for the good grazing land in Goshen. Therefore, they had no strong reason for objecting to Jacob and his extended family living as shepherds in Goshen to escape the famine in Canaan.

The Hyksos rulers of Egypt came from Arabia. As nomadic people, they were likely to be sympathetic to the nomadic Hebrew shepherds in Goshen.

During the one-hundred-fifty-year period when the Hyksos conquered and ruled Canaan and Syria, there were no revolts against Egyptian rule recorded in those lands—a remarkable period of political quietness for that area when under subjugation by foreigners. When the Egyptian Pharaohs replaced the Hyksos rulers, revolts erupted.

There are Egyptian historical records of periods of famine, and there is evidence of ancient granary storage areas. They resemble the biblical descriptions of famine and the granaries in Joseph's plan to store corn to be used in time of famine.

The Hyksos rulers of Egypt who were not as cultivated as the predecessor Egyptian Pharaohs had no interest in building large monuments. As soon as Egyptian Pharaohs ruled Egypt again, the building of large monuments resumed. The foreigner Hebrews would have been a logical source for the large number of slave laborers required for the massive construction projects because of their earlier support of the Hyksos who were hated by the Pharaohs and the Egyptian people.

The favorable treatment the Hyksos rulers gave to the Semite Hebrews may have applied to other Semites in Canaan. If so, they too would have been allowed to enter Egypt in times of famine similar to what drove Jacob and his family to migrate to Egypt. These other Semites most likely also became slaves after the Hyksos rule ended. Under these conditions, they would have taken the opportunity to join the Hebrew Exodus in order to flee from their own bondage—they could have been the Exodus caravan's rebellious people who did not accept the Hebrew God that is described in the biblical Exodus story.

Unfavorable Conditions in Egypt—The Book of Genesis ends with the death of Joseph, and the Book of Exodus starts with "now there arose a new king over Egypt who knew not Joseph." This reflects what actually happened in Egypt. The Hyksos were overthrown and those allied with them lost favor. The Bible indicates that the good Joseph did for the Egyptians was quickly forgotten.

The new rulers of Egypt, the Pharaohs of the eighteenth dynasty, invaded and conquered Canaan and parts of Syria. Rebellions against Egyptian rule erupted there and had an impact on the Hebrews living in Egypt. In reaction to these rebellions, the Egyptians became concerned about an invasion from Canaan. Consequently, the Egyptians started to doubt the loyalty of the Hebrews in Egypt who were originally from Canaan. The hostile Egyptian attitude and concern was magnified by the fact that the Hebrews lived in Goshen, which was between the populated area of Egypt and Canaan. The Bible attributes anti-Semitic remarks to Pharaoh that resemble contemporary anti-Semitic remarks. "There are too many Hebrews." "They are too powerful." "They are likely to be disloyal." These false accusations stirred up Egyptian hatred of the Hebrews.

Ramses II (1301–1234 B.C.E.) was likely the Pharaoh who oppressed the Hebrews the severest. At the beginning of his long reign of sixty-seven years, Ramses initiated the most aggressive Egyptian monument-building program, for which he is most famous. It is most likely that Hebrews and other foreigners were put to forced labor (slave labor), building large granaries and storehouses in Pithom, which is located close to Goshen, where the Hebrews were concentrated. Slave labor also built a large number of temples and public buildings in the city of Ramses, which is at the mouth of the Nile delta not far from Goshen. Ramses also built large temple structures in many places along the Nile River that required slave labor.

Although there is no historical evidence connecting Hebrews to pyramid building, there is reason to believe that the Hebrews were used to build the pyramids as well as the monuments. Pyramid building, which had ceased when the Hyksos ruled Egypt, was resumed when the Hyksos were overthrown. This building activity occurred at the same time that the Egyptians turned hostile towards the Hebrews.

Murals have been found at sites near the Ramses construction areas that depict different cultural types working as slave laborers, including some identified as having Semitic characteristics. Parchment and stone-monument archeological findings of that period contain statements similar to some of the biblical narratives. The Egyptian word for Hebrew has been found in these records.

Moses (ca. 1310–1190 B.C.E.)

There is no historical record of Moses other than what is told in the Bible. Egyptian historians would have skipped over this segment of Egyptian history that included Moses and the Exodus just as they skipped over the entire Hyksos period in Egypt. This is especially true since the Exodus was a defeat for the Egyptians.

Moses was selected by God to convince Pharaoh to allow the Hebrews out of Egypt. After the Exodus, Moses led the Hebrews through the Sinai wilderness for forty years before God allowed them to enter Canaan, God's "Promised Land to the Hebrews." During the Exodus, Moses interacted with God to establish the future of the Hebrews through the Covenant with God and to obtain the Torah.

The Background of Moses—Moses ("Mosheh" in Hebrew) is the anglicized version of an Egyptian name Maose ("boy son") found in hieroglyphic records of that period. He was the great grandson of Levi, who was the son of the Patriarch Jacob.

Moses was born in the bitterest of years of the Egyptian oppression. Pharaoh started an effort to exterminate the Hebrews after forcing the Hebrews into slavery failed to stop their very rapid growth or to break their spirits. First, he ordered the Egyptian midwives of the Hebrew mothers to kill the newborn male Hebrews. When that step did not succeed, the Egyptian people were ordered to drown all newborn Hebrew male infants. The girls were to remain alive to act as a burden on the family. The infant Moses was saved by his mother, who daily hid him in tall grass while his sister Miriam watched over him from a distance. This is where Pharaoh's daughter came across Moses. Having found him hidden and in view of her father's recent edict, she assumed Moses was a Hebrew. She planned to adopt Moses, but wanted a Hebrew woman to nurse the infant. Unknown to Pharaoh's daughter, she had arranged with Moses's own mother to nurse Moses.

Growing up as a member of the royal family, Moses evidently obtained an education and experiences that taught him to be a leader, preparing him for his future role as the liberator of the Hebrews from the Egyptian bondage. Moses went out among the Hebrews, watching them work as slaves. As a young man, he saw an Egyptian killing a Hebrew. In his anger, Moses killed the Egyptian. This forced him to give up the luxury of living with the royal family and to flee for safety. He went to an area occupied by the Midianites in the southeastern part of the Sinai Peninsula, which was outside of Egyptian control. Moses married a Midianite and lived there with his father-in-law for many years until called by God to liberate the Hebrews from their Egyptian bondage.

God Selects Moses to Liberate the Hebrews—God told Moses that he had seen the *"affliction of his people in Egypt"* and he had *"heard their pain."* He told Moses of his plan to get the Israelites out of Egypt and into the land of *"milk and honey,"* and asked Moses to take on the task of dealing with Pharaoh. Moses had several reasons for refusing, but was persuaded to accept the role. God reassured Moses that he would be with him to accomplish the task he described.

The Role of Aaron—On several occasions, Moses expressed his inadequacy as an eloquent speaker and his concern about his stammering. In response, God told Moses to make use of his brother Aaron. Aaron, three years older than Moses, became his brother's spokesman in several important situations. Aaron's first task was to assist Moses in persuading the Hebrew elders to accept God's promise to help the Hebrews leave Egypt. The approval of the Hebrew masses was God's requisite for helping the Hebrews. Aaron then assisted Moses in dealing with Pharaoh for the right to leave Egypt by giving Pharaoh warnings about the plagues.

After the sanctuary in the desert was completed, Aaron's sons served as the priests (*Kohen*) and Aaron served as the high priest. The Levi Tribe served as the assistants to the priests. Males from all the other Hebrew tribes were called *Yisrael*. Traditionally, these three ancestral groupings of the Jewish people, *Kohen, Levi,* and *Yisrael,* were passed down through the ages to all the respective male offsprings. An interesting recent study of two thousand *Kohenim* from different Jewish cultures, living apart with little interaction in the past one thousand years, revealed the common presence of certain genes. This study result suggests that there is a common ancient ancestry for *Kohenim*. A similar DNA technology type study is underway to determine if there is a common gene tying the Jews in India to the Falashas from Ethiopia and the Uganda Jews. It is part of a broader objective of learning more about the Ten Lost Tribes through DNA testing of several newly found Jewish communities in several Asian and African countries.

Moses: the Greatest Prophet—Moses was the forerunner of the Hebrew Prophets. He prophesied the Hebrews' future, reprimanding them for their errant behavior, and preached how they should behave. He essentially prevented the extinction of the Hebrews as a people, when on several occasions, he protected the Hebrews from the wrath of God when they rebelled against God and Moses during the Exodus. Jewish tradition considers Moses to be the greatest Prophet. He had the prophetic capability unique to the Jewish people and is recognized by the Jewish people as the only person to have seen God directly, which he did when he went up to Mount Sinai to receive God's revelation about the future of the Israelites. (The great Rabbi Moses Maimonides formulated this belief as part of his "Thirteen Principles of Faith" in the twelfth century C.E.)

Moses Forbidden to Enter the Promised Land—According to the Bible, God did not allow Moses to enter the *Promised Land* because of his sin against God—Moses had not followed God's instruction to speak to the rock to get needed water. Instead, Moses struck the rock, denying the people an opportunity to see God's miracle at work. Although this did not appear to be a significant sin, the rabbis explain that Moses was being punished by God along with the other Hebrews who transgressed against God because *"The greater the man, the stricter the standard of conduct expected, and the harsher the penalty."*

God did allow Moses to see the Promised Land before he died. Moses viewed all of Canaan from the top of Mount Nebo in Moab. The summit of Mount Nebo, Mount Pisgah Peak, is a high point east of the Jordan River from where you can see as far as the Mediterranean Sea to the west, Lebanon to the north, and the Negev to the south.

The Bible describes the area where Moses died, but his actual burial place is not discussed as was done for the Patriarchs—the Bible says this was deliberate. *The Greatest Prophet and redeemer of the Hebrews wanted to be treated in death as an ordinary person—he did not want to be revered as a hero.*

The Israelites stopped their activity and mourned their great leader Moses for thirty days; this has become the traditional Jewish mourning period for family members. When it was over, they accepted Joshua as their new leader and carried on.

Exodus From Egypt (ca. 1230 B.C.E.)

The major religious message given to the Hebrews in this biblical story of the Exodus is that they should forever celebrate Passover to remember how God redeemed them from physical and spiritual slavery. The

Passover holiday is celebrated by all Jews to remember how God passed over the homes of the Hebrews to be spared from the tenth plague, which would kill all the first-born children and cattle in Egypt. As instructed in the Bible, the Jewish people ate unleavened bread for one week, as a reminder that they were going to leave Egypt the next day, with no time to bake bread. Passover represents a message to the world that everyone should strive for spiritual as well as physical freedom. Because the Passover event, *freedom from bondage,* was so significant to their survival, the Hebrews were instructed in the Bible to establish their calendar with the month in which Passover occurs as the first month of the year.

When Was the Exodus?—The exact date and even the Pharaohs involved in the Exodus is somewhat uncertain due to conflicting secondary historical information. Historians offer different opinions. Based on the biblical statement referring to the "building of Pharaoh's store-cities, Pithom and Raamses," and supported by the general Egyptian historical data, Ramses II is the most likely "Pharaoh of Oppression." The many massive temples and buildings he constructed during his long reign remain preserved until today. The Bible indicates that after the oppressive Pharaoh died, the Hebrews drew hope for the end of their oppression. This suggests that the Exodus occurred under the successor to Ramses II, his son Menremptah, and it took place at about 1230 B.C.E. shortly after Menremptah became Pharaoh. From an historical viewpoint, this timing is likely for two main reasons. The Egyptian army had been weakened by a military campaign in Canaan when the new Pharaoh took over Egypt and the Libyans were beleaguering Egypt on land while other countries were attacking Egypt by sea. These factors were very favorable for anyone trying to escape from Egypt.

One of the confusing pieces of information to historians is a Menremptah victory pillar, dated 1220 B.C.E., found in Canaan with the name "Israel" in its victory statement. It was dated during the time the Hebrews were still wandering in the desert. The year 1220 B.C.E. falls within the Bible's thirty-eight-year gap of information after the Exodus from Egypt. The Israel referred to could have been Hebrews who drifted back to Canaan on their own before the biblical Exodus. It is also conceivable that some of the Israelite tribes left the Moses caravan and actually entered Canaan during the first Moses attempt to enter Canaan in the second year of the Exodus.

Another confusing archeological item is the date in a letter written by Ramses II that was found describing his victory over the "Chief of Asher" in the mountains of northern Canaan in 1270 B.C.E. This date is before the Exodus is likely to have started. An earlier departure from Egypt by members of the Asher tribe before the Moses-led Exodus may be the answer. It is conceivable that some aggressive Israelites would consider escaping the oppression that already existed for possibly one hundred years before the Exodus led by Moses. Goshen, where most Israelites lived, was close to the direct road to Canaan. From historical records, we know that Egypt did not fortify the road until closer to the Exodus period. The fact that the area referred to in the letter was the Promised Land location that Jacob had assigned to the Asher tribe corroborates this aspect of the biblical Jacob story.

Democracy During the Exodus—In probably the first application of the democratic process, the Bible tells of Moses discussing with the Hebrew elders the plan for dealing with Pharaoh and requiring their approval before proceeding.

The Ten Plagues—Moses was instructed by God to be his emissary in dealing with Pharaoh to allow the Hebrews to leave Egypt. Moses, with Aaron's assistance alerted Pharaoh to each successive plague that God was going to impose on Egypt. The first eight plagues were blood, frogs, gnats, flies, cattle disease, boils, hail, and locusts. With each plague, Pharaoh agreed to let the Israelites go, then quickly relented after God ended the plague. These plagues were unsuccessful probably because Egyptians had lived through similar events, which occur frequently in the Egyptian area of the world. The ninth plague was three days of darkness. This plague was unusual and probably had a more drastic effect; solar eclipses do not last that long. (Historians speculate that clouds of volcanic ash from a severe volcanic eruption on a Greek island north of Egypt caused the three days of darkness.)

When it was over, Pharaoh again refused Moses's request, but this time, threatened Moses. In response, God advised Moses to have the Israelites prepare for the Exodus because the tenth plague, the death of all the first-born in Egypt, would be severe enough to certainly convince Pharaoh to allow the Israelites to leave Egypt. God instructed the Israelites to put the blood of a lamb on their doorposts so that the killings would pass over the Hebrew homes (the derivation of *"Passover"*). They were also told to prepare for an immediate exodus by quickly baking bread without giving the dough time to leaven (the making of *matzah*). Affected by the Egyptian children and cattle dying, Pharaoh said yes, and the Exodus started. Three days later, Pharaoh changed his mind and caught up with the fleeing Israelites at the Reed Sea.

Who Participated in the Exodus?—The Bible states that two census counts of Hebrew males over twenty were taken in the desert and both counts were 600,000. This appears exaggerated. When wives and children are included, the total would approximate at least 2.5 million. This total number is much too high, considering the Israelites were a small minority in the much larger Egyptian population, which has been estimated to be only three to seven million.

Some non-Hebrews, who were also under bondage as slaves, viewed the Israelite plan to get out Egypt as an opportunity for their own freedom and joined the Hebrew Exodus. Without any true loyalty to Judaism, they likely contributed to some of the unrest and rebellion in the wilderness described in the Bible. The inclusion in the census of these non-Hebrews who had no alternative but to travel with the Israelite caravan during the duration of the long Exodus may have contributed to the biblical census figures that appear too high. The Book of Judges describes how the Kenites, a non-Hebrew clan related to Moses's father-in-law, joined the tribes of Judah and Simon as they conquered the southern part of Canaan. This is another indication that non-Hebrews joined in the Exodus.

Red Sea or Reed Sea?—Based on the English version of the Bible's Exodus story, we were taught that the Hebrews departed from Egypt thanks to God having parted the "Red" Sea. The Hebrews were left on dry land and the Egyptians and their chariots were drowned in a surge of high water. This version involves an erroneous English translation of the Hebrew name of the sea in the biblical narrative. We now know that the Hebrew name of the sea means "Reed" Sea.

This knowledge has opened a new understanding of how the event could have happened. It is suggested that the Hebrews took a route through a marshy area called the Reed Sea in that period. The Hebrews were able to walk through the marshes, whereas the Egyptian chariots bogged down. A place that fits the circumstances is Lake Balah. It is a papyrus swamp not far from Goshen, where most of the Hebrews in Egypt lived, and it was on the way to the Sinai wilderness. Another suggestion is that a very strong east wind, which occasionally occurs in that area of Egypt, kept the water higher on the Egyptian side of the Reed Sea. That prevented the Egyptians from catching up with the Israelites who crossed the Reed Sea while it was still shallow and before the wind caused the high tide.

Route of the Exodus—The Bible indicates that the Hebrews avoided the coastal road, which was a quick, direct route to the Promised Land. This was for good reason. After conquering most of Canaan in 1286 B.C.E., Ramses II battled with the Hittite army for control of Syria. Although he was victorious, Ramses's army had to retreat to Egypt. Egyptian fortifications were then established along that coastal highway to protect against Canaanite forces attacking Egypt in revenge. These fortifications would have been a deterrent and a danger to the fleeing, relatively unarmed Israelites.

The route taken through the Sinai Peninsula is still unconfirmed. No archeological evidence of the places along the route described in the Bible has been found to date. Sinai archeological expeditions conducted in the past were not very extensive; none has been conducted in more than fifty years.

Based on the biblical Exodus details, the journey started along the western Sinai coast and continued along the Red Sea. Studies of the Sinai terrain characteristics indicate that an interior route is highly unlikely. Before reaching the lower tip of the Sinai, the route went inland to the southern Sinai mountainous wilderness. Mount Sinai, where the Revelation took place, is believed to be in this area, but the specific location is yet unknown. Interestingly, there is a large plain in that area at a 5,000-foot elevation, which in combination with adjacent valleys, could have supported the size of the Israelite caravan described in the Bible. Although there are no archeological findings to confirm the route taken after leaving the Sinai, there is evidence of the existence of those wilderness places in Canaan and the adjacent kingdom areas that are quoted in the biblical Exodus descriptions. Initially, the Israelites tried to enter Canaan from the south but were defeated badly. Moses asked the king of Edom for permission to go north on the Kings Highway to the planned eastern entry point to Canaan and was turned down—it would have avoided the hardship of going through the wilderness. The existence of the *"Kings Highway"* running through Edom and Moab at that time is well established.

Revelation on Mount Sinai—Three months after leaving Egypt, Moses was called up to Mount Sinai to receive God's revelation of what he was going to do for the Israelites. On the first trip, he received from God the Ten Commandments on two stone tablets. After explaining it to the people, he made a second trip and received the Book of the Covenant, which he wrote down and read to the people on his return. This Revelation did not help overcome the people's discontent with the conditions in the wilderness. While Moses was up on the Mount again for a forty-day planned visit, they got rebellious and expressed their unhappiness with the Hebrew God, reaching out for a heathen god. They built the Golden Calf and started to worship it according to pagan practices. Moses went into a rage after learning about it and broke the Ten Commandment Tablets. He then spent another forty days on the Mount, getting a second pair of Ten Commandment Tablets.

The Legacy of Jethro: Moses's Father-in-Law—Early in the Exodus, Moses's father-in-law, Jethro, having heard of the Hebrew escape from Egypt, came to congratulate Moses and bring him his wife and two children. His family had remained behind in Midian while Moses went to Egypt to lead the Exodus.

Jethro watched the hordes of people who, from morning to night, waited outside of Moses's tent for Moses, as the sole judge of the Hebrews in Sinai, to adjudicate their problems by applying the statutes of God and his laws. It was wearing out Moses. He gave Moses advice that was remarkable for that period. He advised Moses to decentralize the judicial responsibility by setting up different levels of wise men (judges). The more serious the crime, the higher the level of authority required. *This legal system did not exist anywhere at that time. There was no justice system for all classes of people and for all types of complaints. Jethro's system was the prototype for the judicial system in today's democratic societies.*

The False Spy Report: Forty Years in the Wilderness—Ten months after their entry to Sinai, the Hebrews left Sinai for the wilderness of Paran in the southern Negev of Israel bordering the Sinai. It was on the way to Moab, which is east of the Jordan River, opposite the Dead Sea and the entry to the Promised Land. In the next year, a group consisting of a leading member of each of the tribes of Israel was sent out to spy on the land of Canaan in order to plan the Israelite entry. They came back with a false report of what they saw, which indicated the impossibility of defeating the Canaanites. The Israelites accepted the report and rejected the Moses plan for invading Canaan. God considered these steps to be a rebellion against Him; the Hebrews had displayed a lack of confidence in God. In reaction, God punished the Israelites for their rebellion, requiring them to stay in the desert for forty years—one year for each day of the rebellious spy mission.

The generation that left Egypt was just not ready for the challenge associated with entering the Promised Land. It required a trust in the God of Moses, which the Hebrew masses lost. After they recovered from the spy incident that incurred God's wrath, the Hebrews ignored Moses's caution against invading Canaan—God would not support them. They attempted a direct invasion of Canaan from the south, which turned into a disastrous military defeat. They could not overcome their disregard for God's instructions for thirty-eight years. A new generation was to be readied for the next attempt to conquer Canaan.

The Bible skips over the next thirty-eight years of wandering in the wilderness while the preparation went on and picks up with the farewell address by Moses before his death. Although the invasion led by Joshua is the only one described in the Bible, it is conceivable that during the long biblical time gap, some Hebrew tribes independently entered the Promised Land along a different route than taken by Joshua.

Rebellions in the Wilderness—Ancient and modern history is replete with rebellions against rulers by their people, by jealous politicians, and by the ruler's family members. The Bible relates that all of these situations occurred during the Exodus. It was a critical period for the survival of the Jewish people. They were suffering during the wandering in the desert and wilderness before they had an opportunity to be strengthened by the biblical teaching. These incidents are told in the Bible to indicate God's desire to perpetuate Judaism by his intercession to end the rebellions:

- The Israelites and the non-Hebrews who left Egypt with them rebelled about having only manna to eat. Craving for the food they ate in Egypt, they were ready to ignore Moses's advice and were preparing to kill the small amount of cattle they had with them. Moses could not cope with the situation and was ready to give up on the Hebrews. God interceded to quell the rebellion.
- In reaction to Moses taking an Ethiopian as his second wife, Moses's sister Miriam said evil things about Moses and aroused the people against Moses. They complained about not having the ear of God as Moses had. Moses was too humble to defend himself. The rebellion ended when Miriam became afflicted with leprosy as God's punishment.
- God had instructed Moses to send a representative from each of the Israelite tribes into Canaan to canvass the situation in preparation for its conquest. These twelve spies came back after forty days with a false report about how impossible it would be to conquer Canaan. After hearing the false report, the demoralized Hebrews rebelled against Moses and Aaron. They complained about leaving Egypt and lost faith in God's promise to give them the Promised Land. As punishment, the angered

God required the Israelites to stay in the desert for forty years so that most of the rebellious generation would die before the Israelites entered the Promised Land.
- Korah, a cousin of Moses, led a group of 250 leaders to stir up the Israelites against Moses and Aaron. Korah was a demagogue who wanted to take over the leadership. It took Divine intervention in the way of an earthquake that consumed Korah and his cohorts to end the rebellion.

The Sin of the Golden Calf—The Hebrew masses reverted to idolatry when Moses was late in returning from Mount Sinai where he met with God. They built a statuette of a calf made out of gold that resembled the god-figure of another Semitic sect. They started to worship it as an idol representing a heathen god. God was outraged, but was convinced by Moses not to punish the Hebrews after they demonstrated their recognition of Him as the God of Israel.

Enemies in the Wilderness

The Hebrews' effort to establish themselves as a people dedicated to the ideals and responsibilities of the Mosaic religion and laws ran into many obstacles in the wilderness before their entering the Promised Land. The previous section described the internal rebellions during the Exodus that threatened the survival of Judaism. In addition to these obstacles, external militant adversaries and competing religions challenged the Hebrews in the wilderness. Battles between small local kingdoms scattered throughout Canaan and battles with neighboring countries were a way of life in the biblical period. The Bible describes such incidents of the Hebrews battling with militant adversaries that interfered with the Israelite goal of getting to the Promised Land.

Brutal Amalekites—Shortly after leaving Egypt, while the Hebrews were still adjusting to the rigors of life in the Sinai, a roving band of the predatory tribe of Amalekites from Canaan started attacking the Hebrew caravan. They assaulted the defenseless people trailing behind the caravan. The next day, the Hebrews, led by Joshua, defeated the Amalekites after a fierce battle.

Uncooperative King of Edom—After failing in an earlier attempt to enter Canaan from the south, the Israelites hoped to enter Canaan from the east. The short route was through the country of Edom. Moses pleaded with the king for passage through his kingdom. Moses tried to arouse the king's sympathy, explaining the ordeal the Hebrews went through before they could get out of Egypt. The king refused. The Israelites were too weak to challenge the Edomites. They were forced to take the long route to their planned entry point into Canaan, going back down towards the Red Sea and a long hard journey through the wilderness on the eastern side of the Jordan River.

Uncooperative Amorites—After being forced to go around Edom, the Israelites sent messages to the king of the Amorites requesting they be allowed to go through his territory to get to the next area, Moab. The king refused the request and attacked the Israelites. The Amorites were soundly defeated, and the Israelites passed through.

Bashan Attacks the Israelites—Led by King Og, the small kingdom of Bashan attacked the Israelites trying to pass through their territory. The Israelites were victorious and occupied the Bashan area until they continued on to Moab a few years later.

The Curse of Balaam—King Balak and the people of Moab felt threatened by the Hebrews who settled in their territory while preparing to enter Canaan. Having a natural enmity towards the Hebrews, the king did not want to cooperate with them. Instead, he approached Balaam, who had a reputation as a prophet, to use his prophetic connection with God to rebuff the Hebrews. He expected Balaam to "curse the Jews into future failure" and to get divine help to accomplish this. It did not happen. Balaam wound up blessing the future of the Hebrews.

The Sin of Baal-Peor—Having failed to destroy the Hebrew morale through the "curse of Balaam," King Balak resorted to another approach: to destroy the Hebrews from within. He had the women of Moab and Midian entice Israelite men to join in the worship of Baal-Peor, their heathen God. This worship involved immoral rites that violated the Mosaic Code. This heresy ended by divine intervention with a plague that killed the Israelites who participated in the heathen rites.

Revenge on the Midianites—After the Midianites caused the Israelites to sin by indulging in the Baal-Peor heathen rites, God encouraged the Hebrews to take revenge on the Midianites. The Hebrews unmercifully slaughtered the element of the Midianites who were involved in the treachery. Rabbis have a difficult time explaining how this sin incident justified the brutal treatment of the Midianites that is described in the Bible.

The Legacy of Moses

Moses was a pathfinder in humanizing and spiritualizing monotheism, translating its basic theme of godliness into laws of ethical behavior and social justice. The Mosaic Code amplified the original Covenant between God and the Jewish people that was established by Abraham. The Hebrew Prophets, followed by the rabbinic Sages, expanded on the principles of the Mosaic Code.

The three thousand-year-old Ten Commandments and Mosaic Code still serve as the behavioral guide to the Jewish people and provide the basis for social morality, ethics, and justice to humankind.

The Ten Commandments—Thirty days after leaving Egypt, the Hebrews arrived at Mount Sinai, where the Covenant between God and the Jewish people was established. There, Moses received 613 commandments from God. The first ten, and most illustrious, are the Ten Commandments given in the form of two stone tablets. The Ten Commandments are simply stated but very comprehensive in scope. They represent the primary set rules of human behavior to be followed by all humankind.

The Ten Commandments

Duties towards God and family
1. Recognize the sovereignty of God
2. Have no other gods
3. Do not take the name of the Lord in vain
4. Remember the Sabbath day, keep it Holy
5. Honor your father and your mother

Duties towards fellow humankind
6. You shall not commit murder
7. You shall not commit adultery
8. You shall not steal
9. You shall not bear false witness
10. You shall not desire or go after your neighbor's possessions

The first five commandments address behavior towards God and family. The Hebrew people are to recognize Abraham's monotheism of a spiritual God as opposed to a physical God. They are commanded not to worship idols and other physical godly concepts such as the sun god or kings—worshipping these as gods was the universal practice among all people at that time. People are not to take advantage of the new respect for God by swearing falsely in God's name. A day of rest is to be taken by everyone—the Sabbath day of rest is to be kept holy in God's name. Children shall show appreciation for the love and care that their parents gave them by honoring both their father and mother with respect and love.

The second set of five commandments addresses the behavior of people towards other people. The commandments present a code of moral and ethical behavior that is the Jewish creed and lifestyle and that has been adopted by the Christian community.

Biblical Sacrificial Laws—Much has been said about the need to judge the relevance of the biblical sacrificial laws in the context of biblical times. In today's world, they sound strange and unworthy of any importance, if not absurd. In the biblical period, when human sacrifices to idols and heathen Gods was common practice, there was an important message to the people of the Middle East conveyed by the biblical sacrificial laws. It was a method of educating the Hebrews to sacrifice animals rather than people. It was premature to attempt to completely end the ritual of sacrifices to God, which remained entrenched in all biblical period societies long after the time of Moses. The message to the people was *"The life of all humans is sacred."*

Dietary Laws—The rules concerning which animals, birds, and fish can be eaten were spelled out as a matter of holiness. Animals that died (interpreted by the rabbis to include animals that were shot) could not be eaten. Dairy and meat could not be eaten together. Those creatures that could not be eaten were called "abominable things," implying they were unhealthy. In times of severe, deathly sickness during the Middle Ages, the Jewish people were apparently healthier than the general population, attributed by sociologists to the Jewish dietary laws.

The Mosaic Code—When taken in the context of the biblical period, the Mosaic Code becomes so noteworthy. It was a time when human life was not sacred, human rights were unknown, and the powerful had unrestricted control over the less fortunate. The Mosaic Code offered radical changes to this code of behavior. The Torah received by Moses contains 613 commandments; 248 are positive (you shall . . .) and 365 are negative (you shall not . . .). They cover domestic life, religious worship, civil law, and government and criminal law. Approximately 200 of these commandments are either obsolete or cannot be observed today. They pertain to priestly duties, temple activities, and animal sacrifices to God that have been replaced by prayers to God in rabbinical Judaism.

The Golden Rule—*"Love thy neighbor as thyself,"* which was espoused by the Jewish sage Hillel and later attributed to Jesus, is actually a major commandment specified in Leviticus. It is expanded upon in the Bible with many other statutes that require considerate and ethical behavior towards fellow man and woman.

God's Creations Are Equal—The Mosaic Code included edicts to be considerate to all of God's creations. The poor were to be helped through tithes. Loans were to be released every seventh year in the Sabbatical Year. Since the early Israelite society was agricultural, this applied to agricultural loans and not commercial loans. Animals were to be treated humanely. Land was to be left fallow in the Sabbatical Year—the land was to rest every seven years, just as humankind was commanded to rest every seven days. This practice has been recognized to be a natural method of revitalizing the soil.

Justice System Laws—The rules for the Judaic justice system were diametrically opposite to the justice system practiced in that period—*the biblical laws of behavior applied equally to the rich and the poor.* The Mosaic Code represents the norms of today's justice system in democratic areas of the world. There must be impartiality; equal justice must be applied to the poor as well as to the rich. There must be truth in the justice system; perjury and slander are forbidden.

Revengeful acts were limited to no more than eye-for-an-eye justice (measure-for-measure retaliation) and the death penalty imposed only for acts of murder.

Benevolent Treatment of Slaves—Cruel treatment of slaves was common in the ancient period. Learning from their own experience as slaves in Egypt, the Hebrews looked at slavery differently from other societies of that period. A Hebrew who could not meet his debts by borrowing could sell himself into bondage to another Hebrew in return for housing and food. Slaves could not be sold in the slave market. Slaves could not be given tasks that would degrade them. A slave's children had to be taken care of by the slave's master. Kidnapping for the selling of the victim into slavery was considered a severe enough crime to be punishable by death, overriding the law allowing the death penalty only for crimes of murder.

To minimize the hardship of slavery, slaves were to be released after six years of bondage, and taken back into society wholesomely. Slaves who escaped their master were not to be returned and were to be aided in making a living. A Hebrew who sold himself into slavery or as a servant to a non-Hebrew also had protection against lifetime bondage. He could be bought out of slavery at any time. He had to be released in the Year of the Jubilee. All slaves were released in this special year, the year after the seventh Sabbatical Year.

Human Kindness in Time of War—Fighting among the cultures and between nations in the area was recognized to be inevitable and was brutal. The Mosaic Code included an injunction that was uncommon in that period, and essentially throughout history. *The Hebrews were required to display human kindness in wartime.* The humane treatment of women, who were subject to rape during warfare, is especially spelled out in the Torah.

Mitzvah—Mosaic commandments are the basis of the Judaic religious practices and the ethical behavioral code of the Jewish people. The word for commandment in Hebrew is *mitzvah*. For Jews, *"doing a mitzvah"* means "bringing goodness to the world." It has become synonymous with *"doing a good deed"* to help make life better for a less fortunate person or for the community. *Whether religious or secular, performing a mitzvah has been the engine that drives the Jewish people to be in the forefront of political and social movements to improve the lot of all peoples of the world.*

Shema—Moses followed his second discourse on the giving of the Ten Commandments with the declaration of loyalty to God that starts with *"Hear O Israel: The Lord Is Our God, The Lord Is One."* This verse, starting with the word **Shema** (Hebrew for *"hear"*), is the keynote of all Judaism. It acknowledges the oneness of God and Israel's undivided loyalty to God. This statement and the remainder of the Moses declaration has been the Jew's "confession of faith" throughout the ages. The Shema is the last statement by Orthodox Jews on their deathbed, and shouted at the point of martyrdom. A full Shema prayer is said daily during morning and evening religious prayer services by Orthodox and Conservative Jews. It is enclosed in the *mezuzah* ("doorpost") mounted on the doorposts of most Jewish homes and religious facilities—to be kissed to honor God. In accordance with the instruction in the Shema prayer, which is to "bind those words on the arm and head," they are also enclosed in the leather boxes called phylacteries (*tephillin*). Observant Jews put *tephillin* on the forehead and on the left hand (to be next to the heart) during daily morning prayer services in order to fulfill this biblical commandment.

Yahweh: the God of Moses—Moses extended Abraham's one-God concept that was based on the Hebrew's loyalty to one protective God. This God established the proper code of behavior for the Hebrews (the Mosaic Code). This God, Yahweh, required the Hebrews to constantly acknowledge His good deeds through the sacrificial system. The ethical and moral code of Moses provided advances in the societal behavior, particularly the Mosaic sacrificial system that eliminated human sacrifice that was part of the pagan rituals. However, the portable sanctuary and elaborate Ark that was the centerpiece of the religious rites and the service that accompanied it came close to resembling the altar worship of the pagan religions that Judaism was to replace. The emphasis was on Yahweh worship rather than on personal behavior that responded to God's commandments.

This Yahweh concept of God, which to many seems out of place in Judaism, must be understood in the context of the mentality of biblical times. All religions of that period worshipped idols that required sacrificial homage. It would have been too much to have the people accept new codes of behavior and give up the type of rituals to which they were exposed by the other cultures and with whom they interacted. Indeed, there were many periods, starting with the Exodus, when Hebrews forgot Yahweh and reverted to idol worship. It took almost eight hundred years before Rabbinical Judaism replaced the ineffective sacrificial system. This new form of Judaic practices that stressed moral and ethical behavior for its own sake was more effective in keeping the Hebrew people from straying from the Mosaic Code of human behavior.

Moses Is Left Out of the Passover Haggadah—The Passover story is told every year at the Passover Seder meal at the home of millions of Jewish families throughout the world. Interestingly, the Prophet Moses, who led the Israelites to freedom from slavery in Egypt for which Passover is celebrated, is not mentioned in the Haggadah that is read to tell the Passover story. The rabbis who developed the Haggadah wanted the Jewish people to remember that God's hand made the Exodus happen. The role of Moses in the Exodus was therefore deliberately omitted in the Haggadah to avoid competition with God for getting credit for liberating the Jewish people.

The Prominence of Number Seven

The number seven has a particular prominence in the Bible. It starts with the biblical creation story; the world is completed on the seventh day when God rested. God then prescribed the seventh day to be the Sabbath, the people's day of rest. This, interestingly, is the first documentation of the concept of seven days in a weekly period. The Greek and Roman aristocracy frowned on the seventh day Sabbath rest for everyone. They viewed working people as not being entitled to a day off from their toils. When Roman Emperor Constantine embraced Christianity in 300 C.E., he adopted the Jewish seven-day week but set Sunday as the day of worship—one of his several Christian practice departures from Judaism. The rest of the world continued to follow the twenty-eight-day lunar cycle.

In the Bible, Noah was instructed by God to take onboard the ark seven pairs of all clean creatures. Jacob toiled for his Uncle Laban for two seven-year periods before getting Laban's two daughters as his wives. Moses was instructed to build a candelabra with seven branches, the first Jewish symbol. It represents the completion of the world's creation in seven days, the central branch representing the Sabbath.

The importance of seven continues with the biblical commandments relating to the Jewish religious holidays. The seventh month is prescribed to be the holy month in the year. Three major holidays occur in the seventh month, New Year's Day, the Day of Atonement, and Succoth. It may seem odd that New Year's Day is celebrated in the seventh month of the Hebrew calendar rather than in the first month. This stems from the biblical commandment that only calls for a "memorial day" to be celebrated on the first day of the seventh month to be followed by the "Day of Atonement" (*Yom Kippur*) on the tenth day of the seventh month. The *Rosh Hashanah* (New Year's Day) concept was adopted much later and became the solemn religious holiday, the Day of Remembrance, when God reviews each individual's behavior during the previous year. God prescribes/seals the individual's fate for the next year on the Day of Atonement. On that day, the Jews atone for their sins against God and fellow human beings to avoid a harsh decree.

The first month being in the spring growing season was consistent with the early Hebrew society, which was agricultural. The rabbis offer a philosophical reason for the emphasis on Passover. The Passover festival, which celebrates the start of the Exodus from Egypt and the redemption of the Jewish people from slavery, was considered to be the most significant event in ancient Hebrew history—it therefore takes precedence for the first month of the year. Passover still has this significance; many secular Jews participate in a Passover Seder but do not attend High Holy Day religious services.

Seven applies to the three festival holidays. Passover and Succoth are commanded to last seven days. The third festival, *Shavuot,* lasts only one day, but it occurs seven weeks after Passover. These seven weeks coincide with the seven weeks between the start of the Exodus from Egypt and when God gave the Torah at Sinai.

The use of seven did not stop with the festivals. Every seventh year was designated as the Sabbatical Year, when slaves were to be set free, debts were released, and the land was to be left fallow. The end of every seventh Sabbatical Year was designated as the start of the Jubilee Year, when all slaves were freed, debts were released, and property taken over by creditors reverted to the original family owners.

The battle of Jericho described in the Book of Joshua is replete with the use of seven. Seven priests, blowing seven ram's horns, blew the walls of Jericho down on the seventh day.

The biblical use of seven carried over to the Jewish life cycle practices. The *tephillin* strap is wrapped around the arm seven times. The *sheva b'rachot* (seven wedding blessings) consecrate the Jewish wedding ceremony. A woman is to abstain from sex for seven days after the end of her menstrual period. *Shivah,* the Jewish mourning period, is seven days long.

Who Wrote the Torah?

For ages, the Jewish people accepted as fact that God gave the current version of the Torah directly to Moses and that it was literally accurate. Then the literal accuracy of some of the Torah stories began to be questioned by rabbis and biblical scholars. By the medieval period, the esteemed Rabbis Rashi and Saadia Gaon had concluded that the Genesis story of the creation of the world was allegorical. In the nineteenth century, the authenticity of the Torah and the biblical books describing the early Jewish kingdoms came under severe attack by many literary critics, led by the German Christian scholar Julius Wellhausen. According to their "higher-criticism," the biblical books were fictitious and were written at least one thousand years after the presumed time of Moses.

After years of acceptance by many scholars, the conclusions of these critics became discredited by archeological findings that verified many biblical events and their approximate period. For example, a stone record has been found that describes the "Ammonite king's victory over the dynasty of David," which confirms the existence of a King David in biblical times. It is interesting to note that there has been no archeological finding that has refuted the Bible's basic accuracy.

Orthodox Jewry and other traditionalists continue to believe that Moses authored the current version of the Torah based on God's input. Contemporary non-Orthodox Jewish religious leaders question the traditional view. Based on references in the Torah to events that occurred after Moses died, they view the current version of the Torah as being "God-inspired" but written after the time of Moses. A current popular view of the Torah's authorship rationalizes that multiple writers adapted various sections from the original Torah to develop the current version. This multiple authorship theory is fundamentally based on the inconsistencies in the narratives that are found within the five books of the Torah and between the books. To some, the consistently simpler writing style throughout Deuteronomy compared to the more complex narrative writing style in the other four books supports the multiple-writer theory.

One theory regarding the authorship of individual biblical sections relates to the use of Yahweh and Elohim as God's name; these names appear in different portions of the Torah. It has been suggested that the author(s) of the sections that use the name Yahweh came from the southern Kingdom of Judah, where God was called Yahweh. Likewise, the author(s) of the sections that use the name Elohim came from the northern Kingdom of Israel, where Elohim was the popular name for God.

A liberal-traditionalist view suggests that Moses wrote Deuteronomy for the benefit of the young Hebrews who grew up in the desert. Its purpose was to strengthen their adherence to the code of conduct that God prescribed in the other biblical books at the start of the Exodus from Egypt, forty years earlier, but which contained less detail. An alternate theory has Deuteronomy written in 622 B.C.E. by *Kohenim* (priests) for King Josiah. Its purpose was to aid in convincing the people of the kingdom of Judah to renew their adherence to the Torah laws prescribed in the other biblical books.

Scholars who suggested that there were multiple authors of sections of the Torah have attempted to identify who assembled the current version of the Torah. The popular conclusion is that the most likely person to accomplish this was the Scribe Ezra, who lived in the fifth century B.C.E. Ezra, an extremely strong leader of the Jewish people, is credited with initiating rabbinical-centered Judaism. He is considered the only one who had sufficient influence over the Jewish people to have them accept a major rework of their holiest document.

Archeological findings of an early version of the Hebrew alphabet that goes back to the Torah time period adds some credence to the likelihood that there was an earlier original version of the Torah.

2
The Jewish Kingdoms

The twelve tribes of Israel entered the "Promised Land" without Moses, their great leader. They faced tumultuous times without a strong leader as a successor. After over a hundred years of turbulent living with their neighbors and fighting between the tribes, the Hebrew people settled on a kingdom form of government. This form of government, which was essentially universal in that time period, brought stability, political growth, and Hebrew religious development. Kings David and Solomon, who followed the initial King Saul as rulers of a united Jewish kingdom, which included all twelve tribes, had lasting fame. This United Jewish Kingdom era was glorious for the Jewish people. It was followed by a long period of political rivalry and hostility between the northern and southern tribes who had formed separate kingdoms. This latter period of Jewish history is primarily remembered for the destruction of the first Holy Temple in Jerusalem, the forced migration of the Judeans to Babylonia, and the historical disappearance of the ten northern tribes of Israel. It was a period when the great Hebrew Prophets tried to counter the moral and religious degradation and the despair that prevailed frequently amongst the Hebrews.

Entry Into the Promised Land (ca. 1190–1030 B.C.E.)

Historical information covering the entry of the Israelites into Canaan is derived from the only two sources available, the biblical Books of Joshua and Judges. These two books, evidently written after the events occurred, mix history with the religious development as the Hebrews settled in Canaan. The first book describes how the cohesive Israelite tribes, led by Joshua, conquered Canaan in one relatively brief but continuous military operation. The Book of Judges, which covers the period after the death of Joshua, starts out with a description of the battles for the conquest of Canaan that contradicts the earlier Book of Joshua. It describes Canaan being conquered in stages by individual Israelite tribes over a longer period.

In conjunction with the descriptions of the battles that took place over the length of Canaan, Joshua assigned territories to each of the twelve tribes of Israel. Archeological records have been found that confirm the accuracy of the tribal locations defined in the Book of Joshua and that verify the existence of the ancient places quoted in these biblical books. They also offer evidence that battles occurred there.

Joshua the Leader—Joshua was the military aid to Moses during the Exodus. His initial military act was to lead a band of Israelites that defeated the Amalekites, who had attacked the Hebrews in the mountains of Sinai shortly after they left Egypt during the Exodus. Joshua was in charge of the mission to spy on the Canaanites in order to plan the Israelite entry into Canaan. Joshua disagreed with the false spy report and supported Moses. According to the Bible, with Joshua listening in because of his loyalty to Moses and to God, God told Moses to appoint Joshua his successor and to groom him to lead the entry into Canaan. God also indicated that, in the future, He would not be there to help the Hebrews out of their troubles as He did during the Exodus while they were wandering in the wilderness.

The Torah narrative describes Joshua as a humble man. After leading the Hebrews to their victories over the Canaanites, Joshua did not attempt to become the political ruler of the Hebrews, as most other victorious military leaders would have done. After Joshua died, the Hebrews went through a turbulent time because they had no other central leader.

Conquering Canaan—Today's historical knowledge of that period indicates that the political situation that existed was most favorable for the Hebrew attempt to conquer Canaan. There was no large country dominating the Palestine area. Egypt had recently lost some battles in Canaan, and pulled out of the area. Assyria, which later became the dominant country, had not yet achieved its greatness and power. The Philistines who became a threat to the Hebrew southern tribes did not come to Palestine until well after Joshua led the Hebrews into Canaan. More importantly, the kings in the Canaan area who were the Hebrew opponents were generally rulers of only a city and its surrounding local area and acted independently. The Hebrews could not have been a match for the well-armed Canaanites when they first started their assault of Canaan.

According to the Book of Joshua, bolstered by their religious zeal, the strong determination of the Hebrews to succeed apparently gave the Hebrews an edge. A wise selection of whom to fight and on which terrain to do battle were other factors that contributed to their success. For example, the Hebrews took the battle to wooded hills, which enabled them to vanquish their enemies with chariots that lost mobility in the woods. The Israelites did not win all the battles. They frequently had to retreat, only to retry years later. The dispossessed Canaanite clans often returned later to challenge the Hebrews. In some areas, the Hebrews just moved into the cities, assimilating into society. In many areas, the Hebrews avoided the cities and established themselves as farmers.

The Book of Judges, written after the Book of Joshua, describes a different sequence of events. With all the independent city-states distributed over the entire land of Canaan, there was a protracted campaign to conquer the areas of Canaan. The Bible describes the brutality of the battles on both sides. Men, women, and children were massacred in captured communities. It was reflective of the barbaric way of life in that period.

Letters between the Pharaoh and Canaanite kings of that period were found at Tel el Amarna, which was the old Egyptian capital. They described how tough and brutal the battles were and how the Hebrew adversaries were formidable. They were better armed and greater in number, entrenched behind fortifications with watchtowers, and equipped with chariots.

Battle of Jericho—The Book of Joshua describes the walls of Jericho crumbling down after seven days of blowing seven ram's horns outside the walls of the city. No archeological confirmation has been found of the destruction of the walls of Jericho by an outside assault as described in the Book of Joshua. The remains of two walls surrounding Jericho in that period have been found. A study of the site by archeologists indicates that the walls collapsed due to an earthquake, suggesting that the book's author used the results of a natural disaster to glorify Joshua's entry into Canaan.

Gilgal—An Israelite shrine has been found at the ancient city of Gilgal. Gilgal served for a time as the center of the Israelite tribes after entering Canaan, and later it was where King Saul was crowned. Based on this historical information and the description of the entry of the Hebrews into Canaan found in the Book of Judges, which omits any discussion of a battle at Jericho, some scholars suggest that the first battle after crossing the Jordan River occurred at Gilgal.

Jerusalem—The city of Jerusalem was located within the territory assigned to the small tribe of Benjamin. However, the Benjaminites were too weak to do battle with the Jebusites, who controlled the city. They elected to leave Jerusalem in the Jebusite's possession and intermingled with them as a way of living in the city without a military struggle.

Living in Canaan—The life of the Hebrews changed dramatically in Canaan. They were no longer the herdsmen of Egypt and the nomads of the wilderness. They needed to learn how to live like the more accomplished Canaanites. They became craftsmen, conducted the business of commerce, and learned to be farmers. They also had to learn the art of defending themselves, amassing arms, training warriors, and building city fortifications.

One major challenge for the Hebrews was to resist the various pagan religions practiced by the people in the area with whom they intermingled. Other than the belief in one God by the Hebrews, many of the Hebrew practices were similar to those of the other religions. There were shrines for Yahweh that were equivalent to idols for pagan gods, sacrifices to God for giving thanks, and reliance on the help of God for their personal good fortune. The Hebrew exposure to the heathen religions, the norm for that time period, brought on religious competition—allegiance to Yahweh or worship of pagan gods, such as Baal, or both.

Another major challenge was to survive the battles with the neighboring clans. Some wanted revenge for losing their territory to the Hebrews. Others waged aggressive battles with the intent of conquering the Hebrews or looting their property. There was constant warfare, with brutality on both sides. The Hebrews struggled hard to maintain life and independence in their newly won communities.

When there was peaceful relations with the non-Hebrew neighbors, there was extensive assimilation into the established community. For example, most of the Asher tribe was lost among the Phoenicians in the north after the Asherites joined them as seafarers.

The Hebrew tribes fundamentally kept separate from each other. Unfortunately, that did not prevent battles between tribes over jealousies that turned into animosities. Their common enemies frequently took advantage of these civil wars to attack the Israelites during periods of weakness.

In some strange, almost miraculous, way, these crude Hebrews living in Canaan made the adjustment from a primitive nomadic lifestyle to a settled society that endured while others failed. This apparent backward society left a legacy of a one-God concept that is the basis of the three major religions of the Western world and an ethical and moral behavioral code that became today's world standard.

Shilo—The Holy Ark, which was carried along during the Exodus wanderings, was brought to the city of Shilo, located in the Ephraim tribe territory. It was the main religious center until destroyed by the Philistines.

The Period of the Judges—The Book of Judges is the only source of history of the 150 year period between the entry into Canaan and the establishment of the Hebrew kingdom of Saul. It describes how a group of individuals known as "judges" surfaced to lead the Hebrew tribes in the perilous time before the Hebrew nation was established. With no king to exercise control, the tribes fought with each other, sometimes brutally. The judges came from all walks of life to serve as seers, judges, and military leaders. Seven major and five minor judges are listed in the Book of Judges. Since those mentioned functioned essentially in the city in which they lived, there undoubtedly were many more such leaders.

Deborah was the most prominent of the judges. She acted as a judge, prophetess, and inspirational leader. Together with the military leader Barak, Deborah led the Hebrews to victory in protracted battles with the Canaanites. However, her attempt to unite all the Hebrew tribes was unsuccessful.

Gideon was another illustrious judge described in the Bible. He led a small force of 300 to a brutal victory over the much stronger Midianite army through a surprise "noisy" attack that caused the Midianites to panic. Gideon was offered the kingship of the Hebrew people but refused.

Samson, of folklore fame, was a judge of Israel for twenty years. The Book of Judges describes how he was groomed for the role of leading the Israelites as a result his mother's religious experience before he was born. The book tells of Samson's personal conflict with the ruling Philistines and describes how Samson was beguiled by Delilah into getting bound as a Philistine prisoner and how the physically powerful Samson got revenge by knocking down the pillars of the prison-house, killing many Philistines with him.

Turning Point After Defeat by the Philistines—The Philistines, driven out of their homeland on the islands of the Aegean sea off Greece, settled on the southern coast of Canaan in 1190 B.C.E. at about the same time as the Hebrews started their entry into Canaan. They were already a cultivated, accomplished society. This enabled them to quickly establish themselves as a strong commercial and military power in the area.

The Philistines constantly put pressure on the Hebrews, conquering more and more of the territory recently won by the southern Hebrew tribes.

When the Philistines embarked on a campaign to take over the hill country of Canaan, the Ephraim and Manasseh tribes united in an attempt to turn back the Philistines. The strong Philistines won a crushing victory, with an enormous loss of Hebrew lives. The Hebrews then attempted to use "the power of God" to help them by taking the Holy Ark into battle with them. This approach failed and they were utterly defeated again. The religious building at Shilo was destroyed. (Archeological evidence has been found indicating buildings at Shilo were burned down.) The Ark was taken by the Philistines and desecrated by being placed in their own temple.

With the Ark of the Lord in a pagan temple, their religious center at Shilo destroyed, and much of their territory overrun by the Philistines, the Hebrews got aroused and concerned. They searched out for a national leader who would lead them to victory over the Philistines. They selected Saul to be king of a united Hebrew country.

The United Jewish Kingdom (1030–933 B.C.E.)

Saul, a young but militant farmer from the Benjamin tribe, led a small band from his clan to overwhelm the stronger Ammonites, who were abusing the Hebrews in the city of Gilead. This was followed by a victory over the Philistines. After these successes that showed his strong leadership, Saul was selected to be king and was anointed king by Samuel, the Sage of Ramah. Saul ruled over a kingdom that included the central part of the country. He laid the foundation for the unification of the entire country under King David, who was his successor.

It is interesting to note that the Hebrew kings were obligated by the Torah to follow the laws of the Bible as well as all the Israelites, whereas other kings of that time considered themselves above the laws of the land and almost godly.

King Saul—The Book of Samuel provides contradictory accounts of Saul's behavior, possibly influenced by the author's bias towards David and hostility towards Saul. (David and Saul becoming antagonists may have caused the writer to lose impartiality.) Saul, on the one hand, is described as a benevolent king, who conducted himself democratically without the trappings of a royal despot. On the other hand, he is described as being a half-crazed, jealous despot at the end of his realm. Saul was so jealous of David that he was ready to kill him and others. It is difficult to sort out the truth about Saul's character from this history.

King Saul had continuing battles with Israel's neighbors, the Philistines, Moabites, Edomites, and Ammonites, who constantly attacked the new state. He fought many battles with these countries that saved the kingdom. Saul died in a battle with the Philistines after a reign of twenty years.

David the Youth—As a boy, David, of the tribe of Judah, received prominence by slaying Goliath, the "Philistine giant." He later joined King Saul's retinue and was in Saul's favor. David married Saul's daughter and became a friend and companion of Saul's son Jonathan. When David's popularity increased as a result of his military victories over the Philistines, Saul got jealous. He tried to kill David. At one point, David had an opportunity to kill Saul, but did not. Saul showed his appreciation, but later again tried to kill David. This time, David went into hiding until Saul died.

King David—Upon the death of King Saul, David reemerged and was made the king of the tribe of Judah at age thirty. Saul's son Eshbaal took over as king of the northern tribes. The southern tribes sided with David. The tribes fought each other for seven years. After Eshbaal was killed, the leaders of the northern tribes came to Hebron and anointed David king over all of the Israelite tribes. He became king of the United Jewish Kingdom, also known as the First Jewish Commonwealth. He ruled as its king for thirty-three years.

The biblical chroniclers paint David as the most splendid of people, but with the full range of personality characteristics. He was tender and brutal, cheerful and despondent, a sinner and a repentant soul. For Jews through all ages of history, David is the most honored Jewish personality other than Moses. He is revered for his accomplishments. He is considered a pious religious leader, credited with composing many of the religious psalms. He founded Jerusalem as the Jewish Holy City and united the Hebrew tribes into one kingdom. Despite his behavior in his later years that tarnished his image while he was king, David never lost the esteem of the Jewish people in later generations. His reputation for having "great goodness" was the basis of the Judaic belief that the Messiah, who will bring "goodness to the world," will come from the house of this peerless king.

King David the Warrior—The powerful Philistines thought they could easily defeat the new King David and invaded Judah. David surprisingly defeated them and went on to become an aggressive warrior who was determined to expand the borders of Israel that would encompass the entire Canaanite territory. He fought and defeated all of the earlier Israelite enemies from the days of the battles when entering the Promised Land. His successful commercial empire stretched from Lebanon to the Red Sea. His influence extended over the larger Syrian world. His kingdom earned the respect of the rulers of the area. The United Kingdom was considered an important Middle East country.

Jerusalem: David's City—David's strategy for having the northern tribes truly unite with him was to establish the capital of Judah in Jerusalem and make it the main religious center for the united Hebrew nation. Jerusalem, located centrally between the two Hebrew factions, had been neutral territory under control of the Jebusites. After conquering it from the Jebusites, he enlarged Jerusalem and created the fortified city of Zion. It became the "City of David." Because of David's desire to connect the nation's prestige with the religious heritage of Moses, he transferred the Holy Ark to Jerusalem and made plans for a magnificent temple to house it in. However, the Prophet Nathan discouraged David from building the Holy Temple because David was involved in so many wars. The building of the Temple was left to David's son Solomon, to be constructed in a period when Israel was at peace.

King David's Moral Degradation—In his later years, David behaved like the typical pompous king of antiquity. He had several wives and established a large harem involving foreign entanglements, a common and acceptable practice in those times. He compounded his adulterous behavior with murders and created an atmosphere of plots and intrigue in the royal court during the last few years of his regime. His wives and sons quarreled and plotted with each other. In his final years, David's esteem was so low, even his son rebelled against him.

King David's Legacy—King David's personality and achievements were the inspiration behind the reformation of Nehemiah and Ezra that saved the Jews after the Babylonian exile. The Maccabee leaders of the Second Jewish Commonwealth drew their strength from David's achievements to fight for an independent unified Hebrew State. David led a religious life dedicated to the God of Moses. Many of the religious Psalms glorifying God are attributed to him. He is credited with being a true poet.

King David has been the most revered religious and inspirational

Jewish personality next to Moses. David is included in many Judaic prayers. The Messiah is expected to come from his family lineage.

Jerusalem, the city of David, has been the spiritual and sentimental center for Jews from King David's time until today.

King Solomon—Shortly before his death, King David appointed Solomon as his successor. Solomon was David's youngest son by his favorite wife, Bathsheba. The very early years of Solomon's rule were full of unrest and even murder at the royal level. Solomon had his own brother Adonijah killed to avoid his threat as a rival.

King Solomon was determined to build the Holy Temple in Jerusalem that his father King David aspired to build. It took thirteen years to complete this massive and magnificent complex that housed the Ark of the Covenant brought from Sinai. Solomon consecrated the Temple in a spectacular ceremony participated in by the thousands of Jews who came to Jerusalem to offer their sacrifices at Succoth.

Solomon extended the consolidation of the kingdom and the country's economic strength and stability achieved by his father, King David. Solomon was spared from fighting wars to protect the nation and avoided his own expansionist wars. His diplomacy in dealing with the leaders of the Israelite tribes, international rulers, and the public was successful in avoiding tensions during the first half of his reign. That gave him the reputation for remarkable wisdom that is described in the Book of Kings. Solomon entered strategic alliances with his neighboring powers that gave the kingdom peace and stability. Frequently these alliances were achieved by marrying a foreign princess. Pharaoh's daughter was one. Solomon's most famous admirer was the Arabian Queen of Sheba.

King Solomon was a great builder. In addition to the magnificent Holy Temple, he built a sumptuous palace and many large fortified cities that were important militarily and commercially. Archeologists have found remnants of copper mines and smelters in the Negev, which were developed by King Solomon. He expanded the kingdom's trade with the world by developing a vast commercial trading enterprise supported by a large shipping fleet. Hebrew ships traveled from Spain to the Indian Ocean.

King Solomon reigned for forty years. During the latter half of his reign, Solomon managed to antagonize many segments of the kingdom, which contributed to the disintegration of the United Kingdom after his death. His massive building activity came with the severe price of forced labor and high taxes that caused discontent among the masses. His administrative governors for the twelve districts into which he divided the country disregarded any input from the Israelite tribal leaders. The antagonized tribal leaders became eager to end Solomon's reign, but they did not have the strength to accomplish their goal. King Solomon also managed to alienate the influential religious element by his tolerance of foreign cults practiced by his many foreign wives who brought their own idols and priests. The Prophet Ahijah denounced Solomon and encouraged separation of the northern tribes from Judah.

Collapse of the United Kingdom (933 B.C.E.)

During the latter part of his rule, Solomon particularly managed to antagonize the people in the northern part of the country, which had a larger and more advanced population than the southern part. Solomon's civil policies, especially the oppressive tax burden on the people, were very unpopular. They also had become discontented over Solomon's lack of religious control, which permitted the worship of Baal and other Phoenician deities. The behavior of Solomon's administrative organization, which controlled the entire kingdom's activity at the exclusion of Israelite tribal leaders, was a political time bomb.

The unrest burst briefly towards the end of King Solomon's rule. Jeroboam, a former royal supervisor of forced labor from the tribe of Ephraim, led a rebellion against King Solomon. After it failed, the other rebellious leaders learned to wait until Solomon's death for their chance to rebel.

Rebellion Splits the United Kingdom—After King Solomon's death, the leaders of the northern tribes, still angered over Solomon's policies, approached Solomon's son Rehoboam, who had succeeded him. As the condition for their loyalty, they asked Rehoboam to end the forced labor policy and reduce the high taxes that Solomon had imposed. Rehoboam unwisely and arrogantly turned them down completely. Following that, Jeroboam, who led the earlier failed revolt against Solomon, returned from his exile in Egypt to lead a successful rebellion against the "House of David."

Two Separate Hebrew Kingdoms—After the rebellion ended, Rehoboam remained king of the southern tribes of Israel in the "kingdom of Judah." Jerusalem, with its Holy Temple containing the Holy Ark, remained in the kingdom of Judah. Jeroboam was installed as king of the northern tribes of Israel. The area they lived in was to be known as the "kingdom of Israel." For the benefit of those northern Israelites who adhered to the sacrificial rituals practiced in the Jerusalem Holy Temple, Jeroboam set up religious ritual centers at both ends of his kingdom as alternates to the Temple in Jerusalem. One was in Dan in the north, the other was in Beth El in the south.

Territorial Differences Between the Kingdoms—The physical division between the two kingdoms was very uneven. Israel was three times the size of Judah. Israel contained the richer territory; it had more large cities and was complete with roads. Judah was rocky and dry, with exposure to the rigors of a desert-driven climate.

Lifestyle Differences Between the Kingdoms—The inhabitants of each kingdom had a different lifestyle. The northerners were farmers, craftsmen, and traders. Their contacts with foreigners weakened their loyalty to the Israelite God, Yahweh. The southerners were mainly shepherds and maintained a stronger worship of Yahweh than the northern Israelites. The Temple in Jerusalem, which was part of Judah, was a significant factor. It enabled the people of Judah to perform the sacrifices that Yahweh required, which shielded them from being corrupted by the region's heathen religions. The kingdom of Israel worshipped the God they called Elohim, who was less demanding in terms of sacrifices than Yahweh. This made the people of the kingdom of Israel more susceptible to reverting to idol worship.

Return of the Big-Power Influence—At the time of the split-up of the United Kingdom, the absence of external pressures that existed during the reign of Solomon ended. Both kingdoms were attacked and overrun by Egypt. Sixty cities in Israel and ninety cities in Judah were captured. Shishak, the new ruler of Egypt, entered Jerusalem as a conqueror. He plundered the treasury and carried off the rich Temple ornaments to Egypt.

After Egypt, the countries of Aram and then Assyria took turns at menacing the country and exacting a heavy tribute from Israel and to a lesser extent from Judah. These actions, in themselves, almost destroyed the demoralized kingdoms.

Fighting Between the Israelite Kingdoms—When the kingdoms of Israel and Judah were not struggling to ward off their larger neighbors, they intermittently fought each other. The ruler's envy of each other and their religious attitude differences were the main sources of friction. Between the external and internal fighting, the lives of many Jews were lost over a several hundred-year period.

The Kingdom of Israel (933–722 B.C.E.)

The northern kingdom of Israel lasted two hundred years. It did not have a very glorious history. It saw nine dynasties of rulers that produced nineteen kings. Most kings got to the throne only after killing their predecessor, frequently, along with royal families and their political allies. Religious transgressions and social unrest were the rule most of the time. Battles were fought periodically with Judah and the larger neighboring kingdoms. The very powerful Assyria finally crushed Israel. Israel, the dominant part of the original United Jewish Kingdom, disappeared as a country along with the disappearance of its population as Hebrews. The words of the Prophets who lived in the kingdom of Israel are a greater historical legacy than the country's accomplishments.

Violent Start—Israel was created when many of the northern tribes rebelled against King Solomon's successor, his son Rehoboam, and established their military leader Jeroboam as the king of a separate country called Israel. In an effort to achieve complete independence from Judah, Jeroboam established two religious centers in Israel as an alternate to the Holy Temple in Jerusalem. They were not very effective in maintaining the Hebrew Yahweh religious fervor. Idolatrous practices crept in, which did not sit well with many of the people in Israel. Nevertheless, Jeroboam ruled Israel for twenty-one years, which was a long time for a king of Israel. During Jeroboam's reign, there was relative stability and only mild battles with Judah. This relatively peaceful period ended soon after Jeroboam's son Nadab became king—anarchy ensued.

Israel at its inception was predominately an agricultural country. This suggested that the country would have a quiet political environment. Instead, ambitious political leaders and the military made conditions in Israel extremely turbulent. For the next thirty-seven years, Israel had six kings. Three died violent deaths. Only twice did a son succeed his father.

Omri Dynasty—Omri fought his way to the throne and established a dynasty that lasted forty years. He served twelve years. Omri restored stability to Israel and expanded its commerce, building many cities. He established peaceful relations with Israel's larger neighbors and with the southern kingdom of Judah, being the first king of Israel to do so.

Samaria: Kingdom of Israel's New Capital and New Name—King Omri, with a soldier's insight, picked the town of Samaria located on top of a hill and overlooking a broad valley to be the new capital of Israel. He expanded it to be the largest city in Israel, and he fortified it so well with a surrounding wall that it took the Assyrians three years to break down the city's resistance when they conquered and destroyed all of Israel. Samaria replaced Israel as the name of the country—which is why ardent Zionists refer to part of the West Bank as Samaria.

King Ahab and His Wife Jezebel—King Omri's son Ahab reigned twenty-two years. Ahab's rule was one of the most successful politically and economically for the kingdom of Israel. He settled the differences with his neighbors peacefully rather than through war, which was unusual for that time and area of the world. However, his rule is probably remembered more for the religious and social unrest that developed and led to the end of the Omri dynasty. The Prophets Elijah and Elisha contributed to the dynasty's downfall by stirring the people against the rulers. They vigorously protested against the expanding Baal worship instituted by Ahab's wife Jezebel, and they condemned the oppressive treatment of the general population.

Jehu Dynasty—The Prophet Elisha consorted with King Ahab's young General Jehu to lead an uprising against Ahab's successor. The people who had been aroused against Ahab by the Prophets Elisha and Elijah supported the uprising that resulted in the kings of Israel and of Judah dying in the fighting. Upon taking over the throne, Jehu followed Elisha's wish for religious cleansing in the kingdom of Israel. Jezebel, who promoted the Baal worship initially, and the rest of the royal family and the lead priests involved in the Baal worship were killed. Baal worship was eradicated, and Yahweh worship was resumed. The Jehu dynasty lasted one hundred years.

Because the king of Judah was killed during Jehu's insurrection, relations with the kingdom of Judah turned bitter and remained that way until the kingdom of Israel disappeared one hundred years later.

Jeroboam II—King Jeroboam II reigned forty years and had an outstanding record for most of his reign. He brought the kingdom back to its former power and wealth and added some territory. Near the end of his reign, moral and social decay again set in. Baal worship resumed. The poor were oppressed and corruption increased. Prophets Amos and Hosea decried these conditions and urged Israel to return to adherence to the Covenant with God in order to avert disaster.

Violent End—The prophetic warnings held true. After Jeroboam II died, chaos and anarchy set in. There were six kings over a thirteen-year period; four kings were assassinated. During that time, mighty Assyria progressively conquered Israel over a ten-year period ending in 722 B.C.E. As territory was taken over, thousands of captured Jews were uprooted and scattered throughout Assyria and foreigners were transplanted to Israel. This combination advanced intermarriage and accelerated the assimilation of the Israelites.

As a consequence of this complete assimilation into Assyrian society, the "ten lost tribes" of Israel simply vanished as an identity. Since Israelites at that time were involved in international trade to the Far East, some migration of former Israelites to East Asian countries appears plausible. This has been suggested as the heritage of the newly discovered "Hebrews of India."

Samaritans—Descendants of Samaria were a mixture of Israelites and foreigners that were brought into the area after the conquest by Assyria. Called Samaritans, they developed and retained a religion that adhered to the Five Books of Moses but with their own variations on the wording of the Torah and how Judaism was to be practiced. They rejected the Oral Law and the later Hebrew biblical books. These issues combined with their active intermarriage policy kept them apart from Judaism.

In approximately 400 B.C.E., the Samaritans built a temple in the city of Shechem to rival the Temple in Jerusalem. They lived apart from the Judeans. Three hundred years later, Samaria was subjugated and their temple destroyed by the Maccabean head of state Hyrcanus. The Samaritans in Palestine went into decline after that. The Samaritans had a following outside of Palestine, but that collapsed with the growth of Christianity. There is a very small remnant of Samaritans in Israel today still practicing their form of Judaism.

The Kingdom of Judah (933–586 B.C.E.)

After the rebellion of the northern tribes of Israel, the remnant of the United Hebrew Kingdom became the kingdom of Judah. Only the small tribe of Benjamin, which lived in the city of Jerusalem, joined the tribe of

Judah. This was extremely significant because Jerusalem was the heart and soul of the Hebrew religion in those times. Jerusalem was a major factor in the longevity of the kingdom of Judah, in the strengthening of Judaism after the Hebrews returned to Zion from their exile in Babylonia, and in the survival of Judaism throughout the ages.

Judah was smaller in size and population than the kingdom of Israel but it was stronger in two respects. Its people were more consistently fervent in their relationship with the Hebrew God Yahweh, and the Holy Temple was located in Jerusalem. These two factors cultivated Judaic nationalism, which, together with the stimulus of the Prophets and the guidance of creative religious leaders, enabled the Jews to overcome Jerusalem's total destruction. They gave Judean life to the people even after Judah's independence was lost. The term "Jew" was derived from the expression, "Judean."

Judah did not experience the many revolutions and assassinations that Israel suffered. Although there were some incidents of violence relating to Judah's rulers, all the kings of Judah came from the Davidic heritage. There were long periods of stability, several Judean kings had thirty-to-fifty-year reigns. Except for the periods under Jezebel's daughter Queen Athalia and the Assyrian vassal King Manasseh, pagan cult worship, which was still popular in the Middle East did not significantly infiltrate into the Judean culture. Judah overcame devastation by Egypt early in its history and experienced a long period of Assyrian dominance in the middle of its history, but kept its independence. At the end, it suffered crushing defeats by Babylonia over a fifteen-year period, which ended the kingdom of Judah's 350-year history.

A Brutal Start: Egyptian Devastation—After the United Kingdom split up, Judah and Israel periodically fought minor battles with each other over attempts to expand their borders. The severe problem came in the fifth year when Egyptian Pharaoh Sheshonk invaded Judah. Egyptian archeological records have confirmed this biblical narrative of history. Judah endured the severe attack. Ninety cities, including Jerusalem, were captured. Many cities were destroyed. However, Sheshonk's campaign was evidently intended only to plunder Judah. Egypt abandoned Judah after the valuables were stripped from the palace and Temple in Jerusalem. Judah remained independent.

Period of Rebuilding—After the Egyptian attack, Judah, the smaller of the two Hebrew countries, became the political vassal of the larger and more politically influential kingdom of Israel. This relationship essentially freed up Judah from foreign entanglements, giving it the opportunity to rebuild and actually grow and prosper. This happened under the forty-year reign of Asa and the twenty-five-year reign of Jehosaphat that followed.

Judah at Its Peak (787–735 B.C.E.)—Judah was at its peak during the fifty-two-year reign of King Uzzia. Uzzia expanded Judah's borders, obtaining an outlet to the Mediterranean. He built new cities and fortifications and expanded the economy. He is credited with the significant expansion of Judah's agricultural economy. Important from a Judaic standpoint, Uzzia kept the kingdom of Judah religiously correct during his long reign, contributing to its stability at a time when the kingdom of Israel was deteriorating due to religious degradation.

Hezekiah: The Good King (726–697 B.C.E.)—Although Assyria was the dominant country in the Middle East at that time, aided by the political guidance from the Prophet Isaiah, King Hezekiah was able to keep Judah's religious and economic freedom by acquiescing to Assyria's political power. Hezekiah, after recovering from a serious illness, became a religious man. He removed the Canaanite altars that were being used by many Hebrews and ended the Hebrew's practice of fertility rites they copied from the Canaanite religion. In 714 B.C.E., this delicate relationship with Assyria changed. Against the pleading of Isaiah, Hezekiah was swayed by nationalists who resented the political subjugation to Assyria. He entered agreements with Egypt and several smaller countries in the area, conspiring with them to oppose Assyria. In 705 B.C.E., the smaller countries were decimated by Assyria, but Judah was spared at that time. Against Isaiah's new warnings, Hezekiah entered foreign entanglements again and a period of political intrigue followed. Hezekiah spent four years building fortifications and prepared to rebel against Assyria. King Hezekiah is best remembered for the tunnel that he built to bring water into Jerusalem, which enabled Jerusalem to cope with the extended siege during his reign and with other sieges during its long history.

Isaiah continued to warn Judah to stay neutral and prophesied the destruction of Judah, Egypt, and the other conspirator countries. Unfortunately, Prophet Isaiah was vindicated. In 701 B.C.E., his prediction came true for Egypt and the other conspirator countries when the new Assyrian ruler, Sennacherib, attacked, conquered, and destroyed most of them. He then turned on the kingdom of Judah and destroyed forty-six Judean cities and attacked Jerusalem. Isaiah changed from encouraging acquiescence to Assyria to encouraging the Jerusalemites to defend themselves with the help of God—God would help them to be victorious.

Miraculously, Jerusalem held out for a long time against the superior Assyrian forces. Then suddenly, the Assyrians ended the siege and retreated home. Prophet Isaiah attributed the unexpected victory to divine intervention. Judah then entered a long peaceful period, but only after agreeing to be a vassal of Assyria.

Religious Backtracking by King Manasseh (697–642 B.C.E.)—King Manasseh ruled the kingdom of Judah for fifty-five years, which started at the end of the long period of Assyrian domination. Whether to appease Assyria and avoid the fate of the kingdom of Israel or because he believed in it, Manasseh allowed Assyrian idolatry to infiltrate back into the Judean lifestyle. Canaanite altars were again built on the highest peaks (the Canaanite custom) throughout the country. The religious degradation reached its peak when the Holy Temple in Jerusalem was desecrated with pagan idols.

During Manasseh's rule, the kingdom of Judah did recover physically and economically from the political devastation by Assyria that occurred early in his reign. However, Manasseh's terrible religious leadership and his own very immoral behavior mark him as the worst Jewish king in history.

Josiah's Religious Reformation: Period of Glory for Judah (640–609 B.C.E.)—Following the long period of Judaic religious desecration under King Manasseh and continued by his son Amon for another two years, there was a remarkable period of religious reform. It happened under Manasseh's grandson Josiah. Only eight years old when he ascended the throne, King Josiah evidently received religious guidance that motivated him by the time he was sixteen to institute the return to Judaic practices. He was probably strongly influenced by the then youthful Prophet Jeremiah. When he was eighteen, King Josiah purged Judah of the heathen altars that had been spread around the country for the Hebrews to participate in Canaanite worship. Josiah went one step further—he removed the priests who had been leading the Hebrews in the idolatrous worship. Finally, after cleansing the Jerusalem Holy Temple of the heathen idols that had been installed by his grandfather, King Manasseh, King Josiah centralized Hebrew worship in the Jerusalem Holy Temple.

In the eighteenth year of Josiah's thirty-one-year reign, a major event in Judaic history occurred. A copy of the Book of Deuteronomy was found in the Temple when the Temple was being repaired. This finding became a significant step in Judaic religious revival. King Josiah assembled the Judeans and the Hebrew priests to Jerusalem and read the Book of Deuteronomy to them. It was the start of a complete return to the adherence to the Covenant and Law of Moses as prescribed in Deuteronomy—some Jewish scholars believe it was truly the initiation of such practices. Josiah capped this religious revival by leading a majestic Passover celebration in Jerusalem that adhered to the Mosaic commandment of a seven-day Passover observance. The people in the kingdoms of Judah and Israel apparently had not observed Passover in this manner for hundreds of years.

Josiah is considered one of the greatest Jewish kings because of his personal moral and religious values and for his restoration of the Judaic religious practices in the kingdom of Judah.

Initial Conquest by Babylonia: Exile to Babylonia—After Josiah was killed in battle as an ally of Assyria against the Egyptians, who had gone on a campaign to conquer the region, the situation in Judah deteriorated rapidly. With Josiah gone, the Judeans started to backtrack religiously by practicing paganism again. Coincidentally, the Chaldeans who became the new rulers of Babylonia under Nebuchadnezzar's leadership rose to power in the area. They defeated Egypt in 601 B.C.E. and proceeded to take over the Middle East. There were four Judean kings in rapid succession, none of which had the skills to challenge Nebuchadnezzar who demanded heavy tribute. When King Jehiakim, against the advice of Jeremiah, rebelled against Babylon in 597 B.C.E., the Babylonians wreaked havoc in Judah. Jerusalem was devastated and plundered. Thousands of captives, including the influential people and all of the artisans and capable craftsmen, were exiled. Intending to weaken Judah so that it would no longer represent a formidable adversary, Nebuchadnezzar left the poorest people behind.

Final Conquest by Babylon: Destruction of the Temple and the End of Judah as a Nation—The last king of Judah was Zedekia, who ruled for eleven years. In 589 B.C.E., his ninth year as king, Zedekia rebelled against Nebuchadnezzar's authority. The powerful Nebuchadnezzar reacted violently, attacking and destroying many cities in Judah. Nebuchadnezzar besieged Jerusalem. Although the people were starving, they held out for a year and a half. The city was finally conquered in 586 B.C.E. and burned to the ground. The Holy Temple was razed and destroyed, its valuables taken to Babylonia. The ninth day of the Hebrew month of Av (*Tisha B'Av*) became a full fast day for the Jewish people commemorating the day on which the Holy Temple was destroyed. This practice started in the Babylonian exile days and continues to be observed by Orthodox and Conservative Jews today.

Another Exile to Babylonia—After Nebuchadnezzar's final conquest of Judah, King Zedekia along with most of the Judean survivors of the Babylonian onslaught were exiled to Babylon. The defeat was followed with more tragedy. Most of the Judean royal family, the priesthood, and many community elders were put to death.

The Tragedy of Gedaliah—Gedaliah, a capable leader from a notable Judean family and an ally of the Prophet Jeremiah, was appointed as the Babylonian governor to rule over the small number of Hebrews remaining in Judah. Gedaliah promoted cooperation with Babylonia and was in the process of developing a following of influential people who started to surface. He tried to restore normalcy to life, turning ownership of the land over to those working the land. Jeremiah was encouraged by Nebuchadnezzar to aid Gedaliah's efforts.

The tragedy occurred seven months after Gedaliah became governor. Judean royalists assassinated Gedaliah, his Judean officials, and his Chaldean guards. Gedaliah had been told what to expect, but he ignored the warning. After the assassinations, Jeremiah advised the people to remain in Judah and to cooperate with Babylon. The conspirators, however, expected a severe reprisal from Nebuchadnezzar and decided to flee to Egypt for their safety, taking Jeremiah and many other Judeans with them. The king did view the murder of his governor Gedaliah and his Chaldean guards as a serious rebellion. He reacted strongly, ending the local Judean authority and exiling most of the remaining Judeans to Babylonia. Gedaliah's death ended any immediate hope for Judah's restoration and independence.

The Fast of Gedaliah—In later years, the Talmudic Sages viewed a Jew killing a Jewish leader for political reasons as a reprehensible, mournful act that is contrary to Judaic principles. (The 1995 assassination of Israeli Prime Minister Yitzhak Rabin by a young Jew who disagreed with Rabin's policies evoked the same rabbinic objectionable reaction.) They established the Fast of Gedaliah (minor fast day) to commemorate the day of his murder. Living under similar political circumstances as Gedaliah, the Sages also wanted to give the message to the subjugated and oppressed Jewish people that Gedaliah's acceptance of foreign subjugation for the sake of Jewish survival was not dishonorable.

Judean Survival—There were several factors contributing to the survival of the Judeans as a people after the kingdom of Judah was destroyed. Strong leaders emerged among the Babylonian Jews to guide the Judeans to retain their loyalty to Judaism. A core of exiled Judeans, with strong feelings towards their all-powerful God Yahweh, considered their future to be in His hands. They considered it necessary to adhere to the sacred biblical commandments to obtain and retain God's blessings, and never lost the will to demonstrate their devotion and respect to God in the Jerusalem Holy Temple—the Temple was rebuilt within seventy years. Judeans had been united in their loyalty only to the Davidian dynasty as the source of their kings. Although the Judean kingdom ended, their past uniformity and respect for central authority prepared the Judeans to accept the urging of the Prophets to repent of their disloyalty to Judaism and, later, to change to rabbinic Judaism under Ezra and Nehemiah.

Babylonian Exile and Return (597–450 B.C.E.)

The period of exile in Babylonia represented very trying times for the Jews as a people. Those who were caught practicing the Hebrew religion were threatened with imprisonment, torture, and death. Because of the pressure of these threats, many Jews, particularly the poorer, unskilled class, succumbed to the immoral Babylonian idol worship, which was conducted very actively through intensive community participation. They felt their own God was not providing them relief from their misery.

The intellectual and artisan class of Jews succumbed to the opportunities that the advanced and successful Babylonian economy offered them. They were lost to Judaism through assimilation into Babylonian society, which came with no governmental penalties. The Yiddish expression *"shver tsu zein ah Yid"* ("difficult to be a Jew") could very well have been created then. It was applicable. Clinging to Judaism brought suffering, abandoning Judaism brought relief.

This negative environment for Judaism lasted over seventy-five years before relief came in the way of a Persian takeover of Babylonia. This oppressive period took its toll on the Jewish population, which dropped dramatically to a low estimated at 200,000.

The Strength of Ezekial—The only countering force to the discouraging Babylonian environment was the Prophet Ezekial. Defying the authorities, he encouraged the Jews to believe God had not forsaken them. His theme was Jews could and should practice their religion without the Holy Temple. As a prophet and a priest, Ezekial became their spiritual leader, stressing the observance of the fundamental Jewish religious practices, such as the rite of circumcision, the dietary laws, and honoring the Sabbath. He taught that obedience of the Mosaic moral laws was more important than temple rituals. Ezekial also offered the hope of the eventual return to Zion of all the twelve tribes, providing visions and plans for a rebuilt temple that would function more ethically.

Use of Aramaic—Aramaic was used as a language in Babylonia because it was easier to write than the cuneiform that preceded it. The Jews learned to use Aramaic when interacting with the Babylonians during their exile. Aramaic became even more important as the common language with the Persians when they ruled over Babylonia.

Aramaic words were integrated into the Hebrew vocabulary and Bible; some parts of the books of Daniel and Ezra were written in Aramaic. It became the language of the lower classes during the Second Commonwealth. Several items in today's Hebrew liturgy are in Aramaic. The most outstanding are the Kaddish (mourner's) prayer, the Day of Atonement Kol Nidre prayer, and sections of the Passover Haggadah.

King Cyrus Permits the Return to Judah—After three years of besieging the well-fortified walled city of Babylon, the very powerful Persian King Cyrus conquered Babylon in 538 B.C.E. Two years later, Cyrus, inspired by the words of Jeremiah expressing God's expectation that the Jews would build a new temple in Jerusalem to serve all humankind, declared *"The Hebrews had the right and duty to go back to their Holy Land."* He even supported the return with money. It turned out to be a long struggle to restore Judaic life in Judah and Jerusalem. The second Prophet Isaiah (the true author's name is unknown) offered hope and inspiration during the lengthy period of rebuilding Jerusalem.

Return to Jerusalem: Disappointment—Shortly after the authorization to return, a small contingent of Jews led by Zerubbabel, a relative of the last king of Judah, returned to Jerusalem with the intent of rebuilding the Holy Temple. He found the city devastated and the Temple in ruins. His plans were to first rebuild the walls of the city in order to give it protection. The neighboring Samaritan and Ammonite leaders protested to the new Persian King Darius, who put a stop to the wall-building activity. Zerubbabel and his followers returned to Babylon disappointed. All work on Jerusalem and the Temple ceased for twelve years.

Renewed Temple Rebuilding Effort—King Darius was finally persuaded to permit the rebuilding of the Temple to continue. However, he did not allow Zerubbabel to lead the effort, suspecting him of trying to restore the monarchy in Judah. Zerubbabel dropped out of the picture, ending all thoughts of the Davidic dynasty continuing to rule over Judah.

The rebuilding effort was very slow. There were few people involved, and the Samaritans again hindered the effort. The old Prophet Haggai and, later, the young Prophet Zechariah provided the stimulus to continue the Temple-rebuilding effort. The ritual emphasis in the rebuilt Temple remained on Yahweh worship, reflecting the Prophets' visions. The rebuilt Temple was finally completed eight years later, in 516 B.C.E. It was not as ornate as the original but served the similar purpose as the focal point for the Hebrew religion.

The Age of the Prophets (750–450 B.C.E.)

Wicked rulers of the two Israelite kingdoms created horrible economic conditions for the people. Frequently encouraged by these same rulers, violations of the Mosaic Code and the worship of idols became prevalent, and the priesthood offered little leadership in overcoming this religious degradation. In addition to these internal troubles, the political climate in the Middle East was turbulent and complex. These conditions imposed the need for frequent decision making on the part of the rulers and the people regarding which country to align with or when to resist—the larger neighboring kingdoms were a constant threat to the existence of the two Israelite kingdoms. The biblical Prophets, unique in history only to the Jewish people, were messengers of God to the Hebrews during this very turbulent period of their history. Their messages of morality, social and political justice, universality of all people under one God, and the hope of future redemption have remained as a lasting inspirational contribution to all civilization.

The Prophets were the conscience of the Hebrew people, recognizing their faults and proclaiming them in public. They offered the Hebrews behavioral advice, consolation for the tragedies that befell them, and hope for their future by:

- Admonishing the people for forsaking their Covenant with God,
- Demanding that ritual observance be ethical and loyal to the Hebrew God,
- Condemning the Hebrew kings for their wickedness and immorality,

- Crying out for social justice and righteousness, especially for the downtrodden,
- Warning the people to repent their ways before catastrophe would befall them,
- Offering the promise of God's forgiveness of the Jewish people and nation if they mended their ways.

There were fifteen literary Prophets whose words are recorded in their respective books that have been passed down through the ages. Isaiah, Jeremiah, and Ezekial are considered major only because of the larger size of their books in comparison with the others. The writings of these prophets are included in the second section of the Hebrew Bible called *Neviim* (Prophets). The writings of three preclassical Prophets; Nathan, Elijah, and Elisha are documented in the biblical books of Samuel and Kings.

In addition to their messages of guidance to their people, the Prophets had the capability to foretell future calamities through divine inspiration. Prophets such as Zephania offered the Jewish people warnings of the destruction of their land. Hosea and Zechariah provided consolation on the defeats the Jewish people were to suffer and the redemption to follow. Prophets also foretold the defeat of Israel's enemies. Obadiah told of the defeat of Edom. Nachum predicted the defeat of Assyria.

Malachi initiated the messianic concept. He prophesied the coming of the messianic era, which was to be announced by the Prophet Elijah. This is the basis for the tradition at the Passover Seder to open the door to the outside and welcome Eijah to come in and announce the coming of the Messiah. Through the ages, this anticipation of the coming of the Messiah provided a measure of strength to Jews during periods of severe oppression, and remains an active hope for some Jews today.

The Prophets got their mission from God to preach God's messages through dreams or visions. They came from all walks of life: aristocracy (Isaiah), priesthood (Jeremiah, Ezekial), farmers (Amos). Some were persecuted and subjected to great hardships (Elijah, Jeremiah). They accepted their role enthusiastically, except for Jonah, who tried to escape from his mission.

Unique for its time, this compact prophetic message provides guidance to the people for all times: ***"God wants people to be moral and to be good to fellow humankind; honoring God through religious rituals must reflect these principles."***

Elijah: Patron Saint of Jewish Life (842 B.C.E.)—Elijah's major challenge was to fight against King Ahab's tolerance of his people worshiping the pagan idol Baal together with the Hebrew God in the Hebrew temples that Ahab established in the kingdom of Israel. King Ahab's Phoenician wife, Jezebel, influenced him to accept this practice; Baal was her god. This pagan worship violated the Judaic laws and was destroying the stability of the kingdom of Israel. Elijah's protestations and those of his successor, Prophet Elisha, ultimately led to the downfall of Ahab's lineage for the kings of the kingdom of Israel.

Elijah has achieved a special place in Judaism's tradition. He is a hero who was responsible for many good deeds, and who will herald good things to happen in the future, including the coming of the Messiah. He is included in Jewish prayers and Sabbath songs, and in the traditional Passover Seder with the fifth wine cup designated as Elijah's cup and the door to the outside opened to let him in with the hope that he will bring the redemption that comes with the Messiah.

Amos: Pioneer Prophet (750 B.C.E.)—First of the literary Prophets who wrote down their messages, Amos set an example for the later prophets. Amos, a Judean, lived at the time of King Uzziah, when the religious and social behavior of the Judean leaders and people were not troublesome from a Judaic standpoint. However, through visits to Israel, he witnessed the widespread religious and social transgressions in the northern kingdom, which was the subject of his prophecies. He preached repentance to the sinful Hebrews of the kingdom of Israel during the reign of Jeroboam II. He strongly objected to the country's Hebrew priests leading the people to heathen worship. He was troubled by the harsh and demoralizing treatment of the people by the corrupt ruling class. Amos warned of Israel's impending doom unless the people repented. Amos was a social reformer who stressed ethics and justice as necessary inherent parts of the true Hebrew religion. His message: *"Seek the Lord that you may live. Seek good and not evil, that you may live."*

Hosea: Prophet of Love and Hope (745 B.C.E.)—Hosea is the only Prophet of the northern kingdom that left written prophecies. His book rebuked the people for their gross idolatry and atrocious sins. He taught that ritual worship is meaningless unless accompanied by an ethical lifestyle. Pained by a troublesome relationship with his unfaithful wife Gomer, who worshiped the idol Baal, Hosea nevertheless continued to love her. He saw in this tragic relationship an indication that *God still loves man in spite of* *man's erratic behavior.* It became the basis of his prophetic mission, to preach love as the heart of religion.

Micah: Prophet to the Downtrodden (740 B.C.E.)—Micah prophesied the destruction of Jerusalem because of its corrupt leaders. He was a spokesman for the common people, avoiding Judah's leaders and distrusting the large cities as being the source of corruption. He had a passion for social justice. Micah's definition of what God requires of man is expressed in his famous quotation, *"Do justly, love mercy, and walk humbly with your God."*

First Isaiah: Statesman Prophet (740 B.C.E.)—The very long Book of Isaiah is attributed to two different authors spanning two different time periods. The first thirty-nine chapters are attributed to the real Isaiah who lived in the last half of the eighth century B.C.E. The last twenty-seven chapters are attributed to an unknown author(s) (Deutero-Isaiah, or second Isaiah) who lived during the Babylonian exile in 586 B.C.E.

The first Isaiah was the "Statesman Prophet." For more than forty years, he provided foreign policy advice to aid Judah in maintaining its independence. When the Judeans did not fall to the strong Assyrians in their campaign to capture all of Judah, Isaiah attributed this success to divine assistance in response to King Hezekia's repentance and his turning to reliance upon the God of Israel. Isaiah's strong leadership saved Judah. Isaiah preached that faith in God was needed in addition to the arsenals of war to survive. Isaiah was a master orator. He condemned the immoral behavior of the people, calling for an end to idolatry, for purity of religious behavior, and for social justice. He warned that sin would not go unpunished.

Isaiah also prophesied the coming of the Messiah, at which time the dispersed twelve tribes of Israel would return to Zion. *"There shall come forth a shoot out of the stock of Jesse. And the spirit of the Lord shall rest upon him."*

His vision of the messianic era was one of peace for all nations of the world. *"The lion and the lamb will lie down with each other. And they shall beat their swords into plowshares. Nation shall not lift up sword against nation. Neither shall they learn war any more."*

Second Isaiah: Restored Faith in God—The second Isaiah section offered the optimism that a small group of Israelites would continue to serve the holy God, preserving a holy Israel, and be capable of rebuilding Zion. It envisioned a time when there will be an end to warfare, when peace and harmony will prevail among peoples and nations. This was to come when the people observe God's laws. These messages have sustained and fortified the people of Israel during its ordeals of cruelty and persecution suffered throughout the ages. These second-Isaiah messages of consolation are read in the synagogue as the Haftorah, reading messages of comfort for seven Sabbaths after the fast of Av, which commemorates the destruction of the Temple and other Jewish catastrophes. Isaiah comforted Israel with his words when the Israelites were preparing to return to Zion after their exile to Babylon, which followed the destruction of Jerusalem.

Jonah: Reluctant Prophet (700 B.C.E.)—The Book of Jonah has a universalistic message. It teaches that all people are equally the children of one God and that the door is open to God's pardon through sincere repentance. God calls on a heathen city, whose people do not adhere to God's Covenant and the Mosaic Code, to repent and be spared. Jonah was given the mission to warn Nineveh, the Assyrian capital, of its impending doom. Because Assyria was Israel's enemy, Jonah was reluctant to undertake this mission and attempted to flee to Tarshish at the other end of the Mediterranean. The story tells of Jonah being thrown overboard from the ship he took, swallowed by a great fish (whale), and getting back to land three days later to complete his mission. Assyria repented and Nineveh was saved.

This book is read as the prophetic portion (Haftorah) during the afternoon service on the Day of Atonement as a reminder of the power of repentance.

Jeremiah: Fearless Prophet (625 B.C.E.)—Jeremiah's period of prophecy lasted forty years. He condemned the wickedness of the Judean people. He assailed the Judean King Jehoiakim for his injustice. He preached against the idolatry that was rampant amongst the priests in the Holy Temple in Jerusalem. Jeremiah incurred the wrath of almost everyone in Judah.

Jeremiah was a political maverick. Initially, he opposed Judah's alliance with Egypt to ward off the rising supremacy of Babylon. Then he advocated submission to the Babylonians who had just conquered Judah as the best approach to Israel's survival. That earned him the wrath of King Zedekiah, getting him imprisoned. Later, after Gedaliah, the Babylonian-appointed Hebrew governor of Judah was assassinated, Jeremiah was taken to Egypt for his safety, where he spent the rest of his life still prophesying.

Jeremiah's basic teaching was that righteousness rather than material prosperity strengthens one's soul: *"Not to glory in wisdom, might, and wealth, but only in the service of God who is just."* He also wrote several "lamentations and consolations" that have been incorporated into the Judaic liturgy.

Zephania: Prophet of Doom (625 B.C.E.)—Zephania started his prophecy aiding the virtuous King Hosia of Judah to reform the moral and religious character of the nation. After Hosia was killed in a battle with Egypt, idolatry and other wickedness returned to Judah. Zephania, along with Jeremiah, predicted the doom of Judah and the other neighboring corrupt nations unless they repented. He predicted a bloody disaster for the inhabitants of Jerusalem. His dire predictions unfortunately came true with the destruction of Judah, including Jerusalem. His prophecy of disaster for the other nations in the area also materialized. A barbaric tribe, the Scythians, invaded many of the Near East countries and the people in these countries were treated brutally.

Zephania's final prediction was for the redemption of the remaining faithful Hebrews in a period of joy and without fear. It took one hundred years, but a small faithful group of exiles from Babylon and Egypt did return to joyously rebuild Jerusalem and the Holy Temple. Unfortunately, the joy and the absence of fear did not last very long.

Ezekial: Prophet of Hope (590 B.C.E.)—Ezekial is the only Prophet to get the prophetic call while away from Palestine. He was a priest among the early exiles sent by the Babylonians to Chaldea. In his fifth year there, he received his mission and started to serve as the center of hope for the exiled Hebrews.

Before Jerusalem fell and was destroyed by the Babylonians, Ezekial denounced the idolatry practiced by the Hebrews in Jerusalem. He prophesied Jerusalem's total destruction if there was no repentance; the Hebrews needed moral and spiritual purification. Like the other Prophets, he warned that if the Israelites did not repent, they would not be forgiven. During the five years of these warnings, Ezekial was hardly listened to. When Jerusalem indeed did fall, it vindicated him and he gained the respect of the Jewish exiles.

Ezekial gave the people new hope. He proclaimed that God had not forgotten them although there was no longer the Temple. He became their spiritual leader, introducing direct religious instructions in the absence of the Temple. He was the forerunner of Ezra who established the synagogue as the center of religious life replacing the worship of Yahweh for the Hebrews.

His last prophecies offered hope for the return of all the land to the twelve tribes of Israel and the restoration of the Holy Temple with a purer form of worship and sacrifices. To his credit, Israel did repudiate forever all idolatrous rites and customs, the nation was purified from its religious apostasy.

Zechariah: Visionary Prophet (520 B.C.E.)—Zechariah returned to Jerusalem after the Babylonian exile. His prophecies aided the leaders in uplifting the spirits of the returning Hebrews faced with the difficult and uncertain task of restoring the Judaic life in Judah and rebuilding Jerusalem. After a strong appeal for repentance, Zechariah offered hope to the people through eight visions. He envisioned Jerusalem restored and serving all nations.

Malachi: Prophet of Religious Reformation (450 B.C.E.)—The Temple had been rebuilt seventy years earlier, the priests had become mercenary, and the people's zeal had faded. Against this background, Malachi, the last of the Prophets, admonished the people for their transgressions of the Mosaic rituals and ethical laws. He denounced mixed marriages and divorces, which became prevalent. He was particularly hard on the priests for not obeying the Mosaic spiritual laws.

Malachi ended by prophesying the messianic days: *"Behold I will send you Elijah the prophet before the coming of the great and terrible day of the Lord. And He shall turn the heart of the fathers to the children, and the heart of the children to their fathers."*

3
Creation of Rabbinical Judaism (450–330 B.C.E.)

Two books of the Bible, Ezra and Nehemiah, represent the only historical source of information for this period. These books were apparently written long after the events, some speculate one hundred to two hundred years later; so the accuracy of the details are somewhat suspect. From these books, we learn that the Scribe Ezra provided the religious leadership that *changed the Hebrew religion from the Yahweh sacrificial system to rabbinical-centered Judaism.* Nehemiah, the Jewish governor of Judah, provided the political leadership to make these changes happen.

The Scribes of Babylon

With the Holy Temple in Jerusalem destroyed, the Prophet Ezekial encouraged the Hebrews exiled in Babylon to practice the Mosaic religious and moral code without the sacrificial rites, which could no longer be performed. Ezekial's work was continued by his disciples, called scribes. They served as learned teachers and holy book writers.

Ezra Establishes Rabbinical Judaism

Ezra was active as a priest and a scribe in Babylon. He witnessed what happened to the various cultures that were a minority in host countries and that did not have religious practices and a lifestyle that differentiated them from the host countries. They were doomed to extinction. He saw it beginning to happen with the assimilated Jews in Babylon. Ezra concluded that the cult-like system of devotion to God through sacrifices prescribed in Leviticus would not keep Judaism alive—it was too close to the other pagan religions in the area. He contended that belief in the Judaic religion alone was insufficient to keep Judaism alive. Jews needed a mode of living that set them apart from the communities they lived in—Jews were assimilating in all the countries they were living in.

Ezra's Religious Reformation (450 B.C.E.)—There were about 50,000 Jews living at that time in Judah; many came with the second group returning from Babylon to rebuild the Temple. The Temple was rebuilt, but it did not keep them from straying from the Mosaic religious and moral codes. After hearing about the moral decay of life in Jerusalem and particularly in the rebuilt Temple's religious rites, Ezra recruited 1,500 Jews to return with him to Jerusalem to change this situation. This small group of Jews managed to keep Judaism alive during those turbulent days.

Ezra concluded that a major source of the degradation in the lifestyle of the Jews in Judah was due to the extensive intermarriage that had occurred in Judah since the Babylonian invasion one hundred and fifty years earlier. Samaritans living in Judah had been intermarrying with Jews. They presented a strong influence on their Jewish spouses. The intermarried Jews were not respecting the temple priests and were violating the Mosaic rituals and laws. Ezra also viewed the temple priests as representing another source of the religious and lifestyle degradation. Some priests, under the influence of neighboring countries, were behaving corruptly and immorally. Some intermarried priests strayed from the proper temple practices.

Ezra, the accomplished scribe, was effective as a teacher. He persuaded the Judeans to make several significant changes that he considered necessary for the survival of the Jewish people as a separate culture. The Jewish people were to start the proper observance of the religious holidays and were to follow the Torah as the guide to living. The intermarriage practice was to end; intermarried families were to be excluded from belonging to Judaism. This was a harsh but bold step that Ezra considered vital. The priests were to agree to not violate the sanctity of their position. Intermarried priests were not permitted; nonconforming priests were removed.

In accordance with Ezra's plan, Jews everywhere were to adopt an ethical and moral lifestyle in conjunction with religious practices that conformed to the Torah guidelines. This behavior would set them apart from non-Jews and give Jews a reason for retaining their Judaism. Based on interpretations of the Mosaic Code in Deuteronomy, Ezra together with other scribes defined comprehensive rules of behavior for the Jewish people. They were kept orally as the *"Oral Torah,"* because the scribes felt a written version would violate the sanctity of the Torah of Moses. To achieve these goals, Ezra introduced Torah readings and Oral Torah discussions at Sabbath meetings that all Jews were required to attend—the beginning of synagogue services. Ezra intended for all Jews to understand the Torah, for without this knowledge, the common Jew would hardly accept the strict new regulations. This led to the age-old practice of an annual cycle of weekly Torah readings on the Sabbath. The reading of a *"Haftorah"* ("conclusion"), which is a lesson from the Prophets associated with the Sabbath or holiday Torah reading, was added some time later. This Torah-reading practice served to establish the Jewish focus on education, which was a mainstay of Jewish survival throughout the ages.

Nehemiah: Enforcer of Rabbinical Judaism

Nehemiah, who had a high-level position within the Persian king's organization, was disturbed about the conditions in Jerusalem. He shared Ezra's views on what changes were needed. He was appointed as the Persian governor of Judah, a position he held for twelve years. In this capacity, he exerted the authority to implement the changes introduced by Ezra and instituted many others.

Nehemiah's first act as governor was to rebuild the walls and fortifications around Jerusalem in order to provide protection against the neighboring countries, which still represented threats to the safety of the Jewish population. He instituted social reforms, getting the debts of the poor voided, and turning ownership of the land over to the poor farmers who were working it. He shared Ezra's view on the harmful effects of intermarriage on Judaism's future and enforced the isolation of the intermarried from Jewish activity. (In later years, it was the Jews who, as a means of Judaism's survival, isolated themselves from non-Jewish society in order to avoid intermarriage.) In this regard, Nehemiah forced the many priests who had non-Jewish wives to leave the priesthood. He increased the Jerusalem population in order to bolster its development by arranging for ten percent of the Jews living outside of Jerusalem to move to Jerusalem. To be fair and acceptable to the people, those required to move were selected by a lottery system. He also enforced the biblical tithe system of supporting the Levites who assisted the priests in the Temple and in the other cities.

Sabbath Becomes a Holy Day and a Day of Rest

Both Ezra and Nehemiah took steps to have the Jews honor the Sabbath as both a holy day and a day of rest. Ezra taught the religious and personal values of this practice, while Nehemiah used his governmental authority to enforce its practice in Jerusalem.

The Great Assembly

Rather than imposing their wishes on the people, Ezra and Nehemiah used a tactic that got the people to voluntarily accept the changes they wanted to institute. They called assemblies of the elders of the communities in Judah to discuss their proposed changes. The assemblies generally involved one hundred and fifty men from Judah and included representatives from the neighboring countries when there were issues that involved them. It turned out to be very effective; the people ended up accepting the changes as their own ideas rather than as changes imposed by the authorities. This "Great Assembly" technique served as a loose confederation of rabbis and sages for providing religious and political leadership to the Jewish people for the next few centuries while they were under foreign domination.

The Legacy of Ezra and Nehemiah

Without historical information that covers the two centuries after Ezra and Nehemiah, there are no details of how their effort to keep Judaism alive was continued. We do know that their efforts succeeded. Three hundred years later, there were determined Jews under the Maccabees who risked their lives fighting the Syrian attempt to wipe out the vestiges of Judaism in Palestine. Without a political homeland after the exile from Palestine in the second century, rabbinic Judaism was still able to survive in Europe for another two thousand years, overcoming the relentless religious oppression and severe Christian proselytizing pressure.

4
The Second Jewish Commonwealth

The events leading to the creation of the Second Jewish Commonwealth provided an important political example to the world. For the first time in history, ordinary people took the initiative to overthrow their tyrannical ruler—previously the action of aggressive, competing kings or scheming politicians and royal family members. This "people's action" was ahead of the times. It was not replicated for almost two thousand years, until the American people's revolution against England.

The success of the Maccabean people's revolt against the mighty Syrians provided another lesson to the world. It demonstrated how effective a poorly armed band of freedom fighters can be when these fighters are highly motivated and determined to fight for their cause at the risk of their lives—events not replicated until recent times.

The fate of the Second Jewish Commonwealth illustrates how a country, born of noble ideals, can deteriorate as a result of tyrannical rule over its people.

Greek Domination: Challenge of Hellenism (326–140 B.C.E.)

Under the tolerant rule of the Persians, the Jews in Judea (the old kingdom of Judah) developed a semiautonomous political system dominated by the religious institutions. The priesthood organization associated with the second Temple, which was the center of religion for the Jews living in Judea, exerted a strong leadership. Also influential and in competition with the priests, were the scribes. They were Ezra's teaching successors, providing interpretations of the Mosaic laws to the people at Sabbath meetings, which was the beginning of synagogue practice. The Great Assembly technique, used by Ezra and Nehemiah to institute their reformation, was apparently allowed by the Persian rulers to settle Jewish political and social issues. The Jewish communities dispersed around the

Mediterranean and living in Babylon were starting to develop their own communal organizations that took advantage of the religious lifestyle promoted by Ezra.

The situation changed dramatically for the Jews with the conquest of the Palestine area in 324 B.C.E. by the Greek Emperor Alexander the Great. Hellenistic (Greek culture) practices were introduced through the establishment of Greek cities distributed throughout Judea and the influx of Greeks into the Jewish populated cities. This culture, opposite to what Judaism stood for, brought challenges to the religious and social fabric of the Jews that also impacted on the political scene. The character of the Hellenism the Greeks brought to Judea had none of the "niceties" of Hellenism practiced in Greece. It was crude paganism, full of lewdness and other forms of immorality.

The Jewish Community Splits: Puritans and Hellenists—The exposure to Hellenism split the Jewish population in Judea into two political groups. The anti-Hellenist Puritans (*Hasidim*) were the nationalists who fought to retain all aspects of Judaism. The Hellenists sought to be fully integrated into the Hellenistic culture, including worshiping Greek idols and taking Greek names. The split was also along social lines. The upper class and city youth tended to be Hellenistic. Hellenism also infiltrated into the priesthood. The farmers and artisans tended to be the Puritans. Although Judaism barely survived Hellenism, this influence left cleavages between the Jews that got more severe in the next phase of Jewish history.

Hellenism's Impact on Jews Outside of Judea—Hellenism had a more limited impact on the large dispersed Jewish community compared to the Judean community. They essentially accepted only the intellectual and cultural aspects of Hellenism such as the arts and literature. The Judeans started taking Greek names and speaking Greek. However, they did not abandon Judaism, maintaining their loyalty to the Temple in Jerusalem by supporting it financially and visiting it. The positive blend of Judaism and Hellenism is reflected in the Septuagint ("seventy" in Greek, after the seventy learned Jewish scribes who contributed to its writing) version of the Torah, written in Greek by Jews in approximately 250 B.C.E. This Torah, written in the language spoken by most people in the Mediterranean countries, was a factor in keeping those Jews who were influenced by the cultural aspects of Hellenism tied to their Hebrew religion. It also was a significant factor in the large conversion to Judaism that took place in the Mediterranean countries over the next few hundred years.

Syrian/Greek Oppression—In 198 B.C.E., the Syrian Seleucus dynasty, with strong Hellenist ties, established its rule over the Palestine area. Under Syrian influence and pressure, the hellenizing of the Jews increased significantly. In 175 B.C.E., it reached a peak under the King Antiochus IV. Antiochus was a tyrant who forcefully imposed Hellenism on Judea and intended to end Judaic practices. The Jewish priesthood mischievously vied for his favors, accepting pagan practices in the Temple. The sanctuary became a Greek temple, and community sacrifices were offered to Greek deities. After a brief unsuccessful revolt against him, Antiochus looted and dismantled the Temple and instituted a systematic persecution of those who resisted hellenization. He imposed the death penalty on those continuing to observe Jewish religious practices, compelling a loyalty to pagan practices. Many Jews were killed and sold into slavery and communities of homes were looted and destroyed under this policy.

The Maccabean Period

The leaders of the battle for independence from Syria were members of the *Hasmonean dynasty*. These families apparently were descendants of an unidentified person named Hasmon. The Hasmoneans became known as the *Maccabees,* after the revolt leader Mattathias' oldest son Judah, who was called "Judah the Maccabee" (*"Judah the hammer"*). Judah led the fight for freedom after his father died within a year after the revolt started. Two other brothers, Jonathan and Simon, successively took over the leadership until the fully independent Second Jewish Commonwealth was established.

In time, the Commonwealth prospered and engaged in international commerce with the Mediterranean countries. This success encouraged many Judeans to migrate to these countries, where they established local religious centers that ultimately became synagogues—the start of organized Jewish life outside of Israel. Jews were given special rights because of their unique religion and the commercial and social contributions they made to the communities. This area of the world found Jewish monotheism and the Mosaic moral code appealing. During this period, which preceded the advent of Christianity, there were many conversions to Judaism. The Jewish population reached a peak during this period.

The Commonwealth ended up with tyrannical regimes that were also led by Maccabeans. Terrible internal dissension between religious and political factions periodically turned into civil war. The Commonwealth ended with a duplicitous takeover by the Romans that was a fallout of the intrigue with the Roman rulers that the feuding Maccabean family members resorted to.

The Maccabean period is remembered by the Jewish people for the liberation and rededication of the Holy Temple that preceded the creation of the Second Jewish Commonwealth. This event gave the Jewish people the reason to celebrate the festival of Chanukah.

Revolt against Syria (168 B.C.E.)—The severe persecution by the Hellenist Syrian King Antiochus raised a new spirit amongst the Judeans. The people became more united and nationalistic. Even those who were drawn to Hellenism became disenchanted with Hellenism because of the severity of the oppression related to those promoting Hellenism.

Mattathias, an aged priest from the village of Modin, located north of Jerusalem, started the revolt against the Syrians. In 168 B.C.E., Mattathias escaped to the mountains from where, supported by his five sons, he waged a revolt against Syria. It appeared to be a hopeless war against the strong Syrian army. Mattathias's army was a small band of poorly armed men, not trained to do battle. Their strength was their determination. Through their battle successes, they conquered Syrian arms and encouraged more to join the revolt. The Maccabeans had a major success in the third year of the revolt. From their mountain stronghold, they ambushed the Syrian army in the narrow Emmaus pass connecting Judea to the coast. They overwhelmed the Syrians, forcing them to flee to the coast. With the Syrian forces in Judea weakened, the Maccabeans were enabled to free Jerusalem. After this victory, the Judeans won their religious freedom. However, it took twenty-three more years of fighting before the Syrians in 142 B.C.E. gave the Judean people their political independence. During this long period of fighting for independence, there were many losses for the Maccabeans. At one point, their army was down to 800 men. Nevertheless, in time, after waging courageous battles led by devoted self-sacrificing leaders, the Maccabeans were successful.

Festival of Chanukah: (Festival of Dedication, or Festival of Lights)—The successful Maccabean capture of Jerusalem in 165 B.C.E. was climaxed with a rededication of the Holy Temple to the worship of the Hebrew's God. The people joyously celebrated for eight days their newfound religious freedom and retaking of the Temple, establishing the Festival of Dedication (Chanukah) lasting eight days. The historical description of events as told in the Second Book of the Maccabees only describes the cleansing of the Temple; the Maccabeans removed all vestiges of Greek idols, installed by the Syrians as part of their Hellenization program, and erected a clean, new altar. The miracle of the one-day supply of oil burning in the menorah for eight days is told only in the Talmud.

Judah the Maccabee (167–160 B.C.E.)—Judah, called the Maccabee, was the military genius of the Hasmoneans. He was the most popular leader and outstanding personality. His main objective was Judean religious freedom, which he won when he conquered Jerusalem from the Syrians.

Judah had established a political alliance with the Roman Republic, which was on the verge of becoming a power in the Middle East. That turned out to be a disappointment. The Roman true interest was increasing their power in the area. They were content to permit Judean unrest against Syria to continue, weakening both parties. After a Syrian civil war ended, Syria was encouraged by Hellenist Jews to overthrow Judah, and Syria became belligerent again. Judah was forced to fight the stronger Syrian army, but without the Roman aid that he expected. Weakened by the desertion of the religious-oriented Judeans, Judah's army lost to the Syrians and fled to Jordan. In a turnaround, the religious-oriented Judeans, who were the main supporters of the Hasmoneans during the initial revolt, had formed an alliance with Syria in return for the Syrian promise not to overturn Judea's religious freedom that Judah had won from the Syrians. After Judah was killed in a battle with the Syrians, his brother Jonathan took over the leadership.

Jonathan (160–142 B.C.E.)—Jonathan's goals differed from his brother's. They were secular rather than religious. His objective was obtaining political freedom for Judea and improving the lot of the people. His strategy was to enlarge Judea in order to achieve greater political power. That would give him the strength to deal with the Syrians for obtaining political freedom. Jonathan's chance came when the Syrian general, victorious in a Syrian civil war, invited Jonathan to return to Judea. Syria allowed him to become the high priest, the position of Jewish authority in Judea, and Syria appointed his brother Simon as governor of the coastal region. Capitalizing on his brother's authority, Jonathan annexed the coastal cities, which gave him economic strength in dealing with the Syrians; Judea started to prosper. He also renewed the alliances with Rome to discourage further Syrian aggression. However, his strategic alliances failed him personally. The Syrian ruler, with whom he had a falling out, assassinated him.

The Commonwealth Achieves Independence (141 B.C.E.)

Jonathan's brother Simon (142–135 B.C.E.) continued the battle with Syria and, in his first year, won complete independence for Judah. Simon's initial action was to convene a group of religious and political leaders to deal with the issue of who was to lead the country. This Great Assembly had few representatives from the previously powerful Hellenist Jews. Without strong opposition from Hellenists who were anti-Hasmonean, the Great Assembly elected Simon hereditary ruler and high priest. This step assured the continuity of the Hasmonian dynasty as leaders of the new Second Jewish Commonwealth. Simon won over pagan cities in the coastal region, contributing to Judea's continued commercial expansion and prosperity. Simon, who was old when he took over leadership, continued to serve as high priest and civil leader but relied on his son, John Hyrcan, to lead the army. Simon's rule ended abruptly when he and two of his sons were assassinated by his own son-in-law who was attempting to take over the leadership of Judea.

John Hyrcan (135–105 B.C.E.)—John Hyrcan, Simon's surviving son, took over the leadership of the Commonwealth. The Syrians immediately attempted to exert influence over the Commonwealth. However, in 134 B.C.E., weakened by internal struggles, Syria gave up their struggle to Hellenize Judea, resulting in the Second Jewish Commonwealth obtaining complete independence.

Hyrcan embarked on an expansionist path with the intent of having a significant Middle East role. In this process, he violated the Mosaic ethics, disregarding the ideal of the Maccabean fight for religious freedom that they had fought for over the previous thirty-five years. Using a mercenary army, he brutally conquered and subjugated the Samaritans, destroying their temple. He forcefully converted the Idumeans (formerly known as Edomites), annexing their country lying south of Judea.

Hyrcanus's forced conversion policies were opposed by many of his countrymen. Later, many Jewish religious leaders condemned these conversion practices.

Hyrcan's reign saw the emergence of two political parties based on opposing religious views for Judaism. One party was the Pharisees, who were the successors of the scribes from the days of Ezra. The Pharisees, representing a majority of the population, were the advocates of rabbinical Judaism, believing in a liberal interpretation of the Torah as expressed in the Oral Torah. In an extension of Ezra's policy of separatism, the Pharisees opposed Hyrcan's expansionist policy of absorbing neighboring nations. The other party was the Sadducees. Their members were the priests who descended from the priests under King Solomon, and the aristocracy who wanted the Commonwealth to be a strong, prosperous nation. From a religious standpoint, the Sadducees advocated a strict interpretation of the Torah, objecting to the concept of an Oral Torah that explained and expanded the Torah. The Sadducees were supporters of Hyrcan.

Aristobulous (104 B.C.E.)—Hyrcan's oldest son Aristobulous became the new leader, lasting one year, after succumbing to drinking and disease. Aristobulous, brought up under Hellenist influence, had changed his Jewish name, Judah, to the Greek Aristobulous. He introduced the radical changes in the Hasmonean leadership that ultimately led to the end of the Commonwealth. In fear of being overthrown by his family members, he imprisoned and killed four of his brothers. This brutal action embittered the people, who did not expect such behavior from Jews—it was a common occurrence in the pagan kingdoms of Egypt, Syria, Rome, and others. His expansionist policies were also resented. Aristobulous gave himself the title of "king," a position most Jews expected to go to a descendant of David, which he was not.

Alexander Jannai (103–76 B.C.E.)—Alexander Jannai continued the expansionist policies of Hyrcan and Aristobulous until essentially all of the Palestine area was under his control. He continued wars of aggression against his neighbors. In the middle of his reign, the Pharisee spiritual leaders who advocated Torah-based Judaism rebelled against his tyrannical rule. Alexander Jannai cruelly and mercilessly crushed them, crucifying and brutally killing many. His policies tore the country in two; Pharisees, who were the advocates of rabbinical Judaism, fighting against Sadducees, who were the aristocracy and advocates of priestly dominated Judaism. The country deteriorated under his tyrannical and disruptive rule. Alexander Jannai is marked as the cruelest leader in Jewish history.

Local and National Governing Bodies (Sanhedrin)—There were councils of twenty-three elders that governed in democratic fashion over local matters in the cities and towns of the Second Commonwealth. There were courts of law at the local level. The National Sanhedrin, a council of seventy-one elders appointed by the king or the Sanhedrin itself, served as a national court of law (the Supreme Court). This arrangement was an extension of the Great Assembly established by Ezra three hundred years earlier. The high priest controlled the Temple organization and operation.

The Decline of the Commonwealth

At Alexander Jannai's death, there was an unusual calm in the Commonwealth after his mother took over the rule as queen. It lasted nine years until her death, when peace between the various religious and political parties deteriorated. Queen Alexandra's two sons, Hyrcanus II and Aristobulus II fought to succeed her. Aristobulus initially was successful and became king. His brother Hyrcanus recruited a "clever statesman" Idumean named Antipater to be his advisor. Ambitious Antipater convinced Hyrcanus to rebel, starting a war between Pharisees and Sadducees that lasted several years. While Roman General Pompey was in the process of conquering other areas of the Middle East for Rome, both sides approached him to select one of the two brothers to be the king of Judea. Pompey appointed Aristobulus as king, but peace did not result.

The Pharisees then interceded with Pompey, requesting that he enter Palestine and change Judea's form of government from a kingdom to one ruled by the religious authorities. Pompey deceived the Pharisees and went further than they intended; he took over the country for Rome. In 63 B.C.E., the Roman army vanquished the Aristobulus loyalist army's fierce resistance in Jerusalem. The battle lasted three months, surprising the Romans who had much easier times vanquishing stronger enemies in their path of conquest. The battle ended when the defenders refused to fight on the Sabbath. Twelve thousand Jews were slaughtered as the independence of the Commonwealth ended and restrictive political and religious regulations were applied.

The rapidly changing rulers in Rome in the period following the defeat in Jerusalem caused the Jewish leaders to change sides in step with whoever seemed to be the Roman leader at the time. Hyrcanus and Antipater replaced Aristobulus as the vassal authority reporting to Caesar. For a short period, the Parthians wrested control of Judea from the Romans and put a rival of Hyrcanus in control. After Antipater was assassinated, his son Herod curried the favor of the Roman leaders. The Roman leaders were convinced that Herod was the right person to keep Palestine for Rome after they defeated the Parthians. In an elaborate ceremony attended by Anthony and Octavian, the Roman senate installed the half-Jew, half-Idumean Herod as king of the Jews in 39 B.C.E. With Herod as king, the Hasmonean dynasty leadership of the Jewish people ended.

5
Roman Domination

The Second Jewish Commonwealth, which lasted 100 years, ended in 39 B.C.E. under the might of the Roman Empire, which succeeded Greece as the dominant power over the Palestine area. The tyrannical Roman rule that followed lasted two centuries. The birth of Christianity, with its tremendous consequences for the Jewish people, occurred in this period.

The Jewish people rebelled twice against the oppressive political climate. After the first rebellion in 70 C.E., the Holy Temple in Jerusalem was destroyed and all semblance of Jewish rule eliminated. After the abortive Bar Kochba rebellion in 135 C.E., the mass of the Jewish people were either killed or exiled as slaves. Except for a small religious community in Jabneh in the northern part of Palestine, Jewish life in Palestine ended.

Roman Rule

During the period of Roman rule, the Palestinian authority changed from the Roman-appointed King Herod to a series of Roman procurators (imperial administrators) and Roman governors.

King Herod (39 B.C.E.–4 C.E.)—The Roman leadership appointed Herod as king in 39 B.C.E. However, a band of Jews loyal to the Hasmonean dynasty did not accept Herod as their Roman-appointed Judean king without a fight. The Roman army had to vanquish the Judean resistance in Jerusalem and the Galilee before King Herod could start his rule—the fierce battles that took place cost many lives.

Half-Idumean and half-Jewish, Herod had little regard for Judaism. Although he personally practiced Hellenism, he tried not to antagonize the Pharisees. Herod rebuilt the Holy Temple; the work was started in 19 B.C.E. and completed after his death. It was made into a magnificent large structure both to please his interest in architectural accomplishments and to ingratiate himself with the Jewish people. He was not successful at the latter.

The Jewish people appreciated the rebuilt Temple, but they generally hated Herod because of his brutality to the people and for his lifestyle that included indulging in pagan and Greek practices. Herod's brutality extended to his own family. He killed his wife and two sons out of fear of their being involved in plots to destroy him.

Herod was a strong ruler who ended the internal chaos and banditry that existed under the previous Hasmonean rulers. Judea did prosper economically under Herod, and the Jews outside of Judea respected Herod for his good political connections to Rome. They credited this relationship to gaining them favorable treatment in the Roman-dominated Mediterranean countries where many Jews lived at the time.

Herod's Sons—Three of Herod's sons shared the rule of Judea after his death in 4 B.C.E. Following their father's example, they were more anxious to please their Roman masters than to serve their own people. Archelaus, the son who was the most capable administrator, ruled as a prince over the most important areas, including Judea, Samaria, and Idumea. His rule was brutal, and he offended the Jews and Samarians alike. After ten years of unrest that saw many killed, Rome replaced him with a procurator. A second son, Antipas, was made duke over the Galilee and parts of Transjordania. His authority lasted thirty-three years, until Rome removed him for severely antagonizing the people to the point of rebellion. The third son, Philip, was governor over a small province and had little impact.

Procurators—There were Roman procurators who ruled over Judea and Samaria between the years 6–63 C.E. During this period, there was constant friction and rebellion. The Roman procurators did not understand the Jews' attitude towards life, their strict moral code, and their religious requirements. The Jews could not accept Rome's aims, policies, and immoral lifestyle. The procurators crucified thousands of Jews for political offenses and thousands of Jewish prisoners lost their lives in the gladiator arenas to satisfy the pleasure of the Romans.

Pontius Pilate—His rule from 26 C.E. to 36 C.E., the longest of the procurators, was very troublesome for the Jews. His soldiers were brutal in subduing revolts against his harsh decrees. It was common for one thousand people to be killed at one time. Pontius Pilate crucified many important people and razed entire villages. He disregarded Jewish religious sensitivities. A major example was his use of the Holy Temple funds to finance the building of an aqueduct to Jerusalem. Pontius Pilate was the procurator associated with the death of Jesus Christ.

Biblical Scholars Hillel and Shammai

Although King Herod was besieged by threats from many quarters throughout his long reign, he maintained a respectful relationship with the Pharisees because he did not consider this group to be a threat. With this benign attitude, Pharisee learning centers thrived in the otherwise chaotic atmosphere in Palestine caused by Herod's oppression of the people. The two outstanding biblical scholars, Hillel and Shammai, flourished during this period. They each led a school of scholars who continued to teach their master's commentaries on the Oral Torah laws for many generations. These two sages each generated hundreds of religious teachings and opinions relating to religious law that are still respected today.

Hillel was the gentleperson, the liberal interpreter of the Scriptures. He advocated interpreting the Oral Laws in a manner that allowed for adapting to changing circumstances without violating the Torah. He laid down the Seven Rules for analyzing contradictory elements of Scripture and deducing the right conclusion. Hillel's principles, with some expansions that rabbis added later, are still followed by Judaic scholars.

Shammai was the stern person, known as the strict interpreter of Scriptures and as an advocate of keeping to the letter of the biblical law. Nevertheless, the rabbinical analysis of Shammai's commentary in the Talmudic period concluded that over twenty of his opinions were more liberal than Hillel's.

While they lived, Shammai was the more respected and popular figure among the Pharisees. In time, Hillel became the more respected sage by the Jewish community and the world at large.

The Spread of Judaism

During the Second Commonwealth period, the Jewish population swelled with the help of conversions to Judaism. Many Jews decided to leave Judea because it developed a high population density. The high international esteem in which the Maccabeans were held and the reputation of the Jews for their capabilities encouraged the countries of the Mediterranean to accept them. Many Jews in these new lands were described as being prosperous artisans and merchants. They ransomed Jews who became Roman slaves after the Jewish revolt in 70 C.E. The Jews in these lands established synagogues to enable them to continue their Jewish worship away from the Temple in Jerusalem. They still maintained ties with the Temple organization, supporting it financially. However not all Jews in the Diaspora (a Greek term for dispersion) were successful financially. Historians also wrote about destitute Jews in these lands, describing beggar Jews in Rome and Alexandria, the two largest cities of that period.

Growth of Jews in the Diaspora continued during the period of Roman rule of Judea. The old Jewish Babylonian community flourished under the Parthian Empire. It was a period of large-scale conversions to Judaism. Jewish seamanship, developed initially by King Solomon, aided the Diaspora movement, with Jewish ships sailing throughout the Mediterranean. By the end of the second century C.E., Jews were living in France, Spain, all along the coast of North Africa, Greece, Italy, Syria, and Turkey.

Many Jews with sailing talent were spared from the customary cruel Roman treatment of Jews as slaves, lion fodder, and gladiator toys. In the first five centuries of the common era, Roman ships sailing all around Europe were manned by Jewish sailors and captains in support of the Roman conquests. They navigated the Rhine River and sailed to Britain, carrying supplies for the Romans. This seafaring role ended with the advent of militant Christianity, when Jews were forbidden to own land or to serve as soldiers or sailors.

The Rise of Christianity

Conditions that existed in Judea and in the Mediterranean countries at the start of the first millennium C.E. were fertile for the growth of Christianity. The turbulent years under the brutal Jewish Hasmonean kings and later under Roman rule caused many Jews to long for the coming of the Messiah to end their oppression and to bring order to the world—as mystical preachers of that period were suggesting. The need to repent before the apocalypse happened was being preached. Based on the Book of Daniel's reference to some dead people awakening to an everlasting good life, the Pharisee religious leaders preached a Jewish belief in the resurrection of the dead when the Messiah comes. This atmosphere, full of anxiety and looking for answers, made Judeans ripe for "Jesus the Messiah." Historical records of that period indicate that several Jews claimed to be the Messiah, only to be rejected by the Jewish people because the improved conditions expected when the Messiah arrived did not materialize.

Information About Jesus—There is no historical information that describes the life and death of Jesus. Contemporary Roman and Greek histories do not refer to Jesus. A contemporary Jewish historian, Joshephus, who wrote in minute detail about Pontius Pilate's reign, also said no word about the life of Jesus, his trial, and his crucifixion. Neither Jesus nor his disciples kept any records. Therefore the life and ministry of Jesus can only be derived from the New Testament books written 40–110 years after the death of Jesus—they were religious books and not historical documents.

The writers of the New Testament, consisting of the four Gospels (meaning good news), the Epistles of Paul, Galations, Romans, and other books, adopted the rabbinical technique of creating stories (Midrash) to enhance the image of the biblical personality. Their references to Judaic practices contain many errors. A Passover meal before Passover starts is contrary to Judaic rules. Roman law and not Judaic law considered any messianic claims to be unlawful and subject to the death penalty. The Gospels attributed the quotation "Thou shall love thy neighbor as thyself." to Jesus, whereas it appears in the biblical Book of Leviticus. The Sanhedrin Court that brought Jesus to trial was not run by the Pharisees, as is stated in the Gospels. The Sadducees ran the court but they had no authority from the Romans to act on capital punishment matters.

There are also inconsistencies from Gospel to Gospel. The first Gospel of Mark, addressed to a Jewish audience, had a simple story about the life and death of Jesus. Jesus was found missing from his tomb by three women, without any explanation of why the body was not there. By the time the last Gospel was written, the Christians had changed their proselytizing targets from Jews to pagans and the story of Jesus became more complex. The Gospel of John, in an attempt to appeal to the new class of converts, describes Mary of Magdala speaking to the resurrected Jesus and her telling of this event to two disciples.

The early Gospel writers mainly tried to encourage the Jews to accept Jesus as the Messiah. They called him Joshua (Hebrew name meaning "salvation"). Joshua became Jesus in later versions of the New Testament. Their writings had roots in Hebrew biblical history and personalities. They originally preached keeping to the Mosaic laws. After meeting little success at converting Jews, the Christian leadership set a new objective: to convert the Roman pagan world. With this change in objective, the later

New Testament writers took on a negative bias towards the Jewish religion and people. They preached nonadherence to the Mosaic laws to show a break with the Jewish people; Sunday replaced Saturday as the holy Sabbath day. Since the Christians turned to proselytizing the Romans, it was not prudent to have a Roman held responsible for the death of Jesus. Therefore, the Roman ruler of Palestine was described in the Epistles of Paul as an almost innocent bystander in the death of Jesus, while the Jews were falsely described as calling for his death. This became the source of Catholic hatred of the Jews for two thousand years.

Birth of Jesus—There is disagreement among Christian scholars as to where Jesus was born. Some are of the opinion that Jesus was likely born in the city of Nazareth, located in the Galilee area of Palestine, where his Jewish family lived. The more popular nativity story is based on the later Gospels, which describe his birth as taking place in Bethlehem. This location was intended to show his connection to King David's lineage, which was Judaism's expectation for the Messiah. Christian theologians developed the "Immaculate Conception" version of his birth in the fourth century. It described Jesus as being conceived by God so that Jesus would not be tainted by man's original sin, which was a new Christian concept at that time.

Year 1 C.E. of the Christian calendar was established to be the year in which Jesus was born. Based on the Gospel narrative that describes Jesus as being born during the reign of King Herod, this birth year is now understood to be incorrect. From other historical data, it has been established that King Herod died in 4 B.C.E., which is more likely the year Jesus was born.

Ministry of Jesus—According to the Gospels, the active ministry of Jesus lasted barely three years. The New Testament tells of Jesus preaching his brand of Pharisaic Judaism to the common people of the Galilee where he lived. Jesus is said to have preached healing in his own name rather than through God, which was contrary to the Pharisee religious principle. This practice would have antagonized the Jewish religious leaders. His claim to be the Messiah also would have made Jews uncomfortable because it violated Roman law.

As told in the New Testament, Jesus was influenced by the preaching of John the Baptist, who urged Jews to "repent for the Kingdom of Heaven is at hand." He offered immersion (baptism) in the Jordan River as a way for individuals to express their willingness to purify their souls. John, who was a Jew, was apparently practicing the Jewish ritual of *mikveh* (purification).

Jesus evidently was also influenced by the teachings of the great Jewish sage, Hillel, who was progressive in his interpretations of the Bible and emphasized social justice. Hillel stressed the practice of the biblical Leviticus statement "Thou shall love thy neighbor as thyself." The Gospels attributed this quotation to Jesus.

Jesus remained a Jew during his lifetime. As told in the Gospels, Jesus wanted to end what he saw as the evils practiced by the hypocritical Jewish leaders. He did not advocate the elimination of Judaism or plan on separating himself from Judaism.

Death of Jesus (30 C.E.)—According to the Gospels, Jesus went to Jerusalem to celebrate Passover in the Jewish tradition. He had a Passover meal (the Last Supper) with his Twelve Disciples two nights before the first day of Passover. The next day the Pharisees brought him to trial in the Sanhedrin Court for his claim to be the Messiah and supposedly caused his execution. No blame was assigned to the Romans.

Church authorities have now discredited blaming the Jews for the death of Jesus that was the basis of much anti-Semitism and suffering by the Jewish people. It is now recognized that Roman law, and not Judaic law, considered any messianic claims to be unlawful and subject to the death penalty. Under these circumstances, the charges and the death penalty had to have been carried out by the Roman ruler, Pontius Pilate, who was responsible for dealing with such crimes.

Jesus died in 30 C.E. at the age of thirty-five. The Romans crucified him, which was a common method of killing people they considered a menace to their rule. To emphasize his guilt, the Roman soldiers put "King of the Jews" on the cross. It marked Jesus as a person considered dangerous to the Romans and subject to the death penalty.

The Spread of Christianity—After the death of Jesus, a small group of Judean Jews led by his brother James accepted Jesus as their religious leader. They were called Nazarenes because they were followers of Jesus of Nazareth. The Nazarenes continued to observe the biblical commandments and Jewish practices. A century later, Saul of Tarses, a Jew who changed his name to Paul, started preaching the teachings of Jesus to the Jews in Greece and Syria. Paul then undertook a long missionary trip throughout the Roman Empire. When Paul concluded that retaining the connections to Judaism became an obstacle in converting the pagan people in the Roman Empire, he created the theological concepts of the new

Christian religion. Paulian Christianity broke all ties to Judaism and replaced Nazarine Christianity. The religion actually was not called Christian until the fourth century, when it became the official religion of the Roman Empire.

The early converts to Christianity in the Roman lands were mainly Jews. They were predominately previous converts to Judaism who had been attracted to Jewish monotheism and moral lifestyle. Without the aid of Talmudic rabbinical Judaism, which came much later, these irreligious Jews were susceptible to Christian proselytizing.

Many pagans in the Roman and Greek communities were becoming eager for a more meaningful religion and a softer God to replace the harsh Greek and Roman gods. They gradually became Christian converts. Pagans found the central theme of life-after-death one of the more appealing Christian concepts. Also appealing to them were the Jewish ideals of human brotherhood and charity giving that were adopted by the Christian religion. Christianity spread most rapidly amongst the pagans living in communities with a large Jewish population where they had been exposed to the virtues of Judaism. By accepting Christianity, many felt they were accepting a form of Judaism that appealed to them. The Christians were more active and determined in their proselytizing than the Jews had been. They did not abandon their missionary work while they suffered brutal persecution by the Romans, as happened during Paul's missionary work.

In the year 300, with so many Christians already in the Roman Empire, Emperor Constantine embraced Christianity and made it the official religion; his mother had already converted. By the year 400, church leaders capitalized on their political strength to encourage the emperor to institute anti-Jewish laws and make Jewish missionary activity a capital crime. This essentially ended conversions to Judaism. Jews were forced into isolation from Christian society. This hostile environment encouraged many Jews to convert to Christianity.

Christianity's Link to Judaism—For almost two thousand years, Christian Church leaders of all denominations were unwilling to acknowledge how much of the Christian faith stemmed from Judaism. One God ruling the entire world and the concept of a Messiah were strictly Jewish concepts at the time of Jesus. Before the time of Jesus, the rabbis had already adopted the concept of reward and punishment in an afterlife. It was dropped later by the rabbis to differentiate Judaism from Christianity, but it is still a Jewish belief for many Jews. The concept of resurrection of the dead at the time of the Messiah is an ancient Jewish concept included in today's central Jewish worship prayers as a "praise to God, who gives life to the dead." The entire Hebrew Bible with its moral teachings, Psalms, and inspiring Prophet quotations are incorporated into the Christian Bible.

Jewish Rejection of Christianity—Throughout the ages, the Christian world has failed to understand why the Jewish people have not accepted Jesus. A fundamental reason for this rejection is that "Jesus the Messiah" has not fulfilled the Judaic expectation for the Messiah. The Hebrew Messiah was to *"bring all the Jewish people back together, bring peace to the Jewish people and to all the peoples of the world, and end all the evils of the world."* In the eyes of the Jewish people none of these events happened. Jewish people suffered and were tortured in the name of Jesus. Neither did they see belief in Jesus bring peace to the Christian world.

The dogma of Jesus the Savior has been a Christian proselytizing theme that also has failed to achieve significant conversion of Jews to Christianity. This Christian faith of exclusiveness runs contrary to the Judaic belief that every individual is endowed with the opportunity to improve their life and that of humankind on this earth. The Talmud teaches universality—people of any faith who do good deeds will be accepted in the world to come.

The Jewish people have not accepted the Christian concept that everyone is the product of the "original sin of humankind" originating with Adam's behavior in the Garden of Eden. The original sin of humankind has no theological meaning to the Jewish people. The rabbinic view is embodied in the Jewish High Holy Day prayers; sinning against God is evil, but every person can avoid the penalty of sin against God by repentance and charity giving.

During the period of domination under the Romans, when Jews suffered badly, the rabbis added the concept of reward in heaven for good deeds on earth to help the Jewish people cope with their suffering. After the Christian stress on accepting Jesus as the passport to heaven rather than being consigned to hell, the rabbis downplayed the realm of heaven and hell in order to maintain a distinction with Christianity, and it lost importance as a Jewish creed. Although the human soul having eternal life is widely accepted by the Jewish people today, heaven and hell represent a vague concept for most Jews other than one is a good place the other bad. The rabbis continue to struggle with the meaning of terminology in Jewish theological literature that might relate to heaven and hell.

Christian versus Jewish Faith—Christians are typically taught to rely on faith in God to overcome their problems. Jews are taught to rely on their own actions, with God's help, to overcome their problems.

For most Christians, the highest virtue is to believe correctly in Jesus—leading to salvation. In Judaism, the highest virtue is to believe correctly in God—leading to doing good deeds. The significant levels of charity, philanthropy, and social action by religious and nonreligious Jews stems from this Jewish legacy of needing to do good deeds.

Expulsion from Palestine

The Roman tyranny that existed during the lifetime of Jesus continued for another hundred years. After two periods of unsuccessful rebellion against Roman rule, the Jewish people were expelled from Palestine. A small remnant of the Jewish community remained in Palestine. Among them was Rabbi Johanan ben Zakkai, who took remarkable steps, which saved Judaism.

Unsuccesful Rebellion Against Rome: Destruction of the Holy Temple (70 C.E.)—After years of tyrannical rule under several procurators, in 67 C.E. the Jews in the Galilee, Samaria, and Judea united in a rebellion against Rome. After the initial Jewish success, the Romans sent in a stronger army under Vespasian and conquered the Galilee. This resulted in a lengthy civil war in Jerusalem between Jewish factions who blamed each other for the defeat. In 70 C.E., Titus, who succeeded his father Vespasian, totally vanquished Jerusalem and subdued the Jews. The Temple was burned down; the only structure remaining was the western wall of the Temple mount. Many thousands of Jews died in the rebellions and thousands were sold as slaves. The Arch of Titus that stands in Rome today has a scene showing Titus's triumphant march in Rome with the Roman soldiers carrying the holy articles they removed from the Temple. The rebellion actually ended two years later when the Zealots were defeated after holding out in the Masada fortress in the Judean desert—960 defenders committed suicide.

Judaism Saved by Johanan ben Zakkai—With the Temple destroyed and most of the religious leaders killed, Judaism was in peril. Rabbi Johanan, a disciple of the great sage, Hillel, believed that Jews must live by the spirit and not by the sword. He convinced the Roman General Vespasian to allow him to open a religious school in the small coastal town named Jabneh in northern Palestine away from the previous centers of Jewish learning. This evolved into a major learning center for the next two hundred years. Through Rabbi Johanan's efforts a council of teachers, the *Bet Din* (Rabbinic Court), was established. The Bet Din took the place of the defunct Sanhedrin council of elders. It ruled on religious matters, studying the more than 300 differences in opinion between the sages Hillel and Shammai regarding the practical law in the Oral Torah; they resolved the differences in favor of Hillel's writing as being more authoritative. The Bet Din also studied how Jews should react to the biblical commandments relating to the Temple sacrificial system. In view of the unlikelihood that the destroyed Temple would be replaced, the Bet Din under Rabbi Johanan's leadership determined that the focus should be on the synagogue as the place for connecting the people with God. With this in mind, the Bet Din instituted synagogue prayers, many of which are still practiced today.

Bet Din Canonizes the Bible—A major accomplishment of the Bet Din was their decree as to which of the religious books should be included in the Hebrew Bible, in the larger sense known as the "The Holy Scriptures" (*Tanach* in Hebrew). They concluded that books covering the time of Ezra (fifth century B.C.E.) would be the last books to be included in the Hebrew Bible. Tanach is a Hebrew acronym derived from the first Hebrew letter of the three sections of the Hebrew Bible, which are the Torah, the Prophets, and the Writings. Writings consists of twelve books of miscellaneous subjects; the Book of Psalms, Book of Proverbs, Book of Job, five *megillot,* and four historical books, including Daniel, Ezra, Nehemiah, and Chronicles (two). Even though the First and Second Chronicles history books were written long after the time of Ezra, these books were included because they were reviews of Jewish history ending with the time of Ezra. The Bet Din ruling disallowed the books of the Maccabees that covered the time of the Second Jewish Commonwealth and the festival of Chanukah commemorating the rededication of the Temple.

Rebellions in the Diaspora: Diaspora Discovers Jewishness (115–117 C.E.)—The Diaspora Jews had not come to the aid of the Judean Jews during their major rebellion against Roman rule in the year 70 C.E. due to their own loyalty to Rome. However, when the war was over, the Diaspora Jews realized that the world made no distinction between the Jews in Judea who fought for their freedom and Jews who remained loyal to the country they lived in. The Diaspora Jews began to endure Roman discrimination in retaliation for the revolt of the Palestinian Jews. When conditions deteriorated further, Jews in Cyprus, Egypt, and Cyrenaica (Libya) belatedly revolted with disastrous results. Every Jew on Cyprus was killed, and Jews were forbidden to enter Cyprus forever under any circumstances. The great Jewish community in Alexandria, Egypt, was decimated and went downhill in size and quality of life forever.

Second Judean Revolt: Bar Kochba Rebellion (132–135 C.E.)—After the initial revolt in 70 C.E., the Judeans remained passive under the influence of the Jewish intellectuals who stressed learning over nationalism. This attitude changed when Hadrian became emperor of Palestine. He started to rebuild Jerusalem but dedicated it to a pagan God. He prohibited circumcision, the fundamental Judaic practice symbolizing the Jewish Covenant with God. These acts incited the Jewish people to again rebel against the Roman rulers. The revolt was led spiritually by the outstanding teacher of Judaism, eighty-year old Rabbi Akiba, who had previously been a strong advocate of peaceful coexistence with the Romans. It was led militarily by the youthful zealot Bar Kochba. After some early successes against the Romans, the stronger and larger Roman army vanquished the Judeans. Rabbi Akiba was martyred after he refused to accept the Roman edict forbidding the study of the Torah. Bar Kochba was killed during the Jews' last stand in the fortified village of Bethar outside of Jerusalem.

Destruction of the Jewish State—It is estimated that a half-million Jews were killed in battle, many thousand civilians slaughtered, and another half-million either sold as slaves or fed to the gladiatorial arenas in the Roman world. All the cities in Judea were destroyed, the remaining Jews were moved to the Galilee. Under the penalty of death, Jews were forbidden to enter Jerusalem. Palestine replaced the name Judea. All Jewish political life ended in Palestine for almost two thousand years. In exile, the Jewish people started to address Palestine as *Eretz Yisrael*, the Land of Israel, after the name God gave Jacob.

6
The Development of the Talmud

Since the time of Ezra's religious reformation in the fifth century B.C.E., the Oral Torah (also known as Oral Law) superseded the Torah as the source of religious and civil laws that the Jewish people adhered to. The ancient Hebrews and today's Orthodox Jews believe that God gave Moses the Oral Torah along with the written Torah.

In the second century B.C.E., the leading rabbis in Judea became concerned that it was too fragile to rely on the rabbis' memory to accurately retain and pass along the Oral Torah from generation to generation. They decided to document the Oral Torah. Rabbis and scholars in Jerusalem started writing down the Oral Torah in about 200 B.C.E. They also started to expand the Oral Torah, adding laws and commentaries to explain the source and rationale for the Oral Torah laws. This work was almost terminated when most of the rabbis and scholars in Judea were killed in the rebellion against Rome in 70 C.E. and the religious institutions in Jerusalem were destroyed. Rabbi Johanan ben Zakkai, who managed to escape the fate of his contemporaries, established a religious learning center at Jabneh, where the documentation of the Oral Torah and its commentaries was resumed.

In the early second century C.E., the outstanding biblical scholar Rabbi Akiba initiated the codification of the Oral Torah documentation. This codification work was interrupted by Akiba's death during the Bar Kochba rebellion and curtailed by the Roman restriction against all Jewish religious study. Three years after the Bar Kochba rebellion ended, the new Roman ruler relaxed the decree against studying the Torah and new learning centers slowly sprung up in the Galilee. Rabbi Akiba's codification work was completed in these academies under the direction of the scholarly Rabbi Meir. Finally, in about 220 C.E., Rabbi Judah Ha-Nasi compiled the Oral Torah into a book, called the *Mishnah*.

As the Mishnah was being developed, rabbis were offering commentaries on the Oral Torah. After the Mishnah's publication, Rabbis discussed the Mishnah and offered commentaries. During this period, unrelated to the Mishnah activity, many stories, legends, and commentaries were being written by other rabbis on subjects considered important to the Jewish people at that time. Rabbis in both Palestine and Babylon decided to collect these commentaries and miscellaneous stories and compiled them into a book, called the *"Gemara."*

The Gemara is generally published with the Mishnah details as the starting point for the discussions and commentaries. The book with the Mishnah and Gemara combined is called the *Talmud.* The Gemara by itself is often called the Talmud as well.

The Mishnah

The objective of the Mishnah was to cover all aspects of everyday living. The Mishnah laws are arranged in six "Orders" (major chapters)—Seeds, Feasts, Women, Damages, Sacred Things, and Cleanliness. The titles are taken from the first subject discussed in each Order. These Orders are divided into tractates (63 total) and chapters (524 total).

The Gemara

The Gemara is fundamentally an explanation and commentary on the Mishnah. The Gemara's "higher purpose" is to seek out the connection between the Mishnah (Oral) laws and the original laws and commandments prescribed in the Torah. It searches for the connection, whether it is legal, ritualistic, historical, or philosophical. The technique of the Gemara is to present the question, followed by all relevant discussions, and ending with solutions to the question, which occasionally are left unanswered. In this attempt to find the truth, both practical and theoretical issues are addressed. The rabbis considered it acceptable to include opinions and solutions from non-Jewish sources. For example, in addressing everyday problems of illness, many pagan society superstitions were offered as solutions to medical problems.

During the early period of the Gemara development, there was a close interaction between Jewish and Greek scholars. This resulted in the inclusion of commentaries and Greek viewpoints. As an example, stories about the hereafter based on Greek mythology have been included in order to satisfy the spiritual needs of the Jewish people of that period who were being exposed to the Christian view of the hereafter. However, in consideration of the anti-Jewish edicts by the political authorities that were influenced by the new Christian Church leaders, the rabbis were careful to exclude any reference to Christianity in the Talmud.

The Talmud

There are two versions of the Talmud, the Babylonian Talmud and the Jerusalem Talmud. The two Talmuds have different Mishnah content. Neither one contains the entire Mishnah. The Jerusalem Talmud is one-third the size of the Babylonian Talmud, which has more expansive discussions and additional tangential material. Although there was some collaboration in the early years of their development, the two versions have different opinions on many laws.

The Babylonian Talmud addresses issues related to life in the city, which was of greater interest to the Babylonian Jews. The Jerusalem Talmud addressed the needs of the Palestinian Jews who were mostly farmers. It contains many agricultural laws and commentaries that are not included in the Babylonian Talmud.

After essentially the entire Jewish population was exiled from Palestine and with Jews in Europe forbidden from engaging in farming, interest in the Jerusalem Talmud waned and the Babylonian Talmud became the authoritative and most-studied version. Only the few scholars who mastered the archaic Aramaic language studied the Jerusalem Talmud, which is written almost entirely in Aramaic.

Babylonian Talmud—By the time the Mishnah was completed there were about a million Jews living in Babylon as a result of several migrations from Palestine and the natural population growth. Supported by this large population and with the Babylonian political environment that respected Jewish sensitivities, Jewish learning academies were established in the large Babylonian cities that became the source of many commentaries on the Mishnah. After centuries of religious toleration, the political environment for Jews in Babylon started to deteriorate in 450 C.E. Concerned over this change, Rabbis Ashi and Rabina led an effort to compile these commentaries, which led to the completion of the Babylonian Talmud in the year 500. It was written in fifty percent Hebrew and fifty percent Aramaic.

Six hundred years later, the Talmud underwent a significant change. Starting in the twelfth century, contemporary rabbinical commentaries on the Gemara were added to the Talmud. The most widely known and respected commentaries are those of Rashi, the notable medieval-period rabbi who lived in France in the eleventh century. Until commentaries in English recently became available, Rashi's Hebrew commentaries were an essential element of all Talmudic studies. His commentaries made the Talmud's sometimes circular and contradictory opinions more comprehensible. Written in easy-to-understand Hebrew and with clear logic, it served as the teaching vehicle for Talmudic students who generally did not understand the Aramaic language of the Talmud. Rashi's commentaries are also distinctive because they cover the entire Talmud.

Jerusalem (Palestinian) Talmud—Although the academies that edited the Palestinian version of the Talmud were in northern Palestine (Caesarea, Sepphoris, and Tiberias), this Talmud is called *The Jerusalem Talmud*.

Jewish life in Palestine became more difficult as the Christian clergy got more powerful. With a very small Jewish population remaining in Palestine, the quality of the rabbis and students in the Palestinian learning academies deteriorated in time. These two factors brought about a premature end to the development of the Jerusalem Talmud in the years between 350–400 C.E., leaving unaddressed the last two Orders of the Mishnah.

Halachah—The laws dealing with Jewish religious and civil life on a personal and societal basis that are in the Mishnah and partially in the Gemara are referred to as Halachah. One-third of the Talmud consists of Halachah. Orthodox Judaism only permits these laws to be changed by a Bet Din, a religious organization of the most learned rabbis in the greater Jewish community. The Bet Din concept was established in the first century C.E., by Rabbi Johanan ben Zakkai. He recognized that laws might need to be changed to accommodate changes in the lifestyle of the Jewish people.

The Judaic dietary law requiring six hours between eating meat and dairy is an example of a law changed by a Bet Din. There is rabbinical agreement that this law prohibiting meat and dairy to be eaten together was derived from the commandment stated three times in the Bible, "Thou shalt not seethe a kid in its mother's milk." A two-hour dietary separation had been followed since ancient times. In the Middle Ages, a Bet Din changed the interval before eating dairy after a meat meal from two hours to six hours based on their opinion that the longer period was necessary to assure compliance with the Torah. Since this Bet Din was recognized only by Ashkenazic Jews, some Sephardic Jews continue adhering to the original two-hour interval.

Aggada—Two-thirds of the Gemara applies to the rabbinical commentaries on the Halachah and to the many stories, legends, and commentaries that are unrelated to Mishnah topics, but which the Gemara compilers included because they were considered relevant to the life of the Jewish people. The Aggada stories addressed the many subjects that troubled the Jewish people.

The Gemara was written over a 400-year period when life was very harsh for the Jewish people who were under pressure to convert to Christianity. In the aftermath of the Bar Kochba rebellion two hundred years earlier, which was so devastating to the Jewish people, Jews wondered whether God had forsaken Israel. However, there was one unmistakable message: there would be no quick deliverance from their exile from the Jewish homeland. The Aggada included parables that would assure them that their God had not forsaken them, that would make the suffering Jews proud of their history and thus give them the strength to resist conversion pressures, and that offered them hope for the future, as the Prophets did. Judaic views regarding the hereafter were included to compete with the Christian views of heaven and hell. To compete with the Christian angels, myths were created about Jewish angels.

The story of the one-day supply of Chanukah menorah oil burning eight days is an example of a Haggada story that the Jewish people (and the world) have learned to accept as fact.

To aid in the everyday needs of the people at the time the Talmud was written, the rabbis offered medical advice freely consisting mostly of superstitions for curing ailments.

Midrash (Stories/Legends/Folklore/Homilies)—A careful reading and analysis of the Bible's text leads to many questions regarding why certain words are repeated, why the specific choice of words, whether there are missing statements to bridge the gap from one sentence to the next, and why seemingly disassociated thoughts are contained in the same Torah section. A major concern to many rabbis was the isolated dishonorable behavior of the three Patriarchs described in the Torah—their lying and deception was not fitting for the fathers of the Jewish people who are supposed to lead an exemplary lifestyle according to the Mosaic code. The rabbis attempted to answer many of these questions and concerns in a collection of stories, folklore, legends, and homilies called *Midrash,* written from the time of Ezra until 1500 C.E. They were intended to make the Bible more understandable and meaningful.

To "correct" the negative impression of the Patriarchs that some of the biblical incidents present, Midrashim were created that extol Abraham's virtues beyond what is described in the Bible. A popular one, intended to show that Abraham respected his God before he got the calling from God, tells about Abraham's treatment of idols. Abraham's family used to make images representing idols and sold them in the marketplace. There are several stories of how Abraham talked the customers out of buying the images, and one story of how he broke the images.

Some Midrash fill in the information that appears to be missing from the Bible. The Bible enumerates in two places the names of Jacob's children and grandchildren who came to Egypt with him. The long list includes only one female, Serah. It puzzled the rabbis as to why Serah was included in the all-male list, since there is no other reference to her in the Bible. Applying the rabbinical belief that every word in the Bible has a specific meaning and that no word is superfluous, the rabbis created Midrash about Serah that offer a reason for her inclusion, which was to honor Serah for her good deeds. One Midrash tells the story of Serah being the one to break the news to Jacob that his son Joseph was still alive, rather than being told by Joseph's brothers as indicated in the Bible. His brothers were too ashamed to break the news because they previously deceived their father about Joseph. Serah broke the news gently by singing the news while playing her harp so that the elderly Jacob would not be shocked.

Stories that relate to the narrative and ethics of the Bible are called Midrash Aggada. The most famous Aggada is the Passover Haggada, which tells the story of the Hebrew slavery in Egypt and their freedom through biblical quotations and rabbinical interpretations of the Exodus. This Haggada is read annually at the Passover Seder (ritual meal) conducted at Jewish homes the first night(s) of Passover.

The Talmud's Place in Jewish History

The Talmud joined the Bible as religious books to be studied by the Jewish people, who came to be known as ***"The people of the Book."***

The Development of the Talmud

Except for those who have gone to a Yeshiva, or a Jewish day school, today's typical Jew's knowledge of the Talmud is limited to the recognition that such a document relating to Judaism exists. Not only are they not aware that current Judaic practices stem from the Halachah in the Talmud, they have no understanding of the importance that the Talmud played in the continuity of Jewish life since the time it was completed.

The Talmud provided regulations for all aspects of life. The complex and often conflicting rabbinical opinions that provided the basis for the Talmudic laws provided room for endless discussions (still going on among those studying the Talmud) and stimulated commentaries on the commentaries. Many rabbis quoted in the Talmud were willing to give up their lives rather than forsake the Judaic principles. These acts of martyrdom provided the inspiration for many Jews to resist the severe Christian conversion pressures during the medieval period, often to the point of accepting their own martyrdom.

During the Middle Ages, the Christian clergy contended that Talmudic studies were the main obstacle to their missionary work among the Jews of western Europe. They took several steps to eliminate the Talmud. In debates with leading rabbis, they challenged the rabbis to renounce the Talmud. The clergy banned reading the Talmud and publicly burned many Talmud. In spite of these efforts, the Talmud remained the source of Jewish strength during that dark period.

Later, when Poland and Russia became the home of millions of Jews, the study of Talmud was taught in the extensive Jewish education system in these countries. Talmud study essentially kept these Jews from assimilating, while Jews in western Europe were already assimilating in the period of European enlightenment.

7
The Muslim World

Muhammad (570–632 C.E.) founded the religion of Islam. Adherents to Islam are called Muslims. The Western world frequently refers to Islam as "Mohammedanism" and calls the Muslim people *"Moslems."* To Muslims, Muhammad is the most important and last Prophet to the God of Abraham they call *"Allah."* Muhammad's basic precepts were sincere prayer, fasting, alms-giving, and complete submission to the will of Allah. The Koran is the Islamic Bible that contains what Muhammad professes were God's revelations to him as God's Prophet.

Within one hundred years, the Muslims became the rulers of the Middle East and the countries of North Africa, where the vast majority of the Jewish people lived.

The Rise of Muhammadanism (622 C.E.)

Muhammad ("Praised One") was born of a poor family in Mecca, Arabia. Despite little education, he became a leader of caravan routes. Through this traveling, he became exposed to Judaism and Christianity. He called himself a Prophet and recruited followers to the new religion that he established. Initially the pagan Arabian tribes in Mecca rejected him, and he was forced to flee to Medina in 622. This marks the beginning of the Muslim calendar. His militant followers forcefully won converts as they vanquished the tribes in the Medina area. In 624, Muhammad was strong enough to conquer Mecca, and it became the Islamic holy city centered on a large black stone. Muhammad dedicated the "Black Stone," initially a pagan shrine, to the God of Abraham. The stone was encased in a large cubic box known as the *Ka'aba,* and it became the most sacred Muslim religious shrine.

In the short time between Muhammad's conquering of Mecca and his death in 632, Muslims had subjugated all of Arabia. Within a hundred years, they conquered the Middle East, southern Asia leading to India, and all of North Africa. Internal clashes for leadership divided the Muslim community after Muhammad's death. About ten percent of the current Muslim population are Shiites. They are followers of the fourth son of Muhammad who wanted the Muslim political capital to remain in Mecca. Shiites are the Muslim fundamentalists. Approximately ninety percent of the Muslim population are Sunni Muslim. They are adherents of the Muslim political leaders who moved the Muslim political capital to Damascus after Muhammad's death.

Muhammad's Negative Attitude Toward Jews

Jews had been living in Arabia for many years before the time of Muhammad. They likely came from Palestine as exiles after the rebellion against Rome in 70 C.E. They lived as individual tribes with a nomadic lifestyle resembling that of the Bedouins. The Hebrew concept of "one God" influenced some Arab tribal leaders to adopt Judaism as their religion, particularly in Yemen, resulting in a fairly large Jewish population in Arabia at the time of Muhammad.

Muhammad believed in the "One God of the Jews" and claimed descent from Abraham through his son Ishmael. He expected Jews to accept his religion because he designed it to be appealing to them. His Islamic religion initially took on many Judaic practices, such as multiple daily prayers facing Jerusalem and abstaining from eating pork. His Koran had many stories resembling Jewish Bible stories. Despite these efforts, Muhammad was not successful at proselytizing the Arabian Jews. There were aspects of his preaching that were considered unacceptable from a Jewish standpoint. He offered little more to Jewish theology other than his claim to be a new Prophet of God. With Muhammad having no stature in the community and having been rejected by most Arabs, the Arabian Jews rejected his advances.

Angered by the resistance of the Jewish people to join him, Muhammad dropped some Jewish practices from the religion he was still developing and became hostile towards the Jews. After one Jewish tribe near Medina fought a losing battle alongside the Medina Arabs fighting him, Muhammad began fighting other Jewish tribes in Arabia. The Jewish tribes failed to help one another in their battles with Muhammad, which was a major cause of their defeat. His military victories over the Jewish tribes won him many pagan converts near Medina. With these new supporters, Muhammad then planned to attack Mecca, which was the main prosperous city in Arabia. Before the attack, Muhammad won over many pagan converts in Mecca by adopting the formerly pagan Black Stone (*Ka'aba*) in Mecca as his own religious shrine. These new adherents to his religion became Muhammad's soldiers in his battle with the Meccan Arabs who still opposed him.

After Muhammad conquered Mecca, he turned completely and bitterly against the Jews. He again changed the Islamic laws to eliminate more similarities to Judaism; as an example, Muslims were to pray facing Mecca instead of facing Jerusalem.

Jewish Life Under Islamic Rule

By the eighth century, approximately seventy percent of the Jewish population lived in countries under Arab rule, including the lower part of Spain, North Africa, Turkey, Persia, and the Middle East. Islamic rule had a profound impact on Jewish economic and religious practices.

The Muslim rulers considered the Jewish people to be the *"people of the book."* As such, the Arab rulers treated Jews living in the Muslim-controlled areas as *"protected people."* That meant that all males were required to pay taxes, which protected the Jewish property while allowing Jews to freely practice Judaism. Over the next several centuries, this freedom allowed Jews to become merchants, who were able to bridge the Arab community on the south side of the Mediterranean with the Christian community on the north side. Jews, already seafaring people, became major international traders who were known to have traveled as far as China.

The centrality of Arab political rule over this large Jewish population was indirectly a major contributor to the spread of Talmudic Judaism. Copies of the Talmud, written in Babylon and completed in the fifth century, slowly made their way to the European Jews. They had raised many questions about the Talmud over the next few hundred years, which remained unanswered; there had been no central religious authority to resolve Jewish religious issues since the end of the Bet Din in Palestine.

Under the Persian rulers of Babylonia, an Exilarch was the highest authority in the Babylonian Jewish community. When the Arab rulers recognized the Exilarch as the highest Jewish authority under their rule, the European Jews living under Arab domination began to respect the Babylonian Exilarch as their religious authority—the centrality of Arab rule over so many countries in which Jews lived was the influential factor. What was still lacking was a method of communicating between the two isolated Jewish communities. The large number of Jewish international traders that developed under the benevolent Arab rule provided the answer. These Jewish merchants carried messages between the rabbis in the western European areas and the rabbis in the Middle Eastern Babylonian religious centers.

Part II

A History of the Jewish People in Europe

Centuries of Trauma and Accomplishment

Preface to Part II

Europe played a significant role in the history of the Jewish people. It was the main bridge from the ancient land of Israel, where the Jewish people originated, to the countries where the vast majority of the Jewish people live today. The five million American Jews essentially trace their heritage to Europe, arriving within the past two centuries. The five million Jews living in Israel emigrated primarily from Europe within the past century. The two mainstream Jewish cultures, Ashkenazi and Sephardi, originated in Europe. The Chassidic movement started there, as did versions of Reform and Conservative Judaism that developed later in the United States.

The two thousand-year history of the Jewish people in Europe is a story of unrecognized Jewish accomplishments, periods of tolerance followed by intolerance and of major tragedies inflicted on the Jewish people. This history is replete with expulsions of Jews from the major European countries, migrations from country to country to seek improved living conditions, and of periodic mass killing of Jews. It was climaxed by the Holocaust in 1941 to 1945 that took six million Jewish lives. The ability of the Jewish people to survive these periods of extreme oppression, disappointments, and disillusionment is a testament to the survivability of the Jewish people.

European Jewish history started approximately in the era of the Second Jewish Commonwealth, 100 B.C.E., when Jewish seafarers and international traders left Israel for the western lands of Europe accessible by sea. For the next thousand years, the Jewish population in Europe expanded to England, France, Holland, and Germany without making much impact on Jewish culture. This changed at the start of the next millennia. Under Muslim rule of Spain, Spanish Jews experienced their *Golden Age* of Jewish cultural life, which ended with the Spanish Inquisition and the expulsion of the Jews from Spain. The rabbinical giants of that period—Maimonides, Rashi, Gershom—made their mark on Jewish religious, philosophical, and educational practices. The Jews in the medieval world were forced to live in Jewish ghettos, but found this insulation from the Christian world and the Talmud educational tool developed by Rashi to be the sources of strength that enabled them to survive and retain their Judaism in the depressive atmosphere that encouraged conversion to Christianity.

The religious oppression and poor economic conditions that prevailed after the end of the Middle Ages constantly influenced Jewish religious behavior and outlook. Masses of Jews fell prey to several false Messiahs over a two-hundred-year period. This was followed by Chassidic Judaism that blossomed as a way of having spirituality enable one to cope with the hardships of Jewish life in eastern Europe.

In the nineteenth century, Reform Judaism emerged as an opportunity for German Jews to adhere to a form of Judaism in an atmosphere of assimilation. Jews enjoyed the benefits of the political enlightenment and open commercialism that replaced feudalism in western Europe. The inability to achieve the same liberties in Russia had a severe impact on Russian Jews that led to secular Judaism. These secular Jews were the driving forces behind Zionism that emerged in Europe at the end of the nineteenth century.

The twentieth century started as a period of contrast for the Jewish people in Europe. Jews in western Europe had essentially achieved full political and economic liberty, whereas the large Jewish population who lived under Russian control still lacked economic and political freedom. World War I represented a particular trauma for the Jewish people—they fought for both sides in the war, with family members fighting each other.

The rise of Hitler in the early 1930s raised a storm cloud over the Jewish people worldwide, but the very nationalistic German Jews elected to ride out the storm until Kristallnacht, after which half the German Jews fled Germany before the Holocaust began. The other European Jews were less fortunate. The very efficient German genocide program took six million Jewish lives while World War II took place and the Germans were conquering most of Europe.

The twentieth century history of the Russian Jews is another illustration of the survivability of the Jewish people. Under Soviet Communist rule, millions of Russian Jews lost their Jewish identity for almost seventy years. Then, led by a small courageous group of Soviet Jews, called *refuseniks,* who fought for the right of Soviet Jews to emigrate to Israel, these Soviet Jews awakened to their Jewish heritage; to date, one million Russian Jews have emigrated to the State of Israel.

1
Initial Jewish Migration to Europe

The earliest Jews came to Europe during King Solomon's reign in the 900 B.C.E. period. They started as seafarers who were part of King Solomon's plan to make his kingdom a commercial success through international trade. The first major migration to Europe occurred during the Second Commonwealth. Because the agrarian lifestyle could not accommodate the Commonwealth's large population growth, the country changed to a commercial society and became highly successful economically. The Jews reestablished their seafaring expertise that they had gained during the King Solomon period a thousand years earlier, which brought them to the Mediterranean countries that welcomed the Jews for their talents as merchants and artisans. Over the next several hundred years, this mercantile activity brought Jews as far north as England and the Rhine River valley in Germany.

Rome—At the start of the first century B.C.E., Jews were an important commercial element of Roman society. By the second century C.E., it is estimated that ten percent of the Romans, approximately one million, were of the Jewish faith. In addition to the large number of Jews who had emigrated from Judea (old kingdom of Israel), there were many Roman pagan conversions to Judaism. Seeking a religion with a higher purpose, they were attracted to the monotheism of Judaism with its philosophy of moral behavior, doing good deeds, and charity giving. Prosperous Roman Jews ransomed many Jews who were brought to Rome as slaves after the failed Bar Kochba rebellion in 132 C.E. Jews enjoyed religious freedom in the Roman controlled areas until after Emperor Constantine embraced Christianity and made it the official religion in 300 C.E. The practice of Judaism became progressively more difficult over the next two hundred years and became subject to the death penalty. Large numbers of Jews, particularly those whose ancestors had been converts to Judaism, converted to Christianity; the population dwindled to less than one hundred thousand.

Spain—Jews lived in Spain from the time of King Solomon. Their ranks swelled when life in Rome started to become unbearable. After a few hundred years of comfortable living as merchants and landowners, they experienced the first expulsion incident when in the year 700 the Visigoth rulers of Spain ordered them to convert to Christianity or leave. Most fled to southern France or North Africa. The climate for Jews in Spain changed when the Muslims rapidly conquered Spain in 711. Whether because the Jews were their allies or because of the fundamental Muslim tolerance towards Jews in that period, the Jews were granted political and religious freedom; many Jews returned to Spain. It began the period of the Golden Age of Jewish life in Spain that lasted five hundred years until expulsion in 1492. The Spanish Judaic lifestyle was retained by the Jews who fled Spain and continues today as *"Sephardic Judaism."*

France—Jews had settled in France while it was still a Roman province. Jewish artisans and merchants joined the Romans as they invaded France, concentrating in the central French cities of Paris, Troyes, and Lyons. The rulers were tolerant towards the Jews, allowing them to practice their religion freely and to engage in commerce with minimum restrictions. This tolerance prevailed even after the Franks conquered France. In the year 749, the new French ruler followed the pattern set fifty years earlier by the Visigoths, who, when they took over northern Spain, required the Jews to convert to Catholicism or be exiled. Dagobert exiled the Jews from central France, where no Jews lived for the next hundred years. Many fled to the Provence section of southern France, which became a thriving Jewish community for the next several hundred years.

Germany—The earliest Jews came as sailors and merchants with the Roman army that invaded Germany. They lived along the northern Rhine River. Others came when the French ruler Dagobert exiled the French Jews. They populated cities, such as Cologne, Mayence, and Speyer. Ashkenaz was the early Hebrew name for the area of Europe now called Germany. Most European Jews other than those from the Mediterranean countries and the Middle East trace their heritage to this area. In time, this group of Jews became known as *Ashkenazi Jews*.

Kingdom of the Khazars—Jews from Persia had migrated to the southern portion of Russia bordering the Black Sea and the Caspian Sea, called Khazaria. At around the year 600, the pagan king of Khazaria wanted to adopt a monotheistic religion. Influenced by the form of Judaism practiced by Jews living in the region, the king selected Judaism over Christianity and Muhammadanism. The country remained a Jewish kingdom for about two hundred years.

2
The Medieval Period

In the early Middle Ages, the aristocracy in many countries were friendly to the Jews, offering them protection and the opportunity to conduct commercial business as merchants. Notable was the French Emperor Charlemagne and his son (768–840). Another example was the bishop of Speyer, Germany, who invited Jews to settle in his town in order to aid in its prosperity. Because of their religious and cultural characteristics, Jews were treated as a distinct class. They were generally granted some autonomy, such as having their own communal organization and education system. However, it came with the price of extraordinary taxes levied on them. Jews were still considered aliens in western European societies. The granting of any rights and their safety always depended on the ruler's attitude toward them. Occasionally, a Catholic high cleric came to their aid.

Initially, there was mostly constructive interaction with the Christian community. This peaceful coexistence ended with the First Crusade in 1096. The advent of Protestantism in the sixteenth century was another cause of political discrimination against the Jews by the Catholic clergy as they waged their battle to fend off its growth. Martin Luther, the priest who turned religious reformer, attacked the Pope and other Catholic clergy for their harsh treatment and accusations against the Jews. When the Jews failed to convert to his form of Christianity, Luther turned violently antagonistic towards the Jews. Then, as Protestantism grew in political strength, it followed Martin Luther's bitter anti-Semitic pronouncements and became another source of Jewish persecution.

Life in the Medieval World

Economic life of the Jews deteriorated in the Middle Ages, driven by the changes in the economic lifestyle of that period. The new *guilds,* which controlled who engaged in handicrafts, excluded Jews from the handicraft occupations. Jews were forced out of land ownership and farming. They were also eased out of the professions, including medicine. With most of their previous occupations gone, the majority of the Jews barely survived. Peddling and clothes-mending became the most popular occupations.

Christianity did not permit charging for moneylending, called usury in that time (whether at a reasonable or exorbitant interest). However, moneylending was necessary to expand the economies of all the growing communities, but there were no sources of Christian money to be lent without a fee. Under these circumstances, wealthier Jews found lending money with interest a rewarding practice. (Moneylending practices were restricted but not prohibited by Judaic law.) Most rulers encouraged moneylending by Jews. The rulers were big gainers in other ways. They taxed the Jews heavily for this opportunity. When the outcry against Jewish "usury" became severe, they periodically expelled the entire Jewish community, appropriating their wealth.

A few Jews, using contacts with Jewish communities in other countries, were successful as merchants in international commerce. Many European rulers, seeing other countries benefit economically from this activity, encouraged and sometimes facilitated this Jewish activity in their own country. There were wealthy Jews at various times in European countries. Although some achieved high positions as financial advisors to the rulers, they held little political influence and were of little aid to the Jewish people. Claims of "rich Jews having too much influence" were circulated by those looking for an economic advantage over their Jewish competitors. These claims were in step with the other negative and false accusations that many influential anti-Semites made during the Middle Ages.

At the end of the Middle Ages, Jews of western Europe were driven into such a state of poverty that there was a massive migration of Jews to eastern Europe in search of opportunities to improve their economic conditions. The one country where opportunities increased was Holland, which was attributed to the contributions to Dutch international commerce made by the Marranos who fled Spain and returned to Judaism.

Badge of Shame (1200)—After the Crusades, the Pope issued anti-Jewish decrees that affected all Jews in Christian Europe. Jews were forbidden to hold office, were not to interact with Christians commercially, and had to wear a symbol identifying themselves as Jews (a patch on their clothes or a pointed hat). The intent was also to cause psychological harm by its shame. These steps were a prelude to the expulsions and forced-living in ghettos that followed in the next two centuries.

Ghetto Life—During the "Black Death" plague period (1348–1350) many Jews were either massacred or expelled from the cities and towns. Jews were falsely accused of causing the plague. Several years after the plague ended, Jews were slowly permitted to return to their former hometowns, but they were restricted to live in separate areas that were frequently walled in to keep them from interacting with the Christian community. This forced isolated living of Jews was later designated *ghetto* based the Jewish ghetto in a gun-factory district of Venice in 1516, which was called *geto* in Venetian.

Life was a struggle in these cramped, unsanitary living areas with nominally restricted access and exit. Trading in secondhand clothes and pawnbroking were the main business options available. Family togetherness and religious study and practice sustained their Jewishness. The few Jews in each ghetto who were somehow successful economically became the community leaders.

Religious Life—Study, prayer, and charity were the activities that gave strength to the Jews during this difficult Middle Ages period. Every community stressed learning and had supervised elementary education. Talmudic study was supported whenever there was a suitable rabbi available. Each Jew felt the need for personal prayer that was offered in the in the communal synagogue. Personal and organized communal charitable activity made certain that no Jew had to rely on the charity of a non-Jew.

At the beginning of the medieval period, the academies in Babylon were the centers of Jewish religious learning and development. These were replaced by the Jewish centers of learning in Spain during the Golden Age period and by those in the Provence region of France (until the expulsion of all Jews from France in 1305). Other major academies were in Mayence and Worms, Germany (until the devastation to Jewish life in Germany during the Black Death period). Many important Judaic religious documents were created at these academies during this period.

Religious intolerance towards the Jews was an aftermath of the Crusades that began in the twelfth century. Starting in the thirteenth century, the Jewish religion was attacked by high-ranking clerics, some notorious ones being Jewish converts to Catholicism. The Talmud was repeatedly put on trial, frequently banned and burned. Pressures to convert to Catholicism increased, and many Jews converted to find relief from the oppression. Of those, some secretly kept the Jewish practices and some actually returned to Judaism when the anti-Jewish political atmosphere subsided.

Karaism—Around the year 760, a group of rebellious Jews led by a disgruntled nephew of the deceased Exilarch (highest Jewish authority in Babylonia) set up a sect of Judaism based on strict adherence to the words of the Bible. Karaites were fundamentalists who denounced the Talmud and Jewish traditions based on rabbinic interpretations of the Bible.

Saadiah Gaon (950)—Saadiah ben Joseph was the last leader (called Gaon, meaning His Excellency) of the great Sura academy in Babylon. He answered Jewish philosophical questions at a time when the Jewish religious community lacked the creativity it had during the years prior to the completion of the Talmud several centuries earlier. He wrote in Arabic, the language of the Jews living in the Muslim world, reaching and impressing a large number of Jews including those living in Spain. As a strong defender of the Talmud, Saadiah Gaon ended the threat to Judaism posed by the Karaites.

Rabbi Gershom of Mayence (1000)—A leading religious authority of his time, Rabbi Gershom promulgated many regulations affecting Jewish lifestyle and social attitudes. Two important ones dealt with women. He forbade polygamy and required the wife's consent for a divorce initiated by the husband. He exhibited unusual tolerance for his time, easing the severe Jewish reaction to those forced to convert to Christianity and required the Jews as a community and as individuals to wholesomely accept forced-converts that elected to return to Judaism.

Rabbi Rashi of Troyes (1090)—The name of **Ra**bbi **Sh**lomo ben **I**tzchak, known as **Rashi,** is not too familiar to the typical Jew today. He was a brilliant interpreter of Jewish religious documents and one of the greatest Jewish educators. His complete set of commentaries on the Bible and Talmud became a standard addition to all printed versions of these two documents. His commentaries enabled the average Jewish student to fully understand the Scriptures and the Talmud. Written in a clear and concise manner that was easy for all to understand, his commentaries were accepted by his contemporaries without challenge. His commentaries, which were integrated into the Talmud text, gave life to the Talmud, which was written in Aramaic and difficult to follow. Rashi's study technique was to have the student enjoy learning, stimulating the students to arrive at their own answers. *"Rashi"* became the important tool for teaching Bible and Talmud in all the academies of Jewish learning.

Learning by the Jewish masses became their pillar of strength during the dark days of the Middle Ages and into the twentieth century.

3
The Golden Age in Spain

During the years 900 to 1200, there existed an ideal combination of religious and political freedom for Jews in Spain. This environment resulted in the most creative Judaic religious, cultural and intellectual creativity in Jewish history, referred to by Jewish historians as *"The Golden Age of Jewish Life."*

Muslim Conquest of Spain: The Golden Age—Jews lived in Spain from before the days of the Roman conquerors. They suffered few hardships under the succession of invaders who ruled the country until the Visigothic king accepted the Catholic faith in 589. A century of severe political and religious persecution followed. When the Arabs from Africa invaded Spain in 711, they found the Jews to be the only ones to welcome and aid them. In return, the persecution ended and opportunities for Jews opened. Under the enlightened rule of the Muslim rulers, Spain became a glorious place physically and intellectually, while the rest of Europe was in the political and intellectual darkness of the Middle Ages. Jews participated in all aspects of this creative atmosphere and made significant contributions to the medieval civilization. Jewish political leaders, poets, and philosophers served as intermediaries between the Arabs and the Christians. They translated the great works of Arab mathematicians, astronomers, philosophers, and physicians into Latin for the rest of Europe. The Jews of Spain of that period were a proud and wealthy community. They supported magnificent synagogues and high quality centers of Jewish learning and culture initially in Cordoba, later in Granada, and finally in Toledo. These moves from city to city were the result of a despotic Caliph taking over the rule in each city, forcing most Jews to leave for more hospitable cities.

Statesmen Who Were Also Jewish Leaders—Hasdai ibn Shaprut and Samuel ibn Nagdela were two notable statesmen of this period. Though they achieved high positions of authority, they were devoted to the Jewish communities and became their leaders.

Hasdai ibn Shaprut (915–970) became the vizier of the Caliph Abd Ar Rahman, who ruled Spain, enabling him to be a benefactor of Jewish life in Cordoba. His most important achievement was the founding and financing of a Spanish academy for Talmudic study that took over this activity just as the Talmudic study academies in Babylon went into decline.

Samuel ibn Nagdela (993–1056) served as the leading statesman to the king of the state of Granada for three decades. During this period he dealt with the problems of the Jewish community and served as its leader. In gratitude, he was given the title, *"Nagid"* ("prince"). He presided over the rabbinic school, wrote commentaries on the Talmud, and kept in communication with the Talmud scholars in Babylon and North Africa. Nagdela was generous financially, supporting poor scholars and teachers who flocked to Granada.

Religious Poets—The freedom of thought under the Muslim rule in Spain, coupled with the Arabic love of good poetry, stimulated Jews in Spain to write both secular and religious poetry. These writings in Hebrew became worthy of being called "The Golden Age of Hebrew Literature." These writers also wrote important philosophical works in Arabic:

Solomon ibn Gabirol (1021–1069), perhaps the most accomplished of the poets, wrote many religious hymns and poems that are included in the Sephardic Jewish liturgy. He also wrote ethical and philosophical works. Gabirol's *Fons Vitae* (The Fountain of Life) was a favorite philosophical book used by medieval thinkers.

Moses ibn Ezra (1080–1139) was a prolific writer of 220 Hebrew liturgical poems, many of which were incorporated into the Sephardic liturgy. He also generated philosophical works dealing with the Scriptures and Judaic practices. After a despotic ruler took over his home city of Granada, he spent a good part of his life wandering through the countries of western Europe, where he did many of his writings.

Judah Halevi (1086–1145) is perhaps the most famous of the Hebrew poets. He turned from writing secular poetry to religious hymns, writing hundreds of religious poems. He is most famous for his poems expressing his love of God and his love of Zion. Halevi's *"Songs of Exile"* and *"Ode to Zion"* best expressed the feelings of the Jewish people of his time. His *Kuzari* was a philosophical work extolling Judaism over Christianity and Islam.

Moses Maimonides (1135–1204)—Jews have the saying, *"From Moses to Moses, there was none like Moses."* The foremost Jew of the Middle Ages was Moses ben Maimon, called Rambam (abbreviation of his name) by Jews and known as Maimonides to the world. Forced to leave his home in Cordoba at the age of thirteen, he went to North Africa, where he continued his studies with his father. From these hostile surroundings, he went on to become a master of so many subjects that he became the marvel of the world. Maimonides became a physician of such capability, he was appointed as physician to the vizier of Egypt and consultant to the famous Saladin family that ruled Egypt. While conducting this work, he found time to be the leader of the Jewish Egyptian community, continue his studies, write his many religious, scientific, and philosophical books, and become a jurist and legal philosopher. His works made a major impact on Judaism and had a strong influence on European philosophy.

His major religious book was the *Mishneh Torah,* which codified all the laws of the Talmud in a way that a lay person could understand the laws without having to deal with the massive Talmudic commentaries. He formulated the *Thirteen Principles of Faith,* which were incorporated into the Orthodox and Conservative daily prayers and has essentially become the Jewish creed.

Maimonides attempted to apply reason to Judaic principles and reconcile Jewish faith with scientific principles. This thinking was opposed by many rabbis of that period who held to the traditional view of the Bible. The most famous was Nahmanides (who defended the Talmud in debates with Spanish clergy and became a leading Jewish mystic). Maimonides's major philosophical work is the *Guide for the Perplexed.* It attempted to show the compatibility of Judaism with Aristotelian logic. He provided a rational interpretation of the biblical miracles, sacrificial system, and prophecy, eliminating many of the superstitions that prevailed.

4
Four Centuries of Terror (1100–1500)

At the end of the eleventh century, Jews in Spain were enjoying the *Golden Age,* while life for the Jews in the rest of Europe had reached a comfortable level. Jewish life changed drastically at the turn of the twelfth century with the Crusades. Jews went through a succession of political, economic, and religious oppressions that culminated in massacres and expulsions. It marked the end of settled communal life for Jews in western Europe. It was the beginning of a long period of political and economic uncertainty in a hostile atmosphere filled with racial tensions for Jews—*the age of the wandering and depressed Jew.*

This horror started with the First Crusade. It lasted for 400 years. No Jewish community throughout Europe was spared the violence and death. It ended with the aftermath of the Black Plague that struck Europe and the Inquisition in Spain.

The Crusades (1096–1270)—History books describe the Crusades as noble Christian expeditions. They were hordes of common people led by knights and noblemen. The main objective was to return Palestine to Christian rule. The emphasis was on capturing the Holy Sepulcher, where the Christians believed Jesus was buried. In reality, the Crusades were a failure for the Christians. Only the first of eight Crusades restored Jerusalem to Christian rule, which lasted less than one hundred years. The other Crusades, except one, did not get close to Palestine, and Jerusalem remained under Muslim control during this period. The knights and noblemen gained fame, but the Crusades caused grief for the common Crusader. For the Jews, the Crusades were a disaster. The Crusaders' religious zeal resulted in the massacre of thousands of Jews and many hundreds of Jewish communities destroyed. One hundred thousand Jews converted to Christianity in order to escape the disaster that the Crusaders were imposing on the Jewish people.

The First Crusade initiated a 400-year period of clergy-led persecution and killing of Jews. Fired up by the religious fervor of the clergy, the

First Crusaders marched through the northern French and German cities with large Jewish populations, slaughtering Jews by the thousands. This killing spree continued as the Crusaders marched into Prague on the way to Palestine by land—the last place these Crusaders got to. The Crusaders who went to Palestine by sea did manage to get the control of Jerusalem away from the Muslims. In triumph, the Crusaders put all the Jews in Jerusalem to a violent death. Jews in Europe barely got over the horrors of the First Crusade when the Second Crusade occurred fifty years later—it was not as severe. The Third Crusade saw a return of very brutal treatment throughout Europe and in the small towns of England. The most serious English incident was in York, where five hundred Jews took refuge in a castle. Most of them committed suicide when the food ran out rather than succumb to the crowds threatening to kill them. The others were slaughtered. This pattern followed with the later Crusades. With each failure, the Crusaders took vengeance on the Jews; with each victory, they celebrated by killing the "infidel" Jews.

Persecution Continues After the Crusades End—The thirteenth century was the beginning of other forms of persecution of the Jews. To demoralize the Jewish people, Pope Innocent III forced Jews to wear the degrading "badge of shame." It consisted of a distinctive garment, such as a pointed hat or a special patch on the front and back of the clothing. To destroy their economic life, under the Pope's guidance, the Fourth Lateran Council in 1215 passed severe restrictions on the commercial and societal activity of the Jews. Pope Gregory outlawed the Talmud in an attempt to destroy the Jewish religion. When many rulers ignored his edict, the Talmud was brought to trial in Paris, France. In a court setting attended by royalty and high clergy, four leading rabbis were required to answer the list of charges that the Talmud blasphemed God and Jesus. Not satisfied with the answer that the Talmud commentaries in question do not refer to Jesus, the court decided that all copies of the Talmud should be burned in a public demonstration.

The brutality against the Jews continued after the Crusades ended. The flourishing Jewish communities in southern France were completely destroyed and eliminated under Pope Innocent's war against heretics in that region. Over a one-hundred-fifty-year period, there were various events that triggered many riots and massacres of Jews in Germany, England, France, and elsewhere in central Europe. False blood libel claims, bad crops, invasions by the Mongols, false accusations of Jews interfering with Christian religious rituals became reason for these riots. It got worse for the Jews during the next major event to hit Europe, the Black Death.

The Black Death Brutality—In 1348, the terrible bubonic plague (*Black Death*) struck Europe. It is estimated that twenty-five percent of the population died. For the Jewish population, it was worse. The Jews were falsely accused of causing the plague, which aroused the suffering masses against the Jews. Pope Clement VI sent letters to all the European rulers urging them to protect their Jewish population. His explanation that the Jews suffered with everyone else and could not have caused the plague was to no avail. In the next three years, thousands of Jews were brutally massacred as never before by the uncontrolled mobs of people, frequently incited by the clergy. Eighteen hundred Jews burned alive in Strassburg and six thousand killed in Mayence are examples of the horror. Between the deaths due to the plague and the wanton killings, it is estimated that there was a fifty percent loss of the Jewish population. Six large communities and one hundred fifty smaller Jewish ones were destroyed.

Horrors of the Spanish Inquisition—While the persecutions were going on in the rest of Europe, two hundred fifty Jewish communities in Spain lived in comfort and security. The Jewish population reached 250,000. The transition from Moorish (Muslim) rule to the Christians did not affect the Jews until the fourteenth century. For the next hundred years, while Christian monarchs were fighting for control of Spain, acts of brutality against the Jews occurred in several provinces of Spain. It reached a peak in 1391. Thousands of Jews were killed in Seville, Cordoba, Toledo, and elsewhere, in a three-month orgy of bloody killing by uncontrolled mobs. Hundreds were sold into slavery to the Moors. The mob fury initiated the process of conversion to Christianity that many Spanish Jews were to accept in the years to follow. Several thousand Jews accepted baptism to save their lives.

After 1391, the pressure on the Jews increased, resulting in entire Jewish communities converting to Christianity; Jews were offered conversion or death. Professionals and people influential in all facets of public life converted. The old-Christians became jealous of these new-Christians, called *Conversos,* many of whom retained positions of influence. Some Conversos called themselves Christian, but secretly practiced some form of Judaism. To insult these nonconforming Christians, the Spaniards called them *Marranos* ("pig"). The Spanish Jews accepted the Marranos as "crypto-Jews." The clergy, resenting the influence of the new Christians, became antagonistic towards the Marranos. There were periodic massacres of Marranos, spurred on by the clergy. All too often, Jews who converted and became clerics led the anti-Jewish attacks.

This situation got worse when King Ferdinand and Queen Isabella became joint rulers of the states of Aragon and Castile. That gave them the power to initiate the Inquisition in 1479. It was promoted and run by Queen Isabella's confessor, Torquemada. The Inquisition was directed against the new-Christians. Its advertised purpose was to "purify the Catholic attitude of all Spaniards." The Inquisition process consisted of rooting out new-Christians who secretly practiced some form of Judaism. The Inquisition relied on informers, many of whom were driven by jealousy. Torture to force confessions was common. The court trials were shams and unjust. The penalty was the *auto-da-fe* (act of faith) process consisting of public burning of the victim at the stake. For three years, the Inquisition was confined to southern Spain until Torquemada was appointed Inquisitor General. He tightened the Inquisition process and applied it to all of Spain. This brutal process under Torquemada killed thousands over a sixteen-year period. (The Spanish Inquisition laws were finally officially abolished in 1834.)

5
Expulsion and Migration

During the Middle Ages' 400-year period of terror against the Jewish people, the persecution in several countries ended only when all the Jews were expelled from the country. This happened in England, France, Spain, and Portugal. In Italy and Germany, the expulsions were less complete—Jews were expelled only from some sections of these countries.

Most rulers took advantage of the precarious position of the Jews in their country during this period. They all taxed the Jews heavily. Bribery to achieve protection and holding leaders and rabbis for ransom by the Jewish community were techniques the rulers used to extort money from the Jews. False libel claims and clerical condemnation of the Jews as infidels became common. At the end, the kings eagerly used these pressures to expel the Jews from their countries. It gave them the opportunity to confiscate the departing Jews' property and financial possessions.

Expulsion from England—After a century of torture, massacre, and conversion, the surviving Jews were expelled from England in 1290 by King Edward I. He was a popular king to the British people for his fairness and accomplishments, but he was a tyrant to the Jews. The "Statute of Judaism" preceded his expulsion edict. This law essentially denied the Jews all forms of their livelihood. After Italian bankers replaced the Jewish banking services, the Jews lost their value to the king, leading to their expulsion. Sixteen thousand Jews were sent to France with only the possessions they could carry.

Oliver Cromwell, who took rule of England away from the crown, allowed Jews to return to England in 1656. He encouraged Jews from Amsterdam to come because of their international trade capability; Jews were given a lot of credit for Holland's commercial success during that period. Jews could now participate freely in economic activity but not in governmental activity, which required being Christian. When the throne was restored in 1660, these conditions for the Jews did not change. During this period of liberalization, many Marranos who had been living in England openly professed their Judaism.

Expulsion from France—Life in France, particularly in the southern part, had been very favorable for the Jewish people until 1230. Jewish religious and economic life had thrived there for the previous three hundred years. The French rulers then started a process of expelling the Jews from their provinces and then inviting them back after a few years when they realized that lost taxes exceeded the money they gained from expropriating the Jewish property. Every few years the process was repeated by expelling the Jews again and allowing them to return later. Most went to Germany. Some went to Spain or other parts of France. In 1394, the Jews were expelled completely, not allowing them back for almost two hundred years. The expulsion ended twelve hundred years of creative Jewish life in France.

Expulsion from Southern Italy—In 1288, a French king also ruled the Naples area of southern Italy. At the same time that the king expelled the Jews from his province in France, the king issued an expulsion order for all Jews in southern Italy. Over a five-year period, the ancient Jewish community in southern Italy was wiped out.

Expulsion from Spain—After conquering the last Moorish kingdom in southern Spain in January 1492, King Ferdinand and Queen Isabella became rulers of all of Spain. They then felt free to quickly deal with the problem of the Jews, which spilled over from the Inquisition against the Marranos. Ignoring the pleas of several Jews who held prominent positions in their government and disregarding the concerns over losing a very wealthy, creative group of people, the Spanish rulers gave in to the clergy led by the Inquisitor-General Torquemada and issued an expulsion order for all Jews. Torquemada, who was angered by Jews helping Marranos secretly practice Judaism, gave up all hope of converting the Jews and wanted Spain to be free of heretics. The Spanish monarchs saw it as a way of acquiring the wealth of the Jews who were to leave Spain without their possessions. The expulsion order, issued on March 31, was to be effective on August 1. Ironically, that day was the ninth day of the Jewish-calendar month of Ab. That is the same day of the previous major catastrophes in Jewish history; the destruction of the First and Second Temples in Jerusalem. The last Jews actually left Spain on August 2, the same day the three ships led by Columbus left on the first voyage to the New World. Several Jews and Marranos were in his crew.

The Jews had to give up practically all their possessions when leaving

Spain. They faced an unknown future, not sure of where they could go, who would accept them, and how they would get to their destination. Thousands of Jews could not accept the hardships ahead of them and voluntarily accepted baptism. Many Jews, given the choice of baptism or death, chose martyrdom. The opportunities for the Jewish exiles were filled with danger and disaster. A group of twelve thousand Jews from northern Spain entered the adjacent Navarre Province of southern France. The king of Navarre, previously very tolerant, was persuaded by King Ferdinand to give the Jews a choice of expulsion or baptism. The entire group chose baptism. Possibly as many as one hundred thousand Jews left for Portugal.

A large number of Jews made it to the eastern Mediterranean countries, whose Turkish rulers welcomed them—they were the most fortunate of the exiles. They had to overcome the hazardous long voyage, which was full of other dangers. Pirates and unscrupulous sea captains took their wealth and sold many into slavery. Of those Jews who thought they would find Muslim North Africa a safe haven, only the luckiest and sturdiest were able to survive the dangers they were actually exposed to when they got there. Many were killed on arrival. They faced starvation, disease, and being sold into slavery.

Jews lived on the Iberian Peninsula for over 1,500 years. During the Golden Years in Spain before their expulsion, Jews contributed significantly to Spain's cultural, intellectual, and economic growth. It is interesting that after the expulsion, Spain lapsed into a period of political and economic decay that lasted 400 years.

Expulsion from Portugal—The Spanish Jews who thought Portugal would be a safe refuge were in for a shock. The Portuguese king allowed only the wealthier ones to stay. The mostly poorer ones were given a few months to find a new refuge, threatening those who stayed beyond the time limit with becoming slaves if they did not convert. Not enough ships were available, so many who could not leave and would not convert became slaves. The new king who ascended the Portuguese throne in 1495 was initially more humane to the Jews, freeing them from slavery. A year later, as part of King Ferdinand and Queen Isabella's condition for allowing the king to marry their daughter, the king issued an order requiring all Jews and Moors to leave the country within one year. It was not an unconditional choice. The king forced all the young Jews under twenty-five to be baptized; he assumed their parents would follow. Those that could not leave became his slaves; he forcefully tried to convert them. The only Jews who remained in Portugal became Marranos, practicing Judaism secretly. After 400 years of this steadily decaying Marrano practice, some of their descendants have nevertheless recently discovered their Jewish roots.

Migration from Germany—During the Middle Ages, Germany was a divided country ruled by many kings. These kings competed with each other, resulting in different treatment of the Jews in the various sections of the country. When Jews were expelled from one section, Jews in the nonhostile sections welcomed them. Jews were frequently permitted to return to cities they were expelled from, but only for limited periods. The price for return was high fees for protection or heavy taxation. Expelled French Jews were welcomed in Germany because the rulers anticipated that the Jews would contribute to the development of their area's economy.

Due to the brutal attacks on them during the Crusades, small numbers of Jews left Germany for Poland and western Russia. In the aftermath of the Black Plague, when the brutality towards Jews got harsher, larger numbers of German Jews and central European Jews in the thousands fled to these countries. The emigration was also encouraged by the rulers of these backward eastern European countries who envisioned the Jews contributing to achieving the form of commercialism already accomplished in western Europe. However, many Jews remained in Germany throughout the turmoil of this period. Through birth records and Jewish cemetery tombstones, Jewish families have been able to trace a continuous family history in Germany going back to the fourteenth century and ending with the Holocaust period.

6
Religious Degeneration

From the twelfth through the eighteenth century, Judaism experienced degradation from the traditional form of the religion. Jewish mysticism that was popular in Palestine and Egypt during the birth of Christianity period became alive again. Known as Kabbalah (or Cabbala), it started as an esoteric teaching of Judaism to be practiced only by those trained to understand it. After the expulsion from Spain, forecasts of apocalyptic events were added to the Kabbalah movement. This, in turn, led to an increase in messianism among its followers. The Kabbalah leaders then changed their attitude regarding who should be exposed to the Kabbalistic teachings and spread this mystical brand of Judaism to the people at large.

Jewish economic suffering and religious oppression made Jews vulnerable to those who promised the elimination of worldly ills and a restoration of Jewish life worthy of the people of the Covenant. The teachings and predictions of the Kabbalah movement stirred on the longing for a Messiah. Several "false Messiahs" took advantage of this mood. Until they were exposed, these Messiahs had large Jewish followings and even captured the imagination of several Catholic religious leaders and rulers. A large number of Jews, estimated to have been up to a million and to have included fervently religious people, were taken in by several opportunists claiming to be the Messiah. Messianic popularity was widespread among the Jews in Europe, Turkey, and North Africa. This messianic fervor was so strong that even after the pretenders were exposed, many Jews continued to believe in them as the Messiah.

Kabbalah—*Kabbalah,* meaning *"receiving,"* offered answers to the mysteries of the universe and the hidden meanings of Jewish life and teachings. Man's relationship to God and the meaning of life were presented in combinations of Hebrew sacred names, letters, and numbers. The messages were conveyed in symbols arranged in diagrams. Kabbalah was intended to replace the traditional religious inspiration and was far removed from the rational and intellectual approach to Judaism practiced particularly by the Sephardic Jews at the time.

The movement started in southern France among the intellectual Jews in the vibrant community that existed there before the expulsion. In the twelfth century, the movement migrated to Spain. The major book presenting kabbalistic teachings that gave strength to the later Kabbalah movement was the ***Zohar*** written by Moses de Leon of Granada, Spain in 1268. It presents mystical teachings of the Five Books of Moses, offering insights to its messages beyond those derived from literal interpretations. ***The Book of Creation,*** one of the earliest philosophical books in the Hebrew language, was another significant kabbalistic book of that period. Although the kabbalistic teachings departed significantly from traditional Judaism, the traditional rabbis and leaders spared them from attack because Rabbi Nahmanides, the highest legal and religious authority of that period, gave some of the kabbalistic teachings his endorsement.

After the Jewish expulsion from Spain, Safed, in Palestine, became the center of the Kabbalah movement. In the late 1500s, Isaac Luria, who lived in Safed, popularized the Kabbalah movement with his way of life and messianic teachings. The movement lost its appeal with the Jewish enlightenment movement that started in the early eighteenth century, which brought a return to rational Judaism.

David Reubeni—In 1524, David Reubeni came to Rome with the claim that there were thousands of descendants of the ancient tribe of Reuben living in Arabia who were intent on assisting in the reconquest of the Holy Land from the Turks. Reubeni's ideas captured the imagination of Pope Clement VII, who sent Reubeni to see King John III of Portugal. While plans were being made for a new "crusade," the king ceased the persecution of Marranos in his country. Jews saw this unanticipated relief to be a sign of heavenly intervention and looked to Reubeni as the Messiah. Whole communities of Jews started to adhere to Reubeni's strange practices and beliefs. The impostor Reubeni left Portugal for Italy before the truth of his claims was determined to be false.

Solomon Molcho—Molcho was a Portuguese Marrano who had taken up Kabbalah and was convinced that the Messianic era was coming. He returned to Judaism, adopted the name of Solomon Molcho, and became a messianic messenger. He later tried to sell himself as the Messiah, a man with mystical powers. When calamities hit Portugal and Italy, his earlier forecasts of doom gave credence to his claims in the eyes of many. After he joined Reubeni in trying to sell the new crusade to the Portuguese rulers, he was turned over to the Inquisition in Italy, where he was burned at the stake for being a renegade Christian.

Shabbetai Zevi—Shabbetai Zevi was the most outstanding and popular of the false Messiahs. A Sephardic Jew from Smyrna, Turkey, he was immersed in Kabbalah at an early age. After recruiting a band of adherents, he started living an ascetic life expected of the Messiah, and made many messianic predictions. When he actually claimed to be the Messiah in 1648, the year kabbalists had predicted the coming of the Messiah, he was driven out of Smyrna by the Jewish community, who would not accept his messianic claims. Shabbetai Zevi and his disciples then roamed westward, advancing his claim and winning adherents in many countries. The widespread and horrible Chmielnicki massacres in the Ukraine and Poland had many Jews looking for a Messiah for their salvation. Shabbetai took an unchaste woman as his bride to play out the biblical story of the Prophet Hosea taking unchaste Gomer as his bride. This event swayed thousands of Jews to his cause. Word of his "miracles" and "achievements" persuaded many in the English and Dutch Jewish communities to believe in him as the Messiah.

Shabbetai Zevi's stirrings among the Middle Eastern Jews got him invited to Turkey by the Sultan. For a few months, he lived an honored and regal life there. Jewish congregations around Europe were offering Sabbath prayers for "Shabbetai the Messiah." When another pseudo-Messiah convinced the Sultan that Shabbetai was a conspirator against the Muslim country, the Sultan imprisoned Shabbetai. Given a choice of conversion to Islam or death, Shabbetai became a Muslim. His abandonment of the Jewish faith was a terrible shock and embarrassment to many prominent Jews who believed in him. Incredulously, some Jews refused to accept that his apostasy really happened.

Jacob Frank—Frank was the last of the false Messiahs and probably the most troublesome to the Jews. Active in the mid-eighteenth century, he sold himself as the incarnation of the previous Messiahs, including David, Elijah, Jesus, Muhammad, and Shabbetai. He developed some mystical theories that related him to the Holy Trinity, which spawned the "Frankist" movement. After this sect was excommunicated by the Polish rabbis for its many beliefs and practices that violated Judaism, the Frankists attacked Talmudic Judaism. It came at a low point in Jewish religious leadership. No rabbi was successful in defending the Talmud, resulting in the public burning of almost two thousand of copies of the Talmud. In 1759, Jacob

Frank became a Catholic. After still voicing his claim to be the Messiah, he was arrested and imprisoned.

7
Oppression in Poland

The name is unknown to the Jews in the United States, but Bogdan Chmielnicki was a name that all Jews in Eastern Europe were taught to remember and fear. He was the Hitler of the seventeenth century. He was bent on removing all the Jews from the Ukraine and almost succeeded. Under his leadership during the Ukrainian rebellion against Poland, many thousands of Jews were massacred and hundreds of Jewish communities were destroyed or devastated. When the Chmielnicki rebellion ended, Jewish life slowly returned to the destroyed villages.

Bogdan Chmielnicki—Bogdan Chmielnicki was a Ukrainian Cossack chieftain at a time when Poland ruled the Ukraine. The Greek Orthodox Ukrainians were bitter against the Catholic Polish rulers. The Ukrainians and the Polish people generally hated the "heathen" Jews.

Jews living in Poland and the Ukraine had achieved a good relationship with the Polish rulers of these countries, which was very unusual for Europe in that period. They served the Polish rulers and nobles in many capacities, such as tax collectors, estate overseers, and financiers. As workers for the Polish nobility, the Jews were caught up in the Ukrainian revolt. To defend themselves against the brutal Cossacks, they fought on the side of the Poles.

In 1648, Chmielnicki led a Ukrainian uprising against their Polish rulers to obtain improved conditions and rights for his people. Spurred on by Chmielnicki, who was also seeking personal revenge against Poles and Jews, the violent Cossacks went on a two-year rampage of rape, brutal killings, and pillaging, with the Jews bearing the brunt of the harm. The Cossack horsemen massacred entire villages of Jews in southern and eastern Poland in vicious pogroms. Jewish communities were obliterated. Almost every village where Jews lived was attacked. Many Jews were captured by the Tartar allies of Chmielnicki and sold as slaves to North African Muslims. Compassionate North African Jews who showed solidarity with their downtrodden brethren bought their freedom. Entire villages of Jews were forced to convert to Christianity—when the Poles retook a village, they permitted the Jews to revert to Judaism. It is estimated that nearly 500,000 Jews perished and 700 Jewish communities were destroyed over a ten-year period.

Polish Pogroms—The major Jewish suffering in southern Poland and the Ukraine ended when Poland had a one-year peaceful period with Chmielnicki. Then the Jews in northern Poland and Lithuania became victims of the new problems for Poland when the Swedes invaded Poland. Shortly after, the Russians invaded Lithuania, with the problems of this war spilling over into Poland. When these invasions ended in eight years, the Polish peasantry blamed the Jews for their own suffering. In spite of the good relationship the Polish Jews had with the Polish nobility, there was no one to defend the Jews against a series of pogroms conducted by Polish ruffians over the next few years.

Economic Impact—After living in these lands for about 300 years, in the seventeenth century, the Jews in Poland and Lithuania had achieved a political relationship with these governments that was unmatched elsewhere in Europe. The Jewish communities were granted a high level of autonomy. They were free to appoint central councils who represented them in dealing with the government for establishing taxes. In turn, there were councils for each province who sent representatives to the central council. The councils were responsible for collecting the taxes and managing the welfare of the Jewish townspeople. The councils consisted of rabbis for religious and legal matters, and laymen to handle taxation and other business matters.

After Poland's ten-year war ended, the Polish economy slowly returned to normalcy. That was not the case for the Polish Jews. With Jewish communities destroyed, many Jews forced to relocate, and reduced opportunities to work for the nobility, the Polish and Lithuanian Jewish population became impoverished. The councils had difficulty in meeting taxes and were burdened by the need to feed the many orphans left by the ten years of widespread pogroms. These economic problems brought on disunity among the Jewish elements. The impoverished, suffering Jews had reason to accept the promises of the false Messiahs of that period.

8
Oppression in Russia

Life for the Jews in Poland turned oppressive during the early eighteenth century. Inhospitable rulers, intolerant clergy, aggressive foreign merchants, and demanding nobility combined to make conditions difficult for the Jews. The melancholy caused by the suffering influenced the masses to first revere false Messiahs and then respond to the Chasidic movement to uplift their spirits. At the end of the eighteenth century, conditions for the Jewish people took a turn for the worse when Poland was partitioned between Russia, Austria, and Prussia, and Russia took over the major part of Poland. Over a million Polish Jews, whose ancestors came there to escape oppression in Central Europe during the Middle Ages, now came under the barbaric Russian rule. Russians were still living under the serfdom tyranny of the Dark Ages. Russia, hating the quarter-million Jews already living in their country, forced the Jews to live in restricted areas under difficult economic conditions and an oppressive political environment. Russia now had to find a way to deal with a million more Jews. The answer was czarist type tyranny that lasted until the Communist revolution, when Communist tyranny towards Judaism took over.

The Pale of Settlement—Russian Empress Catherine II continued the oppressive Polish policy towards Jews when she took over the large area of Poland with its million Jews. She developed a reputation as an enlightened despot, allowing forms of culture to develop in Russia. Towards the end of her reign, she feared the liberalism promoted by the French Revolution would be a threat to the Russian tyrannical rule, and so she rescinded all progressive measures for the Russians. She was particularly harsh on the Jews. The Pale of Settlement was formally established, defining where Jews could not live and where they could. Jews were forced out of the countryside where they maintained small businesses and served as artisans and into crowded cities under difficult economic conditions; there were economic restrictions and restricted areas even within the Pale of Settlement areas where Jews were allowed to live.

Topsy-Turvy Conditions Under Alexander I—The nineteenth century started with the new Czar Alexander I offering hope for a more benevolent Russia for all Russians, including the Jews. He was a tolerant person who surrounded himself with liberal advisors. Alexander established a commission to investigate the Jewish question. The results were conflicting. New laws permitted Jewish agricultural settlements in previously prohibited territories. Russian schools at all levels were opened to Jews, and Jews could have their own schools provided the teaching was conducted in Russian, Polish, or German; his objective was to break down the separativeness he believed Talmudic education fostered. On the other hand, he imposed economic restrictions for Jews conducting businesses in the countryside, particularly operating taverns. Alexander was very impressed by the attitude of the Russian Jews who ignored Napoleon's pleas for support and dismissed the oppressive Russian policies towards Jews to staunchly help defend Russia against the French army's attack in 1812. In appreciation, Alexander extended some favors to the Jews. After Napoleon's defeat at Waterloo, when all Europe turned reactionary, Alexander abandoned all liberalism. He reinstigated the old expulsion policy, which caused thousand of Jews to be ruthlessly evicted from territories and left in horrible living conditions. By the end of his reign in 1825, most Russian Jews had been forced to live in poverty in restricted areas within the Pale under political and economic repression.

9
The Age of Jewish Enlightenment

The eighteenth century was the era of European political intellectual enlightenment. This renaissance of rational thinking did not infect the masses of the Jewish people who were still weighed down by the decadent mood of the Middle Ages. They were obsessed by Messianic impostors, steeped in superstitions, and subdued by the lack of Judaic leadership in the earlier century.

Within this dark cloud hanging over Jewish life, three Jewish leaders emerged who had a profound affect on different segments of the European Jewish community. The Baal Shem Tov lifted the spirits of the downtrodden eastern European Jews with his mystical offerings that started the Chasidic movement. The Vilna Gaon established the concept of rational Talmudic study to uplift Jewish life and to serve as a counter to Chasidism, which de-emphasized formal prayer and Talmudic study. Moses Mendelssohn introduced the German Jewish community to the cultural world and stressed the opportunity for Jews to make personal decisions about their religiosity, leading to the creation of the Jewish Reform movement.

Birth of Chasidism: Baal Shem Tov (1700–1760)

Israel Ben Eliezer (1700–1760), who became known as the *Baal Shem Tov* (Master of the Good Name), called *Besht* based on the Baal Shem Tov initials, lived in the Carpathian mountain area of Moldavia in eastern Europe (southern Poland) at the beginning of the eighteenth century. From humble beginnings, he started as a Hebrew school teacher of young children. He went on to minister to the Jews living in the area who were poor, had little self-respect because of their lack of Talmudic scholarship, and found little happiness in life. It was an area where most Jews honored the false Messiahs of the earlier period because of their suffering and unhappiness. He preached that God was everywhere and accessible to anyone who reached to Him through deep faith in Him and personal fervent prayer. The Besht's philosophy was that God was served best by being cheerful about life and accepting the inevitable. His strong religious faith, mystical teachings, and faith healing impressed masses of poor, uneducated Jews, who started to revere him almost as a Messiah.

The Baal Shem Tov did not write down his philosophies and ideas. His pupils, who were known as *Zaddikim,* carried on his teachings. They took on the role of spiritual leaders for the Baal Shem Tov's followers, offering religious Jewish communities where Chasidism (*Chasid* means pious one) started to flourish. The category of Zaddikim became hereditary, which occasionally resulted in unworthy people occupying the position and tarnishing the Chasidic movement.

Modern Talmudism

At the time that the Baal Shem Tov was preaching the unimportance of Talmudic study for reaching personal fulfillment, Rabbi Elijah in the Lithuanian city of Vilna took steps to advance the study of the Talmud in opposition to Chasidism which he considered to be a degradation of Orthodoxy. The east European non-Chasidic religious community had the utmost respect for Rabbi Elijah because of his scholarship and noble personality. They called him the *Goan,* which was the title bestowed on the leaders of the Babylonian Jewish learning academies a thousand years earlier. He contributed to the strengthening of Talmudic and Torah learning in many ways.

Rabbi Elijah the Goan (1720–1797)—The Goan of Vilna who grew up in Lithuania, the haven for traditional Judaism, was unusually learned for his time. He was knowledgeable in physics, astronomy, music, geography, and philosophical Jewish literature before he became a master of both the Jerusalem Talmud and the Babylonian Talmud, and the other rabbinic classics. Under his influence, the emphasis on Talmudic study changed from the rigid study of the Talmud's words to a rational understanding of the Talmud's message including the allowance for the application of scientific principles. The same objective and scientific attitude was applied to the study of the Torah and the Oral Law. He also stressed that secular knowledge would help the Jewish people better understand the world and Judaism. The rabbis who studied in the academies that instituted his approach to Jewish scholarship brought to their communities a new understanding of the Torah and the Talmud based on rational reasoning.

Although he promoted rational interpretations of Judaism's holy literature, the Vilna Gaon was a staunch defender of Orthodox Judaism's basic learning values, dignity, and traditions. He viewed the Chasidic practices of open frivolous prayer as disrespect for Talmudic learning and the reverence of Zaddikim as violations of Orthodoxy and fought in public against Chasidism, even to the point of excommunicating Chasidim and forbidding intermarriage with them.

Jewish Religious Enlightenment

The seeds of the Reform Judaism movement were planted in Germany by one of the most unusual Jewish personalities, Moses Mendelssohn. While he was initiating and leading the Jewish intellectual and cultural renaissance, he maintained his attachment to traditional Judaism, promoting changes in Judaic practices with the objective of strengthening Judaism. He moved the Jewish Middle Ages ghetto mentality into the modern world. His objective was to make the culture of the world acceptable to the Jewish people and make Jews acceptable to Christians as their fellow citizens.

During the fifty years following the Jewish cultural enlightenment fathered by Mendelssohn, the Jewish educational system in western Europe took Mendelssohn's lead and moved from strictly Talmudic study to a program that included liberal Jewish education and secular subjects. In addition, several ritual changes were introduced to prayer services to make them more attractive to those who were responding to the Jewish cultural enlightenment. Then two camps emerged among this group of modern-leaning Jews—one to revert to Orthodoxy and the other to completely scrap Judaism as a religion. After a struggle to determine which direction to go between these two groups, Rabbi Abraham Geiger formally established the Reform movement in Germany. It kept Judaism as a religion but scrapped the traditional customs and rituals.

Moses Mendelssohn (1729–1786)—As a youth, Mendelssohn took an unusual step for Jews up until that period. He went beyond the study of the Talmud in Hebrew to learn the German language. Except for a few privileged Jews, German Jews spoke Yiddish (which is a combination of

Hebrew and German with a sprinkling of other languages) for their conversations and interaction with German society. This knowledge of German exposed him to the famous aristocratic art critic and writer, Gotthold Ephraim Lessing, who had published a play, *The Jews,* in which a Jew with fine human qualities was the hero; a bold theme for a Christian of that period. Lessing later wrote the important play *Nathan the Wise* that was a powerful plea for religious tolerance in which the Jewish character was patterned after Mendelssohn.

Mendelssohn went on to study German literature and became a writer of philosophy and a critic of literature, all in the German language. This cultural activity, unusual for a Jew, earned him a respected position in German society, which was unheard of for a Jew. Mendelssohn became a defender of Judaism against attacks by the Swiss preacher Johann Kasper Lavater, who was eager to convert this illustrious Jew that he admired. Mendelssohn tactfully explained the merits of Judaism over Christianity, explained how his loyalty to Judaism was consistent with the preacher's own religious views, and admonished the preacher for trying to convert him. He pointed out that Judaism was tolerant of other religious beliefs, did not proselytize, and believed that "anyone who lived a moral life could attain salvation."

The preacher incident convinced Mendelssohn that the liberal German society still had too many prejudices and was not ready to accept Jews on an equal basis and that he should spend more time addressing the concerns of the Jewish people. The stature of respect that he achieved enabled him to engage in and win battles with German, Swiss, and French authorities over Jewish rights. He was instrumental in revoking a ban on Jewish marriage in several Swiss villages and withdrawing an expulsion order of hundreds of Jews in Dresden, Germany, and for the city of Berlin, he drafted many legal documents beneficial to the Jewish community. In France, Mendelssohn pressed for many civil rights for Jews and exposed bigotry against Jews.

Mendelssohn became convinced that for Jews to earn the respect of the Christians, the Jewish people had to change their culture that was driven by the economic and societal restrictions imposed on Jews by the Christian society in the Middle Ages. They had to end their isolation from German society that their use of Yiddish was fostering. To achieve this goal, Mendelssohn translated the biblical Genesis into German prose, and then, with the help of other scholars, printed in German, using Hebrew letters to make it readable by the Jews who generally only read Hebrew. The entire Bible text was accompanied by commentaries intended to make the Bible more understandable.

In concert with his feelings about Jews having the freedom of choice regarding their religious views, Mendelssohn became the early public advocate of the separation between church and state; a political position that was one hundred years ahead of his time in Europe. These views and an explanation of his concept and philosophy of Judaism, which he considered a rational religion, were presented in his book *Jerusalem*.

Many of the intellectual Jews who followed Mendelssohn's lead and integrated into German society, including his own family, drifted to Christianity.

Jewish Educational Changes—Moses Mendelssohn was very influential in changing the way Judaism was taught. Consistent with traditional Judaism, he viewed the laws (commandments) in the Torah as a contract between Jews and God that are to be honored by all Jews; they guide the Jews' moral and spiritual conduct and enable Jews to maintain their identity and integrity as a distinct group. However, he became a strong believer that Jews should have freedom of choice concerning how they accepted and practiced the Jewish faith.

Mendelssohn established a Jewish school in Berlin that used German as the language of instruction. The curriculum included secular subjects and traditional Jewish studies. Religious instruction included not only the reading of Hebrew but also the study of the principles of Judaism. This educational approach that eliminated the focus on Talmudic study quickly became popular in all the large German cities. Mendelssohn was strongly opposed by the traditional Jewish leadership, who judged his educational approach that took young Jews away from study of the Talmud and taught secular subjects and his freedom-of-choice views to be dangerous for Judaism.

Mendelssohn's translation of the Bible into the vernacular language for German Jews was followed by similar translations in France, Italy, Poland, and other countries, contributing to the religious enlightenment in these countries.

The Modern Reform Movement is Established—During the first quarter of the nineteenth century, several Jewish communities throughout western Europe introduced changes in the religious services. Religious facilities were opened in Germany and were called temples rather than synagogues to influence those Jews who despised "Jewishness" implied by the name, "synagogue," but were unwilling to convert to Christianity. The name, "temple," made them more comfortable. Organ music was introduced. Complex religious poems were deleted from the liturgy and replaced with German poems. Sermons in the vernacular language became popular in most countries.

The battle between the Jewish intellectuals in Germany to either dismember Judaism as a religion or revert to the retention of the full Orthodox traditions ended with the accomplishments of Rabbi Abraham Geiger. In 1840, as chief rabbi in Breslau, Germany, he succeeded in establishing the German Reform movement, which eliminated the adherence to the dietary laws, the practice of wearing phylacteries, keeping separate Passover dishes, and other customs and practices. His philosophy was to offer the enlightened German Jews the opportunity to retain the ethical qualities and values of Judaism without being tied to traditions that outlived their usefulness. After the central European battles for political emancipation in the 1840s failed to win political rights for the Jewish people, the Reform Jewish movement in Europe lost its momentum, and aristocratic and intellectual Jews converted to Christianity in order to "feel accepted" by the community at large. However, Rabbi Abraham Geiger had succeeded in laying the intellectual foundation for Reform Judaism, which was revitalized by Rabbi Isaac Mayer Wise in the United States in the 1870s.

Birth of Historical Judaism: Forerunner of Conservative Judaism—While Rabbi Geiger was promoting the Reform movement, another rabbi was strongly opposing his approach to modernizing the Jewish religion that discarded the Orthodox traditions. Rabbi Zechariah Frankel held that Judaism was a changeable religion; a review of Jewish history illustrates this to be true. In his view, however, the changes should only come about as a result of changes in the life pattern of the Jewish people through the course of history but still conforming to Jewish traditions. This "Historical Judaism" was the view accepted by the Conservative movement in the United States.

Leopold Zunz: Promoter of Historical Judaism (1794–1886)—Leopold Zunz was a member of a group of young Jews who met in Berlin in 1819 to promote Judaism as a religion with a rich culture through a magazine sponsored by "A Society for the Culture and Scientific Knowledge of Judaism." The famous poet Heinrich Heine was a member of this society before his conversion to Christianity. Heine professed to be a convert in order to be accepted in German society as a stepping stone for his professional advancement, but never gave up his admiration for Judaism. Like Heine, many other intellectuals in the organization converted and gave up their goal. Zunz remained loyal to the organization's objectives and continued to promote Judaism for the next sixty-five years. He is recognized as one of the most outstanding intellectuals of modern Jewish thought. Zunz wrote *The Religious Discourse of the Jews,* which showed, through an analysis of the Jewish liturgy, that Judaism was a living religion, changing over the years in concert with the events that took place. It substantiated Rabbi Zechariah's "Historical Judaism" view. He wrote many other books that reflected on Jewish history to extol Jewish accomplishments and engender pride in the Jewish achievements.

Birth of Modern Orthodoxy—Rabbi Raphael Hirsch was a theological schoolmate of Rabbi Geiger who founded the Reform movement, but he went in the opposite direction regarding changing Judaism. Rabbi Hirsch, from a modern intellectual standpoint, took the leadership in advocating an adherence to Orthodoxy. In his *Nineteen Letters About Judaism of Ben Uziel,* a fictitious set of correspondence, Hirsch demonstrates the wisdom of the Jewish ancestors in maintaining the Jewish way of life. His premise is that God rules over the universe and people must live according to God's instructions in the Bible. His philosophy called for the Jewish community to select good over evil as a way of obeying the will of God—this was the mission God gave to the Jewish people. For this reason, the Jewish people must have distinctive laws and customs to differentiate them from the rest of society. Hirsch saw God's spirit in the entire Bible and decreed that no human had a right to change the Torah's religious commandments. He attempted to explain the necessity of adhering to the commandments in a way that was acceptable to the contemporary Jew.

Jewish Cultural Enlightenment

Moses Mendelssohn had a goal to make the culture of the world acceptable to the Jewish people. He took a bold step resisted by the Jewish leadership that he considered vital in meeting his objective. It caused a cultural revolution in Jewish society. It would introduce the Jewish people to the modern world and end the ghetto mentality that kept the Jewish people cloistered in their own closed society. The Jewish people relied on the exclusive study of the Talmud that was shielding them from the exposure to rational thinking and modern philosophy. It was developed in the Middle

Ages before the European Renaissance and liberal enlightenment took place. It provided the Jewish people a sense of security when there was severe oppression of Jews.

To achieve this goal, Mendelssohn translated the biblical Genesis into German prose and printed the entire Bible in German using Hebrew letters. This use of the Hebrew language to translate the Bible opened the study of secular subjects in Hebrew. The Jewish printing firms published many of the European classics in Hebrew, which became extremely popular with the Jewish youth. Jews started studying natural sciences, philosophy, history, and world affairs.

In Germany, the Jewish people quickly took on German as their spoken language. It enabled the German Jews to end the use of Yiddish and gave them the connection to the world of science, literature, and philosophy. Over the next hundred years when the German authorities developed a more benign attitude towards Jews and gave them full citizenship, the German Jews developed a loyalty to Germany that overrode their concerns for the Jews as a people. This attitude is what kept many Jews from leaving Germany during the early Nazi regime when life for Jews became bitter and hope for the future was dim.

Mendelssohn's German-translated Bible commentary language structure provided a new appreciation of grammatical Hebrew. It was particularly effective with the young Russian and Polish Jews who found no intellectual stimulus in Russian or Polish culture. It led to the Jewish nationalist movement and to the Jewish enlightenment movement in eastern Europe known as "Haskalah."

10
European Political Liberalism

The life of the Jewish people in western Europe was affected dramatically by the movement to political liberalism that developed in Europe after the French Revolution in 1789. There were voices for political change prior to the Revolution, but they didn't include advocating benefits to the Jewish people. To the contrary, Voltaire and Diderot, the leading proponents of political change were hostile to the Jews and used the Jews in a derogatory way to promote their ideals. The leaders of the French Revolution, Mirabeau, Abbé Grégoire, and Robespierre, supported the Jewish cause for political emancipation, but they succumbed to the anti-Semitic element who objected and initially refused to grant the French Jews full citizenship. However, in appreciation of how the French Jews were extremely supportive of the Revolution, all the French Jews (about 40,000) were gradually granted full citizenship within the next two years.

As a consequence of the French Revolution, the people of Europe became very nationalistic. The Jewish people in western Europe were swept in by this nationalistic mood, and they became ardent nationalists for the country they lived in and more aggressive at fighting for full citizenship. The Dutch Jews were the first to achieve political emancipation during the era of the French Revolution. The era of Napoleon Bonaparte that followed had a greater impact. The walls of the ghettos throughout western Europe fell in the path of Napoleon's armies as they swept through Europe, and the Jews enjoyed emancipation almost everywhere.

The Impact of Napoleon—Between 1796 and 1815 Napoleon's armies swept through central Europe conquering all the countries on the way to Russia, bringing the spirit of liberation promoted by the French Revolution. It brought momentous change for the Jewish people. The walls of the ghettos in Germany and Italy were in effect torn down. Jews felt safe to freely come and go without restrictions. The ghetto badges of shame were discarded. The medieval, oppressive life ended. Jews in most of the small German states received full citizenship. The Jews living in the large Prussian State received equal citizenship with only some limitations on holding state office positions. Although there were no Jews living in Spain and Portugal, Napoleon abolished the Inquisition laws that were still in effect since 1492, "liberating" the Marranos from fear; in Portugal Marrano families openly returned to Judaism.

Napoleon's treatment of the French Jews was ambiguous. He passed himself off as being a friend of the Jewish people, initially passing some helpful laws and reviving the Sanhedrin (council of seventy-one) Jewish legislative concept of old. His political actions towards the Jewish populace were unfriendly and intolerant. He forced the Assembly of Notables (Jewish leaders) to answer many testy questions to show the loyalty of the French Jews and indicate their willingness to assimilate, and unsuccessfully tried to get the Sanhedrin to force the rabbis to violate Judaic laws. In the end, he passed a set of infamous decrees that caused economic hardship to the Jews. He passed laws that made Judaism a second-class religion.

Resistance to the European Reactionary Movement—With the defeat of Napoleon in 1815, a reactionary wave covered all of Europe except England. The Jewish leaders, aroused and inspired by their new-found freedom, lobbied hard to keep their emancipated status but were unsuccessful. The nationalists and the displaced clerical leaders collaborated to reverse the political changes that took place; alien groups were targets and scapegoats, the Jews were again considered an alien group. Old Austrian restrictions on Jews were reinstated, including the return of ghetto life. Jews were expelled from some German cities, and mob actions against Jews became commonplace again in Germany.

The liberation movement engendered initially by the Napoleon's march through Europe built up an opposition to the reactionary forces in power. Jewish professional luminaries, such as Gabriel Riesser, and two converted Jews who achieved fame for their writings, Heinrich Heine and Karl Börne, were influential in including Jewish rights in the platform of the new German liberal party called the "Young Germans."

The New Liberalism—The Liberalism counterreaction first took hold in France after the Revolution of 1830; Judaism was placed on an equal footing with Catholicism and Protestantism. In 1848, the Liberation movement succeeded in Germany, Hungary, and Austria; ghettos were again torn down and Jews were extended the same privileges as the other citizens. Jews were allowed to join the governments of the countries and German states that instituted political reforms. The Liberation movement quickly received a setback in Austria and Hungary; all freedoms were abolished. It took another twenty years before the rights and privileges were restored in these two countries. Freedom came to the Italian Jews piecemeal, first in northern Italy after the Austrians were expelled, then in Naples and Sicily under Garibaldi's revolution, and finally in the Papal States including Rome when the governing authority was taken away from the Church.

Moses Montefiore: Product of Liberalism in England—England was ahead of the rest of Europe in granting rights to Jews. By the time of the French Revolution they were treated as equal citizens, being allowed to participate in all forms of commerce but could not hold public office and attend English universities. The forces for Liberalism finally succeeded in England. These restrictions were removed in 1831. This gave Moses Montefiore the opportunity to become the sheriff of London and a knighthood by Queen Victoria, which came with the position. It was the start of fifty years of public service to Britain and humanitarian service to the worldly Jewish community. The British honored him for his intense loyalty to England and his philanthropic work. He is honored and remembered by the Jewish community for his efforts to bring relief to his Jewish brethren around the world, his devotion to reestablishing Jewish life in Palestine, and maintaining his allegiance and support to Judaism.

Montefiore is distinguished as the one Jewish leader who could speak for the three traditionalist segments of Orthodoxy. He was from an old Italian-Jewish family whose Orthodox traditions preceded the Ashkenazi and Sephardi traditions, grew up in the London Sephardic community, and married an Ashkenazi, which was highly unusual for a Sephardi of his stature. His strong adherence to traditional Judaism was influential in the lack of success of the Reform movement in England.

Moses Montefiore interceded to obtain the freedom of Jews unjustly held for crimes based on false anti-Semitic accusations in Syria, Italy, and Morocco. His mission to Damascus in 1840 succeeded in obtaining the release of the imprisoned Jews and a statement from the Turkish sultan condemning the false ritual murder accusation (monks falsely accused several Jews of killing a monk for religious reasons, whereas he was killed in a quarrel with a Muslim). This was the first instance where Jewish political strength could help fellow Jews in trouble. He had sufficient stature to have an audience with Russian and Rumanian authorities, pleading for improving the deplorable conditions the Jewish people in these countries were under.

Montefiore was an early Zionist, applying his wealth to promote his ideals. He believed that "Palestine must belong to the Jews, and Jerusalem is destined to be the seat of the Jewish empire." As early as 1838, he had plans for establishing Jewish agricultural colonies, which the authorities initially considered but rejected. He made several visits to Palestine in later years, during which time he instituted agricultural and industrial undertakings to improve the economic life and morale of the small Jewish community in Palestine.

Moses Montefiore was the prototype of today's Jewish philanthropist. He gave generously to the Jewish poor and religious institutions at home in England and abroad.

Adolophe Crémieux: Product of Liberalism in France—Adolophe Crémieux personified the emancipated Jew who could fight for rights of his countrymen while also fighting for rights of his fellow Jews. He won fame as a defender of the ideals of the French Revolution during the post-Napoleonic period, while, at the same time, he won back the rights of equal citizenship for French Jews after they were abrogated during the reactionary period that took hold in Europe. He was a prominent member of the Chamber of Deputies both within the government and as an opposition member but continued to be a defender of the rights of Jews and interested in their welfare throughout his lifetime.

Crémieux was disturbed by what became known as the Mortara affair. After the Jewish infant Edgar Mortara was secretly baptized by his Catholic nurse, the Church authorities forcibly took the infant away from the parents and required that he be reared as a Catholic. Despite protests from world governments, including the Catholic community, Pope Pius IX rejected the pleas to return the child to his parents. Later, Crémieux went with Moses Montefiore to the Middle East on their successful Damascus mission that freed the unjustly accused Jews. He was aroused by these two incidents and concluded that the unified position that the world Jewish community took with respect to these two incidents should not go to waste. Crémieux established the worldwide Alliance Israelite Universelle in 1860 that would defend the human rights of the Jews, wherever they were threatened, and also aid in the education of Jews in North Africa and the Near East, which was another of his personal interests.

Haskalah Movement in Eastern Europe—At the start of the nineteenth century, Russia and Lithuania were still shrouded in intellectual darkness. The European forces of enlightenment rising in Germany became the modernization stimulants for the east European Jews. The transformation of east European Jews to adopt this liberal enlightenment was called Haskalah.

Moses Mendelssohn's translated the Bible into German and provided stimulating commentaries in German. Several of Mendelssohn's colleagues then translated his commentaries into Hebrew, with the objective of encouraging Jews who did not know German to use the Hebrew as a source for their cultural enlightenment. The commentary language structure provided a new appreciation of grammatical Hebrew and facilitated the integration of Hebrew culture with the culture that had overtaken western Europe. From this beginning, Jewish intellectuals, such as Solomon Rapoport and Nahman Krochmal, published documents in modern Hebrew that covered Jewish cultural interests, including biographies of great Jews of the past. They provided philosophical explanations of Judaism as a living, changeable religion. The Haskalah movement grew rapidly with the emergence of many writers who wrote novels and poems in Hebrew.

The Haskalah movement took a step to move Jews away from Talmudic-centered study and towards secular education by endorsing the universal education plan offered by Czar Nicholas I. When it became apparent that Nicholas's intent was Jewish assimilation and not enlightenment, other liberal and conservative Jewish leaders denounced the Haskalah leaders for being taken in and steering Jews away from Judaism. The ill intent of the Russian government became evident when they forcefully moved Jews from the smaller towns into the larger overcrowded villages and cities, forcing many Jews into starvation.

The Haskalah movement reacted to the reactionary policies of the czar's successor, Nicholas II, by turning nationalistic. The foremost Jewish nationalist of that period was Perez Smolenskin. He promoted the Hebrew language, spoke out against assimilation, and encouraged Jews to maintain their self-respect. He published *The Eternal People* in 1873, in which he called the Jewish people a nation that needed to have a home in Palestine in order to develop their talents properly.

As a result of the Haskalah movement, Hebrew and Yiddish periodicals and newspapers appeared throughout eastern Europe. Russian Jews became actively creative writers of colorful Jewish folklore and philosophical histories of the Jewish people, written in Hebrew and Yiddish. Besides Smolenskin, among the famous Maskilim writers are Nahman Haym Bialik, Judah Leib Gordon, Ahad Ha'am, Mendele Mocher Sefarim, Sholom Aleichem, Isaac Loeb Peretz, and Sholem Asch.

11
Renewed Anti-Semitism

Starting in the eighteenth century and for the first three-quarters of the nineteenth century, social and political liberalism that overtook western Europe also benefited Jewish society. Jews were allowed to participate at all political levels of society and engage in all economic activity. By 1870, the forces of nationalism grew stronger; neighboring countries started to stake claims for the border territories, which frequently contained minorities of nationals from the neighboring countries. Countries prepared for war, nationalism got more intense, and bitterness towards their neighboring countries got more severe. In the midst of all this political turmoil, the Jewish people lost the gains they had made in the previous seventy years. Jews became the scapegoat for all reverses each country suffered. The antagonism towards their Jewish countrymen erupted in violence towards Jews in many countries. Middle-Ages type of false ritual murder accusations against Jews surfaced. Violent anti-Semitism also occurred in southern Russia, where state-sponsored *pogroms* (riots against Jews) resulted in hundred of Jews being murdered; the pogroms prompted worldwide governmental protests including one from the United States.

German Anti-Semitism—Germany profited financially from their victory in the Franco-Prussian war. Financial prosperity led to speculation in the stock market, which ended in a crash in 1873—Jews irrationally took the blame for this event. Christians who lost money became Jew haters. Prussian Prince Otto von Bismarck, battling with the Catholics and the Liberal party while maneuvering to unify Germany, found the Jews the convenient scapegoat for all the ills the country faced. It was easier to rally the Germans to his side by condemning the Jews than to pick on the Catholics or the Liberal party. The Liberal party failed in its attack on the Catholics, so they turned against the Jews. The Catholics reacted to Bismarck's anti-Catholic legislation by accusing the Jews of leading the battle for the legislation, while Pope Pius IX denounced the Jews as enemies of Jesus Christ. The chaplain to the kaiser attacked the Jews, hinting that the anti-Semitism was approved at the top level of government. This former Socialist party leader proclaimed moderate Christian Socialism was acceptable but Jewish socialism was subversive. The public acceptance of these political attacks on Jews prompted the creation of a new political party that used anti-Semitism as its rallying cry.

Anti-Semitism became widespread, fueled by many German intellectuals. They replaced the religious motivation for their anti-Jewish bigotry with the new scientific analysis that was in vogue. Jews were Semites, not Europeans; they never contributed any value to civilization. All forms of science were concocted to degrade the Jews. William Marr, a noted journalist, wrote that Jewish penetration into every form of German life was wicked. Richard Wagner, the great composer who earlier accepted aid from Jews interested in promoting German music, forcefully denounced the Jews for their influence on German music.

This widespread anti-Semitism provided the background for the Germans to be so receptive to Hitler's rise to power in the 1930s with his diatribes that mimicked many of the anti-Semitic diatribes of this nineteenth-century period. The Jewish people had learned to enjoy and participate in the nineteenth-century prosperity that Germany enjoyed. Their new German nationalism had overridden their Jewish consciousness; this applied to the assimilated Jews and to the Orthodox Jews. Suddenly they now found they could do nothing right for Germany. Their political contributions were distorted by their political enemies and ignored by the political parties they supported. Their prosperity had contributed to Germany's growth; now envious Christians sought to bankrupt them. German Jews who were popular for their artistic accomplishments were described as being exceptions to the evil Jews. The Jewish people were unfairly accused of being responsible for all German ills.

Anti-Semitism in Austria-Hungary—The Austro-Hungarian Empire, created in 1867, included many nationalities that vied to obtain local control of the area where they were the majority, and German minorities seeking ties to Germany. Austria had its German minority. Hungary had the Magyars fighting for independence. The Poles wanted to control Galicia. The Czechs vied with the German minority for control of Bohemia. Slovakia had multiple nationalities competing for power. The German financial crisis of 1873 spilled over into Austria-Hungary, and the resulting political, nationalistic turmoil created an oppressive situation for the Jewish people in all of these areas.

The center of this empire was the city of Vienna, where the Jews had contributed immensely to the vitality and charm of the city, providing the intellectual and scientific leadership. They had fought on the side of the liberals for justice for all the peoples of Austria. When the financial panic hit Austria, the Jews bore the brunt of the blame. The Austrians accused the Jews of being the leaders of the Liberal party that caused the depression. Jews were attacked in the parliament and in the streets of Vienna. Jewish students in the universities were attacked. The Jews who backed the German cause for power over Austria now were disowned by the Germans and vilified by the Austrians for having backed the Germans.

The Jews in the other lands of the empire suffered the same fate. In Hungary, they fought for Magyar independence but did not receive full rights when independence was achieved and had to flee with the Magyar patriots when the independence was lost. Jews had sided with the German minority in Bohemia but were disowned by them when the nationalistic battles erupted—the Czechs despised the Jews for their backing of the Germans.

Romanian Treachery—Romania was one of the poorer European countries, where the population lived in poverty under the grip of wealthy landowners who taught the peasants to blame the Jews for their misery. Jews, primarily those who came in from other countries, essentially were the only commercial-oriented element of society. The discrimination that existed against Jews turned to violence in the midst of blood libel accusations and other vicious false claims.

In 1878, European powers were ready to grant Romania along with other Balkan countries full independence from Turkish rule. Because of the previous history of political anti-Semitism, Romania had to agree to include full rights for Jews in their constitution. After independence was granted, the Romanian government defaulted on their pledge and the restrictions and persecutions not only continued but also got more severe.

The Dreyfus Case Illuminates French Anti-Semitism—Since the third French Republic was established in 1870, there were serious political clashes between the Royalists and Clericalists on one side, and the liberal French government in power on the other side. Several ugly events that took place over the next twenty-five years resulted in clashes between these two forces that took on violent anti-Semitic overtones by the clerical forces.

Alfred Dreyfus, the only Jewish officer on the French general staff, was falsely accused of selling military secrets to the German government. He was sentenced to solitary life confinement on Devil's Island in the Caribbean. Even after the accusations against him were revealed to be forgeries, frenzied mobs in the streets of Paris shouted "death to the Jews." Emile Zola, Anatole France, and Georges Clemenceau rallied to Dreyfus's defense to get him a retrial. The case dragged on for years while the army officers in charge refused to accept the uncontestable evidence of Dreyfus's innocence. The overt and widespread anti-Semitism that prevailed in public places aroused many liberal forces. It had a pronounced affect on many Jews in Russia and other central European countries, stimulating their Jewish nationalism and Zionism.

Protocols of the Elders of Zion—The "Protocols of the Elders of Zion," purporting a conspiracy by rabbis to take over the Aryan world, was first circulated in Russia in 1904 and then in many other countries of the world. Both Jews and intellectuals who recognized it to be a vicious anti-Semitic diatribe quickly denounced it. Even after it was disclosed to be a forgery and a falsehood in 1921, anti-Semites continue to quote it, and Henry Ford's newspaper, the *Dearborn Independent,* published it. The Arabs quoted the protocols as a part of its anti-Israel propaganda in the year 2000, while the Israeli-Palestinian peace negotiations were taking place.

12
Birth of Zionism

Jews who attend religious services generally recognize the prayer for returning to Jerusalem that accompanies the last sounding of the *shofar* (ram's horn) at the close of the Yom Kippur High Holiday services. This prayer, probably stemming from the time of the exile from Palestine during the second century, did not encourage Zionism. Religious Jews accepted the words of the Prophets that it was God's wish that the Jewish people would return to Palestine, but also believed God would determine when.

Early Zionist Movement—The first stirring of Jewish nationalism came from the German Jewish Socialist, Moses Hess, in the middle of the nineteenth century. He rationalized the logic for Jewish nationalism, underscoring its importance over Jewish emancipation. Indeed, as Jews steadily enjoyed political and economic liberty in western Europe, the Jewish nationalist spirit waned there. At the end of the century, the reaction to the return of virulent anti-Semitism to western Europe coupled with the enlightened Jewish writers of the Haskalah movement in eastern Europe were two forces that energized a Jewish nationalist spirit. The leading spirit was the Russian Jew Leo Pinsker. In his "Auto-Emancipation" booklet published in 1882, he argued that Jews were foolish to believe that their growing nationalist feelings for the country they lived in would give them true satisfaction—they would still be treated as strangers. Jews needed a homeland in Palestine or elsewhere to achieve self-respect. The nationalistic callings of the enlightened Russian Jewish writers stimulated the creation of the Lovers of Zion movement in Odessa, Russia, which by 1890, spread to other countries. Although this organization spawned the creation of several settlements in Palestine, the trying conditions the pioneers faced in the inhospitable Palestine of that period dampened any Zionistic enthusiasm among world Jewry.

Herzl Fathers the Zionist Movement—The essentially dead Zionist movement was reactivated and ultimately fulfilled by the charismatic

Theodor Herzl. He had the talent required to bypass the resistance to Zionism expressed by the Jewish leaders, whose economic and political support was considered necessary, and negotiate with the leaders of countries that he considered capable of fulfilling his dream of a Jewish national homeland. This gave Herzl the air of statesmanship, which was necessary to give the Jewish nationalist movement he was promoting a touch of authenticity and realism.

Although he was exposed to traditional Judaism in his youth in Budapest, during Herzl's young adult life in Vienna, he was interested in journalism, being a playwright, and story writing—he expressed no interest in Jewish-related causes. This background made it more remarkable for Herzl to father Zionism.

In 1891, at the age of thirty-one, he settled in Paris as the correspondent for an Austrian newspaper. This exposed him to several anti-Semitic incidents that rocked the French nation—false claims of Jewish involvement in French national scandals that were echoed and supported by high-ranking French officials and by public masses. He slowly developed his Zionist outlook expressed in his 1895 book, *The Jewish State*. The accompanying anti-Semitism of the Dreyfus case the following year strengthened Herzl's goal of establishing a Jewish national home, which he considered to be the blessing of Jewish destiny.

Herzl's initial tactic was to involve rich European Jewish bankers, such as Baron de Hirsch, the Rothschilds, and the Montagues, but they had no interest in any movement that would give a political voice to Jews as a *people*. He then approached the leaders of the early Zionist movement in Russia and other Jewish leaders, approaching them as a world Jewish leader. With newfound support, he embarked on rounds of negotiations with many European and Turkish rulers to enlist their support for establishing Palestine as a Jewish State. The many rejections he received would have depressed anyone else, but Herzl had the unusual talent of not despairing and not quitting. To achieve the necessary political and financial support, he conceived the idea of a worldwide Zionist organization to be inaugurated by a congress. After the first World Jewish Congress adapted the national home concept, Herzl embarked on many campaigns to establish a Jewish home in Palestine. Over the next several years, he negotiated with the Sultan of Turkey, who ruled over Palestine, seeking more Jewish rights in that country, and with the German kaiser, the king of Italy, the pope, and other rulers, seeking political support for his objective of a Jewish homeland in Palestine.

Herzl died suddenly at forty-four, likely worn down by his Zionistic political efforts and the trauma that hit him at the Sixth Zionist Congress when Uganda was under consideration by many at the congress, including the influential British writer, Max Nordau, who was Herzl's deputy. He didn't achieve his goal of a Jewish national home during his lifetime. He did succeed in establishing a Jewish renaissance, awakening the Jewish nationalist movement and a love for Hebrew as a secular language and Hebrew literature as a Jewish national treasure.

The Zionist Congresses—The First Zionist Congress was convened in Basel, Switzerland in 1897. Almost two hundred delegates from fifteen countries attended. Thousands of Jews around the world expressed their support. However, many western European Jews opposed the idea as a delusion and a myth. Orthodox Jews insisted only the Messiah could reconnect the Jewish people with Palestine. American Reform Jews maintained that Judaism had outgrown the need for a Jewish national home anywhere. Nevertheless, the movement remained alive and gained strength. The congress convened almost yearly, interrupted by the two world wars. Herzl acted as if the movement was a worldwide success. He established the Jewish National Fund as a voluntary fund-raiser to buy land in Palestine for the entire Jewish people.

The Sixth Zionist Congress in 1903 experienced a serious dilemma that almost wrecked the Zionist movement. After many rejections, Herzl received an offer for a Jewish homeland in Uganda, Africa, from a sympathetic British colonial secretary, who thought it would offer a haven for oppressed east European Jews. The fervent Zionists who insisted on Palestine for the homeland prevailed over the territorialists, who were willing to accept any territory as a homeland. Palestine remained the only Zionist objective thereafter. The movement never achieved the strength to achieve its goal on its own. Parts of Palestine became the Jewish national home in 1948 as a result of many other influences.

13
Life in the Twentieth Century

Life for the Jewish people in Europe went though dramatic changes over the span of the twentieth century. When it started, Europe was the continent with the largest Jewish population. When it ended, Europe's Jewish population ranked third behind the United States and the State of Israel, which did not exist at the turn of the century. Six million European Jews perished in the Holocaust during World War II.

The twentieth century started with the growth of the World Zionist movement that ultimately led to the establishment of the State of Israel. In the second decade, World War I traumatized the European Jewish world when Jews, loyal to the respective country they lived in, fought for both sides in the war—Jews fighting against Jews and against their relatives. World War I put a damper on the Zionist movement objectives until Great Britain offered the Balfour Declaration, which appeared to provide the political basis for Jews reestablishing their national home in Palestine.

The next three decades were difficult, particularly for Jews in the east European countries. The economic recovery from the effects of World War I was slow in the countries created at the end of the war; it was a victory for nationalism and democracy but came with increased bigotry towards Jews. The economic trouble for Jews in these countries was compounded by the increasing economic restrictions imposed on their Jewish citizens and by the rising anti-Semitism. The political and economic life of the German Jews turned disastrous after Hitler's rise to power. Hitler planned to eradicate all Jews from the world and almost succeeded in Europe, where six million Jews perished as part of Germany's "Final Solution for Jews." The promise of the Balfour Declaration faded, and Palestine was closed to Jews escaping Nazism in the late 1930s until the State of Israel was established. Communist rule in Russia turned into a Soviet program of eradicating the Jewish culture and eliminating Judaism as a religion. Until the refusnik movement started in the 1960s, almost three million Russian Jews lost every connection to their Jewish heritage.

The second half of the century witnessed the determined efforts of the Holocaust survivors to leave Europe followed by the departure of one million Soviet-area Jews to Israel. The intensive Jewish central European communities of Poland, Germany, Czechoslovakia, Hungary, Lithuania, and Romania disappeared.

14
World War I

The World War I period was a very troubling and painful time for the Jewish people in Europe. They were losers in every respect. On the western front, they fought valiantly on both sides but it did not shelter the Jews from attacks of disloyalty. Thousands of Jews who had migrated from the east to western countries but had not been naturalized were expelled as dangerous, disloyal foreigners. On the eastern front, the Jewish civilians were caught in the middle of the Russian and German army's advances and retreats. Many Jewish lives were lost due to these reversals of military fortunes, killed due to incidental military action by anti-Semitic mobs and by expulsions. Anti-Semites attacked the Jewish people on both sides as being the cause of each misfortune.

Western Front—Although the thought of Jews fighting and killing other Jews was painful, the Jewish population in the western Allied countries and in Germany and Austria were intensely patriotic and loyal to their home countries. Jews volunteered quickly in the British Commonwealth and in France and fought in proportion to the size of the Jewish population. It did not stop the anti-Semites from accusing Jews of disloyalty. One out of six German Jews fought in the German army, a higher percentage than the general population. One-third were decorated for bravery. During the war, there were accusations that the Jews in Germany and Austria were underrepresented in the armies. The loyalty and bravery of the Jewish soldiers did not stop the many German anti-Semites from blaming Jews for Germany's defeat, a theme continued later by the Nazi party.

Eastern Front—Jewish soldiers were casualties on both sides. The major disaster, however, befell the Jewish civilians. Three and one half million Jews lived in Poland under Russian and German control and in Galicia under Austrian control. An equal number lived in the Russian Ukraine. The Russians initially attempted to evacuate Jews to the Russian hinterlands before the initial German advance, but the Germans advanced so rapidly that the plans were aborted; many Jews were trapped in the boxcars waiting to be moved and perished. There were massive battles on this front covering both areas, with each side making major advances, then being forced to retreat at various times. The Jewish population in towns overrun by both armies at different times suffered many casualties. The economy of the Jewish communities in Poland, Galicia, Romania, and the Ukraine were devastated; mostly poor to begin with, they became penniless. It took a massive relief effort by the American Joint Distribution Committee to prevent starvation and to help rebuild lives.

Russian Revolution—For the previous one hundred fifty years, the several million Jews living under the Russian tsars were tormented and oppressed because they insisted on living as Jews rather succumb to the Russian way of life. The Jewish masses were therefore ready to accept anyone who would overthrow the autocratic Russian Empire. For that reason, during the war, the sympathies of the Russian Jews were mainly with the Germans.

In the early twentieth century, many Jews became active in the east European socialist movement that advocated improved working conditions, which were deplorable. This class of Russian Jews actively supported the Bolshevik revolution, some as leaders of the Communist party. Leon Trotsky, formerly a socialist, joined Lenin as the revolution began and shared the leadership of the Soviet Union until Stalin succeeded Lenin. Trotsky and another Jew, Rosa Luxemburg, became leaders of the international wing of the party that advocated an end to individual countries with national identities. There was also no room for Jews as a separate class of people in the Communist ideology.

A Russian civil war and battles with Polish and White Russian forces followed the 1917 Communist revolution. As the civil war progressed, the White Russians and Ukrainians fighting the Communists took their vengeance out against the Jews through a series of pogroms—almost 1,000. Many thousands of Jews were killed in the pogroms. Russian Jews who mostly lived as craftsman and small business people were not supporters of the Communist ideology. The majority practiced Orthodox Judaism and feared Communism, which advocated a godless society. However, as a defensive measure against these pogroms, Jews in the many of the large cities and towns formed Red army units that took an active part in the battles against the counterrevolutionaries.

The Balfour Declaration—The political efforts of the World Zionist Organization to achieve a Jewish homeland in Palestine had been unsuccessful until a breakthrough occurred during the war when Great Britain issued the Balfour Declaration. Although Britain had no control over Palestine at that time, the event of a major world power now being supportive of a Jewish national home in Palestine invigorated the Zionist movement. The wording of the Declaration even won support of many influential non-Zionist American Jews. Although the British practically abandoned the Declaration after the war ended, it represented an historical basis for the Jewish position in future political negotiations for a Jewish home in Palestine.

The Balfour Declaration of 1917 expressed the British government's endorsement of the establishment in Palestine of a national home for the Jewish people. It was drafted by Foreign Secretary Arthur James Balfour with the support of Dr. Chaim Weizmann, the British Jewish Zionist leader and chemist who had contributed significantly to the British war effort with his gunpowder developments. This gesture to the Jewish people was also somewhat in appreciation by the British of the Jewish support of the British army in the ongoing war effort. Early in the war, the "Zion Mule Corps," led by Vladimir Jabotinsky, fought a brave effort on the side of the British army in the unsuccessful battle of Gallipoli, Turkey. Later in the war, the "Jewish Legion" of about 3,000 mostly American volunteers fought gloriously for the British in their military campaign against the Turks in Palestine. Politically, the British government considered winning support of the Zionist movement would help them get control of Palestine when the war ended.

The Balfour Declaration, approved by the British Cabinet, was sent to Lord Walter Rothschild, the head of the prestigious Rothschild family and a member of the House of Lords. It read:

> His Majesty's Government view with favour the establishment in Palestine of a national home for the Jewish people, and will use their best endeavours to facilitate the achievement of this object, it being clearly understood that nothing shall be done which may prejudice the civil and religious rights of existing non-Jewish communities in Palestine, or in the rights and political status enjoyed by Jews in any other country.

The declaration contained an important point that made it acceptable to the world at large, including the Allied powers, Germany, and Turkey. It protected the civil rights of the Palestinians, and religious rights of the Christians and Muslims. In 1918, Dr. Weizmann even persuaded Emir Feisal of Arabia to accept the notion of a Jewish homeland that protected the rights of the Arab population. (This sympathy evaporated after the rise of Arab nationalism, and the emir aspired for leadership of the Arab world.) The last clause in the declaration about the "rights and political status in any other country" was intended to make it acceptable to the non-Zionist American Jews. It implied Jews who did not go to the homeland in Palestine would not be considered second-class Jews.

When the declaration was formally made, hundreds of thousands of Jews celebrated in the large American cities with mass rallies. Because the declaration included the statement protecting the rights of Jews outside of Palestine, it received endorsements from normally non-Zionist groups. The Reform rabbinate gave its endorsement (lukewarm) of the national home idea. Louis Marshall urged his fundamentally non-Zionist American Jewish Committee members not to obstruct any attempts to establish the Jewish national home as a Jewish refuge from persecution. A year later, the Zionist Organization of America was formed and its membership soared.

In 1918, a Zionist commission headed by Chaim Weizmann was established to work with the British army in Palestine to resolve Jewish-related issues related to the British takeover of the country. Before the full impact of the Balfour Declaration was yet known, and fighting in the area was still going on, the committee showed its optimism about a revitalized Jewish society in Palestine by laying the cornerstone for the Hebrew University on Mount Scopus in Jerusalem. In 1925, the university was formally opened in a colorful and inspiring ceremony featuring Lord Balfour and Weizmann and attended by university representatives throughout the world.

Lord Balfour had come to believe that in view of the harsh treatment the Jewish people received from the Christian world over the past two thousand years, they were deserving of a homeland in Palestine. He demonstrated his feelings by his constant support of the Jewish cause after he left office.

Brandeis's Contribution to the Balfour Declaration—British Prime Minister Lloyd George and Foreign Secretary Arthur Balfour were reluctant to proceed with the Balfour Declaration without an endorsement by the United States. Chaim Weizmann solicited the support of Justice Louis Brandeis, who was known to have President Woodrow Wilson's respect. Brandeis, with the aid of Rabbi Stephen S. Wise, convinced President Wilson to override his State Department's objection and announced the U.S. support—Wilson had previously been persuaded by the State Department to recant an earlier promise to support it.

15
Period Between the Two World Wars

Shortly after the war ended, the world community met in Paris to reshape Europe that had been devastated by four years of war. Political boundaries were rearranged, several new countries were created. Minority rights in all European countries were established and guaranteed. The League of Nations was established in 1920 as the mechanism to resolve future issues between nations. Although President Wilson was the leading advocate of the League, the isolationist Congress refused to endorse U.S. membership.

Russia, which was in the midst of the civil war over the communist revolution, was not included in the World War peace treaty. After the Russian civil war ended, Jewish religious and cultural life was slowly eliminated. After Stalin took control of Russia, brutal anti-Semitism reappeared in the Soviet Union.

The high hopes and the noble achievements of the Paris peace accords were short-lived. The harsh reparations against Germany resulted in economic turmoil, providing a breeding ground for Nazism. Minority rights in central and eastern Europe quickly evaporated. Reactionary military rulers came to power in several counties; they imposed new anti-Jewish edicts and economic restrictions that brought their Jewish communities to economic ruin. The Great Depression of 1929 also affected Europe—it added to the misery of the Jewish people. For a variety of reasons, anti-Semitism became revitalized throughout Europe. The League of Nations was tested on several occasions—it failed to curtail aggressive dictators or resolve international conflicts. Hitler came to power in 1933, having openly advertised his aggressive political intentions and his aim to wipe out the Jews. The world community did not oppose or curtail Hitler until forced to by his attack on Poland in 1939. For the Jewish people, this period culminated in the worst catastrophe to befall the Jewish people; the Holocaust costing six million Jewish lives.

The Paris Peace Conference—A huge international peace conference was convened in Paris in early 1919. Its aim was to rectify the problems that plagued Europe before the war. Two Jewish groups from the United States were represented, the American Jewish Committee, and the American Jewish Congress. Through the skill of Louis Marshall, who was a member of both groups, agreement was reached for the two groups to cooperate and avoid public exposure of disagreement. It was an effective arrangement, which enabled Marshall to take a strong role in the negotiations of minority rights affecting the Jews in Europe.

The treaties guaranteed full civil and political rights to all religious, racial, and linguistic minorities. Citizenship was to be granted to these groups. A share of public money was to go to the minority educational or charitable organizations. Jews were to be allowed to observe their Sabbath.

There was an effort by the Zionist delegation to include the Balfour Declaration in the peace treaty being negotiated with Turkey. The opposition by pro-Arab members of the British and French delegations almost doomed this effort had the treaty with Turkey not been delayed because of events that occurred. There was an attempted *coup d'état* by the Syrian legislature to take Arab control of Syria, Palestine, and Mesopotamia by naming Arab kings of these countries. Coinciding with the takeover attempt, there was Arab rioting in Jerusalem that resulted in a number of Jews being killed. The attempted coup and the disturbances in Palestine infuriated world leaders. Consequently, at the San Remo conference in 1920 that finalized the treaty with Turkey, Britain was made the mandatory authority over Palestine, and the Balfour Declaration was incorporated into the treaty.

The Russian Revolution Impacts Millions of Russian Jews—The Communist assumption of power in the Soviet Union after the revolution of 1917 had a major impact on the economic and cultural lives of all Russians. For the millions of Jews living in Russia, it led to the loss of identity with their Judaic heritage and had an economic impact far greater than those on other ethnic groups. Eighty percent of the Russian Jews were traders and shopkeepers, and as such, this hated class of bourgeoisie that could not be Bolsheviks was the first victim of the new regime.

Communist Suppression of Judaism—Marxism called religion the tool of the capitalists and the enemy of the proletariat. After the civil war ended and they finally took full control over the Soviet Union, the Communist party initiated the policy suppressing all religious activity. The Jewish section of the Communist party was particularly fanatical and ruthless in the treatment of observant Jews who clung to Judaism. They were influential in the closing of religious schools and synagogues and the exiling of leading rabbis and lay persons. Communist leader Ester Frumkin was representative of Jews bent on the elimination of Judaism, whom the non-Communist Jews labeled "anti-Jew Jews." She was a once married to a rabbi, then became a leader of the Bund. (The Bund was a strong east European Jewish socialist workers' party that was anti-Zionist and rejected Judaism as a religion.) Frumkin told this to her fellow Jewish communists. "The danger is that the masses may think that Judaism is exempt from anti-religious propaganda, and therefore, it rests with the Jewish Communists to be even more ruthless with rabbis than non-Jewish Communists are with priests." For all her loyalty to Bolshevism, Stalin later exiled her to Siberia, where she perished in a labor camp.

Under communist rule, it was forbidden to teach religion to all youth under eighteen. For the Jews, it also meant no Hebrew could be taught. In some areas, the Jewish Communist leaders promoted Yiddish schools to replace the Yeshiva and Talmud Torah religious schools that were a basic part of the Jewish culture. It was not an effective venture. Since these schools could not teach Judaism, they were not popular with the observant Jews. With all the Soviet propaganda encouraging Jews to assimilate into the Communist society, Yiddish schools were not the school of choice for the secular Jews. By the mid-1930s, these Yiddish schools went out of existence.

By the time Hitler attacked Russia in 1941, the anti-religious Communist policy was very effective in causing Russian Jews to lose their Judaic religious identity and their Hebrew/Yiddish culture. It took a confluence of Nazi persecution, inbred anti-Semitism among the Russian masses, and Russian political anti-Semitism to remind the Russian Jews of their Jewish heritage. It was exemplified by the astonishing view expressed by Leon Trotsky in 1938. He was living in exile but still a leader of the internationalist wing of the Communist party and one who essentially denied he was Jewish. He previously ignored Jewish problems. He had objected to Zionism and advocated Jewish assimilation into a classless Communist society as the way to end the discrimination against Jews. Trotsky was so moved by the anti-Semitic Moscow trials of 1936–1938 and the harsh Nazi treatment of the German Jews that he changed his lifelong view about assimilation. Admitting that assimilation was not the answer, he contended that Jews would continue to be a national group of people and suggested that a form of immigration was the only real solution to the Jewish problem in Russia.

Economic Impact—Under the economic restrictions of the tsarist rule, the Russian Jews were forced to make their livelihood as craftsmen and tradesmen between the industrial town people and the farming masses and villagers. With the Communist changes to the economy, the Jewish people essentially lost their role in the economy. The collectivization of Russian farms and the worker takeover of industry did not directly affect the Jewish people who were previously prevented from working in these areas. However, with the farming and industrial segments of Russian society having a new stronger economic position that effectively eliminated the need for middlemen and small craftsman, millions of Jews lost their livelihood and became destitute. It took years before the Jews were able to take advantage of the advanced education opportunities that did open for them under the Communist Soviet Union. They became trained for professional, technical, educational, and governmental employment areas.

Birobidzhan: the Jewish Autonomous Region—The Jewish Communist leader Abraham Bragin proposed establishing a Jewish republic in the Soviet Union in 1924. It met with opposition from various Jewish elements. The Zionists opposed the idea because it competed with Palestine as the Jewish homeland. The religious Jews would not have anything to do with Godless communism. The Jewish section of the Communist party, who was trying to erase all remnants of a Jewish identity, opposed the idea. Nevertheless, the Soviet government slowly took to the idea. In 1926, under the leadership of Soviet President Michael Kalinin, a project was initiated to develop the province of Birobidzhan, located in Far Eastern Asia, as a Jewish homeland. In 1928, Birobidzhan was designated as a Jewish settlement, and in 1934, it was declared a Jewish autonomous region.

The aim was to relocate about 250,000 Jewish former middle-class bourgeoisie and convert them into proletariat farmers. The effort was a public relations success with the American Communists, but in reality, it was a failure. At most 50,000 Jews moved there. The area did not have good soil for farming. The younger Jews, after receiving an education, left for the new industrial opportunities in the large Soviet cities. Several of the Birobidzhan Jewish leaders were executed during the 1936–1938 purges. By 1970, only 20,000 Jews out of a total population of 175,000 remained in Birobidzhan. The Birobidzhan community never achieved the Socialist Jewish culture that was anticipated when the project was initiated. With all these problems, the American Jewish defenders of Communist Russia continued to laud Birobidzhan as a great accomplishment for the Jewish people.

Russian Anti-Semitism Returns—When he took over power, Lenin declared that there was no room in the Soviet Union for anti-Semitism. Although there were instances of anti-Semitic utterances by Lenin, while he was alive, anti-Semitism was absent for the most part. There were no pogroms instigated by Soviet authorities or tolerated by others. Jews had equal opportunities for jobs and education, and Jews held many government positions. The Soviet leaders considered themselves anti-Jewish but not anti-Semitic. For example, they allowed Yiddish, which they considered the vernacular of the Jewish proletariat, but did not allow Hebrew, which they considered a subversive political, religious language. Hebrew books, whether religious or literature, could no longer be printed. Baking of matzah, the symbol of Jewish freedom from slavery in Egypt was forbidden.

The Soviet five-year industrialization plans placed a new emphasis on large industrial cities and in the mining of the enormous mineral wealth found throughout the Soviet Union. Millions of Jews who lost their previous livelihood migrated from the Jewish *shtetls* (small villages heavily populated by Jews) to the large cities in search of job opportunities. This competition for jobs awakened the dormant anti-Semitism among many workers. The fact that the educated Jews rose to management positions was another source of irritation. Until the purges of 1936–1938, Jews achieved a greater number of government positions than their population percentage. This situation also fed anti-Semitism.

After Lenin's death and the assumption of power by Stalin, the reign of pre-Soviet official Russian anti-Semitism resumed. It started when Stalin started to destroy his political opponents, many of whom were Jewish. Appealing to his anti-Semitic loyalists in Jew-baiting style, he condemned Trotsky and other Jewish opponents by their original Jewish names, names these Communists wanted to disown and names not known to the public. Stalin was clever in hiding his anti-Semitism from the public. For foreign consumption, he officially condemned anti-Semitism, but in reality, he turned into a bitter anti-Semite who was behind the official Soviet anti-Semitism. It was an effective approach. Most American Jewish Communists and Communist supporters defended Stalin from accusations of anti-Semitism associated with the purges of mostly Jewish Communists during the 1936–1938 Moscow trials. The trials ostensibly "eliminated Jewish internationalism from Russian society," even though Trotsky's internationalist Communist faction no longer represented a threat to Stalin. Stalin's daughter, Svetlana, shed light on her father's anti-Semitism in her books published in the West after her defection from Communism. She stated, "Stalin developed his anti-Semitism after years of struggling for power with Trotsky. It gradually changed from political hatred to hatred of all Jews as a racial class."

Suppression of Zionism—One of the first acts of the new Soviet government was to prohibit general Zionist activity while Communist Zionist groups like Poalei Zion were allowed to continue. General Zionist activity did continue underground for several years. Zionists, whose activity was monitored by the secret police, were periodically arrested; several thousand were exiled to Siberia and eastern Asia. The leader of this anti-Zionist movement was again the Jewish section of the Communist party spearheaded by the notorious Ester Frumkin. The Zionist Hehalutz movement to develop Jewish farmers was outlawed in 1926 and the Communist Poalei Zion movement was shut down in 1928.

16
World War II History

Prior to World War II, Europe had a long history of societal anti-Semitism bred by bigoted religious attitudes and economic jealousy. Frequently this led to violent attacks on Jews, and during crises or climactic periods, it led to mass slaughter of Jews. The First Crusade in the eleventh century, the Black Death, and pre-Spanish Inquisition period of the fourteenth century and the battles between the Russian Cossacks and the Polish people in the seventeenth century were the most severe—hundreds of thousands of Jews were killed. At other times, Jews were attacked and killed because of local vicious anti-Semitism. Often Jews were given the option of converting to Catholicism to save their lives. An untold large number accepted the offer but many accepted martyrdom.

The World War II period ushered in the most severe anti-Semitic period. The Germans carried out Adolf Hitler's plan to eliminate the European Jews, outlined in his book, *Mein Kampf,* written in 1924. The "Final Solution for the Jewish People" spared no Jews in Europe, including those who had partial Jewish heritage. No options for conversion to spare lives were offered. Six million Jews were killed in a five-year period. The centuries-old Jewish communities in Germany, Poland, Russia, and Greece were essentially eradicated; the Polish centers of Yiddish culture gone forever. This Holocaust, an event not to be forgotten, so significant to the Jewish people, is treated separately in Part IV of this book.

17
Post World War II History

World War II ended with Hitler dead, the Nazi regime eliminated, and a quarter-million Jewish concentration camp survivors placed in Displaced Persons camps in Germany and Austria, occupied by the western powers. A like number of survivors were liberated by the Russians. Barely alive and with no means of support, they were left on their own to reconnect with society. Almost all the survivors were desperate to get to Palestine. The British prevented this, turning back many who tried to enter illegally with the help of Jewish underground organizations. The three-year period between the end of the war and the creation of the state of Israel (which took them in) was a trying period for the survivors. The world community offered no havens for them. The rehabilitation and resettlement of the survivors is covered in Part IV.

The Short-Lived Yishuv in Poland—The country where Hitler almost completely accomplished his objective of eradicating the Jewish people was Poland. When the war ended, over ninety percent of the prewar 3.3 million Jews had been killed, and every vestige of the Jewish community was destroyed. As the survivors emerged, a small band of Jews were determined to nullify Hitler's objective of a *Judenrein* (Jewish-free) Europe. They set out to establish a *Yishuv* (Jewish-controlled settlement) in southern Poland. The area they selected was Lower Silesia, bordering Czechoslovakia and East Germany. Except for its capital, Breslau, the area was spared the war's devastation. It was an industrialized area, rich in natural resources and farming. The departing Germans left many opportunities in this rich environment.

Of the three hundred thousand original population, ten thousand Jews from that area had managed to survive the Holocaust. Under the leadership of Jacob Egit, this group appealed to the new Communist rulers of Poland for the right to establish an autonomous Jewish community. The Polish governor, who was sympathetic to the plight of the Jews, and with the encouragement of his Jewish deputy, granted their request in the summer of 1945.

The Central Committee of Jews in Lower Silesia was formed to organize and run the Yishuv. They were immensely successful. All of the prewar Jewish lifestyle was renewed, including synagogues, schools, and full Jewish cultural life. ORT (Organization for Rehabilitation Through Training) vocational training schools were quickly implemented to equip the members of the Yishuv to take advantage of the work opportunities. Special attention was given to aiding the youth, which were mostly orphaned by the Holocaust. Jews from other Polish areas and from Russia joined the Yishuv, raising the total population to fifty thousand after four years. Approximately one hundred Jewish cooperatives employing 2,000 workers and 150 farms of two hundred and fifty families were created.

This remarkable rebirth of Jewish life was unfortunately short-lived—the new anti-Semitic attitude of the Polish government was its undoing. It started with the forced resignation in 1949 of the Yishuv leader, Jacob Egit, who was accused of running a Jewish nationalistic settlement aligned to the state of Israel. The pressures on the Yishuv increased as the Polish government mimicked the strong anti-Semitic Soviet policies. It peaked with the 1953 Soviet "Doctors Trial" that falsely accused Jewish physicians of a conspiracy to poison Soviet officials, after which overt Judaism in Poland became unsafe; it ended in 1957.

Soviet Repression of Jews Continues—Thirty years of religious and cultural repression had been successful in eliminating any sense of Jewishness among Russian Jews. They knew they were Jewish only from the entry on their identity card. Remarkably, when the State of Israel was declared in 1948, a feeling of Jewish nationalism was aroused among many Soviet Jews. In October 1948, although Zionism had been banished for twenty-five years, a sense of solidarity with the Jews of Israel was shown by thousands of Jews outside a Moscow synagogue as they greeted Golda Meir, the head of the new Israeli legation in Moscow. Although the Soviets recognized the new Jewish State, Stalin quickly ended any thoughts of immigration to Israel. Anti-Jewish measures were put into effect. All Jewish publications were abolished and all Jewish cultural institutions disbanded. The Jewish Anti-Fascist Committee was closed down. This group of Soviet Jewish intellectuals was organized in 1942 to appeal to the Jews of the world to aid the Soviet Union in its struggle against Germany—at a time when the war was going badly for the Soviet Union.

In November 1948, the arrest began of hundreds of Soviet Jewish writers, actors, musicians, and artists. These arrests continued into 1949, disregarding the Soviet Union's signing of the Declaration of Human Rights the previous December, a pledge to allow the right of every individual to leave any country and return to their country. Some of the finest Yiddish writers were executed after being tortured. Some had survived the Soviet efforts to stamp out Jewish culture in the twenties and thirties. Jews were being condemned for disloyalty to the Soviet Union. The fact that 500,000 Jews fought in the Soviet army against Hitler, with over two hundred becoming generals, and hundreds awarded medals honoring their heroism and contributions to major Soviet victories was never mentioned to the public and was not a consideration in Stalin's brutal treatment of the Jews.

In 1952, twenty-four Jewish writers were accused of foreign espionage and sentenced to death. In 1953, Stalin contrived the "Doctors' plot," as Jewish doctors were accused of a trumped-up plot to poison Soviet officials as part of an anti-Communist conspiracy under the leadership of American Zionists. Jews were attacked on the streets, and many Jews were dismissed from their jobs. Stalin's death fortunately ended the trial and ended Stalin's plan for the mass deportation of Jews to Siberia. Human rights were still not extended to Soviet Jews.

The Soviet Jews became prisoners of silence. They were reluctant to express their Jewishness for fear of reprisal, which took several forms: arrest and imprisonment, loss of jobs, children exposed to reduced education, harassment by the KGB, and harassment by anti-Semites.

Resurgence of Jewish Identity in the Soviet Union—The reaction of the Soviet Jews to the continuous repression of Jewish culture and religion is another manifestation of the survivability of the Jewish people. By the start of World War II, Jews in the Soviet Union had almost completely lost their ties to Judaism. During the war, almost a million Russian Jews fled to Siberia and central Asia to escape the Germans who had penetrated deep into the Soviet Union. Uprooted from their homes, this group of Jews lost all vestiges of Judaism.

As the Soviet Jews learned about the details of Hitler's genocide of the Jews, they started to rekindle their Jewishness. They disregarded Stalin's oppressive policy towards the Jews in favor of volunteering to join the Soviet army in order to help defeat Hitler for the sake of saving Jewish lives. They were exhilarated by the opportunity to participate in the liberation of Jews from the German concentration camps.

The establishment of the State of Israel stirred the young Soviet Jews.

They became interested in studying Hebrew, which was still not permitted, and flocked to the few synagogues remaining in the large cities to celebrate the Jewish holidays; there were only two synagogues in Moscow with a Jewish population of 500,000. Although no longer required to state their ethnicity on the Soviet identification card, over two million Jews chose to identify themselves as Jews in the 1959 census. They were completely assimilated, and their Jewish identity was likely to bring trouble. Evidently, they took this step because they were still proud of their Jewish heritage.

Anti-Semitism continued to surface in the workplace. For many children it was also present in the schools, as it was at the university level for adults. This atmosphere depressed many, particularly the well-educated. Zionism became their answer. They longed to live in Israel where being a Jew was a not a cause for hostility, but immigration to Israel was unattainable.

The Refusenik Era—The ban on immigration to Israel continued under Stalin's successors until 1966, when Soviet Prime Minister Alexei Kosygin, in response to worldwide protests, announced that Jews who submitted exit applications would be permitted to join their families in Israel. Within a year, the restrictive emigration policy returned. After the Arabs armed by the Soviets lost to the Israelis in the 1967 Six Day War, the Soviets cut off emigration rights. Only 3,000 were allowed to leave in all of 1969, compared to 24,000 the year before. The applicants knew that their requests were likely to be refused. They were also at risk of being falsely accused of state crimes, such as disloyalty for being Zionists, spying for Israel or the United States, and slandering the Soviet Union. This did not deter thousands of Jews from submitting requests for exit permits to immigrate to Israel. It was the start of the *rufusenik* period. (A refusenik was a Jew whose emigration request was refused.) These exit requests continued for twenty-five years. Refusenik activists maintained and posted an annual list of current refuseniks to aid the network of refusnik supporters.

The refusenik situation was a paradox. The refuseniks maintained they were not dissidents who wanted to change the country but only wanted permission to leave the country. However, Jews requesting emigration to Israel sufficiently displeased the Soviet government. The requests were turned down, and the government undertook a considerable effort to conduct the oppressive KGB harassment treatment of the refusniks and to imprison them. These abusive actions aroused the concern of human rights activists throughout the world and complicated foreign relations with the United States, who passed the Jackson-Vanik amendment that tied Soviet trade rights to Jewish emigration rights. All of these negatives for the Soviet government would have been avoided if the same Jews whom the Soviets objected to were granted exit permits. The Soviets did use some refuseniks to their advantage. They swapped the freedom of some leading refuseniks for the release of important Communists held in foreign prisons.

The refusenik situation became a contest between the government and the refuseniks. The Soviets tried to break the will and emotions of the refusenik leaders. The refuseniks fought back by accepting imprisonment, torture, exile to Siberia, and loss of jobs and income as a price to pay for retaining their determination to leave for Israel. Many Soviet Jews took up the cause of the refuseniks and suffered the same fate of harassment and imprisonment. The Soviet harsh treatment of the refusenik leaders and those who stood up to the government by protesting against the Soviet emigration policy and against the cruel penalties imposed for unjustified accusations imposed on the refuseniks violated the 1975 Helsinki Human Rights Agreement that the Soviets signed. This behavior intensified the world sympathy for the refuseniks. Joining in requests for reduction in refusenik penalties and for permission to emigrate were many United States and British government officials. Elie Wiesel was among the U.S. human rights activists working for the freedom of imprisoned refuseniks and for the right to emigrate. Russian human rights activists, including Andrei Sakharov and Elana Bonner, joined in protesting against the harsh treatment and unjust penalties imposed on leaders of the emigration movement.

The courageous leaders of the refusenik movement were true heroes. They risked their lives and withstood brutal punishment not for their own sake but for the freedom of others. They stood tall among others in history that fought for freedom. They withstood physical and mental suffering to keep to their mission of helping others. Never bending under Soviet pressures, they always kept their personal integrity. Four outstanding refuseniks were Vladimir Slepak, Iosef Begun, Ida Nudel, and Natan Sharansky. Each one represented a different aspect of the refusenik movement:

Vladimir Slepak—In March 1970, the Soviets claimed that Soviet Jews really did not want to emigrate to Israel. Forty Jews responded with a letter to the contrary. One was Vladimir Slepak. It was his first step in becoming a leading refusenik activist and spokesman for the Jewish emigration movement for the next seventeen years. He wrote many letters of protest, organized protests, and was a contact with the Western world on behalf of the emigration movement and human rights for Soviet Jews. The

KGB harassed Slepak's family in many ways, but it did not stop his activism on behalf of the refuseniks. A five-year exile in a remote Siberian village near the Chinese border for "malicious hooliganism" did not dampen his enthusiasm.

Twenty years his senior, Slepak became a friend and mentor of Natan Sharansky. He tried to protect Sharansky from Soviet oppression. His home was open to Sharansky, and he corresponded with Sharansky during his prison stay. He shared many protest activities with Sharansky, including serving as a member of the Soviet Jewish Helsinki Watchdog Group that monitored Soviet adherence to the Helsinki Agreement for Jews and non-Jews alike.

Iosef Begun—Dr. Begun applied for his exit visa in 1971. It cost him his research position with the Moscow Engineering Institute. At that time, the movement to emigrate to Israel was growing. In Begun's view, the best way for the Soviet Jews to prepare for this move was to study Hebrew and Jewish culture. He had devoted the previous three years to training himself on these subjects and decided to teach them to prospective emigrants. Although his request to be allowed to teach Hebrew was denied, he defied the Soviet authorities and undertook the teaching of the Hebrew language and Jewish culture illegally.

Five years later, after his reputation as a teacher grew, the Soviets arrested him on the pretext that he was a parasite because he had no job. They refused to grant him permission to teach Hebrew. He was exiled to Siberia for two years because of his staunch defense of the right of Soviet Jews to teach Hebrew. At his trial, Begun persisted in arguing for the right to teach Hebrew although he knew his defense would result in a severe penalty. His devotion to teaching Hebrew resulted in another three-year exile to Siberia. In 1983, after being caught with Hebrew books, Begun was sentenced to seven years in prison followed by five years in exile for "keeping literature for slandering and defaming the Soviet Union." Refuseniks who admired Begun for his courage and his devotion to their cause had gone on a hunger strike in protest, and World Human Rights activists had sent letters requesting his trial be dropped. It was to no avail.

Ida Nudel—Although she was exposed to Russian anti-Semitism in school during the year of Stalin's Doctors' plot and later as an economist at her place of employment, she was content to live as a Soviet citizen. In 1970, the attempt of Jews to illegally leave Russia for Israel by stealing a plane in Leningrad stirred her feelings for her fellow Jews. It also prompted her to study Hebrew. In 1971, she was fired from her job for phony security reasons after applying for an exit visa. Her exit permit denied, Nudel became a refusenik for the next sixteen years.

Ida Nudel devoted herself to opposing the tactics of the Soviets against the refuseniks. She was one of the strongest refusenik advocates of demonstrations—to request emigration rights and to protest against refusenik prison sentences. She advised refuseniks on how to defend themselves against charges by showing how their behavior was within the Soviet laws. Ida Nudel provided constant support to Jews who were sent to prison. She wrote and visited them, which frequently required lengthy trips to Siberia. It was customary for her to keep in touch with their families at home, which was a tremendous morale booster. Her home in Moscow became a meeting place for Jewish activists coming to Moscow for protest activity.

Courageously, she irritated the authorities with all her different forms of protest. Banners requesting human rights for all citizens and for the right of Jews to go to Israel that were displayed in prominent places always caused the authorities to take notice. In her seventh year of this type of activism, she was charged with hooliganism and sentenced to five years of exile in a remote Siberian village. This diminutive woman had to learn to survive in the bitter-cold temperatures. The hospitality was also ice-cold. She had to contend with aggressive drunks and anti-Semitic townspeople. Nudel refused to give up her request to emigrate, so upon her release, she was not allowed to return to her home in Moscow. The KGB never ceased to monitor her during her five-year exile to Moldavia.

Ida Nudel's sister and family were granted exit permits to Israel in 1972. Her sister became a tireless advocate for Ida's freedom, writing to the Soviet government for her release and appealing to the United States government for help in obtaining her release. Ida Nudel's activity as a human rights activist and the ordeal she was suffering became well known worldwide. When she finally received her exit permit in 1987, Dr. Armand Hammer, president of the Occidental Petroleum Company, flew her to Israel in his private plane. When she arrived in Israel, she received telephone calls from Secretary of State George Shultz and President Ronald Reagan congratulating her on her newfound freedom. *She rejoiced over being home with her people.*

Natan Sharansky—The most honored and respected refusenik is Natan Sharansky. He is more widely known today than the other refuseniks because of his current political activism in Israel. Sharansky is the leader of the Russian immigrant party and has served as a cabinet minister in several capacities.

Sharansky was exposed to Russian anti-Semitism at the early age of five when anti-Semitism flared after the death of Stalin. It was then that his father told him of Stalin's harsh treatment of Jews and cautioned him that to survive in Russia it was vital not to speak negatively about Russian society to anyone. Sharansky kept his thoughts privately for the next twenty years until he joined the *Aliyah* (upward) movement that advocated emigrating to Israel.

He grew up without any connection or feelings about Jewishness and succeeded in getting into the prestigious Moscow Institute of Physics and Technology. There, open discussions about the political environment exposed him to an article by Andre Sakharov about the Committee for Human Rights. Sharansky's translation of this article was reported to the authorities and it initiated the long encounter with the KGB. Sharansky had already been impressed by the Israeli Six-Day War victory—he concluded, along with many other Russian Jews, that assimilation was not the answer to personal freedom in Russia. When he applied for an exit visa to Israel in 1973, he ran into trouble with the KGB. He was denied a visa and prevented from joining his new wife Avital, who left for Israel the day after their marriage. Avital became a tireless fighter for Sharansky's freedom after he was sentenced to thirteen years in prison on trumped-up charges of being a traitor spying for the United States. A devout Jew, Avital gave her husband a book of Psalms, which became his source of strength while incarcerated and was his only possession when he left the Soviet Union for Israel in 1988 thanks to international pressure on the Soviets that resulted in his early release from prison.

A fighter for human rights for all people in the Soviet Union and a spokesman for Moscow's dissidents, Sharansky risked his life so that other refusniks could get their freedom. He had the courageous and stout ability to resist the KGB's efforts to break him through torture and long solitary confinements during his ten years in the horrible Soviet Gulag prison system in Siberia. He came out of this imprisonment with renewed psychological strength in a remarkable display of outstanding courage. He received his freedom as a result of world pressure on the Soviet Union to release this exceptional human rights activist. *Natan Sharansky is a true hero of our time.*

The pattern of the Soviets increasing and decreasing the number of exit permits in reaction to protests or Soviet foreign policy issues continued for the next twenty-five years. With the democratization of Russia that was started by Communist party Premier Mikhail Gorbachev, this restrictive immigration policy changed. As part of his Glasnost policy, Soviet Premier Mikhail Gorbachev relaxed the restrictions on exit permits for Soviet Jews wanting to emigrate to Israel. By the end of 1988, over 65,000 Jews left the Soviet Union for Israel, twenty percent higher than the previous high set in 1979. By the end of the decade, there were 900,000 emigrants to Israel from former parts of the Soviet Union.

18
Contemporary History

Jewish life in England and France, the western European countries with the largest Jewish population, continues to be vibrant. There has been a slight movement to restore Jewish life in Germany and Poland, mostly by Russian Jews seeking better economic opportunities. The largest European Jewish population remains in the old Soviet Union countries even after more than one million Jews emigrated to Israel. The end of Communist rule in Russia brought favorable economic opportunities for Jews along with the general population. It resulted in almost a shutdown of Jewish emigration to Israel. Soviet-style nationalism, which contains anti-Semitic elements, did not fare too well in recent Duma lower chamber elections, but its widespread support poses a risk to the Russian Jewish community in the future.

Vatican's Self-Appraisal of Its World War II Holocaust Attitude—Directed by Pope John Paul II, the Vatican conducted a ten-year internal study of the Vatican's behavior towards the German persecution of the Jews during World War II. Concurrent with the study, the Vatican conducted a dialogue with Jewish religious and community representatives to aid the Vatican in understanding the issues from the Jewish standpoint.

The study report, published in the spring of 1998, received a mixed reaction by the Jewish community. They were extremely pleased that Pope John Paul was concerned enough to call for the study and applauded his interest in further dialogue and reconciliation between the two religious groups. The study gave credit to individual Catholics who aided Jews and went so far as to admit that the behavior of many Catholics went against the teachings of the Catholic religion. The study's comment that hundreds of thousands of Jewish lives were saved through Pope Pius XII's personal action or through his emissaries received the scorn of the Jewish community.

The report was seen as attempt to whitewash Pope Pius XII, who had remained silent about the genocide of the Jews both during and after the

Holocaust. The historical record shows that very little Catholic aid to the suffering Jews came about directly as a result of Vatican efforts, and there was an absence of Vatican leadership towards providing relief to the Jewish Holocaust survivors.

Release of Holocaust Victims' Swiss Bank Accounts—Many dormant Swiss bank accounts belonged to Jews killed in the Holocaust. Swiss bankers have presented unreasonable obstacles for the release of these bank accounts to descendants of the original account holders. They require death certificates and wills—impossible documentation to obtain from Holocaust victims. The Nazi Germans deposited money in Swiss banks that was obtained by selling gold and other valuables taken from the Jewish Holocaust victims—these assets also justifiably belong to Holocaust survivors.

Starting in 1996, the World Jewish Congress aided by the U.S. Senator Alfonse D'Amato took the lead in questioning Swiss Banks about these accounts. The Wiesenthal Center conducted an independent research of this subject and filed a class action lawsuit on behalf of Holocaust survivors. The Volcker Commission chaired by Paul Volcker, former chairman of the U.S. Federal Reserve, was created to investigate all aspects of this banking situation that was turning into a scandal for the banks and to recommend a resolution. In 1999, the Swiss banks accepted responsibility for these injustices to the Holocaust victims; the final restitution arrangements are still being worked out.

Compensation of World War II Slave Laborers—Almost two million people were forced to work as slave laborers for German industry and the German war machine during World War II. Pressed by several Jewish organizations and a class action suit, the German government at the end of 1999 finally acknowledged its debt owed to these slave laborers. The German government under Chancellor Gerhard Schroeder, together with German industry, agreed to pay $5.2 billion to the approximately 1.7 million slave laborers which included mostly non-Jews from eastern Europe and a large number of elderly Jews still living in eastern Europe. U.S. Deputy Treasury Secretary Stuart Eizenstat led the U.S. government's participation in the complex negotiations.

Rise of Neo-Nazism—Far-right political parties embracing Nazi anti-Semitism and other racist policies have shown increasing political strength across Europe. In the 1980s, Jewish world organizations were the only voice to object to former U.N. Secretary Kurt Waldheim's ascension to the Austrian presidency because he hid his Nazi past. In February 2000, fourteen European Union countries voiced their concern about the Austrian parliamentary leader inviting the far-right Austrian Freedom party headed by Joerg Haider to join his ruling coalition. Although he claimed not to be personally anti-Semitic and a believer in democracy, Haider expressed pro-Nazi views and praised the Nazi SS troops along with his strong anti-immigrant policy. This expression of European public opposition to politicians embracing Nazi sympathizers was accompanied by the reminder that the world and not just the Jewish people should remember the lesson of the Holocaust—Nazi Germany's evil ways should not be repeated. Their reaction was compounded by the unwillingness of the Austrian people to recognize their support of Hitler starting with the Anschluss (joining) of Austria in 1938 when they enthusiastically welcomed Hitler. Many Austrians now claim they also were victims of Hitler. The State of Israel also voiced its strong disapproval by recalling its ambassador to Austria. The United States expressed a mild concern regarding this development but also recalled its ambassador.

Part III

A History of the Jewish People in the United States

Jewish Immigrants' Dreams Come True

Preface to Part III

Jews have lived in the United States a relatively short time when compared to the 4,000-year span of Jewish history. It has been less than four hundred years since the first Jewish settlers set foot in New Amsterdam (now New York City). They were formerly Marranos (secret Jews) living in Brazil, who had openly returned to Judaism. They came to escape from the vicious intolerance towards Marranos, which came to the New World in Brazil. Their victorious fight with Peter Stuyvesant for the right to stay in America with religious freedom paved the way for 5.6 million Jews to live in the United States four centuries later and become the largest Jewish community in the world.

The heritage of the Jewish-American population has essentially changed three times. The first Jewish immigrants had a Spanish heritage with a Sephardic Orthodox religious culture. Then came the German Jews in the nineteenth century. They introduced the American version of German Reform Judaism. The early twentieth century brought the large wave of east European Jews with their Ashkenazic Orthodox religious heritage. They drifted to secular Judaism and then established the new Conservative Judaism movement. The latter half of the twentieth century witnessed a strengthening of Orthodox Judaism.

Jewish communal organizational life developed and grew in an effort to protect the increased freedoms and rights that the Jewish people continued to obtain during the growth of the United States. The leaders of these organizations and many individual Jews fought for improved benefits and freedom of opportunity for all Americans. Snapshots of the major organizations are provided for educational purposes.

The Jewish people in the United States today enjoy unlimited economic opportunities in an atmosphere essentially free of anti-Semitism in the workplace. A short sixty years ago, this was not the case. World War II influenced the growth of economic opportunity for the Jewish people, the reduction in anti-Semitism, and the elimination of economic bigotry towards Jews.

Jews, having no political influence where they lived since their exile from Palestine in the second century, were in no position to fight discrimination and intolerance towards fellow Jews in foreign lands. This lack of political influence changed slowly in the United States. It first became evident in the role that the American Jews played in finding relief for the Holocaust survivors and in helping to establish the State of Israel. It became more evident with the fight to gain the emigration rights for Russian Jews anxious to escape Soviet intolerance towards their Jewish citizens.

One objective of this section is to give the younger-adult Jewish generation an opportunity to become familiar with the historical aspects of Jewish life in the United States. It will give them an insight to the earlier hostile economic and social environment for Jewish Americans and instill a greater appreciation of life in the United States today for the Jewish people.

1
Jews Arrive in America

Historians identify the first Jews to arrive in the Americas to be the Marranos, who were Jews that converted to Catholicism during the Inquisition period but secretly retained their ties to Judaism. They left Spain and Portugal for Brazil in the early seventeenth century. Many Marranos had actually joined the Spanish conquistadors who roamed across North and South America to conquer and/or colonize the territories and remained there. Amazingly, remnants of these former Jewish people have now been surfacing in the former Spanish colonial areas of New Mexico, Peru, and elsewhere—they are being aided by several Jewish organizations in their quest to return to Judaism.

The Jewish connection to the United States, surprisingly, may have started much earlier than with the Marranos from Brazil. During the past twenty years, several historians have suggested that Christopher Columbus had a Spanish-Jewish heritage and that this connection was additional motivation for him to explore a route to the Far East that could be an outlet for the Spanish Jews preparing to leave Spain.

Christopher Columbus: A Possible Jewish Connection—Although born in Genoa, Italy, and outwardly a practicing Catholic, there are many historical anecdotes that provide credence to the suggestion by some historians that Columbus was of Spanish-Jewish heritage, which influenced his voyage to America.

The belief is that Columbus (Latin name for Colombo, his family name) was of Spanish-Jewish heritage, whose grandfather was a Converso (forced convert) and fled Spanish Catalonia to Italy a hundred years earlier during a period of violence towards Jews in northern Spain. Colombo was a common name among Spanish Jews. This Spanish background presumably is what enabled Columbus to learn Spanish fluently before he left Italy at the age of twenty-five; Columbus spoke and wrote Spanish; he never wrote in Italian. It is suggested that this connection to his Jewish background was the reason why, when living in Spain, Columbus wanted to be known as Cristobal Colon. Colon was a common family name adopted by Conversos in order to be accepted by the Inquisitors as converted Jews.

Columbus was an adventurer whose search for a new route to India by sailing west rather than the conventional east was driven by his motive for fame and the wealth that would come with it. His pursuit of this goal involved many interactions with the Jews of Portugal and Spain. It started ten years before his actual voyage to America. Wealthy Portuguese Jews tried to persuade the Portuguese king to authorize Columbus's search for gold in the West by financing Columbus in return for easing the harsh laws against Jews. The plans failed when the king was killed. Columbus then approached the Spanish King Ferdinand and Queen Isabella. After several years of rejection because the Spanish treasury was essentially emptied by the cost of the final defeat of the Moors in Spain, Columbus received the monarchs' backing, but only after two wealthy influential Jews, Don Isaac Abravanel and Don Abraham Seneor, contributed most of the required funds.

The historians who speculate about Columbus's Jewish background suggest that a desire to find a haven for the Spanish Jews who were undergoing severe repression at that time motivated both Columbus and the Jewish financiers. The order expelling all Jews from Spain was issued shortly after the voyage was approved. Columbus left Spain on his first voyage to America the day after all Spanish Jews were leaving Spain by a flotilla of ships in response to the 1492 expulsion order. Columbus wrote in his log, "After the Spanish monarchs expelled all the Jews from their kingdoms and lands, in the same month they commissioned me to undertake a voyage to India." Columbus, a practicing Christian, was strangely motivated to associate the start of his adventurous journey with this special day in the plight of the Jewish people.

An interesting item is this quote in a letter Columbus wrote to a nurse friend: "I am a servant to Him that elevated David from sheep tender to king." Columbus at that time envisioned himself being elevated to a high position after his major discovery of the New World. Columbus evidently was alluding to his connection to the Jewish God and wishing for help from the "Jewish God" rather than from the "Christian God." His weak tie to Catholicism was also indicated by the fact that a priest did not accompany Columbus on his first voyage to America. At the height of the Inquisition period in Spain, conversion of the heathens that Columbus expected to encounter would have been a natural objective, as it was on his later trips.

Jews were involved in many aspects of Columbus's voyage to America. A Jewish astronomer provided Columbus the navigation astronomical tables that enabled him to successfully cross the Atlantic. Five recent Conversos accompanied Columbus on his first voyage to the New World; they were his most trusted aides. The first to set foot on American soil was a known Marrano, Luis de Torres, who joined the crew to serve as the interpreter for the East Indians they expected to find. After returning to Spain, instead of writing to his sponsor, Queen Isabella, Columbus first wrote about his discovery to a Jewish friend who was his supporter.

First Jewish Colonies in America—Many Marranos joined the Spanish and Portuguese invaders of America. They settled in the conquered territories covering South America, Mexico, and the West Indies. Unfortunately, the Spanish Inquisition came to the New World searching out Marranos; hundreds were killed. When the Dutch briefly seized Brazil from the Portuguese in 1631, many Marranos openly returned to Judaism and prospered under Dutch rule. This freedom lasted a short period. The Portuguese retook Brazil in 1654, causing the Jews to flee from forced conversion or death by the Inquisition. Some went to the Netherlands where, thanks to the influence of some Dutch Jews, they were accepted. Many fled to the islands of Barbados, Jamaica, Martinique and Santo Domingo where they became farmers who successfully promoted the area's sugar cane industry. They were able to live there openly as practicing Jews. The Marranos living in South America, Mexico, and in the southwestern United States were forced to continue to hide their attachment to Judaism. After five hundred years, remnants of these Marrano societies have been discovered clinging to traces of Jewish practices such as treating the Friday night dinner as a special family occasion.

First Jews in the United States—A group of twenty-three Jews, fleeing from Portuguese intolerance towards Jews in Recife, Brazil, arrived in New Amsterdam (later known as New York City) in 1654. Peter Stuyvesant, the governor of the Dutch colony, was unwilling to let them in because of his intolerance to Jews. Another obstacle was that they were destitute because of having to pay an exorbitant boat passage fee that was for more money than they had. The standoff was ended when Stuyvesant was ordered by the Dutch East India Company, who were the owners of the colony, to allow the Jews to enter; Jewish members of the board of directors had a hand in the order. Stuyvesant's intolerance persisted after the order. He did not permit the Jews to build a synagogue, but they bypassed him by organizing the Shearith Israel (Remnant of Israel) Congregation that conducted services in private homes. They bought a tract of land in 1656 for the first Jewish cemetery in the United States. Stuyvesant still made life difficult for the Jews who slowly won some economic rights through protests with the Dutch and the support of the Dutch Jews. Britain captured New Amsterdam in 1664, but the civil rights for Jews in New York City did not improve for another one hundred years.

New England's Hospitality—In the late seventeenth century, a small number of Jews, mostly Marranos who returned to Judaism and assumed their original Jewish names, started living in New England. They concentrated in Rhode Island because of the religious tolerance offered by its leader, Roger Williams. The Touro Synagogue in Newport, Rhode Island, named after its first Cantor, Isaac Touro, was dedicated in 1763. It is the oldest Jewish building existing in America.

Southern Hospitality—Before the American Revolution, the only place in the South where a large number of Jews lived was the colony of Georgia founded by the liberal-minded James Oglethorpe in 1732, when ninety Jews joined the original 4,000 settlers. They lived mostly in the city of Savannah.

2
Jewish Immigration From Germany

After the defeat of Napoleon, the spirit of equal rights in western and central Europe was replaced by renewed intolerance to minorities in central Europe. In 1815, this hostile atmosphere caused an increase in the emigration of German Jews, a pattern that was to be followed for many years. Frequently, the father came first, bringing the rest of the family later after accumulating enough money. Families helped other relatives and friends to emigrate and get started in this country. With this migration, Ashkenazic Jews began to outnumber the Sephardic Jews in the United States. The peak emigration of German Jews occurred in 1848 after the failure of the liberal revolutions in Europe. The German Jews who supported this movement joined the non-Jewish liberals fleeing to the United States.

The influx of German and Austrian Jews slowed by 1880, with 250,000 having arrived. Although most remained in the eastern cities with established Jewish communities, many more adventurous ones followed the "pioneers" first to the Midwest and then to the West Coast. They went to the large cities as well as to rural trading posts. Many went through the success story of starting as small-town merchants and covered wagon peddlers to reach financial success as owners of large department stores in major cities around the country and started prominent families that lasted for generations. Some of them did achieve successful careers as bankers and owners of financial institutions. Contrary to the claims of anti-Semites, Jewish financiers represented a small percentage of the total financiers in the country. Opportunities for employment in banking institutions for Jews were severely restricted until after World War II, when employment barriers to Jews went down in most fields.

The German Jews were particularly active in establishing synagogues and Jewish communal organizations such as charitable societies, orphanages, hospital boards, social clubs, and welfare organizations. Loan societies advanced funds to the needy without charging interest. All of these activities derived from the biblical commandments (*mitzvot*). In 1843, the B'nai B'rith (Sons of the Covenant) was organized by twelve recent German immigrants as a mutual aid society to help sick and unemployed members. It was first called by its German name, *Bundes Bruder*.

3
Jewish Immigration From Eastern Europe

In the early nineteenth century when the German Jewish immigration was at its peak, Jews in eastern Europe barely knew about life and opportunities in America, and few came. This changed by many factors. It started with the unsuccessful Polish rebellion against Russia in 1863, which was followed by political unrest against the Russian czarist regime. The Jews lost what little liberty they had. It was heightened by the organized pogroms against the Jews, which killed many Jews and caused their economic destruction. By the end of the century, almost one-third of the Jews in Russia became paupers. This led to a massive immigration of six hundred thousand Jews from eastern Europe between 1881 and 1900, bringing the total in the United States to one million Jews. Several attempts were made to limit the immigration of Jews into the United States, but Presidents Cleveland, Taft, and Wilson vetoed the measures. In 1924, the Johnson Act was passed by Congress that severely limited Jewish immigration through a system of quotas for preferential countries that did not account for much Jewish immigration. This law kept out the Jews fleeing Europe from the Nazi Germany persecution. However, thanks to the unrestricted immigration before this law and natural growth, at the end of World War II there were four million American Jews.

These new eastern European immigrants were different than their German predecessors. They concentrated in the large cities. Initially not assimilating too well, they lived in their own ghetto areas. These immigrants were mostly industrial laborers. Employed mostly in the clothing industry, Jews influenced this field both as entrepreneurs who advanced the productivity of the industry and as labor leaders who developed labor unions and were advocates of improved working conditions. Out of economic necessity, they worked on the Sabbath and lessened their affiliation with the synagogue and other Jewish communal organizations. The hardships of living in crowded tenements and working in the uncomfortable "sweat shops" did not deter them from encouraging and assisting family and friends to join them in this country. The more industrious immigrants, who saved their wages and with little education, became owners of small garment businesses themselves.

4
Contributing to the Development of the United States

The American Jews, who always represented a small minority of the United States population, made significant contributions to the United States growth in many political and social areas. Starting in the colonial days, Jews had a hand in the westward expansion of the United States through their trading skills. The actions of Jewish patriots that contributed to the success of the American army in the Revolutionary War were taken into account by the framers of the U.S. Constitution. The strong Jewish support of all the American wars is a matter of record. Judaic values influenced the contributions to U.S. society made by several Jewish Supreme Court Justices and Jewish Labor Leaders. Jews motivated by Judaic values established the future pattern of philanthropy; giving to charitable, educational, and religious organizations, to Jewish and non-Jewish beneficiaries, and to white and black beneficiaries.

Opening Up of the West—In the colonial days, adventurous Jews became Indian traders. They provided the commerce to support the westward expansion of the colonies. The Jewish peddler was a familiar sight in almost every town that sprung up from the East Coast to California between 1820 to 1860. These peddlers served as the commercial link, frequently the sole contact, between the dispersed farmers and the trade centers, providing much needed supplies. As the towns grew into cities, these peddlers opened the country stores, and Jewish artisans joined the westward trek to provide many services. As the peddlers prospered, they opened general stores and then department stores that became well-known family operations. Many a Jew became a respected citizen of these western communities, serving as law enforcement officials and principal office holders. This was especially the case during the hectic and turbulent Pacific coast Gold Rush days when Jews joined the forty-niners.

The War Periods

European countries treated Jews as second class citizens, allowing them no political role, restricting their economic opportunities, and frequently expelling them. Up until the liberalism enlightenment of the nineteenth century, these circumstances did not engender a sense of nationalistic loyalty to the country they lived in among the Jewish population. The attitude of the Jewish people towards the United States was different from the start. They were appreciative of the opportunity to escape the prejudices in the country they left and were willing to make personal sacrifices to support the United States in every war starting with the Revolutionary War. Jewish Civil War veterans established the Jewish War Veterans organization in 1896 to foster recognition of the role Jews played in the American wars. The JWV continues to be an active organization representing the American Jews who fought in the twentieth-century wars.

Revolutionary War—By the time of the Revolutionary War, there were approximately 2,500 Jews living in the United States. Many leading Jewish figures provided important Revolutionary War support. Because the Jews in the colonies had no ties to England as many Colonists had, there was no dual loyalty problem for them. The vast majority were "patriots." They welcomed the religious and economic freedom principles of the Revolution. Many Jews had become wealthy since coming to America, and they used their resources to finance and support the Revolution in many ways. Jewish Indian-traders became outfitters of the civilian army. Jewish financiers advanced money in return for risky IOUs to pay the soldiers in the Continental Army. Some Jewish traders, such as the Gratz brothers of Philadelphia, signed pledges not to trade with the British while manufacturing uniforms. Some Jewish traders armed their vessels with cannons and destroyed British shipping.

The most notable Jewish figure who played a leading role in the Revolution was Haym Solomon. As an immigrant from Poland who was familiar with the Polish revolutionaries Kosciusko and Pulaski, he settled in New York, joining the Sons of Liberty organization that helped prepare for the Revolution. In 1776, the British arrested and condemned him to die for his involvement in the destruction of British arms in New York City. He escaped to Philadelphia, where he quickly became wealthy as a skillful currency trader. His success and his willingness to accept a trivially low commission got him appointed by the French as their official currency trader and paymaster of their troops supporting the Revolution. He then essentially became the semiofficial financier of the Revolutionary effort. He was very generous with his personal wealth during and after the war, making loans without interest to many government officials, including Jefferson and Madison. Solomon was also a leader of the Jewish community. He persuaded the wealthy Philadelphia Jews to support the Revolution financially. He helped finance the first synagogue in Philadelphia. He also fought to repeal the Pennsylvania law requiring all office seekers to swear that they believed in the Old and New Testaments, which effectively kept Jews out of office.

In appreciation of the contributions Jews made to the Revolutionary cause, liberal-minded James Madison and Thomas Jefferson were instrumental in defining the religious rights embedded in the United States Constitution—they applied to Jews without specifically addressing Jews. These two presidents were good friends of the Jews. In appreciation of Jefferson's relation to the Jewish people, Commodore Uriah Levy purchased and restored Jefferson's home, Monticello, in Virginia, which had been left to decay after Jefferson's death. Captain Levy at one point had been discharged from the Navy by a board that had several members prejudiced against him because of his "Jewishness." A Congressional Commission of Inquiry later completely vindicated him of all charges, and he was appointed the first Jewish Commodore in the U.S. Navy. In this capacity, he fought for and won the elimination of the Navy's corporal punishment by flogging with a cat-of-nine-tails.

Civil War—The estimated 150,000 Jews living in the United States at the start of the Civil War were as divided as the rest of the country. In both the North and the South, there were vocal and occasionally fanatical Jewish abolitionists and slavery defenders, including the clergy. About twenty-five percent of the Southern Jewish population owned slaves. Before the Civil War, many elected to free their own slaves to voice their objections to slavery. A small number of Jews were involved in the slave trade. Three Jews, August Bondi, Jacob Benjamin, and Theodore Weiner took part in John Brown's attempt to free slaves. Rabbi's Sabato Morais of Philadelphia and David Einhorn of Baltimore were threatened for preaching antislavery sermons.

Jews were mainly loyal to the side where they lived. About seven percent of the Jewish population fought for both sides of the Civil War, which was the same percentage as the general population. There were Jewish generals on both sides.

A Jew, Judah Benjamin, was the trusted advisor to Jefferson Davis, the president of the Confederate States. Because of his skills, Benjamin was shifted to various cabinet positions as the war progressed and new problems needed resolution. After the war ended, Benjamin "the Jew" became a convenient scapegoat for a vocal minority seeking to blame the Confederacy losses on someone.

The majority of the Jewish soldiers fought for the North, which had the larger Jewish population. There were several all-Jewish regiments. Seven Jewish enlisted men earned the Medal of Honor. However, Jewish chaplains were not permitted until Congress passed a law in 1862 that only required chaplains to be "an ordained minister of some religious denomination." This change was influenced by the intensive lobbying by all the Jewish organizations and rabbinical leaders, and had the support of President Lincoln. Lincoln was a friend to American Jews. He had some personal Jewish friends. The Jews, and particularly the German Jews, had become active in politics as supporters of the Republican party, "the party of free men and free soil, and of vigorous business enterprise." Two of the three delegates who placed Lincoln's name in nomination at the 1860 Republican convention were Jews. The entire Jewish population mourned Lincoln's death through special synagogue services for several months as if he was a leading member of the Jewish community.

There were isolated instances of anti-Semitic actions throughout the war. The most serious incident was General Grant's edict in December 1862 requiring all Jews to leave the Tennessee border area dividing the North and South positions within twenty-four hours. It was treated as an important issue by the Jewish community, which raised a storm. Although Jews were a small percentage of those Grant considered a problem, the order unfairly singled out only Jews for punishment, and it was imposed on all Jews regardless of any involvement in the troublesome incident. After the protest, the order was quickly withdrawn by President Lincoln, but many Jewish lives had already been torn apart by the edict.

World War I—Most American Jews supported the German side at the beginning of World War I primarily because all Jews disliked the czarist oppression of the Russian Jews. The German Jews also felt a loyalty to their former homeland, which at the time treated Jews favorably, and they gave Germany political and financial support. The Russian Revolution changed the attitude of many Jews, engendering support for the "Free Russia" movement. They envisioned freedom for the Russian Jews, not realizing the Soviet Union would turn out to be a new oppressor of Jews, denying them religious freedom. When the United States entered the war a month after the Russian Revolution started, except for a group of pacifist Socialists concentrated in New York City, the American Jews had no difficulty in ardently supporting the U.S. war effort. Jewish labor movement leaders, led by Samuel Gompers and political leaders, such as Louis Marshall and Samuel Untermeyer, rallied the Jewish support. Even the eminent Rabbi Stephen S. Wise, who was a staunch pacifist, became an ardent supporter of the U.S. role in the war.

When the United States entered the war, President Wilson appointed his Jewish financial advisor Bernard Baruch to head the War Industries Board. Baruch's success at developing the U.S. industry's capability to meet the wartime needs earned him the reputation as the nation's most respected civilian personality.

Although Jews were 3.3% of the population, 250,000 Jews, representing 5.7% of the armed forces, fought in the war. There were 51,000 Jewish enlistees.

When the United States entered the conflict, the Jewish Welfare Board (JWB) was established by a conference of Reform, Conservative, and Orthodox leaders to address the social and religious life of the Jewish soldiers and sailors. The JWB recruited rabbis as chaplains, provided prayer books, and established Jewish recreational centers. After the war, the JWB served as the central organization for the Young Men's and Young Women's Hebrew Associations and other community centers that were being established throughout the country.

World War II—Early on, American Jews recognized the dangers to the world that Hitler represented. They were strong supporters of Roosevelt's efforts to aid Great Britain when it became the sole country opposing Hitler after the fall of France, while at that time, half of the country was isolationist, opposing Roosevelt's activist support program. The America First organization was the leading isolationist force. Charles Lindbergh was one of their leading spokesmen who joined in with anti-Semitic remarks and threats. Jews were accused of dragging the United States into the war. The Japanese attack on Pearl Harbor reduced the hostile environment to the Jewish people in the United States. The hostility essentially ended only well after the invasion of Normandy, when the American people could see victory down the road.

The American Jewish leaders were not very effective in influencing Roosevelt to aid the Jews fleeing from Hitler, very few Jews were admitted into the country. His inaction was mainly due to his political concern about antagonizing the influential isolationists in Congress, who, along with many influential public isolationists, had little sympathy for Jews. This inaction to rescue survivors continued long after the administration gained knowledge of the German plans to eradicate the European Jews and persisted for several years after the Holocaust survivors were liberated from the Nazi concentration camps. The U.S. aid program was hostage to the anti-Semitic State Department and the anti-Semitism that existed around the country. Senators and leading newsmen opposed permitting refugees into the country.

In 1943, the State Department issued a policy statement about Palestine that was intended to placate Saudi Arabian King Saud. It advocated allowing only a small number of Jews into Palestine after the war ended; this plan contradicted previous U.S. endorsements of the British Balfour Declaration promising a Jewish State in Palestine. In 1944, Congress introduced resolutions advocating a Jewish commonwealth in Palestine. The State Department opposed the measure, and it was killed. Efforts to change the U.S. immigration laws to allow Jewish Holocaust survivors to enter the United States were not successful until 1952.

Six hundred thousand Jews fought in all the services on all the war fronts. That was eleven percent of the Jewish population, a little higher than the national average. There were 35,000 Jewish casualties, including 10,000 deaths. Thirty-six thousand Jews were decorated, sixteen Jews became generals or admirals.

Jewish physicists played a leading role in the U.S. atomic energy program during the war. The notable Jewish scientist and Jewish community leader, Albert Einstein, originally a pacifist, joined two other refugee Jewish physicists, Leo Szilard and Eugene Wigner in encouraging President Roosevelt to develop the atomic bomb in order to beat the German effort to develop one. The scientific development aspect of the secret "Manhattan Project" that developed the bomb was led by the American Jewish scientist J. Robert Oppenheimer who, although relatively young at thirty-eight, had already gained the reputation as an accomplished physicist and administrator. He was joined by hundreds of American and notable former European Jewish physicists, including the brilliant Harold Urey, I. I. Rabi, John von Neumann, Leo Szilard, Victor Weisskopf, and Edward Teller. The latter went on to head the hydrogen bomb program. Einstein was denied a secret clearance and kept out of the Manhattan Project by its director, General Leslie Groves. Groves, suspicious of all Jews, considered Einstein to be a communist because Einstein lauded Stalin out of thankfulness for the Soviets fighting Nazi Germany, who Einstein hated for what they were doing to his fellow Jews.

General Groves was never told of Einstein's role in proceeding with the bomb; Roosevelt had confided only to his closest associates that it was Einstein who had persuaded him to proceed with the atomic bomb development. Roosevelt feared this information about Einstein's role would have been grist for the anti-Semites among those who opposed him politically. In 1947, after having been lauded by the government for his masterful management of the complex atomic bomb development program and respected by his peers for this effort, Oppenheimer was subjected to a strong personal indignity. Spurred on by FBI Director Hoover's long-time suspicions and Joseph McCarthy's impending accusation of Oppenheimer's loyalty, the Atomic Energy Commission removed Oppenheimer's security clearance and brought him up on disloyalty charges. After a vicious attack by the AEC lawyer, a three judge panel found him entirely loyal. Another three judge panel also vindicated him but refused to restore his clearance primarily because Oppenheimer would not endorse the hydrogen bomb program.

The Jewish community was one of the strongest American supporters of the United Nations concept being formulated after the war ended. Authorized by President Truman, pro-Zionist representatives of several Jewish national organizations attended the UN organizational sessions. Their major contribution was the successful lobbying to eliminate the resolution that all *mandated land* (Palestine territory under British control authorized by the defunct League of Nations) go to the majority element after the UN trusteeship ended, which would have resulted in Palestine becoming an Arab state. They persuaded several countries to endorse another resolution calling for the partition of Palestine, enabling it to pass.

Vietnam War—United States involvement in the war in Vietnam gave rise to the New Left movement. This strong activist group resorted to violent actions in protest against the Vietnam War, and secondarily to express their dissatisfaction with the country's social welfare system. Jews coming mainly from the college campus played leading roles in several New Left organizations. Left-leaning Jewish writers and journalists of the radical underground newspapers joined the cause. They claimed to be promoting Judaic ideals as the basis of their cause. In reality, they were opposing the Jewish religion and the Jewish community structure.

The Jewish community opposed the protesters' viewpoint and actions, and particularly objected to their anti-Judaic philosophies and lifestyle. Because Jews were very vocal leaders of the movement, the number of Jews participating was misleading. Only a small percentage of the Jewish university students were involved (about 5%).

Jewish mainstream commentators warned that the New Left's disruption and intimidation tactics could destroy all the freedom-gains achieved by Jews in the United States. With so many Jewish leaders of collegiate antiwar organizations, Jewish community leaders warned that there might be an anti-Semitic reaction by middle-America families whose noncollege children fought in the war, whereas college students were granted deferments. Some of this concern materialized. Although Jews were well represented in the military units fighting in Vietnam, and Jews were a minority in the secular protest movement, mainstream Jews were exposed to negative criticisms by the public. After the war lingered on for many years, several prominent members of the Jewish clergy did encourage an end to the fighting to prevent what started out to be a Vietnamese civil war from escalating into a World War III.

The Israeli victory in the 1967 Israeli Six Day War brought a crisis to the Jewish involvement in the New Left movement. Battles rose between those who favored the Palestinian cause and those who favored the Israeli position. Many New Left Jews formed radical peace groups that advocated Middle East peace solutions detrimental to Israel. The situation worsened when the major New Left organization, the Students for a Democratic Society (SDS), was taken over by Third World spokesman Stokely Carmichael, who later changed his name to Kwame Ture. He denounced Israel as Western imperialism and equated Zionism with racism. His anti-Semitic attacks resulted in a significant dropout of Jewish participation in all New Left organizations.

Societal Benefits and Labor Rights

Society in general and the rights of the American worker were strengthened by the combined efforts of Jewish members of the Supreme Court, Jewish civil activist lawyers, and Jewish labor leaders. The Jewish jurists applied the principles of Judaic law to American law, introducing humanism into the court system and advancing social justice. Four Jews, Brandeis, Cardozo, Frankfurter, and Goldberg, who made significant contributions to American society that earned them appointments to the Supreme Court, were also dedicated to Jewish causes.

Louis D. Brandeis—Brandeis, from Louisville, Kentucky was an active Zionist throughout his lifetime. Professionally he was an activist lawyer concerned over monopolistic practices, corruption in political affairs, and labor problems. He earned the reputation as "the peoples' lawyer." Before the turn of the twentieth century, Brandeis had won legal battles in these areas. The arbitration board that he devised as part of his 1910 Protocol of Peace for ending chaos in the ladies garment industry served as a lasting model for solving labor industry disputes. This experience also strengthened his ties to Judaism, which he considered the guide to his professional behavior. He won a precedent-setting case that defended Oregon's maximum-hours legislation for women based on massive labor statistics and medical and social evidence.

President Wilson appointed Brandeis at age fifty-nine as the first Jew on the Supreme Court—only after a lengthy battle in Congress that had anti-Semitic overtones. He spent twenty-three years on the Supreme Court working as a two-man team with Chief Justice Oliver Wendell Holmes to apply social justice in the court rulings and to use contemporary facts rather than personal prejudices as the basis of their rulings. In his late seventies, President Franklin Roosevelt frequently consulted Brandeis on legislative matters. He helped shape Roosevelt's "New Deal," which incorporated many of Brandeis's social reforms; until fifty years ago, it was acceptable for members of the Judiciary to provide legislative advice to the executive branch.

Benjamin N. Cardozo—A practicing Sephardic Jew who supported Jewish education in New York City, Cardozo was a "lawyer's lawyer." President Hoover appointed him to the Supreme Court in 1932 where he continued his practice as a liberal lawyer. He defended the Roosevelt New Deal legislation and is noted for his opinion declaring the Social Security Act of 1937 legal. He emphasized that a judge should look beyond legal authorities to serve those seeking justice.

Felix Frankfurter—He spent twenty-five years as a professor of law at Harvard University. Frankfurter was an advisor to President Wilson and a participant in the Versailles Peace Conference in 1919. He was a legal protégé of Louis Brandeis and supported Brandeis's Zionist activity. After contributing to the development of Roosevelt's New Deal programs, he was appointed to the Supreme Court by President Roosevelt in 1939. Until he retired in 1962, he served as an independent, forward-looking, and judicial-minded member of the court.

Arthur J. Goldberg—He first became famous as a skillful mediator of labor-management disputes. He became general counsel of the Congress of Industrial Organizations (CIO) and of the United Steel Workers of America in 1948. In 1955, he helped negotiate the merger of the CIO and American Federation of Labor unions. In 1962, President Kennedy appointed him to the Supreme Court. He served only three years, resigning in 1965 to accept President Johnson's appointment as Chief American Delegate to the United Nations, succeeding the late Adlai Stevenson.

Labor Leaders—Most of the large number of Jewish immigrants that came from eastern Europe, starting in 1880, remained in New York City. Many worked in the clothing industry, which had miserable working conditions; sixty-five hours a week was normal. Health and safety conditions were deplorable. These conditions coupled with the socialist background brought from Russia encouraged these workers to seek improved working conditions. The national American Federation of Labor and two of its largest unions rose as a result of these conditions. They were organized and led by dynamic Jewish leaders who were devoted to the cause of labor. It was through their leadership that unionizing became effective and working conditions improved for the union labor force and other workers.

In 1886, Samuel Gompers helped form the American Federation of Labor (AFL) and became its first president. Through his leadership, it became the first national craft union. The AFL was initially strengthened in 1890 when it was joined by the United Hebrew Trades organization, which was started by several Lower East Side Jews under the leadership of Morris Hillquit. It consisted of twenty-two unions in the New York City garment industry and several unions involved in other trades employing Jewish workers.

By 1900, the number of new Jewish immigrants had already increased significantly. This new wave of immigrants brought many females into the workforce, which, coinciding with the expansion of the ladies clothing industry, contributed to the growth of several independent local unions. These unions were associated with the various subsidiary aspects of the garment industry, such as cloak makers, shirtwaist makers, cutters, and pressers. Samuel Gompers brought these small independent unions into an umbrella organization within the AFL and called it the International Ladies Garment Workers Union (ILGWU). In 1909, a precedent was set when all the women of the citywide shirtmakers' union joined the strike by the shirtmakers' local against one large company. This total shutdown of the industry in New York City influenced the employers to settle the strike in favor of the union. Workers received significantly improved working conditions and, for the first time, compensation benefits. The workweek was reduced to fifty-four hours and workers were paid for four holidays.

The next major ILGWU accomplishment occurred in 1910. It resulted from influential Jewish community leaders applying pressure on Jewish garment business owners to end a long and bitter strike—a pattern that was to be followed several times in the next four years. The employers and unions agreed to accept Louis D. Brandeis, at that time a successful lawyer in industrial relations, to help settle the long impasse. His Protocol of Peace resulted in a fifty-hour workweek and many rights and benefits for the workers.

In 1911, there was a horrible fire in the ten-story Triangle Shirtwaist Company building in New York City in which 147 women and twenty-one men were killed, and over 200 burned and maimed. It was a tragic day for the Lower East Side Jewish community. Because of the terrible safety violations that contributed to the catastrophe, union members resolved to fight for improved working conditions, and unionism gained strength.

In 1914, Sidney Hillman organized the Amalgamated Clothing Workers Union for the men's garment industry. He led it into being a force for achieving improved labor rights through several successful strikes over the next four years. He then focused on developing union membership benefits such as medical care, unemployment benefits, life insurance, day care center services, vacation opportunities at union-run resorts, and education center services.

ILGWU union membership had been reduced seventy-five percent due to the high unemployment at the start of the Great Depression, and the union was practically out of funds. In 1932, David Dubinsky assumed the ILGWU presidency and restored its health. He eliminated the leftist element of the union and allied himself with President Roosevelt, helping to formulate the New Deal labor legislation. A major piece of this legislation was the 1934 National Labor Relations Act that made collective bargaining a federal law. It reinvigorated unionism in the country.

The Great Depression Period—The Jewish immigrants who entered the United States in the forty years before the 1930s depression worked mainly as laborers in the garment industry and industrial trades. They suffered along with the rest of the workers in the country as business contracted severely (50%) and unemployment rose sharply (30%) during the Great Depression that started in 1929 and ended in 1941.

During the 1930s, many of the first-generation American Jews went on to higher education seeking employment in the professions. This group of highly educated Jews suffered more than the general college-educated population because the existing discriminatory practice of not hiring Jews in many professional and commercial fields accelerated with the depression. Jews were virtually excluded from the legal, engineering, industrial, and banking fields. Major universities had quotas limiting Jewish enrollment, which also applied to medical schools.

Many Jewish professionals took advantage of the employment opportunities that opened under the Roosevelt administration and were contributors to the programs advanced by his administration. Jews were attracted to President Roosevelt's labor and social action programs and almost ninety percent supported him in the elections.

Philanthropy: Jewish Style

Early in the nineteenth century, a Jew, Judah Touro, became the first philanthropist in the country to give large donations to charities and religious institutions of both his own religion and other religions. A century later, another Jew, Julius Rosenwald, expanded the broad scope of Jewish and non-Jewish philanthropic generosity by being the first to donate millions to miscellaneous black institutions.

Today there is a new level of Jewish philanthropy. A group of the nation's wealthiest and most influential Jewish businessmen meet twice a year as a study group to consider topics relating to philanthropy and Judaism. By their interaction, they find areas of common interest that help them establish partnerships for philanthropic support of Jewish causes. They conduct this activity quietly behind the scenes, without fanfare and publicity. Formed by Leslie Wexner of Limited Inc. and Charles Bronfman of Seagram Co. in 1991, the group has grown to about twenty. Projects they have supported included the refinancing of the Hillel organization; the Partnership for Jewish Education, which makes matching grants for Jewish day schools; and the Birthright Israel project which helps send Jewish youth on trips to Israel. Several projects intended to draw assimilated young adults to Judaism are underway. The Jewish Campus Service Corps is an example. It funds recent college graduates to spend a year or more on a college campus creating a Jewish lifestyle through speakers, literature, Jewish film series, and kosher meal parties.

Judah Touro—Judah Touro was the son of Cantor Isaac Touro of Newport Rhode Island fame. As a young adventurer, he went to New Orleans in 1801 while it was still an inhospitable city for Jews under French control. Nevertheless, through prudent investing, engaging in the international shipping business, and diligent saving, this bachelor amassed a fortune. He gave money to many Jewish institutions, including almost every synagogue in the country, the Jewish hospital in New Orleans, and a hospital in Palestine. He left money for the upkeep of the Newport synagogue, where his father was cantor and which was renamed in his father's honor, and left money to maintain the Jewish cemetery in the city. He also contributed to many American Jewish charities and, following the tradition of Jews in the Diaspora, gave to the poor Jews in Jerusalem.

In 1812, Judah Touro, a volunteer in the American army, was severely wounded in the Battle of New Orleans. A Christian soldier saved him and became his friend for life. In further appreciation, Judah Touro gave money to many Christian institutions and charities both in New Orleans and around the country. When he died, Touro left his fortune to be divided between Jewish and Christian charities.

Judah Touro also gave to patriotic and civic causes. He gave money to help finance the Battle of Bunker Hill monument, founded the New Orleans Free Public Library, gave money to a sailor's hospital in New Orleans, and contributed to many other more civic institutions.

Julius Rosenwald (1862–1932)—Julius Rosenwald had a remarkable career, working his way up from clerk to become the president of Sears Roebuck. He amassed a large fortune, which in the tradition of Judah Touro, he gave to Jewish and Christian charities and to many civic and social causes. He gave money to Jewish war relief during World War I, money to promote Jewish agricultural settlements in the Soviet Union, and supported the Hebrew Union College and the Jewish Theological Seminary. Living in Chicago, he contributed millions to the Chicago University and to the Chicago Museum of Science and Industry.

Julius Rosenwald included one additional beneficiary category to his philanthropic generosity, the African-American community, which received a large share of the $63 million he donated to charities. From 1910 on, he subsidized the erection of YMCA buildings for blacks in twenty-five cities, established thousands of rural black schools in the

South, and supported black health-care and cultural activities. He gave $2.7 million for the construction of model housing for blacks in Chicago. Rosenwald's philanthropy to black institutions remains unmatched.

Social Welfare Organizations

Almost from their first arrival, social-minded Jews responded to the Judaic ethic of being charitable to the poor and being concerned about the elderly. They supported a variety of community charitable and social organizations, and some of national scope. Old-age homes, orphanages, and Jewish education facilities were established in the largest cities. Before the city and federal welfare systems came about, Jewish indigents were helped by the Jewish Welfare Board and free-loan societies provided source money to those trying to get out of financial binds or start small businesses. Even Jews trying to get into farming or raising chickens commercially could get financial help through Jewish Agricultural Loan Societies. Jewish philanthropists sponsored hospitals with a Jewish environment in the largest cities that also serviced the public. There were also Jewish tuberculosis rehabilitation hospitals created in the early twentieth century, when the disease was prevalent, that went on to become national health research centers for other diseases.

Immigrant Support Organizations—In 1902, several immigrant aid societies merged into the Hebrew Immigrant Aid Society (HIAS). This became the main organization helping Jews getting established in this country—they located relatives, provided temporary lodging, assisted with employment opportunities, and provided train tickets to those intending to settle away from New York City. The National Council of Jewish Women organization supported the poor immigrants. The Clara deHirsch Home for Women in New York City provided short-term safe shelter to female newcomers. HIAS and the Joint Distribution Committee (JDC) collaborated in assisting Holocaust survivors leave the European transition camps. Starting in the 1970s when Jews were permitted to leave the Soviet Union in large numbers, HIAS and JDC again collaborated on immigration support activities.

Communal Organizations—By 1880 there were already sixty Young Men's Hebrew Associations (YMHA) offering Jewish cultural activity. When the massive immigration of east European Jews started in the mid-1880s, the emphasis shifted to the Americanization of the new Jewish immigrants by offering English instruction. In 1900, Jacob Schiff, the philanthropist who was extremely involved in improving the conditions of poor Jews in New York, built the large YMHA in New York City and funded it to provide commercial and vocational courses in addition to the cultural activity. It became the prototype for YMHAs and Jewish Community Centers in other cities that also offered gymnasium and swimming facilities, employment assistance, and summer camps.

Settlement Houses—These were philanthropic-supported facilities located in poor Jewish-immigrant neighborhoods. There were many in New York City, with a concentration in the Lower East Side. Christian missionaries sponsored some; most were secular but supported financially and operated by the Jewish community. Ultimately there were approximately seventy-five Jewish settlement houses across the country. They concentrated on providing immigrants with basic welfare services and courses in English reading and writing. Some even provided training in the manual trades. A few larger ones functioned as a YMHA, including offering free summer camp to the poor.

The most famous of these settlement houses is the Henry Street Settlement, located in the Lower East Side of New York City and still in existence today. Lillian Wald organized it in 1893. She was a middle-class Jew from Cincinnati who took up a career in nursing. She was horrified by the poor health of the immigrant Jews living in the squalor of the tenements of the Lower East Side. With Jewish and non-Jewish financial aid, she set up the free visiting nursing service for the area that ultimately covered the entire city. She operated the settlement for forty years, expanding it to offer full settlement house social services.

The most unusual communal center for immigrant Jews was the Educational Alliance, also still operating today. The large building located in the heart of the Jewish immigrant ghetto of the Lower East Side was built in 1893. Sponsored by several wealthy Jewish community leaders, the Alliance was committed to advancing the education and lifestyle of the Jewish immigrants. It provided a host of social services that included lecture programs, club facilities, library, gymnasium, and workshops. Its night course program enabled the immigrants to continue working while getting an education. It became an example to be followed by many communities and organizations. The New York Board of Education adopted it. The City College of New York adopted the program for its evening adult-education program. Arthur Murray, the famous dance instructor got his first dancing lessons at the Alliance. David Sarnoff, who as chairman helped make RCA a leading American corporation, was a graduate of the Alliance's science courses.

Civil Rights

The Jewish people came to this country to escape intolerance, bigotry, and persecution. Throughout Europe, Jews were denied basic civil rights. This background made them very sensitive to the occurrence of civil rights abuses. Starting with their arrival in New Amsterdam when they fought against Peter Stuyvesant to obtain religious and economic freedom, Jews were in the forefront of American civil rights battles for the Jewish people and for the non-Jews. Rabbis pursued the Judaic principle of social justice for all people. Jewish organizations devoted their efforts to civil rights. Jewish social welfare organizations and many individual Jews acting on a nonsectarian basis expressed concern about social injustice issues. These Jewish groups generally fought for the civil rights of all ethnic minorities, believing that an issue affecting another minority would soon affect Jews. The Jewish people's Judaic culture and their heritage of being denied civil rights essentially unified the Jewish people in support of civil rights for all. However, there was no uniformity amongst the Jewish people as to what the appropriate steps were for achieving these goals. No single group speaks for all the Jewish people.

In the early twentieth century, lawyer Louis Marshall, the "spokesman" for the German-Jewish community, was the leading Jewish civil rights activist. In the twenties and thirties, Herbert Lehman gave up his relationship with the family banking business to go into Jewish communal affairs and then into politics. From his position as N.Y. lieutenant governor under Governor Franklin Roosevelt, and then as governor of New York, he was a strong advocate of civil rights. In the forties and fifties, Jacob Javits as a liberal Republican congressman and senator from New York was a leading civil-rights and labor-rights advocate.

Probably the greatest American rabbinical fighter for social justice was Rabbi Stephen S. Wise. Rabbi Wise believed Jews were divinely dedicated to seek justice for all people. He transformed this ideal into the principles of the "Free Synagogue" that he established in New York City: Freedom of the pulpit; synagogue providing full community services; no distinction between rich and poor with regard to synagogue membership and seating arrangements; and complete identification with Judaism. He responded to every social issue that arose in his day and became one of the major outspoken civic reform leaders. He spoke forcefully for Jewish rights, labor rights, and justice for blacks. He helped organize the NAACP and lent his prestige to raise funds for the organization.

Black-Jewish Relations—The Judaic principles of equal justice for all people motivated many Jews to recognize the abuses imposed on the black people in this country, which went beyond the intolerance towards the Jewish people; in addition to being denied their basic civil rights, blacks were brutalized and lynched wantonly. Starting with the Jewish abolitionists of the Civil War period, Jewish leaders and civil rights organizations fought for bettering the rights of blacks, and Jewish philanthropists provided significant financial support to civil rights efforts and to black organizations. Jewish lawyers defended blacks in the judicial system and supported the voter-registration drives in the South in the 1960s.

The alliance between Jews and blacks essentially started with the creation of the NAACP in 1909. This relationship started to deteriorate when the black Muslims' anti-Semitism and anti-Zionism accelerated in the 1950s. The cleavage increased due to several factors. Starting in the late 1960s, black activists excluded whites from their organizations and were increasingly hostile to Jews. The black riots of the sixties were a major setback in relations. In taking out their grievances against the country regarding conditions in the black ghetto areas, blacks scapegoated Jews as a class of people responsible for their troubles. Jewish businesses that were considerate to blacks were destroyed along with those that may have been guilty of abuses. These actions reminded Jews of what frequently happened to Jews in Europe when riots against Jews and destruction of their businesses were the vehicles of Polish and Hungarian nationalists intent on eliminating Jews as commercial competition after their countries won political freedom.

In 1967, the African-American Teachers Association in Brooklyn, New York accused Jewish teachers of miseducating the black schoolchildren as a ploy for taking jobs away from Jewish educators. This action aroused the Jewish community because of the bigotry in the accusations and the unfair economic impact. Although it was a local problem, it was amplified by the concern that it would set bad precedent. In the 1970s, quotas insisted by blacks as part of the new national affirmative action program was generally opposed by the Jewish organizations concerned about

Jewish civil rights since it would deny Jews and others from opportunities based on qualifications and merit.

A major issue surfaced later that is also still lingering, preventing the return of the Black–Jewish coalition fighting for civil rights. The continuous virulent anti-Semitic remarks by Louis Farrakhan, the present leader of the black Muslim group, has been a major irritant to the Jewish people and an obstacle in mending relations. He has vilified the Jewish religion, equated Zionism with racism, and accused Jews of essentially causing all the ills of the world. Farrakhan and other black militants have made Black–Jewish relations on many of the college campuses contentious. The weak response by the black community to the repeated anti-Semitic remarks by Farrakhan and alike has been disappointing to the Jewish community. It gives evidence of lack of sensitivity to the feelings and rights of the Jewish people and a disregard for the previous Jewish contributions to black civil rights.

Jewish Support to the National Association for the Advancement of Colored People (NAACP)—In 1909, a small group of black and white social activists, including several Jews, established the NAACP. The NAACP's strategy was to use publicity, protest, and legal redress to fight for equality and justice for African-Americans. Rabbi Stephen S. Wise, a member of the group, was the leading fundraiser. A Jewish lawyer, Joel Spingarn, was the very effective chairman of the NAACP for the next ten years. He acted as the integrationist and worked together with the black leader W.E.B. DuBois as the nationalist to make the NAACP the most forceful organization for black civil rights at that time.

One of Spingarn's major accomplishments was to get the army to establish a separate training camp for the World War I black soldiers so they would have better opportunities to get commissions—it was almost impossible with the bigotry that existed in the regular Army training camps. His lawyer brother, Arthur Spingarn, was the NAACP legal counsel for many years, and was president when the NAACP won its landmark Supreme Court case outlawing school segregation in 1954.

Louis Marshall, the leading Jewish civil rights activist of the time, also supported the NAACP on legal matters. Industrialist Kivie Kaplan, a leading Jewish philanthropist, was NAACP president for over ten years. He served as a fundraiser and was himself a major contributor. Jews sat on the NAACP Board of Directors since its founding until black militants took over the NAACP and excluded white participants.

American Civil Liberties Union—The ACLU is the leading secular civil rights organization in the United States. It has no connection with the Jewish community. Because so many of its officers and legal staff are Jews, reactionary organizations with an anti-Semitic agenda frequently express their objection to the ACLU with bigoted remarks suggesting it is a Jewish organization. They disregard the fact that all ACLU investigations are conducted from a nonsectarian perspective and that the Jewish communal organizations frequently forcefully oppose the ACLU civil rights positions.

Early Motion Picture Industry: Absence of Jewish Values—In the early days of motion pictures, a group of nickelodeon movie makers in New York City controlled the production and distribution field as a closed monopoly. In 1909, a Jewish entrepreneur, Carl Laemmle, broke the monopolistic trust in a court battle and set up his own production studio outside of Los Angeles called Universal City. With the trust broken, another Jew, Adolph Zukor, who started by producing quality films in a Brooklyn studio, moved to California, where he made Paramount Pictures the leading filmmaker. Jewish film producers such as Sam Goldwyn, Louis B. Mayer, and Jack Warner established other major film companies. These Jewish film moguls were mostly new immigrants who started out as youngsters, mostly penniless. They became successful through ambitious entrepreneurship. They were strictly businessmen, who happened to be Jewish but without Judaic convictions. They portrayed Jews in degrading stereotype character roles as they did Indians, Afro-Americans, and other ethnic minorities on a business-judgment basis rather than due to any ethnic bias.

The motion picture business was very competitive and had no moral standard or guidelines. The motion picture industry produced films that they believed appealed to the movie-going audience. There was no "Jewish conspiracy" to control the industry or to destroy ethnic character, as some anti-Semitic hate-mongers have asserted. These Jewish motion picture producers certainly did not favor the Jewish people; they rarely produced a movie that had Jewish value.

5
Religious Development

The Jewish religious denominations in America today developed in relation to the European area from where the successive immigrant groups came from. The economic conditions each group of immigrants faced were other factors.

The earliest arrivals were Sephardic Jews, whose descendants originated from Spain before the expulsion in 1492. Generally becoming economically comfortable after settling in this country, they were content to continue their heritage of the Sephardic style of Orthodox Judaism.

Next came the Jews from Germany, influenced by the Reform Judaism that already had developed in Germany. The leading German Jews were wealthy and socially progressive. They were looking for a style of Judaism that enabled them to satisfy their intellectual needs without being burdened by the rigid religious behavioral pattern of Orthodox Judaism. The American version of Reform Judaism resulted.

The next large wave of immigrants was from eastern Europe. Their religious heritage was Ashkenazi Orthodox, but many were socialist politically and lost their religious beliefs before coming to the United States. The available economic opportunities, predominately in the garment industry and other related trades, generally forced the majority to work on the Sabbath. These Jews lost their adherence to Orthodox practices and passed on their irreligious behavior to their offspring. They offered their children very little, if any, Hebrew religious education. Their emphasis was on how to make use of the public education system to prepare their children for the American opportunities.

Out of these conditions sprung Conservative Judaism. It was to offer Jews the opportunity to practice a form of Judaism that included some acceptable changes of Reform Judaism, such as mixed seating, but retained many Orthodox practices such as *kashrut* (kosher-food preparation and consumption rules) and Sabbath services, which Reform Judaism had eliminated.

The last group of immigrants was the ultra-Orthodox Chasidic Jews from eastern Europe, who believed that only separation from secular society could assure Jewish survival.

The newest mainstream Judaic denomination is Reconstructionist Judaism, organized in 1960 by Rabbi Mordecai Kaplan. Reconstructionism stresses activist Judaism over religious Judaism. It replaces the concept of a supernatural God that controls one's destiny with a God who gives life meaning and purpose.

Reform Judaism

In the first half of the nineteenth century, the German-Jewish immigrants established congregations in the largest cities. The rabbis they brought in from Germany independently introduced changes in the religious practices similar to the Reform movement in Germany, such as prayers in the language of the country instead of Hebrew and the elimination of kosher-eating rules. Early attempts to organize the Reform Judaism movement failed. The individual who ultimately succeeded in promoting and organizing the Reform movement was Rabbi Isaac Mayer Wise.

Rabbi Wise advocated changes in the religious practice through flexibility in applying the Orthodox rules for controlling change. The changes he proposed were in the context of continuity with the Judaic past history, its Bible, and Talmud. For example, *kashrut* was dropped because some elements of this practice were extrapolated from vague statements in the Bible that did not contain any specific reference to this requirement, whereas the specified biblical mandate to honor the Sabbath caused him to retain Saturday prayer services. His flexibility-concept allowed him to eliminate prayers relating to the obsolete temple sacrificial system. He introduced his proposed reforms in his own Cincinnati congregation. The most innovative change was the introduction of mixed-sex seating. (In Orthodox synagogues, the women are required to sit separately from the men; either behind a curtain or in a balcony.)

Rabbi Isaac Mayer Wise lectured widely on the merits of the Reform movement, which contributed to its increased membership and its public recognition. Primarily because of his efforts, the Union of American Hebrew Congregations was established in 1873. Two years later, he started the Hebrew Union College for ordaining Reform rabbis and served as the president. Located in Cincinnati where he served as the rabbi of a congregation that already adopted his Reform practices, he wrote and taught most of the courses. The Reform movement organization was completed in 1899 with the establishment of the Central Conference of American Rabbis.

Since its inception, the Reform Judaism movement adopted three platforms that provided the principles that guided its members. The Pittsburgh Platform of 1885 stressed Judaism to be a rational, progressive religion, geared to the views and habits of modern civilization. It frowned on the adherence to the Mosaic Rabbinical Laws, and forbade the use of the traditional garments such as skullcaps and prayer shawls. The Pittsburgh Platform, the product of Rabbi Kaufmann Kohler, who was considered to be the champion of Reform Judaism, set the Reform movement ritual and behavioral standards for the next fifty years. The Columbus Platform of 1937 put a new stress on the Torah to complement the social justice objectives of the Reform movement. The Centenary Perspective issued in 1976 encouraged the optional adherence to the Judaic traditions of study, prayer, and keeping the Sabbath and the holy days, and the practice of other activities that promote the survival of the Jewish people.

Through the years, many Reform congregations reversed some of the ritual reforms they instituted earlier. They went back to Saturday services instead of holding them on Sunday, and some Hebrew was reintroduced into the prayers. Bar mitzvah replaced confirmations at age thirteen. Skullcaps and prayer shawls became optional rather than being forbidden at services. Three major changes were instituted under the advocacy of Rabbi Alexander Schindler who presided over the Reform movement from 1973 to 1996. Reform Jews were encouraged to persuade their non-Jewish spouses to accept Judaism through a Reform movement outreach program and the Jewish community was urged to accept intermarried couples into synagogue life. The most controversial change was the acceptance as a Jew the child born to a Jewish father and a non-Jewish mother (patrimonial descent)—Orthodox and Conservative Judaism only accept as Jewish the child born to a Jewish mother (matrimonial descent). Today there is no ritual standard among the Reform temples. With no intention of dictating a single mode of religious expression, the Central Conference of American Rabbis in 1999 accepted a new Pittsburgh Platform promoted by Rabbi Richard Levy, but contested by other Reform rabbis. It provides ten principles that will reclaim many of the Judaic practices previously rejected by Reform Judaism. It affirms the importance of studying Hebrew, promotes lifelong Jewish learning, urges observances in some form of the Sabbath and holidays, encourages *Aliyah* to Israel, calls for the observance of mitzvot, and makes the synagogue central to Jewish communal life. The platform continues to encourage social action and charity giving.

Conservative Judaism

In the 1880s, several prominent Reform rabbis expressed their discontent with how far the Reform movement was moving away from traditional Judaism. A traditional Sephardic rabbi, Sabato Morais, uncomfortable with the version of Orthodoxy practiced by the east European Jews, took up the call. He opened the Jewish Theological Seminary in New York's Shearith Israel Synagogue. The objective was to teach Conservative Judaism based on a model of Conservative Judaism already developed in Europe for German Jews who were not happy with the extremes of the German Reform movement. After ten years, it did poorly, not having received much support from the community. The seminary was on the verge of collapse in 1897 when Rabbi Morais died. Oddly, several wealthy German-Jewish community leaders saved it. Although staunch Reform Jews, they did not want to see the seminary fail. They envisioned the new form of Judaism to be an attractive spiritual vehicle to the newcomers and one that would help to reduce the crime that had become prevalent amongst the newcomers.

This group established a $500,000 endowment fund and recruited Rabbi Solomon Schechter, a proven teacher and scholar at Cambridge University in England, to head the institution. Rabbi Schechter had discovered the Geniza (Judaic religious item hidden storage facility) in a Cairo, Egypt, synagogue that produced over 1,000 manuscripts that filled many holes in the previous thousand years of Jewish history. He preached change within the spirit of the Torah, winning over many congregations. They accepted Reform movement practices of mixed-sex seating and driving to synagogue on the Sabbath, but retained Orthodox practices of *kashrut,* wearing skullcaps, prayer shawls, and Hebrew as the basic prayer language. The position of rabbi was elevated to one who conducted the services and guided the congregation. The focus was to be on Jewish life and peoplehood rather than Jewish doctrine and liturgy, which made it attractive to Zionists. Schechter was extremely successful at getting synagogues to join the Conservative movement. He stimulated the creation of the Rabbinical Assembly of America for Seminary alumni. In 1913, he encouraged the network of Conservative congregations to form the United Synagogue of America, which became the national institution of Conservative Judaism in the United States.

In the last decade, the Conservative Jewish movement adopted another major departure from the Orthodox with its acceptance of egalitarian religious practices. Women now have equal status with men in many Conservative congregations that have chosen to follow egalitarian practices. Women serve as rabbis and cantors, and participate in all aspects of the religious services, including being called up to the Torah reading (*Aliyah*) and being counted as one of the ten people (*minyan*) required to conduct a formal group prayer service (formerly only men were counted towards the minyan).

Orthodox Judaism

The East-European immigrants were Yiddish-speaking Orthodox Jews. The vast majority lived in New York City, where they built hundreds of "hole-in-the-wall" synagogues and a few larger ones, *cheders* (private teacher, one-room Hebrew school), Talmud Torahs (community-organized afternoon religious-education classes), and full-day yeshivas. In 1886, Rabbi Jacob Joseph, a respected European rabbi, was hired by a group of rabbis in New York City to serve as "Chief Rabbi of New York," similar to the custom in European cities. The concept failed, it was mired in controversy due to factionalism among the rabbinical groups in the city.

There was a rabbinical intellectual effort to sell orthodoxy conducted by the father and son Soloveichiks. The father, emigrating from Germany in 1932, was shocked at the quality of orthodoxy he found here and attempted to invigorate traditionalism at the Yeshiva University that he headed. His son, a professor of Talmud at Yeshiva, lectured around the country about the philosophical merits of traditionalism. Their efforts failed to change the drift away from orthodoxy.

The Young Israel Synagogue modern-Orthodox movement was started in the early 1930s. It brought English into the sermons and introduced cultural lectures in English into the Orthodox synagogue environment; it achieved limited growth. By the 1950s, Orthodox Judaism lost many of its adherents and the Orthodox religious education system decayed.

Between 1947 and 1960, one hundred fifty thousand Jews, mostly Holocaust survivors, entered the country, bringing in a new form of Orthodoxy. Half of them were ultra-Orthodox Chasidic Jews. They brought their dynasties and Chasidic lifestyle with them to Brooklyn, New York. The two largest groups were the Lubovitch and Satmar Chasidim.

The Lubovitch, with Rabbi Joseph Schneerson as the leader, settled in Crown Heights after escaping from Poland in 1941. He was the most respected and influential Chasidic leader. His missionaries went all over the world to win Jews back to the Orthodox faith. After his death, his son-in-law, Menachem Mendel, took the name Schneerson upon assuming the head of the dynasty. With an engineering degree background and as a believer in hard work and the value of intellect, he established the international Chabad movement. It was a network of Lubovitcher yeshivas, schools, youth activities, and college organizations. They taught Orthodox practices and the performance of good deeds. The rabbi won many adherents among intellectuals by his lecturing and personal interaction. Under his influence, the Lubovitch accepted the State of Israel but fought to keep its religious regulations strictly Orthodox. With Rabbi Schneerson's death in 1996, the Lubovitch have been without a leader because his followers, who revered him as the Messiah, expected his quick return as the Messiah. They have been disappointed.

The Satmar Chasidim, with Rabbi Joel Teitlebaum as head, settled in Williamsburg. They practice the strictest separatism from secular society of all the Chasidic sects. The Satmars have been against Zionism since its beginning at the turn of the century. They have violently opposed creating the State of Israel and will not recognize it. In their view, "God will return the land of Israel to the Jewish people when he sends the Messiah to the people of the world. Jews should not be forcing the hand of God with their political ownership of Israel."

While the Chasidic ultra-Orthodox movement was gaining strength, the conventional Orthodox movement regained its strength, particularly among the more educated and younger Orthodox. In the last forty years, there has been renewal of mainstream Orthodoxy by second- and third-generation Jews who adhere to the traditional Orthodox practices and commandments while living and working in a modern lifestyle.

Reconstructionist Judaism

Rabbi Mordecai Kaplan believed that Judaism should be more of a "civilization" and less of a religion. He argued that the social habits and standards, lifestyle, and spiritual ideals should be the characteristics that differentiate Judaism from other peoples—"Judaism should be a Peoplehood." Addressing the rational views held by the educated, he rejected the ideas of the hereafter and of salvation. He proposed individuals be free to practice the Orthodox rituals and customs as they see fit, and when convenient rather than as religious doctrines. He lectured and wrote about the "reconstructed" form of Judaism for twenty years before individual synagogues adopted his principles in 1945. His new prayer book dropped references to Jews being the "Chosen People" and references that gave folklore interpretations to God's miracles. In 1960, Kaplan finally organized the Fellowship of Reconstructionist congregations. Since then, some of the Reconstructionist synagogues have adopted traditional Judaic religious practices.

6
National Communal Organizations

In the past century, Jewish people around the world never had a respite from political, economic, and religious problems. Helping Jews escape from persecution and establishing a Jewish homeland in Palestine were additional dimensions to the concerns and needs Jews faced. American Jews responded to this multitude of problems through the many national communal organizations they developed and supported. These activist organizations often were in the forefront of legal and political battles to win rights for all persecuted and downtrodden people while fighting for Jewish rights.

Agudath Israel of America

Founded in 1922, it is the nation's largest grass-roots Orthodox coalition in the United States. It has a large rabbinical membership who provide community-wide Torah-learning leadership. Its legal department is an advocate of the Orthodox community in the judicial process, defending the rights of American Jews in the court system. Agudath Israel also provides religious education and communal social services in America and abroad. It is a major voice for the Orthodox community on public issues and in its interaction with the Reform and Conservative leaders on common issues.

American Jewish Committee

Founded in 1906, it consisted of fifteen of the most prominent German-Jewish community leaders and thirty-five representatives from organizations around the country. Its purpose was to "prevent infringement of the civil and religious rights of Jews and to alleviate the consequences of persecution." Its first main effort was to work through the U.S. political process involving pressure on President Taft to obtain more freedom for Jews in Russia. In the 1920s, the American Jewish Committee, with Louis Marshall as chief spokesman, led the battle against Henry Ford's anti-Semitic activities. It was originally anti-Zionist, but became supportive of efforts to allow Jews into Palestine before the start of World War II. The committee concentrated on reacting to Nazi activities affecting Jews.

American Jewish Congress

Under the stimulus of Louis Brandeis before he became a Supreme Court justice and the leadership of Rabbi Stephen S. Wise, this umbrella organization of mostly Zionist-leaning groups was established to address the forthcoming World War I peace process with a unified Jewish position. Dissolved after the Paris Peace Conference, the American Jewish Congress was resurrected in 1922 by Rabbi Wise, who fought to have an organization with a democratically selected group of representatives as opposed to the American Jewish Committee, which self-appointed its membership. Civil rights for all Americans became the new agenda. The congress got involved in issues of anti-Semitism, black civil rights, employment discrimination, and church-state relationships. It publicly led a strong Jewish stance against Germany before the Nazi genocide began. However it was ineffective in convincing President Roosevelt to aid the Jews being persecuted by Germany. The American Jewish Congress was a strong voice in the American Zionist movement.

Anti-Defamation League

The Anti-Defamation League (ADL) was established by the B'nai B'rith in 1913 "to protect the good name of the Jewish people." Since its beginning, the ADL has been involved in fighting anti-Semitism in this country. In the 1930s, ADL was the major organization countering the negative view of Jewish-Americans painted by the many anti-Semitic organizations that were active at that time. The ADL lectures around the country also served to bolster the spirits of the Jewish people. ADL fought the economic bias against Jews in the business and professional fields, and opposed the restrictive access of Jews to resort hotels and country clubs.

Perhaps its most important contributions are the reports and assessments of the many anti-Semitic situations and events that have occurred in this country over the past eighty-five years.

B'nai B'rith

Established in 1843 as a Jewish social and benevolent society, the B'nai B'rith changed its scope as it grew. The educated and experienced members intended to pass their wisdom on to the newer immigrant members in order to help improve the image and acceptability of Jews in America. The early German-Jewish leadership of the B'nai B'rith opposed the East European Jewish immigration and was anti-Zionist. In the mid-1930s when the membership became heavily East European, the policies changed to pro-Zionist. B'nai B'rith lobbied for increased immigration laws, and before the start of the Holocaust, for the right of Jews to enter Palestine. In 1939, President Henry Monsky vigorously condemned the British White Paper that kept Jews escaping Hitler's Europe from entering Palestine. President Philip Klutznick became the chief American Jewish spokesman supporting the State of Israel during the hectic days of the Sinai War when the U.S. government had a pro-Arab tilt and President Eisenhower threatened unfair sanctions against Israel. In 1951, the Israeli government came out with its first bond drive at the same time as a massive UJA fund drive, making it difficult to sell. B'nai B'rith's multi-million-dollar purchase of Israeli bonds then encouraged many other institutions to buy bonds, making the bond program a success that year and in the future.

In 1925, B'nai Brith established the Hillel program, which, through its Judaic-oriented programs, would help keep Jewish college students tied to Judaism and provide an opportunity for Jews to meet on campus. There are currently over 125 Hillel foundations in the United States, Canada, and Israel that provide this environment. Hillel has undertaken a new initiative to encourage Jewish college students to become involved in community social action programs as a fulfillment of the Judaic mission of improving the world through justice and righteousness.

Hadassah

The remarkable Henrietta Szold founded Hadassah in 1912 as a women's Zionist organization dedicated to providing high-quality health care to Palestinian Jews. It operated as a nonpolitical organization that accomplished its goals through undertaking specific medical missions in Palestine that included providing health care to the Palestinian Arabs as well. At sixty, Henrietta Szold went to Palestine in 1920 and remained there until her death twenty-five years later, personally directing the Hadassah-funded medical activities and serving as the president of Hadassah. The Hadassah Hospital on Mount Scopus in Jerusalem, opened in 1938, became the premier hospital in the Middle East providing expert health care to Palestinian Jews and Arabs alike, and to underdeveloped countries that lacked adequate medical facilities.

In 1940, when the Holocaust began, Hadassah joined the pro-Zionists in pressing the United States and the other free countries of the world to aid the escapees from the German terror. Hadassah President Szold was an advocate of a Palestinian binational state during the early Israel-statehood UN deliberations. Hadassah has been a vigorous supporter of the State of Israel since it was established in 1948.

With 300,000 members, it is the largest Zionist organization and the largest Jewish woman's organization in the United States today. Hadassah continues to serve the health needs in Israel. The Hadassah Medical Organization operates two Hadassah hospitals and supports five medical schools in conjunction with the Hebrew University.

Hadassah has expanded its goals. It is striving to meet the challenge of continuing Jewish identity and to improve the health, safety, and education in the United States, Israel, and throughout the world by taking actions (empowered by Jewish women) to improve these causes that reflect the best of Jewish values.

Jewish War Veterans of America (JWV)

Jewish Civil War veterans organized the JWV in 1896 to foster recognition of the role Jews played in the American wars. Membership increased significantly after each of the two World Wars, making JWV a respected voice on issues affecting veterans and the Jewish community in general. In 1933, the JWV was one of only two major Jewish organizations to endorse the Non-Sectarian Anti-Nazi League's counterboycott of Hitler's boycott of Jewish businesses in Germany. In March 1948, the United States UN delegate Warren Austin announced that the United States was backing away from the Palestine partition plan that had been passed by the United Nations in November. A massive Jewish community protest to President Truman was initiated by the JWV, which paraded 150,000 members down Fifth Avenue in New York City. From the JWV ranks came pilots and military specialists who volunteered to fight with the Israeli armed forces in the 1948–49 War for Independence, making a significant addition to the Israeli fighting capability.

Joint Distribution Committee (JDC)

The large number of Jews who had emigrated from eastern Europe were distressed by the impact World War I was having on their families in their original homelands. The severe fighting on the eastern front left many Jews killed and the area economically devastated. In response, the American Jewish community established the Joint Distribution Committee in 1914 to provide emergency relief to the area; almost three-quarter million Jews in Poland and the Baltic countries relied on the J.D.C. for survival. The formation of the J.D.C. established the precedence for American Jewry taking on the responsibility for the welfare of unfortunate Jews throughout the world. After the war ended, the J.D.C. supported Jews in the European communities ravaged by the war and the postwar anti-Semitic riots. Sixteen million dollars was raised in the United States during the war, and $27 million was raised in the first two years after the war ended to support the J.D.C. relief efforts.

The J.D.C. repeated this massive relief effort after the end of the Holocaust. In 1946, under the leadership of Dr. Joseph Schwartz, the J.D.C. administered the privately funded the "*Jewish Marshall Plan.*" The plan provided meals and clothing and operated secular kindergartens and higher level schools in the Displaced Persons camps in Germany, Austria, and France. In addition, the J.D.C. operated many facilities that supported the Jewish communities in Eastern Europe such as canteens, clothing warehouses, and clinics. All this was funded by a $100 million dollar United Jewish Appeal in 1946.

Kulanu ("All-of-Us")

This is a relatively new organization dedicated to finding and aiding lost Jewish communities around the world. They report on Crypto-Jews in the American Southwest, Marrano Jews in Brazil and Peru and Africans with Jewish heritage in Ethiopia (Falashas), Uganda, Mali, and South Africa, and the "lost tribe" communities in India (Bene Israel, Cochin Jews).

National Council of Jewish Women

Hannah Solomon organized the National Council of Women in 1896. Its aim was to unite women interested in the work of religion, philanthropy, and education. The council has organized and encouraged the study of the principles of Judaism, the history, literature, and customs of Jews, and their bearing on world history. Studies were conducted under their auspices to improve Sabbath schools and social reform work. In the early days of the council, when persecution of Jews in the United States was prevalent, the council strove to secure the interest and aid of influential persons to prevent persecutions.

North American Conference on Ethiopian Jews (NACOEJ)

NACOEJ has been deeply involved in the various campaigns and arrangements to relocate the Ethiopian Jews to Israel. They provide aid to the small number of Jews remaining in Ethiopia and provide political representation for the Ethiopian community in Israel to aid in their conversion process, and to receive improved education and government benefits.

Organization for Rehabilitation Through Training (ORT)

ORT is a Jewish movement organized to promote social and economic change affecting Jewish people in all parts of the world. This international organization, established in Russia in 1886, has a large U.S. support organization. ORT is dedicated to helping Jews whose economic life has been disrupted by political conditions. It establishes a network of trade schools and agricultural training schools in the countries where the help is needed. Jews in Poland, Lithuania, and Romania left destitute at the end of World War I were the initial recipients of U.S. ORT aid. From 1924–1938, to aid Jews whose livelihood was destroyed by communism in the Soviet Union, ORT helped Jews build hundreds of farming communities in the Ukraine and Crimea. These were destroyed by the Germans after they quickly advanced into the Soviet Union in 1941. More recently, ORT training projects have been conducted in Israel for newcomers from underdeveloped countries.

Simon Wiesenthal Center

This center is named after the Nazi hunter Simon Wiesenthal. Organized by Rabbi Marvin Hier in 1977, it is devoted to fighting anti-Semitism and bigotry around the world. It is currently active in the actions to get Holocaust survivors restitution for the assets seized from Jews by the Nazis and held in Swiss banks. The Simon Wiesenthal Center also conducts interracial conferences to explore ways of reducing hate crimes and improving intergroup relations.

United Jewish Appeal (UJA)

The United Jewish Appeal was organized between several Zionist and non-Zionist organizations in 1934 as a coordinated way of raising funds to support both the American Jewish community and the Jewish national home. It is the major Jewish Federation organization in the large cities. UJA raises funds annually that are distributed to local Jewish communal organizations and to the State of Israel for humanitarian applications. In the year 2000, the United Jewish Appeal name was changed to the Jewish Federation to indicate a closer association with local charitable and other community service organizations than with overseas special mission funding.

World Jewish Congress

In 1936, after the American Jewish Congress, the American Jewish Committee, and the B'nai B'rith turned down his appeal to join in an effort to combat international anti-Semitism, Rabbi Stephen S. Wise organized the World Jewish Congress. It linked organized Jewish communities in several countries to present an international front to address anti-Semitic incidents worldwide. In 1942, the WJC Geneva representative presented to Rabbi Wise and to the U.S. government the first corroborated details of the Final Solution (Nazi plan for the extermination of the European Jews) in process. More recently, WJC President Edgar Bronfman led the effort to get the Swiss government to do justice to Holocaust survivors with respect to the assets in the Swiss banks left over from the Holocaust period.

7
Zionism in the United States

The American Zionist movement developed very slowly before it played the significant role in the creation of the State of Israel. The early Zionist movement that existed in Europe between 1880 and 1900 found very few Jewish supporters. Theodor Herzl's invigoration of the Zionist movement in 1901 had little impact on American Jews. There were few American attendees at the eleven Zionist congresses held in major cities in Europe between 1897 and 1913. The Orthodox rejected Zionism because it was too secular. The socialist Jews saw little value in Zionism to the worker movement. The Reform Jewish leaders vociferously opposed Zionism. They saw it as threatening the gains Jews made in the United States, and they objected to what they perceived to be the Zionist requirement that all Jews live in Israel.

Many Zionist organizations were organized that had different perspectives on what they preferred the future national home to offer. It included religious Zionists pushing for an Orthodox religious state, labor Zionists stressing a socialistic worker-dominated country, and general Zionists with no fixed agenda. It also included a revisionist Zionist movement that was pressing for action by the Jews in Palestine, violent if necessary, to bypass the slow political process. The largest general Zionist group was the Zionist Organization of America, which was an amalgamation of several smaller groups.

Hardships the Jews in East Europe suffered during and after World War I stimulated the initial growth of the American Zionist movement. The need for Jews in America to react to the Nazi anti-Jewish actions in the 1930s, the horrors of the Holocaust, and the world indifference to the plight of the survivors aroused the American Jews to join the Zionist movement in larger numbers. The movement peaked in the period when the State of Israel was being established, with the membership of Zionist-affiliated organizations reaching almost one million.

With the State of Israel now in existence for fifty years, the impetus for the Zionist movement of creating a Jewish national homeland is gone. The mature State of Israel is now anxious to conduct its foreign affairs without external influences, including World Zionist organizations—this Israeli coolness to the World Zionist organizations has contributed to reduced Zionist affiliations. The absence of major Israeli security issues that previously aroused the concern of American Jewry and competition between internal U.S. needs and Israeli needs for philanthropic funds are other factors that have contributed to a diminished enthusiasm for Zionism.

Although the American Zionist movement has lessened, the majority of the Jewish people remain ready to support the State of Israel because it represents the "haven" for the Jewish people around the world. How to proceed with the Israeli-Arab peace process in the context of protecting Israeli security is as much a divisive issue among American Jews as for the Israelis. Conservative and Reform movement objections to the restrictive Orthodox religious rulings that prevail in Israel represents a challenge to them for achieving internal change within Israel. However, none of these issues present a reason for breaking their link to Zion.

Brandeis Stimulates American Zionism—Louis Brandeis became the first American Jewish leader to embrace Zionism. From a background devoid of contact with Judaism, he developed an understanding of the Jewish people's problems when he helped negotiate the garment industry strike in 1910, and after interacting with several prominent European Zionists. He induced prominent and wealthy Jews to support Zionism by assuring them it would not affect their loyalty to this country and by giving them the opportunity to contribute philanthropically to the poor in Palestine. He recruited Rabbi Stephen Wise to join him. The two became the powerful coleaders of the American Zionist movement until Brandeis bowed out after becoming a Supreme Court justice. Brandeis and Wise were instrumental in convincing President Wilson to support the British Balfour Declaration that endorsed a Jewish national home in Palestine.

Brandeis's motto was: **"To be good Americans, we must be better Jews, and to be better Jews, we must become Zionists."** The small American Zionist movement grew thirteenfold in five years thanks to his inspiration and recruiting efforts.

Rabbi Stephen S. Wise: Zionist Advocate—In the early twentieth century, Rabbi Wise became the leading Reform rabbi who influenced the German-Jewish Reform community to accept Zionism and more social activism, including being more sympathetic to the problems of the east European Jews. He was intensely involved in the American political process, fighting for U.S. government support of the Zionist positions regarding the many critical events confronting the Jewish world community—Rabbi Wise had access to Presidents Wilson and Roosevelt. Rabbi Wise was the spokesman for the American Jewish Congress, which was the leading U.S. Zionist organization protesting Germany's anti-Semitic policies in the 1930s.

Rabbi Abba Hillel Silver: Militant Zionist Orator—At Zionist conferences held towards the end of World War II, Jewish leaders were planning for the Holocaust survivor needs that would be required when Hitler was defeated. At these conferences, Rabbi Silver was the strongest advocate of an independent Jewish commonwealth as the only guarantee of free immigration. Rabbi Silver replaced Rabbi Wise as the leading Zionist spokesman. He was appointed the chairman of the American unit of the Jewish Agency that represented the Palestinian Jews in negotiations regarding Palestine and refugees. He became a fiery preacher of Zionism from his Cleveland pulpit and around the nation, being an advocate of militant political action to achieve Zionist goals.

In 1945, there were 100,000 Jews cramped in squalor DP camps who were anxious to get to Palestine. Under Foreign Minister Ernest Bevin's decision to ignore the Balfour Declaration, the British government would allow only two thousand entry permits a month. It was his strategy for placating the Arabs in order to get connections for their oil. Rabbi Silver became the contact with President Truman to put pressure on the British to change their stance. In 1948, he led the campaign to put pressure on President Truman to end the arms embargo on the new Israeli government. Unfortunately, neither effort succeeded.

American Council for Judaism: Anti-Zionist Movement—This 16,000-member organization was started by a small group of Reform rabbis who objected to the Reform rabbinical organization adopting a pro-Zionist position. With Rabbi Elmer Berger as its director, it conducted a well-advertised campaign against establishing a Jewish state, and expressed this view at State Department and congressional hearings. The council, whose membership included well-respected Reform rabbis and high-stature individuals, was the most influential anti-Zionist organization during the governmental discussions of what type of Palestinian state the United States should endorse after the British Palestine mandate was to end. Its membership and influence decreased sharply two years after the

State of Israel was established, and the council went out of existence after the Israeli Six-Day War.

8
Support of the Creation of the State of Israel

The full knowledge of the horrible, unbelievable Nazi treatment of the European Jewish community shocked the American Jewish community when they learned about this as the war with Germany was about to end. For the next few years, the immediate concern was helping the half-million desperate survivors stranded in the "Displaced Persons" (DP) camps recover from their ordeal and rebuild their lives. Finding a refuge for these homeless DPs was essential. To achieve this goal, the American Jewish community at large addressed the issue of opening up Palestine to these survivors. They pressed for the establishment of a Jewish State in Palestine as the implementation of the Balfour Declaration in the United Nations. After much consideration, the United Nations approved a Palestine partition plan, but then considered rescinding the plan after rioting broke out in Palestine in conjunction with the Arab rejection of partition. The American Jewish community devoted its energy along with many sympathetic non-Jews to lobby at the United Nations and with the American government to support the Zionist goals.

United Nations Deliberations—In 1947, United Nations deliberated what to do when the British mandate over Palestine ended. The partitioning of Palestine into a Jewish state and an Arab Palestinian state was one of several considerations. Although the territory to be under Israel's jurisdiction was rather small and did not include Jerusalem, the Palestinian Jewish leaders and the American Zionist organizations favored the Palestine partition plan alternative while the pro-Arab U.S. State Department favored a UN Trusteeship. White House liaison official David Niles, who had Zionist inclinations, informed President Truman of the maneuvering of the State Department officials, which he considered detrimental to Truman's policy and prestige. He convinced Truman to override his State Department and approve the partition plan.

It took frantic lobbying of many Jews to convince several of the countries that were initially inclined to reject partition to change their vote.

Niles called a friend Tom Papas who in turn called Twentieth Century-Fox President Spyros Skousa, but he was unsuccessful in persuading the Greek prime minister to change his vote. Justice Frankfurter, alerted by Niles, recruited his fellow Justice Frank Murphy to jointly call on the Philippine ambassador. This call, together with a cable from ten senators to the Philippine president, was successful. Niles and Robert Nathan, a former New Deal lawyer, persuaded former Secretary of State Edward Stettinius, Jr. to contact the president of Liberia, who changed his vote. Alerted by Jewish Agency liaison Nahum Goldman, former Assistant Secretary of State Adolf Berle cabled the Haiti president, changing Haiti's vote. The partition plan passed in November. The two states were to come into existence in August 1948, two weeks after the mandate was scheduled to end.

U.S. Recognition of the State of Israel—The Palestinians, who rejected the plan, started to battle the Israelis after the partition plan was approved. The severity of the fighting gave the U.S. State Department Arabists an opportunity to undo the partition plan. It led to several months of political maneuvering between the State Department officials and Truman's staff supporting partition, each trying to win Truman's approval.

In an effort to swing President Truman to the Zionist position, Truman's former Kansas City haberdashery business partner Edward Jacobson was brought in to use his influence. In 1946, Jacobson had arranged for the eloquent Rabbi Arthur Lelyveld to brief Truman on the importance of Palestine to the Jewish people. This time in March 1948, Jacobson met directly with Truman and persuaded him to meet with Chaim Weizmann. Truman and Weizmann had a cordial meeting, ending with no promises being made beyond Truman's commitment to continue support of the partition plan. The meeting established a mutual trust between the two, with Truman easing his anti-Zionist stance that was triggered by recent Zionist aggressive lobbying that antagonized him.

President Truman had a meeting with Chaim Weizmann at which he expressed support for the United Nations Partition Plan. To President Truman's surprise, shortly after the meeting, UN Ambassador Warren Austin delivered a speech to the UN Security Council expressing the United States's recommendation that in view of the violence in Palestine, the partition plan be shelved in favor of a temporary UN trusteeship. The public reacted with outrage. UN Secretary General Trygve Lie and American delegate Eleanor Roosevelt threatened to resign. It made Truman feel like he lied and double-crossed Weizmann. Truman sent Weizmann a note explaining that when they had met, he was not aware of what Ambassador

Austin was going to say. Truman appreciated Weizmann's public response that he believed Truman. The rest of the Zionist community and its sympathizers were outraged about the UN speech, which represented a grave defeat for Zionism. Protest parades were held, and Truman was deluged with hundreds of thousands of letters and telegrams.

The Jewish Palestinian leaders took a more positive proactive stance. The Jewish Agency in Jerusalem announced it would establish a provisional government three weeks later, on May 15, 1948, the date the British had announced for their advanced departure from Palestine. The Israeli main concern was whether the United States would recognize the new Jewish State when its independence was proclaimed. Weizmann and Truman's former special counsel Samuel Rosenman met to discuss a strategy for achieving U.S. support. This was unnecessary, Truman had made up his own mind without further encouragement. When Truman approached Rosenman on the subject, Truman confidentially advised Rosenman that out of respect for Weizmann's wishes, if a Jewish state was declared, he would recognize it.

On May 2, the State Department initiated a new effort to delay Jewish statehood by offering a cease-fire in Palestine and U.S.-supported peace talks in Palestine. It tempted many of the Zionist leaders, but Chaim Weizmann, who insisted that the Jewish state be declared without delay rejected it. The State Department did not give up their fight. They warned of the danger of an Arab victory, they warned of the consequences of an Arab oil embargo, and they warned about the uncertainty of the Israeli State's behavior towards the United States. Truman kept his intentions quiet.

On May 12, Niles and Clark Clifford, who was President Truman's new special counsel and extremely helpful to the Zionist cause, met with Secretary of State George Marshall and Undersecretary Lovett to thrash out the government's position. Clifford argued in favor of recognition of the Jewish state, Marshall violently objected. There was no resolution. Clifford and Marshall then met directly with President Truman—again no resolution.

Early on May 15, Clifford first inquired of the Jewish Agency whether they intended to proceed and what boundaries they were declaring. Receiving the answer, Clifford drafted the formal United States approval of the new Jewish State; Truman had accepted Clifford's position and rejected Marshall's. He expressed the view that the Jewish people had suffered so much under Hitler and needed a place to go to. The declaration of the State of Israel was announced at 6:00 P.M. The official White House recognition was announced at 6:11 P.M.

9
Political Support to the Soviet Jews

Since the Communist revolution, there was a stringent repression of the Jewish religion and customs in the Soviet Union. The Communists wanted the Jews to assimilate and most Jews did. Nevertheless, the Jewish community and its religious and intellectual leaders were under constant attack. At the time of Stalin's death in 1953, out of the thousands that existed before the revolution, there were 400 synagogues remaining in all of the Soviet Union; ten years later only 100 remained. The Jewish people had lost their identity with their religion and their heritage, except for the "Jew" nationality tag on their identity card. The repression, at a peak under Stalin, continued under his successors. In spite of the near-total assimilation, the Soviet rulers did not extend the human rights to the Soviet Jews that other ethnic groups received. Jews were removed from government positions and were restricted from many job categories. Emigration requests were not merely denied. They were accompanied by trumped-up disloyalty charges that resulted in prison and labor camp sentences. With all this repression, there was no noticeable objection to this denial of human rights raised in the United States by the Jewish community. Their efforts were concentrated on supporting the State of Israel which went through one crisis after another.

Reaction to Soviet Repression—The first world reaction to this denial of human rights to Jews in the Soviet Union came in 1960. A group of fifty scholars, writers, and academicians met in Paris to express their concern about the plight of the Soviet Jews. It included world-renowned individuals respected for their concerns about denial of liberties to subjugated people around the world, such as Martin Buber, Bertrand Russell, Albert Schweitzer, and Reinhold Niebuhr. The Soviets were not moved; the repression of rights and the denial of exit permits continued.

In the United States, the first reaction to the Jewish oppression situation in the Soviet Union came in 1962 when the Agudath Israel organization voiced its concern over the harsh treatment of the Soviet Orthodox

Jews, who by now represented a very small number of Soviet Jews. A major reaction to the plight of the Soviet Jews developed at the "Conference on the Status of Soviet Jews" in October 1963. Cosponsored by Reverend Martin Luther King and Supreme Court Justice William O. Douglas, this nonsectarian meeting was effective in exposing the plight of the Soviet Jews to the American public. It ended with a strong appeal for follow-up action. It led to the American Jewish Conference on Soviet Jewry in early 1964, at which follow-up actions and funding plans were coordinated among the participating organizations that included the American Jewish Congress, the American Jewish Committee, the B'nai B'rith, and many other smaller organizations. The National Conference on Soviet Jewry was formed; it became the main American organization to publicize the cause of Soviet Jews.

The publicity about the treatment of Soviet Jews aroused a group of Jews who previously had little interest in Jewish affairs. In April 1964, a group of Jewish students met at Columbia University to protest the treatment of the Soviet Jews and held a silent march to the Soviet Mission to the United Nations. It was the start of the Student Struggle for Soviet Jewry, an organization that campaigned for rights for Soviet Jews over the next twenty years.

In reaction to the active protests against the government's rejection of emigration requests, the Soviet announced stiffer laws against protest demonstrations, strikes, subversive writings, and slander against the Soviet Union. Many refuseniks (name given to Jews who refused to accept the Soviet position against emigration to Israel and the harassment that accompanied the Soviet policy) were arrested under this law. When other Jews protested, they were arrested for slandering the Soviet Union. The American Jewish community was aroused by the Soviet edicts and the penalties imposed on the refuseniks. In 1966, the National Conference on Soviet Jews organized rallies protesting the Soviet suppression of spiritual and cultural rights of Jews. The Zionist Organization of America and various rabbinical councils joined in the protests. Twenty-two American writers, including six Pulitzer Prize winners, urged Soviet writers to use their influence in restoring Jewish institutions in Russia.

The Soviets reacted with denials that these oppressive conditions existed. In October, Hadassah President Marion Jacobson visited the Soviet Union for a first-hand view and reported that conditions were bad and that the Jewish cultural and religious life was weakened despite efforts to preserve them. Responding to the protests, at the end of the year, Soviet Prime

Minister Alexei Kosygin announced that Jews who submitted exit applications would be permitted to join their families in Israel.

The joy of the announcement was short-lived. In the aftermath of the Israeli Six Day War of 1967, the Soviets, who were shocked by the Arabs loss in spite of the massive arms provided by the Soviets, cut off emigration rights; in all of 1969, only 3,000 were allowed to leave compared to 24,000 the year before. The Jews in Russia were energized by the Israeli victory; Jewish nationalism exploded, the Zionist network in Russia expanded, and the emigrationist movement grew. In 1969, thirteen Jews planned to hijack a plane in Leningrad, fly to Sweden, and continue on to Israel. They were intercepted before takeoff and brought to trial. When the Soviets sentenced two of the Jewish hijackers to death for treason, the American and Israeli Jewish communities rose in protest. The National Conference on Soviet Jewry launched a massive campaign to free them and to allow Jews to have the right to leave the Soviet Union. Congress was persuaded to sponsor a joint resolution denouncing the verdict and requesting mercy. The Israeli Liaison Office convinced twenty-four governments to send diplomatic requests for easing the penalty. The pressures succeeded; the Soviets commuted the death sentences to life imprisonment and reduced the sentences of the other hijackers.

The protests against the Soviet treatment of the Jews expanded in the summer of 1971. Rallies were held with slogans like "*Let My People Go*" and "*Save Soviet Jewry.*" A candlelight vigil was initiated outside the Russian embassy in Washington, D.C. and consulates around the country that lasted for several years. Thousands of Soviet Jews applied for visas; many were highly educated, intellectual Jews. This once privileged class of educated Jews was now frozen out of government positions and universities. They rose in protest against the ban on emigration. The Soviets responded by relaxing the ban on emigration, but then they levied a crippling exit tax, requiring emigrants to pay for receiving their college education.

Jackson-Vanik Amendment to the East-West Trade Pact—The crippling "diploma tax" caused the Jewish community's effort on behalf of the Soviet Jews to turn to the political arena. Two Jews, Richard Perle and Morris Amitay, triggered a push among senators to link freedom of emigration of Soviet Jews to trade relations between the United States and the Soviet Union. It was an effort that took two and one half years to accomplish. Democratic Senator Henry Jackson, who proposed this arrangement as an amendment to the pending Soviet-American trade bill, took it up. Jackson skillfully got Republican President Nixon's agreement and started to push the amendment through the senate. Jackson got Congressman Charles Vanik to cosponsor the amendment in the House of Representatives. It took another year of intensive lobbying to get the amendment passed in spite of the Russian attempt to get it scuttled by eliminating the diploma tax and offering to increase the number of exit visas.

With these two Soviet actions, President Nixon took on a campaign to drop the proposed amendment. Under Nixon's encouragement, two leading Republican Jews, Jacob Stein and Max Fisher, attempted to persuade the Jewish Presidents Conference to drop their support of the amendment. In addition to counterarguments raised at the conference, a letter from one hundred leading activists in Moscow urging continued support of the amendment convinced everyone at the conference, including Stein and Fisher, to renew their support of the amendment.

In May of 1973, Soviet Premier Brezhnev convinced the U.S. National Security Advisor Henry Kissinger to drop the proposed amendment by offering to allow emigration to continue at the rate of forty thousand a year. Brezhnev also reminded Kissinger that significant restrictions on emigration had already been dropped. The offer broke the uniformity of support for the amendment within the Jewish leadership. However, the majority of the Jewish community decided that they could not fail their European brethren this time as they did in the thirties, and they continued to urge passage of the amendment. Senator Jackson and the other congressional amendment supporters held firm.

The next attempt to scuttle the amendment came in conjunction with the Yom Kippur War in October 1973. Secretary of State Henry Kissinger tried to get the Jewish community and Congress to show their appreciation for President Nixon's granting 2.2 billion dollars to rebuild Israel's defense forces. Congress did not go along, prompting more bargaining between Congress, Nixon, and the Soviets. After President Nixon resigned in August 1974, President Ford and Congress came to terms and the amendment passed in January 1975. The results were mixed. For the first several years, between 25,000 and 50,000 exit permits were issued annually. Starting in 1980, the number was progressively reduced, going below 1,500 for five years.

Immigration to the United States—In the late 1970s, Soviet Jews started to show a preference for immigrating to the United States rather than to Israel. This resulted in clashes between Israel and American Jews, and within the American Jewish community itself, as to where Russian

Jewish immigrants should be directed. In the 1980s, more Russian Jews settled in the United States than in Israel.

10
Bigotry Against Jews in the U.S.

The fundamental reason that Jews left Europe for America was to escape the persecution and anti-Semitism that haunted them from the past and that kept resurfacing in their own lifetime. Indeed, the United States fulfilled their hopes, providing a home free of religious persecution and government-sanctioned anti-Semitism. Throughout the existence of this country, the Jewish people have expressed their appreciation for this hospitable environment by helping to defend the country in time of war and helping to make it a better place for all Americans in times of peace.

Life for the Jewish people in the United States, however, was not exactly free of anti-Semitic bigotry. Until several decades ago, Jews were exposed to various forms of bigotry and hate bias. It was particularly bad during the latter part of the nineteenth century and the first half of the twentieth century. This bigotry was painful to many individual Jews economically and psychologically, but it did not stop the Jewish people as a group from fully integrating into American society. With so little bigotry against Jews in today's society, this almost-forgotten, uncomfortable aspect of life for many Jews in America is difficult for younger Jews to imagine.

Nineteenth-Century Bigotry—Small in number and concentrated in a few northern cities during this period, Jews were disliked by many Christians who never actually met a Jewish person. This antagonism stemmed from the old Christian religious teachings that the Jews were the killers of Jesus Christ. This religious-driven hatred of Jews was particularly strong in the South. The Southerner's distaste of all Northerners strengthened their feelings—to them, a Northeast Jew was the worst kind of person. This intolerance did not extend to the Jews who lived in the South, where Jews lived mostly in harmony with their Gentile neighbors.

This personal anti-Semitism generally did not interfere with the Jewish immigrant's ability to share in the growth of America. Jews freely migrated to all corners of the United States without being exposed to organized anti-Semitic prejudice. Jewish-owned enterprises, including many department stores sprung up in most major cities, helping the country's economic development. Jews freely participated in the opening of the West in almost every capacity. Some small western towns were even organized by Jews, and named after them.

The existing underlying bigotry periodically surfaced under different circumstances. Some mid-century presidential candidates resorted to the age-old anti-Semitic practice of accusing Jews of being responsible for the country's ills (although Jews had so little influence on economic or political issues) and denigrated their opponents for having Jewish associates. Southern Jews actively supported the Southern cause in the Civil War, with a high percentage of the Jewish population fighting with the Confederate army. This did not stop bigoted accusations of disloyalty against Jewish merchants appearing in leading Southern newspapers. When the Civil War was being lost, the leading Jewish Confederate official became a scapegoat for many people in the South. Anti-Jewish bigotry also surfaced in the North during the war. Although Jews played an active role in the Union army, Jewish soldiers suffered harassment. General Grant issued a bigoted expulsion order applying only to Jews. Wealthy Northern Jews who were members of the Democratic party (that had favored the Southern position in the Lincoln election) were singled out for unjust accusations of disloyalty to the Northern cause.

Bigotry Against Judah Benjamin—In 1852, Judah P. Benjamin from Louisiana was the first Jew to be elected to the United States Senate. Because of his very effective career in the Senate, when the Civil War erupted, Benjamin was asked to join the Confederate president's cabinet. He served as attorney general, secretary of war, and secretary of state. President Davis credited Benjamin with making major contributions to the early successes of the Confederacy. When the Civil War started to go badly for the South, many Southerners found "Benjamin the Jew" a convenient scapegoat, viciously attacking him in hate-monger terms for being the cause of the South's problems.

Northerners also found Benjamin a convenient scapegoat. Of all the Confederate leaders, they selectively picked on Benjamin, denouncing him for his "Jewishness" in supporting the Confederate cause. Earlier as a senator, Vice-President Andrew Johnson had denigrated his fellow senator, Judah Benjamin, in anti-Semitic tones (using the same anti-Semitic diatribes against another senator who had long-before converted to Christianity). Because of this background of anti-Semitic hatred against him, when the war ended, Judah Benjamin felt that he had to flee the country in order to save his life—the only Confederate official who feared for his life when the war ended.

General Grant's Bigotry—In the winter of 1862, there were many black marketers in cotton that were interfering with the Union army's efforts to defeat the Confederate army in the greater Tennessee Valley area. Although Jewish traders represented a small number of those involved in this traffic, General Grant first issued an edict that "required all cotton speculators, Jews, and other vagrants having no honest means of support to leave the area under control of the Tennessee military government within twenty-four hours." Shortly afterwards, Grant changed it to an army order that "Jews as a class were expelled from the Tennessee military area within twenty-four hours of receiving the edict," dropping any reference to the others covered in the original edict. Approximately 2,500 Jewish families living in an area that covered Tennessee, Mississippi, and Kentucky were uprooted, irrespective of whether they were involved in the cotton trade or how long they lived there.

Northern Jewish communal leaders reacting quickly to this cruel, bigoted edict that applied only to Jews, convinced President Lincoln to revoke the order. General Grant's bigotry was denounced in many newspapers, but many others attacked the Jews as Copperheads (a slur for Northerners who sympathized with the south) for slandering General Grant. This issue carried over to the 1868 presidential election. The Democratic party strongly urged the Jews in the North to abandon the Republican party because of Grant's treatment of the Jews during the Civil War, which they did not do. After the election, the Jewish leaders dropped their animosity to President Grant, and he in turn, as president, became responsive to Jewish sensitivities.

Twentieth-Century Bigotry—In the last half of the nineteenth century and in the first part of the twentieth century, Jewish immigration increased significantly. They crowded into large city Jewish "ghetto" areas. Jews suffered personal attacks and property desecration due to white ethnic intolerance in the predominately poor slum areas of the large northern cities where large numbers of Italian, Irish, and Polish immigrants lived in their respective ghetto enclaves adjacent to the Jewish ghettos. Competition for scarce jobs and Jewish intrusion into work fields those ethnic groups considered their exclusive domain were major factors for the antagonism that arose. Some of the hate bias was also due to the anti-Jewish teachings of the Roman Catholic Church in that period. The threat of power-sharing in cities like New York and Boston added to the antagonism of Irish Catholics towards Jews. Colloquial slurs against all ethnic groups were common. "*Kike*" was the most popular derogatory name for Jews.

Bigotry against the Jews by the white Anglo-Saxon Protestants (WASP) which started in the late nineteenth century became more intense in the early part of the twentieth century. They discriminated against Jews at the social level. Jews were restricted from living in WASP communities through restrictive covenants that excluded Jews and blacks. Jews were excluded from country clubs and civic organizations and prevented from registering in resorts and hotels. This social discrimination had little impact on the Jewish people—with little political strength, Jews accepted this bias.

WASP discrimination against Jews at the business and university level did hurt. Many business fields including industrial, WASP-owned banking, and the legal profession were closed to Jews. Teaching positions at the university level, particularly at the prestigious schools, were nonexistent for Jews. Most colleges and universities had quotas restricting Jewish enrollment. The City College system in New York City was the prime exception. This school had a no-tuition-cost open enrollment policy, admissions were limited to New York City residents who had the highest high school academic grades. It provided a higher education to a large number of the poor Jewish New York City residents who otherwise would not have had a college-level educational opportunity. Many City College Jewish graduates turned out to be well-recognized personalities in the professional and artistic fields. Many of the City College Jewish graduates also went on to join President Roosevelt's New Deal "brain trust."

Bigotry against Jews started to diminish during World War II. The large number of Jewish servicemen who carried their burden and showed their bravery earned the respect of many who never had contact with Jews before but previously had a dislike for Jews out of ignorance. The war effort at home required all the human resources available, so most of the employment discrimination evaporated. After the war ended, Jews shared in the prosperity that followed. The WASP social discrimination evaporated as the WASPs sought to capture the newfound wealth of the Jews who were bypassing the restricted social facilities and residential areas with their own nonrestricted alternatives. The exposure of the Holocaust horrors resulting from Nazi anti-Semitism undoubtedly effected many Christians, arousing their sympathies and changing their attitudes towards Jews. Surprisingly, another factor that helped to end this silent WASP discrimination was a book that exposed to middle America the depth of America's prejudice against Jews. *Gentlemen's Agreement,* Laura Z. Hobson's best-selling book, converted to the 1947 award-winning motion picture starring Gregory Peck, revealed the discrimination that a Gentile family that assumed a Jewish identity faced when working and living in a prestigious restricted Connecticut community.

In the past thirty years, ethnic antagonism against Jews has shifted from the whites to blacks. Two major incidents occurred. During the widespread 1965 urban riots, the destruction of white-owned property was concentrated on Jewish property. In 1991, pogrom-like rioting by blacks against the Jewish Chasidic community occurred in Crown Heights, Brooklyn. A black killed the young Jewish driver of an automobile that accidentally killed a black youth. Three days of rioting by blacks ensued with no intervention by authorities. The friction between blacks and Jews flares up periodically on the college campuses in the form of bitter expression of opposite views, accompanied by bigoted tirades against Jews by anti-Semitic black activists.

The Anti Defamation League started auditing anti-Semitic incidents in the United States since 1980. The total number of vandalism, harassment, threats, and assaults reached a peak in 1994; the 2000 total number of incidents was double the number of incidents when the statistics were first accumulated. Although there have been 150 fewer incidents each year since then, the high level of incidents on the college/university campus remained constant.

Leo Frank: the American Dreyfus Case—In 1913, Leo Frank was accused of murdering the thirteen-year-old Mary Phegan, an employee of the pencil factory in Atlanta Georgia, partially owned by Leo Frank. The Atlanta newspapers joined in inflaming the public against Frank with anti-Semitic remarks. Although there were several witnesses testifying that he was home with his family at the time of the murder, the prosecutor, who spouted anti-Semitic remarks to buttress his contrived case, convinced the jury of Frank's guilt—he was sentenced to be hung. The mob outside the court shouted and rejoiced at the verdict. The American Jewish community became alarmed over the unfairness of the trial and the bigotry that surrounded the incident; they came to Frank's aid. The leading Jewish lawyer, Louis Marshall, took up his case, which went all the way to the Supreme Court, where Frank was denied the right to a new trial. Anti-Jewish sentiment intensified in Georgia over the next two years as the bigoted masses reacted to the Jewish defense of the unjustly accused Leo Frank.

The American Jewish Committee mobilized influential non-Jewish legislators, businessmen, and other community leaders to protest against the death penalty. The Georgia governor was finally persuaded about the prosecutor's irregularities and commuted Frank's sentence. The anti-Semitic frenzy in Atlanta intensified with the commutation. Two months later, a group of twenty-five men, including clergymen, former justices, and the sheriff, broke Frank out of the jail and hung him, an act hailed by Georgia newspapers and public officials as heroic and just. The aftermath of the Frank incident case continued over the next few years. The anti-Jewish sentiment that surrounded the case entered the political scene in the South and spread over many parts of the country. The KKK used its accusation of a Jewish conspiracy in Frank's defense as its rallying cry.

In 1985, the governor of Georgia granted Leo Frank a posthumous pardon after it was determined that previously suppressed evidence showed the murderer to have been a black porter. The governor's investigation was triggered by a man's deathbed confession that he witnessed a man other than Frank carrying Phegan's body. The witness indicated that he did not reveal this information at the trial because he feared the real murderer would kill him.

11
Anti-Semitism in the U.S.

The general population of the United States offered a tolerant atmosphere for the Jewish people from the time of the earliest Jewish immigration. Bigotry toward Jews only existed as anti-Semitism at the personal level. This situation changed with the Leo Frank trial in 1915, when the Ku Klux Klan exploited anti-Jewish sentiment that prevailed in the South over this trial to spout organizational anti-Semitic bigotry. Two individuals who achieved fame because of their personal accomplishments later inflamed organizational bigotry. In the 1920s, Henry Ford spouted anti-Semitic bigotry to his hate-group followers. In the 1930s, Charles Lindbergh spouted his anti-Semitic bigotry. In the 1990s, Minister Louis Farrakhan, with a large Afro-American constituency and a national audience, has been a significant vocal anti-Semite that has affected Black-Jewish relations.

Ku Klux Klan—Taking advantage of the anti-Jewish sentiment that developed during the Leo Frank trial in 1915, the reconstructionist-era Knights of the Ku Klux Klan was reactivated in several Southern states and in Indiana. The focus changed from terrorizing blacks to warning the country about the dangers of Jews and Catholics, who were destroying the country with their immorality and radicalism. By 1925, the Klan membership reached four million, with 75,000 people attending its rallies. The Klan even had its own "One Hundred Percent American Store" in Indianapolis. However, the exposure of the Klan's dishonest bigotry and the increased prosperity of the country combined to lessen the Klan's popularity such that by the end of the decade, its membership was less than 10,000. At the end of the twentieth century, the Klan is still active, spouting anti-Semitism on the World Wide Web.

Henry Ford's Anti-Semitism—In 1920, industrialist Henry Ford surprisingly became a dispenser of anti-Semitic hate literature and a sponsor of nativist hate-groups and rabble-rousers who opposed immigrants. He continued his anti-Jewish posture for many years. Because of his stature as an accomplished industrialist, his attacks on the Jews were most painful to the Jewish community while it influenced many anti-Semites to become hate-group supporters.

In 1920, the *Dearborn Independent* newspaper, owned by Ford and managed by Ford's right-hand cronies, published the "Protocols of the Elders of Zion" as part of an article that attacked the Jewish people. The caption read "The International Jew, the World's Problem." This scurrilous article, first published in Russia in 1904, purported to be the details of the "Elders of Zion" plot to destroy the Aryan world. Even after it was disclosed to be a forgery and a falsehood in 1921, the newspaper continued to write Jew-baiting articles that expanded on the Elders of Zion plot. It was not until Ford felt the pain of the Jewish economic reaction of avoiding the purchase of Ford automobiles did he arrange peace terms with the Jewish community through the American Jewish Committee in 1927.

Hate-Group Anti-Semitism—Hate groups increased in number in the late 1930s such that, according to the Anti-Defamation League, there were twelve hundred by the end of the decade. Jews were blasted over the radio and in newsletters for being communist, un-American, financial conspirators planning to take over the country, and worse. This was at a time before television when radio had an enormous listening audience.

The most popular figure was the political rabble-rouser priest, Charles E. Coughlin. He used a weekly radio address to inflame anti-Semitism. Other national-level anti-Semitic hate-mongers included Gerold B. Winrod with his Defenders of the Christian Faith, William Dudley Pelley with his Silver Shirt movement that emulated Nazism, and the far-rightist General van Horn Mosely who linked Jews to the communist conspiracy that he claimed was preparing to take over the country. As World War II started, two new hate groups joined in, the German-American Bund (American supporters of Germany infused with German agents), and the America First Committee (isolationists opposed to Roosevelt's policy of helping Great Britain). These two groups very actively dispensed anti-Semitism during the depression and up until the United States entered the war. The famous and popular Charles A. Lindbergh joined them. The main effect of these hate groups was to reinforce the nativists ability to block any congressional attempt to change the restrictive immigration laws and bring relief to Jews looking for a haven from Nazi Germany. For the Jews in the United States, the inability to stop the ever-increasing tirades politically took on depressing, ominous tones.

After the United States' entry into World War II, hate groups lost popularity along with the general decline in bigotry toward Jews. For a short period after the war ended, the long-time hate-monger Gerald L. K. Smith did try to capture the support of the old anti-Semites. However, after the war's end, as anti-Semitism in this country began to disappear, this flagrant anti-Semitic movement lost its appeal.

Charles A. Lindbergh: Anti-Semite—Lindbergh and his wife became admirers of Hitler in 1936 after being wined and dined in Berlin. Lindbergh evidently was disillusioned with democracy after his child was abducted and killed in 1932. Before the United States entered the war in 1941, Lindbergh became a forceful speaker for the America First Movement. He accused the Jews of pushing the United States into the war and warned of the danger to the country of the Jews having too much ownership and influence over the press, radio, and government. Most of the thoughtful, important people aligned with the isolationist movement disassociated themselves from Lindbergh's anti-Semitic remarks. However, this American hero's incitant remarks influenced millions of ordinary people. Lindbergh preferred to let Germany win so they could be the protectors against Russian Communism. He was essentially disgraced by his pro-German attitude, which continued after the United States entered the war against Germany.

Anti-Semitism at the Government Level—Anti-Semitism surfaced at the congressional level in the 1940s to 1960s. On the floor of Congress, several congressmen viciously and falsely blamed the Jews for being responsible for the country's economic ills and conducting international banking conspiracies that threatened the United States. They used anti-Semitic conspiracy and all-Jews-are-communists theories to argue against efforts to aid the Jewish refugees from Nazism. Representative John Rankin and Senator Theodore Bilbo were the most notorious. Several congressmen running the late 1940s Hollywood-witch-hunt for communism had an anti-Semitic bias to their probes.

The recently released Oval Office tape recordings made by President Richard Nixon disclosed that anti-Semitic comment and actions even exists at the presidential level. President Nixon used nasty anti-Semitic tones when he referred to his Jewish opponents and planned retaliatory actions in the same context. Historians have documented that other presidents before Nixon expressed dislike of Jews in confidential deliberations.

Anti-Semitism in the 1990s—Bigotry towards Jews continued to decrease in the 1990s. A 1998 Anti-Defamation League poll indicated that the number of Americans who hold strongly anti-Semitic views has dropped from twenty percent to twelve percent since 1992. The

Anti-Defamation League reported that the number of anti-Semitic incidents in the United States dropped from 2,066 in 1994 to 1,571 in 1998. It was as low as 906 in 1986 but progressed higher since then until the peak in 1994.

Hate groups have not gone away, although their impact is diminishing. Many are using the World Wide Web sites to spread their hate. The most notorious active nationwide groups include the Aryan Nations, the neo-Nazi National Alliance, and the White Aryan Resistance. The Ku Klux Klan is still active at the local level in several states.

David Duke, the Louisiana racist politician, is the current most influential white anti-Semitic bigot and hate monger. Minister Louis Farrakhan, black leader of the Nation of Islam, is the major black vocal anti-Semitic bigot with a large national following. The Jewish community is skeptical of his offers to mend relationships with the Jewish people because he has not indicated recognition that his earlier remarks were offensive to the Jewish people and he continues to spout virulent anti-Semitism with outlandish accusations of Jewish responsibility for most of society's ills—for instance, being responsible for the world's AIDS epidemic. Another influential black anti-Semite is Reverend Al Sharpton, a high-visibility black activist in the New York City area who likes to include anti-Semitic rhetoric in his inflammatory remarks against the white community.

12
Contemporary History

Enormous favorable change has taken place in the political and economic environment for the Jewish people in the past fifty years.

Political Change—Whereas Jewish congressmen were previously elected only in districts having a large Jewish population, in the latter half of this century Jews were no longer ostracized from political consideration and were able to compete in the national, state, and local political arenas without prejudices against them. After the 1998 elections, there were eleven Jewish senators and twenty-three Jewish representatives in the House, including several from states with a very insignificant Jewish voting population. There were five Jewish women in Congress, including both senators from California, who were active in promoting social causes for improving conditions in the United States and in continuing the strong U.S.-Israel relationship. Connecticut Senator Joseph Lieberman, a practicing Orthodox Jew, earned the respect of the country by asserting moral leadership during the President Clinton impeachment considerations.

Economic Change—The economic opportunities for the Jewish people in the United States have increased dramatically. Jews are no longer restricted from employment in the large industrial companies, and job opportunities are available to Jews in all fields and areas of the country based on their personal merit. In 1998, twenty-three percent of the Fortune 400 companies had Jews in the capacity of chief operating officer and fifteen percent of the top forty chief executive officers were Jewish.

Release of Holocaust-Victim Swiss Bank Accounts—Many dormant Swiss bank accounts belonged to Jews killed in the Holocaust. Swiss bankers have presented unreasonable obstacles for the release of these bank accounts to descendants of the original account holders. They require death certificates and wills—documentation impossible to obtain for deceased Holocaust victims. The Nazi Germans deposited money in Swiss banks that was obtained by selling gold and other valuables taken from the

Jewish Holocaust victims—these assets also justifiably belong to Holocaust survivors.

Starting in 1996, the World Jewish Congress, aided by U.S. Senator Alfonse D'Amato, took the lead in questioning Swiss banks about these accounts. The Wiesenthal Center conducted an independent research of this subject and filed a class action lawsuit on behalf of Holocaust survivors and victim's families. The Volcker Commission, chaired by Paul Volcker, former chairman of the U.S. Federal Reserve, was created to investigate all aspects of this banking situation that was turning into a scandal for the banks and to recommend a resolution. In 1999, the Swiss banks accepted responsibility for an injustice to the Holocaust victims; the final restitution arrangements are still being worked out.

Compensation of World War II Slave Laborers—Almost two million people were forced to work as slave laborers for German industry and the German war machine during World War II. A class-action suit was pressed by several Jewish organizations and the United States government. At the end of 1999, the German government finally acknowledged its debt owed to these slave laborers. The German government, under Chancellor Gerhard Schroeder, together with German industry agreed to pay $5.2 billion to the approximately 1.7 million slave laborers, including a large number of elderly Jews still living in Eastern Europe. U.S. Deputy Treasury Secretary Stuart Eizenstat led the U.S. government's participation in the complex negotiations.

The Jonathan Pollard Case—Jonathan Pollard, a former U.S. naval intelligence clerk, was sentenced in 1987 to life imprisonment without parole for spying for Israel. This sentencing has become a contentious issue between many in the American Jewish community and the U.S. government. It also became an issue between the U.S. government and the Israeli government during the Wye negotiations in 1998.

Pollard contended that he felt a loyalty to Israel just as he did to the United States. Those favoring a release of Pollard through a presidential pardon or parole argue that his crime was helping an ally of the United States, and so, the punishment did not fit the crime, particularly in comparison to others guilty of spying for the Soviet Union. They also argue that Pollard pleading guilty after being offered a plea bargain that was less than a life sentence; the prosecutor did not ask for the life sentence.

The U.S. intelligence community argues that Pollard was guilty of more than just spying for Israel, he did great harm to U.S. Intelligence. They contend that he did his spying for money and not for a noble cause of spying for Israel. There is no way of testing the accuracy of his detractors, since there was no trial.

During the Wye peace talks, the Israeli government acknowledged Pollard spied for them and requested that the U.S. government reconsider the case, reminding the U.S. government that Pollard expressed his regret for the spying activity, which was a necessary step for his release. After the U.S. Intelligence community forcefully objected, President Clinton dropped the consideration.

Part IV

Holocaust History (1939–1945)

Six Million Jews Exterminated for Only One Reason—They Were Jews

Preface to Part IV

The Jewish people have a four-thousand-year history marked by many contributions to world society that outlasted the periods of tragedy they suffered throughout the ages. The most recent tragedy is the Holocaust of 1939–1945. It has become an important part of Jewish history. What started out as Nazi Germany's ethnic cleansing of their German-Jewish citizens turned into the **genocide** of the Jewish people. Hitler almost accomplished his goal in Europe. Six million Jews were killed in sixteen countries, or sixty-five percent of the Jewish population. In Poland alone, three million perished, or ninety-two percent of the Polish Jewish population. For this reason, the Holocaust Remembrance Day, *Yom Hashoah,* has been added to the Jewish calendar.

Because of the powerful message of the Holocaust and its impact on the Jewish people, the Holocaust history merited being a separate volume in this book. Although relatively brief, it is a rather comprehensive treatise of the subject—it would require reading several books to acquire the equivalent information.

The volume starts with the 1875–1933 period in Germany to provide an insight into the German culture that allowed the Nazi regime to convert one of the most educated, cultured, and tolerant societies into a brutal one—a German variety of anti-Semitism was always present. It describes the increasingly harsher phases of the German oppression of their Jewish citizens leading to the "Final Solution of the Jewish Problem." German Jews considered themselves German first and Jewish second; they were prepared to remain in Germany despite the oppression. Kristallnacht was the turning point. The synagogue burnings, business destruction, and concentration camp incarcerations alarmed the German Jews to the dangers ahead for them. After this frightful event, half of the German Jewish population fled Germany before the Holocaust began.

The Final Solution, kept secret from the Western free world for two years, was a carefully planned and well-executed German process for the mass extermination of the European Jews. My father's family living in the Ukraine were victims of the Holocaust—all thirty-three relatives perished in his home city, Vladimir Volynsk. Two survivors independently wrote their story of the total destruction of this city, which had been turned into a Jewish death ghetto—140 people survived out of the original 27,000 population. Their story is included to illustrate the total devastation of almost every Jewish community in eastern Europe.

With war's end and the liberation of the concentration camps, one would have expected the Holocaust survivor's lot to improve, aided by a sympathetic world. Unfortunately, these expectations did not materialize. The reader will learn of the survivors' struggles to be rehabilitated and to find refuge away from the European disaster scene, and of their determined effort to enter Palestine, which was officially closed to them by a hostile Great Britain.

Several Holocaust-related subjects were included that I felt would be of interest to many readers. The results of a study of what type of personality had a better chance of survival in the concentration camps and to whom or what the survivors attributed their survival is discussed. The apparent reluctance of the Jewish people to offer resistance during the Holocaust is analyzed and misconceptions regarding the actual resistance offered is explained. The efforts of some leaders of European countries and individual gentiles to save Jewish lives are discussed, illustrating that there were many noble people who, at their personal risk, rejected the evil Nazi treatment of the Jews. Also covered are some subjects of renewed interest, such as the American government's response to the Holocaust, criticism of President Roosevelt and American Jewish leaders for their reaction to the news of the Holocaust, and the Nuremberg trial after World War II that brought justice to leading Nazi officials.

Introduction

The Holocaust (*Shoah* in Hebrew) was a Jewish tragedy that the Jewish people will never forget. More than one half of the European Jewish population perished, equal to one-third of the world Jewish population. They were tortured, worked to death, shot, gassed, burnt alive, and buried alive. They were made to suffer the greatest emotional pain, witnessing the brutal killing of their children and parents. These six million Jews were killed for one reason—they were Jews.

Five million non-Jews died in the concentration camps and death camps. They lost their lives for several reasons: they opposed the German regime politically; Hitler considered them misfits, unworthy of living; they were caught in the path of the German army's onslaught in Eastern Europe and did not welcome the Germans.

Germany, probably the most cultured country in the world at the time, was the source of the most horrible, unimaginable brutality ever imposed on human beings. Hitler and his staff masterminded the Holocaust, but it took many Germans and their non-German allies to carry it out. Businessmen, professionals, and ordinary Germans enthusiastically supported the Nazi brutal anti-Jewish measures. Many Protestant and Roman Catholic officials openly supported the Nazi regime. Only dissident Protestant leaders declared that unquestioning obedience to the state was not compatible with the Christian faith. Fifty years after it happened, we are still learning about the complicity of other "silent" participants. While it was happening, except for a courageous few, the world was quiet.

When the Holocaust ended, the countries of the world offered little aid and few opportunities to the survivors. 500,000 Jewish survivors had to languish in Displaced Persons camps for several years before they were allowed permanent refuge away from the scene of the horrors that befell them. *The ability of these Holocaust survivors, who had lived through hell on earth, to overcome their personal trauma and once again lead productive lives is evidence of what a human's positive determination can accomplish.*

The Holocaust was a Jewish tragedy that offers a lesson to the non-Jewish people of the world who believe in justice and value human life, *which is to stand up to impending acts of genocide and prevent the slaughter of innocent people before the evil expands.*

1
Beginning of the Evil (1875–1933)

For a hundred years before the Holocaust, Germany was the most favorable European country for Jews to live in. It was tolerant religiously and offered open opportunities for economic growth. Such was the situation at the start of the Nazi regime in the early 1930s. The enlightened Jewish community that accepted secularism along with its Judaism was vibrant in all aspects of society. Economically, Jews who were integrated into all business fields seemed to suffer less than the typical German during the days of high inflation and economic instability in the post-World War I period. Jews were an integral part of the high level of culture, science, and education that existed in Germany. Jews were proud to be German, and most Germans were proud of their fellow German Jews who achieved fame in music, literature, medicine, and physics. That is the irony of what happened to the Jews in Germany.

In the background of this hospitable environment, however, was the German variety of anti-Semitism that developed in the latter half of the nineteenth century. Starting to take hold among the nationalistic Germans was the political anti-Semitism that stressed the superiority of the Nordic (Aryan) race and the inferiority of the non-Aryans, especially the Jews. It was espoused earlier by several notable philosophers, such as Immanuel Kant and Friedrich Nietzsche, and by the eminent composer Richard Wagner. The powerful Chancellor Otto von Bismarck who was instrumental in unifying Germany and creating the powerful German Empire of that era offered encouragement to political anti-Semitism. Although he did sponsor civil and religious rights for the German Jews, Bismarck said nothing to refute the anti-Semitic oratory in order to gain favor with the nationalists. At the end of the century, anti-Semitic literature was very abundant. Several small political parties representing various factions of society adopted anti-Semitism as their rallying cry as an approach to achieving public support for their individual agendas. The atmosphere was troublesome, but the actions of these groups, which included university-student political parties, small-business organizations, and small-farmer organizations, did not result in the loss of rights for the German Jews.

Anti-Semitism intensified in Germany during the last two years of World War I. The war was dragging on, the people were suffering, and the casualties were mounting. The anti-Semites rose in strength, finding the Jews as handy scapegoats to blame the war losses on. The military joined the anti-Semites, resulting in legislation curtailing Jewish rights. The Weimar Republic created after the war ended restored full equality to the Jews. A Jew, Walter Rathenau, who as a civilian kept the German war industry going during the four years of war, became the foreign minister of the Republic. The nationalists denounced him for conceding too much to France, and the Prussian militarist condemned him for a treaty with Russia. Although Rathenau was stoutly German with no Jewish interest, "Kill the Jew" was a common cry among the anti-Semitic groups. Nazi party assassins murdered Rathenau in 1922. Jews were the most liberal group of the period and the strongest supporters of the Weimar Republic, which lasted until Hitler took power. That contributed to the wrath of the nationalists against the Jews. The nationalists objected to the Weimar Republic and became the early supporters of Hitler.

Adolf Hitler, an Austrian, volunteered to fight for the German army in World War I—he considered himself German. After the war, he joined the small Nazi party in Germany and soon took over its leadership. In 1923, he attempted and failed to establish his own republic in Munich, Bavaria (known as the Beer Hall Putsch). In 1924, while in jail for this crime, Hitler wrote his autobiography, *Mein Kampf.* In his book, Hitler argued for the glorification of the Aryan race and the elimination of Jews from Europe without any consideration of justice or respect for human values in how it was to be accomplished. He saw war as the only salvation to Germany's problems and viewed democracy as standing in the way of Germany achieving its growth. He would lead the way to Germany's restoration to glory. This book told the world in advance about Hitler's aims and the Nazi creed. In the early years of Hitler's rise to power, the political world saw Hitler as an eccentric who would get nowhere, and therefore, no action was taken to restrain him.

Poor economic conditions developed in Germany after World War I mainly resulting from the war reparations imposed on Germany. This contributed to the turbulent political atmosphere that existed during the Weimar Republic that succeeded the fallen German Empire. The Communists and the National Socialists (Nazis) fought to win the public's support from the Socialists running the Republic who were rather unsuccessful at leading Germany out of its economic depression. It was a difficult, no-win situation for the Jews. The Communists found it convenient to condemn the Jews as being the capitalists who were ruining the country although Jews were far from being the main capitalists of the country. The Nazis, with the German industrialists on their side, also found it convenient to blame the Jews for losing the war and for the harsh peace terms. They accused the Jewish bankers of causing the economic problems, whereas Jewish bankers had little influence in that era. The Nazi "race card" combined with their fear of Communism won over the middle and upper classes and the Prussian aristocracy. Jews became handy scapegoats for the Nazi march to power.

2
Degradation of Jewish Life (1933–1939)

In 1932, Hitler under the Nazi party got thirty-two percent of the vote for president. In 1933, Hitler persuaded the aging President von Hindenberg to appoint him chancellor and to grant him dictatorial powers to save the Republic. Soon after, Hitler initiated the policies he advocated in *Mein Kampf.* The socialist and communist leaders were sent to newly established concentration camps. Nazi bands attacked Jews, a small number were murdered. A short boycott of Jewish businesses was instigated; Storm Troopers prevented Aryan Germans from entering Jewish stores, which was a sign of what was to come. The Nuremberg Laws of September 1935 deprived the Jews of German citizenship. Under these laws, Christians whose parents or grandparents were Jewish were considered to be Jewish and subject to the same restrictions.

Thereafter, the ability of Jews to maintain their livelihood diminished; to many, it vanished. Hitler promised to ethnically cleanse the German Jews out of Aryan Germany and enrich Germany by transferring the wealth of the German Jews to the Aryan Germans. Many Germans became eager to take over the confiscated Jewish businesses and homes and to replace Jews evicted from all government positions. In essence, Germany's climb out of economic depression that most historians credit to Hitler was not accomplished through economic policies but by stealing the wealth of the German Jews. This was a pattern followed later by other nationalities in German-allied countries.

The Nazi regime took a variety of steps to encourage the German masses to support their anti-Jewish policies. Starting with propaganda minister Josef Goebbels presiding over a public bonfire, the books of Jewish writers, such as Heine, Einstein, and Freud, and non-Jewish books sympathetic to Jewish issues, such as by Mann and Zola, went up in flames. This was followed by a contrived research project by several respected professionals describing how Jews like Einstein corrupted science and how books by Jews were degrading to Germany. Jewish literature and music by Jewish composers officially then became unacceptable to Germans.

Religion was another tool used by the Nazis to inspire the German public to despise the Jews. The Christian Nazi Institute was created for eliminating all references to Jewish influences in the Christian theology, including Jesus Christ's Jewishness. A major propaganda instrument was the Institute for the Exploration of the Jewish Question. It was created to train the German public on anti-Jewish behavior as a step to glorifying Germany and the Aryan race. These propaganda practices were very effective. German anti-Semitism became the norm. The "Horst Wessel" song became the rallying cry of the masses at Nazi rallies, effectively becoming the national anthem. Its words suggested that killing the Jews was an honor. *"When Jewish blood flows from the knife, things will go much better"* is one of the milder song stanzas.

The anti-Jewish measures spread to the eastern European countries—Poland, Lithuania, Latvia, Romania, and Hungary. These countries, with a tradition of anti-Jewish feelings, were quick to institute their own repressive Jewish measures. By 1939, millions of Polish Jews were turned into paupers, living off charitable contributions and donations from overseas relatives. Anti-Semitism had become official and widespread in Poland. The dictators who ruled the central European countries sanctioned killing of Jews by political bullies, such as the Iron Guard in Romania. By 1941, most of the Romanian Jews became destitute like their Polish brethren.

Hitler's early strategy was to degrade the German Jews and destroy them economically. He intended to accomplish this with a minimum of bloodshed and isolated violence so as to not arouse the world community and not antagonize those Germans who still had a sense of decency towards all human beings, including Jews. It was successful. The world remained quiet except for protests by the Jewish community that heard his worldwide radio broadcasts in fear. The American Jewish business community voiced its protest by boycotting German businesses, but it had little effect. The brutal anti-Jewish policies that drove thousands of Jews to commit suicide did not interfere with the European politicians' intent to keep peace with Hitler. The United States officially offered no meaningful opposition to Hitler. U.S. policy was hampered by the lingering effect of the Depression and the powerful isolationist movement that prevailed. This force coupled with the active anti-Semitic element that included many influential politicians, counteracted considerations to oppose Hitler.

Four Year Plan—In August 1936, Hitler drafted this plan. It called for Germany to take the next four years to prepare for war against "Jewish Bolshevism" and to regain its glory. Germany would expand through a *Lebensraum* (living space) policy, which aimed at taking over old land formerly occupied and governed by Germans (Austria and Sudentenland in Czechoslovakia) and seizing new land in eastern Europe. The German Jews would be required to pay for the cost of the war when it came.

Kristallnacht—In March 1938, Hitler militarily took over Austria, and immediately a quarter-million Jews were put under the same German repressive measures. There was a quiet world reaction to the *Anschluss* (joining) of Austria to Germany. In its aftermath, in September, Chamberlain of Britain and Daladier of France joined with Hitler in the Munich Pact, which permitted German takeover of parts of Czechoslovakia and repudiated the British and French defense pact with Czechoslovakia. It was again, peace with Hitler at any price. These events in 1938 emboldened Hitler to change his strategy towards the Jews. He used the event of the assassination of a German diplomat in Paris by a young Jew, Herschel Grynzpan, to enter a more violent phase of Jewish persecution. Seventeen year old Grynzpan became distraught over how the Nazis deported his parents to Poland. The elder Grynzpans had left Poland in 1911 and settled in Hanover, Germany where they became firmly established as Germans. In October 1938, the Nazis decided to expel 60,000 Polish Jews who had fled from the anti-Jewish Polish policies between 1918 and 1933. Although they had entered Germany well before 1918, the Grynzpans were included in the expulsion. Their business was confiscated, and they were sent out penniless. Because Poland would not accept the return of these 60,000 Jews, they were stranded on the border between the two countries with no shelter and little food. The young Grynzpan took revenge for this harsh treatment of his family.

On the night of November 9, 1938, the Gestapo (secret police) organized and orchestrated a nationwide pogrom that lasted two days. Almost every synagogue (191) was burned. Much Jewish property was destroyed (7,500 stores, 800 large department stores, 170 apartment houses, and many thousands of homes). Jews caught in the streets were beaten, several thousand killed. Jews were arrested without cause. Thirty thousand, mostly wealthy, male Jews were detained and beaten in German concentration camps, which were initially set up for Hitler's political enemies and converted to slave labor camps at Dachau, Buchenwald, and Sachsenhausen. World War I veterans with medals of honor were not spared. The Gestapo allowed families to bribe their loved ones out of the camps; this was a deliberate Gestapo fund-raising plan. The prisoners were released with the warning that if they told anyone about what happened in the camps, the Gestapo would kill them. It was very effective. Many of the prisoners kept their treatment silent, even from their immediate family.

Incredibly, the Germans ordered the Jewish population, already impoverished by the impact of the Nuremberg Laws, to pay a fine of four hundred million dollars to clean up the destruction that the Germans caused. It was decreed that Jewish businesses would not reopen until they were taken over by Aryans. To belittle the meaning of the event, the Germans called it *"Kristallnacht,"* the "night of the glass"—the shards of glass from the broken windows glittered like crystal. Since the Germans claimed Kristallnacht was retaliation for the assassination, the world was, again, quiet about the German action. Kristallnacht did, however, cause a reaction among the German Jews—it woke them up to the danger of living in Nazi Germany.

Jewish Reaction to Kristallnacht—In the first year of Hitler's "Third Reich," all Jews in civil service were fired and the entertainment industry was made *judenrein* (free of Jews). In the second year, Jews were *verboten* (forbidden) from journalism, radio, and other media. In the third year, the Nuremberg Laws took away the legal rights from the Jews. The German Jews had an almost incredible reaction to these events—less than a third left Germany. They were mostly the famous Jews who had help getting out, and the young who had weak ties to Germany. The others were willing to stick it out; they believed Hitler was a short-term aberration. The government-organized violence of Kristallnacht was a turning point for the Jews in Germany and Austria. After Kristallnacht, the ability of Jews to maintain a livelihood completely vanished.

Recognizing how desperate their fate was if they remained in Germany, many of the remaining Jews quietly managed to leave Germany. Many Austrian Jews followed suit. Most of them left penniless and uncertain as to where their final destination would be, but they were thankful to be out of Germany and Austria. Half of the Jewish population, approximately 300,000, had left Germany by October 1941, when Jewish emigration was prohibited. Some departures were possible even during the first two years of the war because, up until that point, the Germans encouraged emigration of the Jews after taking their money and valuables. Whereas before Kristallnacht, some Jews who had found it difficult to adjust to their place of refuge returned to Germany, none came back to Germany after Kristallnacht.

Czechoslovakia Takeover—With the world leaders so passive in reaction to his actions, Hitler ignored the Munich Pact, and engineered the takeover of Czechoslovakia in the spring of 1939. Another quarter-million Jews saw their lives turn bleak under the Swastika. The world remained quiet over the loss of one of the finest democracies. The impact on the Jews who shared in this democracy of course was inconsequential to the world.

Scarce Places of Asylum—The free world expressed a lot of sympathy over the plight of the Jews in Germany, but it ended there. The major countries of the world each had an excuse for not being able to take in the essentially penniless Jews who wanted to flee from Germany. The British allowed in a small number of children (7,500), as did other west European countries (3,500). The U.S. immigration quota for Germany was actually one of the highest. However, since it covered all Germans, Jews were actually a small percentage of the Germans who entered the United States during the 1930s. The leading Jewish community members and many non-Jewish political and social leaders constantly urged Congress to increase the very restrictive immigration quotas that were in effect since 1924, but Congress refused.

Many famous German Jews were fortunate to find sponsors who managed to circumvent the western-country immigration obstacles facing the ordinary Jew trying to escape from the Nazi grip over Europe. Others, out of desperation, accepted refuge in countries throughout the world where previously there were few, if any, Jews. Jews managed to find refuge in South and Central American countries and in many underdeveloped countries of Africa. The city of Shanghai, China, became a haven for several thousand Jews. However, the largest number of escapees (100,000) went to Palestine in spite of the British White Paper of 1937 that restricted Jewish immigration to the small number of 12,000 per year, and the 1939 White Paper that restricted the total immigration to 75,000 over a five-year period. Illegal entry into Palestine was accomplished through the efforts of several organizations that conducted underground operations to aid the fleeing Jews.

Britain had deliberately kept the legal immigration below their authorized quota. By the end of 1943, there were still 30,000 (40%) entry visas not granted. The underground organizations forged transit papers, arranged transportation to get the escapees inconspicuously through country borders, and outfitted mostly small, hardly seaworthy boats to smuggle them out of Europe. The boats left from ports in Southern France, Italy,

Romania, and Bulgaria. The operations ended by smuggling the refugees onto the shores of Palestine.

Clever bribing of officials at all levels of government, including the Gestapo, was required for the missions to be successful. Jews were rescued in this fashion from Poland, Germany, Czechoslovakia, and Romania. The largest organization involved in these operations was the *"Mossad le Aliyah,"* the (Institute of the Illegal Immigration) founded by the Histadrut labor organization in Palestine. This effort continued through 1941, when the German takeover of France and penetration into the Balkans made these efforts impossible.

Evian Conference—In July 1938 after the plight of the Jews was expanded by Hitler's takeover of Austria, a conference on the German-Austrian Jewish refugee problem was held at Evian, France. The thirty-two attending nations, all expressing concern for the refugees, were asked to absorb twenty-five thousand refugees. Not one country accepted. They offered these excuses: (1) they could not accept intellectuals who were useless to them; (2) baptism papers were required because it was a Catholic country; (3) they were afraid of anti-Semitic reactions in their own country. Chamberlain proposed Tanganyika in Africa, but that country objected. Angola and Ethiopia were recommended, but Portugal and Italy who ruled these countries refused. Britain did not allow Palestine to even be considered as a place of refuge. The conference ended with a resolution that no country would finance the entry of a refugee. Since Germany allowed Jews to emigrate with only five dollars in their pocket, that essentially closed the door to these countries for refugees.

British Asylum—Former Minister Stanley Baldwin of England established a fund supported by British non-Jews to provide refuge in England to 7500 Jewish children whose families were stateless after leaving Germany and Austria to escape the Nazi terror. Many of these children were housed by numerous Christian families as they moved from the industrial cities to the safer countryside in Britain and Wales during the heavy German bombing of England.

Oil and Compassion Do Not Mix—Most of the British public and, frequently, ruling members of the British government expressed sympathy for the German Jews. However, the British government's desire to protect their access to Arabian oil found in the 1920s overruled this compassion. The British government essentially abrogated their 1917 Balfour Declaration that promised Jews a national home in Palestine when they became controllers of Palestine under the League of Nations Palestine Mandate.

Britain issued the White Papers of 1937 and 1939 that severely limited Jewish immigration into Palestine at the time when Jews were struggling to escape from Nazi terror and were anxious for entry into Palestine. No other countries offered them refuge. During the height of Germany's terrible bombing of British cities in 1940, when Britain got its own share of suffering, the British government still refused to open Palestine to Jews struggling to reach its shores in flimsy boats that were barely seaworthy. The British patrolled the Palestine coastline and forced those caught entering to go back to sea. Unfortunately, many Jews drowned at sea when some boats sank in bad weather. Others drowned in the process of sneaking on shore or were shot by the British as they tried to enter.

The most devastating incident involved the ship *Struma*. In December 1941, this rickety boat with 770 Romanian and Russian Jewish refugees, including seventy children, left the port Constanza on Romania's Black Sea coast for Palestine. When the British refused their entry, the ship anchored off the Turkish coast but the authorities would not permit the passengers to disembark. For two months, they lived under deplorable conditions, surviving on minimum rations supplied by the Turkish Jewish community. Because Britain would still not permit the ship to continue on to Palestine, the Turkish government forced the Struma to leave their shore. Without a working engine, the Struma was towed out to the open sea, where it sank with only one youthful Jewish survivor. Until recently, it was attributed to bad weather. Now it is believed to have been sunk by a Russian submarine.

In 1943, there was a significant opportunity for the American Jewish community to rescue 70,000 Romanian Jews by paying a ransom to Romania, which they were willing to do. Romania suggested that getting the Jews to Palestine was the most practical step. To the British, Palestine was out of the question as a place of refuge for Jews; they did not want to offend the Arabs. The British coerced King Carol of Romania to block the plan by threatening to deny Romania a loan that was part of the arrangement. The reason given was that it would have been too much of a financial imposition on the countries that had to absorb these penniless Jews. Again, to protect British access to Arab oil, 70,000 lives were lost.

The British government's apathy towards the plight of the Jews trying to flee Nazi Germany was also influenced by the personal dislike of the Jewish people by several high British officials in a position to affect the policy towards the Jewish refugees. For example, 1939 correspondence in British archives reveals Prime Minister Chamberlain's disdain for the Jewish people "who are not lovable." Colonial Secretary MacDonald indicated pleasure that his pressure on several East European countries to prevent Jews leaving their country for Palestine was successful in overcoming "the power of Jewish money." To Chamberlain's credit, "he saw no justification for the pogrom-killing of the Jews by the Nazis."

The Saga of the *St. Louis*—In May 1939, the *St. Louis* was last ship to leave Germany with Jewish refugees. It had 930 Jews on board who had scraped together money to pay the passage and the Cuban entry-permit fee. They sailed to Cuba, believing they found freedom. Most of them held American quota numbers enabling them to enter the United States in one to three years. However, when the boat reached Havana, they were shocked to learn that they had no landing rights. The Cuban labor movement had convinced the Cuban government to invalidate the entry permits because "they feared the immigrants would take away their jobs." The Joint Distribution Committee attempted to post a monetary bond assuring that the Jews would not seek employment in Cuba if they were allowed to enter, but the efforts were fruitless, the ship left Cuba.

The German captain of the *St. Louis* was very sympathetic to the plight of the Jews, knowing what would happen to them if they returned to Germany. First, he anchored off Miami in the hopes that the United States would let the Jews in. The Coast Guard, on orders from the State Department, chased the boat away, making certain that no one tried to swim ashore. The captain then requested permission to sail to Shanghai, China, but was turned down by Berlin. He then slowly steamed back to Europe and landed in Antwerp, Belgium. That slow trip gave England, France, Belgium, and the Netherlands the opportunity to negotiate a deal with the Joint Distribution Committee. After the JDC posted a bond, each country accepted a portion of the passengers. Unfortunately, those who remained in France, Belgium, and the Netherlands were caught in the German occupation of these counties and, except for a few, perished in the death camps.

3
"Final Solution" Planning (1939–1941)

In July 1939, Hermann Goering, Hitler's second in command, gave the orders to devise the plan for the "final solution of the Jewish question," which initially was to find the way for emigration of the Jews. At that stage, the Germans thought they could profit financially from an emigration plan and they were not quite ready to face the world reaction to overt mass extermination of the Jews. The machinery for the Final Solution was to be organized by Adolf Eichmann under SS Chief Heinrich Himmler.

When the German army was so successful in quickly conquering most of Europe, Hitler's plan for the Jewish people changed. The Germans saw that the world community was not very interested in the freedom of the European Jews if it required immigration of Jews into their country, and, therefore, they could profit more by a plan for the liquidation of the Jews. The Final Solution was defined in January 1941. Although the plan did not have Hitler's name on it, it surely was in response to his wishes, expressed as early as 1922. He wrote, "The annihilation of the Jews will be my first and foremost task." The high Nazi officials at the Nuremberg war crimes trial attempted to deny Hitler's responsibility for the Final Solution Jewish extermination plan, but the War Crimes Tribunal did not accept their arguments.

Blitzkrieg Success Changes Hitler's Plans—On September 1, 1939, Hitler invaded Poland and conquered it in thirty days. Hitler and the Soviet dictator Joseph Stalin then divided Poland according to the pact they had signed in August. Britain and France had finally responded to Hitler's aggression. They had joined the war on Poland's side but did nothing to help Poland avoid a rapid collapse. After the Polish defeat, the British and French fought a "phony" war with Germany, feeling secure just watching the German forces from the safety of the Maginot Line trenches on the border with Germany. They refused to attack Germany or the German Siegfried Line opposite the Maginot Line. The Germans were content with this *Sitzkrieg* (sitting war), giving Germany the freedom to prepare their next attacks. It came suddenly and forcefully in the spring of 1940.

The Germans used a *Blitzkrieg* (lightning war) tactic. It consisted of a very coordinated air attack that supported the mechanized attacks combined with massive infantry assaults. By the summer, all of Europe was either conquered by Germany or became its satellite ally, except for neutral Switzerland, Sweden, Spain, and Portugal. The British armed forces in France, isolated in a small area off Dunkirk on the English Channel, managed to escape from the German onslaught thanks to a massive armada of small boats from England that rescued them from the Dunkirk beach. Britain remained the only western European country fighting Hitler. Stalin was content to do nothing based on his "phony" peace alliance with Hitler, while Germany was preparing for the invasion of Russia, which took place on June 22, 1941. The German advance into Russia did not end until Germany lost the battles of Stalingrad and Moscow in the winter of 1942–1943. The German army, having had a year of success over the Russian army in the previous year, became overconfident. The Germans did not prepare adequately for the harsh Russian winter, which overwhelmed them.

Except for those in Great Britain, the German European conquests put all of European Jewry under the control of Germany or their allies. With little military pressure on them, the Germans proceeded to develop their Final Solution. The focus changed from emigration to extermination of the Jewish people.

By 1939, the Germans had already instituted the killing of the mentally retarded and physically deformed children. The techniques used were considered too inefficient for the large number of Jews to be killed. Eichmann had death camps built in Poland where techniques of mass killing using different poison gasses were to be developed. While this was going on, special Secret Service forces (*Einsatzgruppen*) under Himmler went through Poland finding and killing the elite Polish and Jewish community including the Polish intelligentsia, clergymen, and nobility.

Wannsee Conference—The "Final Solution of the Jewish Problem" was formally defined at a conference in the Wannsee suburb of Berlin in January 1941. It was chaired by Reinhard Heydrich and attended by representatives of all the major German government organizations and representatives from the eastern occupied territories. The specialists who had devised the efficient gas chambers and the representatives of the special killing squads who explained their methods also attended the meeting.

Heydrich restated Hitler's policy of eradicating the Jews with no mercy to be considered, and it became the basis of the Final Solution. The plan was to ship Jews from the western ghettos to transit ghettos and then to the death camps to be built in Poland. Jews going to the death camps were to be told they were being resettled either to Palestine or to work areas and could even take personal belongings. Forged letters and postal cards were sent from the supposed destinations to support the fiction. It was very effective; many Jews in the Polish ghettos believed the offers and unwittingly volunteered to go to the death camps. Jews in the Russian ghettos were to be killed en masse by firing squads. In the absence of interconnecting railroads between Russia and Poland, the transport of Jews from Russia to the death camps in Poland was too difficult. With the German army tied down fighting the Russians, the plan called for the German eastern European allies to be solicited to support the killing process of their respective Jewish population—most responded.

Ghettos—The large cities in eastern Europe all had areas where the Jews lived in large concentrations that were almost one hundred percent Jewish. These areas were converted into ghettos, cordoned off with restricted access. The Jews from the other areas of the city were forced to move into the ghetto along with Jews from neighboring small villages and towns. The result was that two to three times the normal population had to share living quarters that were cramped to begin with. By the summer of 1942, there were approximately four hundred ghettos of various sizes housing two million Jews throughout German-occupied eastern Europe. The smallest ones in Poland had no enclosures. However, the freedom to go in and out was short-lived. They were the first ghettos to be emptied; the occupants were sent to the death camps in Poland.

The two largest ghettos were both in Poland, Warsaw with a population of 450,000 and Lodz with a population of 200,000. Typically, six people shared a room. The Germans tried to demoralize the population, denying them the opportunity to practice Jewish religious rituals, but they were continued in secret. Despite the oppressive living conditions, with people constantly disappearing and dying in the homes and streets, communal leaders organized many educational and cultural activities to bolster morale. They tried to offer the younger people some hope for the future.

The Germans provided a small amount of food to be rationed and nominally shared by everyone. People with money and others who sold their clothing and meager possessions were able to buy food smuggled in. Food became scarcer with time, money ran out, and people were getting desperate. Begging was common. The poor and the less aggressive people died of starvation. This was in step with the Nazi policy to kill as many Jews as possible by *natural causes* to protect against a later investigation. The ghetto conditions bred many fatal diseases. There were epidemics of dysentery, typhus, typhoid, and diphtheria. The few Jewish physicians in the camps had next to no medicines at their disposal for treating these very sick people. These conditions resulted in many deaths by "natural causes" that the Germans sought. In Warsaw, 83,000 died of starvation and disease in less than two years, and in Lodz, 45,000 died by these causes.

Judenrat—Heydrich gave orders for a Jewish council of elders, *Judenrat,* to be established in each community controlled by the Germans. It was to be constituted by influential community members and rabbis who were to be responsible for precisely and promptly executing the orders of the Einsatzgruppen (iron-fisted group). Failure to do so would result in severe punishment to the community members and/or the elders. The Judenrat had a broad and painful responsibility. It covered ghettoizing the Jewish communities, doling out the food rations, and keeping the ghetto occupants stimulated to want to keep on living under the dreadful conditions of the ghetto. When a German ghetto official called for a number of Jews to be sent to the camps, it was the Judenrat who had to select who went to the labor camps and who went to the death camps. In the end, when the ghettos were closed down, the members of the Judenrat usually wound up in the gas chambers.

Russian Concentration Camps—When Stalin took over the eastern part of Poland in 1939, an area that was under Russian control prior to World War I, he distrusted the Jewish people living in these areas. They were interrogated to determine whether they would be loyal to Poland in the event that the war ended and Poland reclaimed the land back. About 10,000 young men who unwittingly indicated their loyalty to Poland (all their lives they had lived only in Poland) were sent to slave labor camps in eastern Siberia where living conditions were very severe. Many Jewish families from this area were sent to forced-labor communities in central Asia where they lived under very harsh conditions. Starvation and disease took its toll in both locations.

Theresienstadt—This concentration camp in Bohemia was initially set to house aged German Jewish veterans who had been seriously wounded in World War I and distinguished German Jews whose disappearance would be embarrassing if there ever was to be an international investigation of Germany's handling of the Jews. Ostensibly, it was to be run as an autonomous Jewish village. Freedom and normalcy of life was displayed when the International Red Cross visited Theresienstadt. When they left, Theresienstadt returned to being a harsh concentration camp. For most inmates, it was a transit camp on the way to Auschwitz.

Himmler Takes Over—In the spring of 1941, Himmler took charge of the Final Solution. He ordered the expansion of Auschwitz to accommodate 100,000 death camp prisoners and 30,000 slave laborers to work in the nearby munitions plants. The Einsatzgruppen killing squads were authorized to remove Jews from prisoner camps and ghettos and eliminate them. He did not want to use the word "kill" in case there was an investigation later, but these forces knew what he meant. The special killing forces were expanded with Ukrainian, White Russian, and Lithuanian recruits. These forces were assigned to each military unit, and they very efficiently collected the Jewish populations in the towns overrun by the German army.

4
The Final Solution in Action (1941–1945)

Three elements of the German regime had different objectives concerning the Final Solution. The Nazi political element was intent to eliminate the Jews completely and rapidly. The war industry required the Jews to support munitions fabrication, clothing manufacturing, and construction projects—the educated Jews represented the most skilled workforce available in eastern Europe. The finance ministry's objective was to get the maximum financial return extracted from the Jews. The Germans proceeded with the Final Solution in a manner that essentially met all their objectives. ***For the Jewish people it resulted in disaster.***

The extermination camps were to run at full capacity, but the ablest people were to be kept for last—they were to be sent to the concentration labor camps. Special forces having the authority to kill Jews at will were to be assigned to each military unit advancing into Russia. This two-fold killing pace satisfied Hitler and the Nazi hierarchy. Making slave laborers available to support the war effort satisfied the German war department.

The ghetto residents and the labor camp inmates were given the minimum food required for survival. Those assigned to the death camps were either sent directly to the gas chambers or were fed minimally. Medical help and medicines were very limited and reserved for special people. This minimum expenditure for food and medicine was more than compensated for by the monetary value of the goods collected and sold by the Gestapo. The gold teeth taken from the inmates and the cadavers went to the German Reichsbank. The money and jewelry collected from all the camp inmates went to the SS, as did the clothing collected from those about to be killed. This arrangement, which netted millions of dollars, pleased the German finance ministry. When clothing became scarce in Germany towards the end of the war, the clothing taken from the Jews was the primary source of clothing for the German public. These steps satisfied the finance ministry.

The concentration camp officials needed to provide slave laborers.

They also did not want to waste food and medical resources. Under these conditions, young children and older men and women had little chance for survival. When the Judenrat selected people for work camps, this group was left out. When the cattle cars loaded with Jews of all ages arrived at the concentration camps, the elderly and young children were separated out and sent on to the death camps. Because of this Nazi selection process, almost all concentration camp survivors were parentless.

Of the six million Jews who died in the Holocaust, most were killed in the gas chambers, and the next larger number by the special-forces firing squads. The rest died from starvation or disease. When the labor camp workers got too ill or weak to work, they were left to die, to be replaced by newly arrived concentration camp inmates. Towards the end of the Holocaust period, thousands of concentration camp inmates died from weakness or illness when they were marched by the Germans from one camp to another to avoid being freed by the advancing Russians. The inmates were forced to march in the cold, icy winter of 1944 without adequate clothing and frequently without shoes (*The Death March*).

End of the Ghettos—The Germans systematically emptied and razed all the ghettos to the ground from 1942 through 1944. By the beginning of 1944, the Germans had already liquidated all the ghettos except Vilna in Lithuania, and Kovno and Lodz in Poland, where only a small number of Jews were still living.

In July 1944, the last 3,000 Jews in the Vilna ghetto were taken outside of the city and murdered by the Germans. In August 1944, 2,500 of the original 30,000 Kovno Jews remained alive in the ghetto. They were sent to concentration camps in Germany, ahead of the advancing Soviet army, and the ghetto was destroyed. In September, when the Russians seemed to be ready to liberate Lodz, the Germans proceeded with their final liquidation of Lodz, sending 15,000 to Auschwitz and leaving 500 to clean up the ghetto. Three hundred Jews who had hidden during the final liquidation but were discovered when it was over were also allowed to remain in the ghetto—an unusual act of mercy by the Germans. Shortly after this action took place, the Polish underground decided to rise up against the Germans. While the Germans contended with the Polish underground, the Russian army took a break from the fighting the Germans and ceased their advance. The Russians finally resumed their advance in January 1945, capturing Lodz and freeing the last of the ghetto survivors.

Concentration Camps—There were several hundred concentration camps spread throughout Germany, Austria, and Poland. These camps served two purposes. They housed Jewish and non-Jewish prisoners who served as slave laborers supporting the German war effort and performing other tasks for which the Germans lacked German laborers. They also served as holding camps for Jews rounded up by the Germans in the countries they occupied before transshipping them to the death camps in Poland. German doctors conducted their horrible medical experiments on Jews and others in several of these camps in Germany, for which they were convicted of war crimes at the Nuremberg trial after the war ended. The older and larger concentration camps in Germany, such as Dachau and Bergen-Belsen, had small-scale carbon-monoxide execution chambers.

The majority of the concentration camps were in Germany, set up for convenience nearby munition plants and other war-related industrial plants that required slave labor. Several of the larger ones, such as Dachau, Buchenwald, and Sachsenhausen, with a capacity of several thousand prisoners, were established in the early days of the Hitler regime. Many labor camps were small and temporary. They housed a few hundred inmates, lasting as long as the work detail required. Similar slave-labor camps were created in Poland where road-building for the German army was another major task. Conditions in the camps were brutal. There was little food, next to no medical aid, and horrible working conditions. Poorly dressed, undernourished, and frequently sick, prisoners were forced to do heavy manual labor building roads, often under the most severe east European winter conditions. Those who could not keep up were either killed on the spot or sent to the death camps.

Many Holocaust survivors tell of having been at several concentration camps. That happened because prisoners were moved from camp to camp as the workload changed. A large number of survivors started as inmates of the Auschwitz concentration camp. At the war's end, the migration from camp to camp accelerated as the Russian army came close to the camps in Poland, and later, close to the camps in eastern Germany. Fifty-eight thousand ill-clad Auschwitz concentration camp inmates were forced to march to camps in Germany in the bitter cold January 1945 winter. Many did not survive. Ironically, many of the six thousand Jews left behind at Auschwitz by the Germans because they were too sick to leave the infirmary managed to survive.

Holding Camps—In France, Belgium, and the Netherlands, it was not convenient for the Germans to force Jews into ghettos as they did in eastern Europe. The Germans set up holding camps in these countries for the Jews who were periodically rounded up before being sent to the German death camps in Poland. The camps in Belgium and the Netherlands also served as forced-labor camps.

France was a divided country. The Germans occupied northern France while southern France was a "free zone" run by the Vichy France government. Although the French people mostly resented the Germans and resisted the German oppression of the Jews in France, the French police in both sections of France cooperated with the Germans, as did the Vichy France government. The French police rounded up Jews for the holding camps and ultimate deportation to the death camps. One hundred thousand French Jews and a large number of stateless Jews who earlier temporarily came to France in order to escape Hitler lost their lives in this fashion.

A brutal incident occurred in July 1943 when the French police packed 7,000 Jews into the Velodrome d'Hiver sports stadium in Paris. They were penned in without food and with only water from a street hydrant, no sleeping quarters, and only a few latrines. After five days of this ordeal, the police loaded the prisoners onto trains and escorted the trains to the border of Germany from where the trains continued on to Auschwitz. In another incident, four thousand Jewish children were separated from their parents and collected in the French camp at Drancy, only to be sent later to the extermination camp at Auschwitz under orders from Adolph Eichmann. Drancy, a suburb of Paris, became the principal camp used for the deportation of French Jews to Auschwitz.

Death Camps—To carry out their Final Solution of the Jewish problem, the Germans created six large death camps in Poland, where except for Russia, most of the European Jews lived. The camps were located close to the cities with the largest Jewish populations in order to facilitate the mass murder of the Jews who had been forced into the ghettos of these cities after the German occupation of Poland. Each site was chosen because of the railroad connection to a large city so that the mass transfer of the victims to the camps could be accomplished efficiently. The largest camp, Auschwitz, was located on a railroad line that connected to all of the large cities in Europe, except in Russia. It became the death camp for the non-Polish European Jews in addition to Polish Jews from the cities of Lodz and Cracow. There was a very efficient Nazi transportation organization dedicated to arranging the shipment of Jews from throughout Europe to the death camp at Auschwitz. Unventilated box cars and cattle cars were used to transport the victims, which could take several days. Without sanitation facilities and no food or water provided, many died on the way to the camp. Approximately five million of the six million Jews who died in the Holocaust perished in death camps.

Before the death camps got under full operation, the Nazi SS killer squads, aided by the local collaborationists, went through most of the large Lithuanian and some Polish cities, executing hundreds of Jews at a time in killing sprees. German records indicate that over a quarter million Jews were murdered in this fashion.

Initially, apart from Jews shot individually in sadistic fashion, the death camp mass killing was accomplished by gassing in vans and small rooms filled with carbon monoxide fumes generated by diesel engines. When these crude gas chambers failed to work, the Germans used firing squads. The dead were burned or buried in nearby ditches. This gassing method was too slow and inefficient to handle the large number of Jews remaining to be killed under the Final Solution plan for eradicating all European Jews. Under orders from Himmler, a more efficient mass-killing process was developed. Zyklon-B, a deadly insecticide poison gas was discharged into large rooms disguised as shower rooms that the victims innocently entered. This gas, in pellets, was easy to handle. It was efficient, killing in five minutes as opposed to sometimes hours for the earlier methods. Massive crematoriums were built for disposing of the dead. The smell from the crematoriums permeated the air for miles; the people in the neighboring towns could hardly not know what was going on, as they claimed after the Holocaust ended.

The death camp at Auschwitz, and to a lesser extent at Majdanek, also served a secondary role as a concentration camp, housing the slave laborers who worked in the neighboring German factories. Four camps, Treblinka, Sobibor, Belzec, and Chelmno, were strictly death camps. Treblinka and Sobibor had only a very few barracks, which were reserved for the Jews who had to do the camp dirty work of disposing of the dead. Essentially one hundred percent of the Jews sent to these two camps went directly to the gas chambers. They were killed within three hours of arrival at the camp. When it became clear that all the Jews in the Treblinka and Sobibor camps were to be killed, the camp inmates organized rebellions out of desperation. Unfortunately, very few escapees survived. The Germans closed the camps in 1943 after the rebellions.

Auschwitz—Two million Jews (one out of every three that was killed in the Holocaust) died at Auschwitz. Called Oswiecim by Poland, it is located in the Silesia section of southern Poland. The Auschwitz camp facility actually consisted of three separate camps a couple of miles apart:

Auschwitz-I located in Auschwitz, Auschwitz-II at Birkenau, and Auschwitz-III at Monowitz.

When they occupied Poland in 1939, the Germans intended to transform the Auschwitz area into a large new German community as part of the Nazi *Lebensraum* takeover of east-European territory. For that reason, they decided to build the massive IG Farben synthetic rubber plant there. In April 1940, they opened the Auschwitz-I camp with a small gas chamber for killing Polish intellectuals from Silesia who were arrested for "subversion," including many Roman Catholic priests and nuns.

In late 1941, the large Auschwitz-Birkenau (Auschwitz-II) facility with several large Zyklon-B death chambers and massive crematoriums went into operation as part of Final Solution plan. The new killing process was very efficient. Approximately ten percent of the ablest Jews coming off the trains at Auschwitz were selected to be slave laborers. The others were sent to the death camp facility. Groups of victims were marched into large open gas chambers resembling shower rooms on the second floor. They were ordered to undress so the clothing could be collected and sold in Germany before they were soiled in the agony of death. The doors were closed, and they were quickly killed by the entry of Zyklon-B gas through the "shower heads." After large exhaust fans cleared the deadly fumes, Jewish *Sonderkommandos* (shameful commandos) shaved the women's hair (valuable to the German women) and removed the gold teeth (source of wealth to the Nazi regime). Elevators were used to carry the bodies to the crematoriums on the floor below—a very efficient process. Between May and July 1944, most of the 430,000 Jews deported from Hungary went directly to the Auschwitz gas chambers at the rate of 10,000 per day.

When the Nazi leadership could not convince enough Germans to move to the city of Auschwitz to support its plans for the area, the Germans built Auschwitz III at Monowitz. It housed the thousands of Jewish laborers required to support building and operating the massive new rubber and synthetic oil factories, to work in nearby munition factories and rock quarries, and to support various roadbuilding projects.

"Arbeit Macht Frei"—This sign, "work makes free," was posted above the entrance to the death camps in order to deceive the Jews into believing that they were being cleansed in the "showers" in preparation for being sent to work and to encourage them to enter the death chambers passively. The Germans didn't intend this sign to be true, but ironically, the only Jews who survived the Holocaust were those Jews who were sent to the forced-labor camps to work for the Germans.

Death Camp Statistics—Five million Jews perished in the six extermination camps in Poland. The approximate deaths at each of the camps are shown in the table, which also indicates the closest large Polish city from where most victims in each camp came from. Auschwitz, where one-third of the Holocaust killings took place, was the death camp for Jews from most of the European countries in addition to Jews from the two large Polish cities of Lodz and Cracow.

Death Camp (Location)	Deaths
Auschwitz (Lodz, Cracow)	2,000,000
Majdanek (Lublin)	1,000,000
Treblinka (Warsaw)	800,000
Belzec (Lvov)	600,000
Chelmno (Lodz)	360,000
Sobibor (Brest Litovsk)	250,000

Mass Killings in Russia—With the absence of railroad connections between Russia and Poland, Jews from Russia were not sent to the Polish death camps. There were no death camps established by the Germans for exterminating the large number of Russian Jews captured by the German army after its invasion of Russia. The Germans just slaughtered them periodically in the ghettos that they established in the large cities and towns. The largest killing spree was at the Babi Yar ravine outside of Kiev, the Ukrainian city with a large Jewish population, where 35,000 (probably many more) were killed.

Shortly after the Germans occupied Kiev in 1941, the Jews were told to assemble at Babi Yar for resettlement to a work camp. Believing the Germans, they obediently left Kiev for Babi Yar. However, in production line fashion, the Germans marched the Jews into the ravine where they were machine-gunned by German and Ukrainian soldiers. A few miraculously survived to tell the tale.

Roughly one million Russian and Baltic country Jews who failed to escape ahead of the German army's occupation were slaughtered by the Germans in the Russian and Baltic city ghettos that the Germans created after the occupation of these territories.

Brutal Treatment—Jews in the concentration camps were exposed to the most inhumane treatment imaginable. Torture techniques surpassed those of the Middle Ages. Dogs were trained to bite at the most sensitive areas of the body. Women and young girls were brutally raped. Survivors have described the sadistic treatment, including cruel medical experimentation on humans conducted by Dr. Joseph Mengele at Auschwitz. Barbaric, perverse medical experiments were conducted for the army and the SS at several concentration camps located in Germany, including Dachau, Buchenwald, and the Ravensbruck concentration camp for women. The German medical profession at the time praised the physicians conducting these inhumane experiments. The world community thought otherwise; they were convicted and executed by the postwar war crimes commission.

For many survivors, what they personally experienced or witnessed was so painful that they could not tell their own families about it for many years. Even today, some still cannot talk about it. The trauma never ends for others; they still live in fear. Primo Levi, the accomplished Italian Jewish author who wrote about his personal ordeal in Auschwitz, took his own life after being tormented for fifty years by why he survived and others perished in the camps.

Vladimir Volynsk: Ancestral Home—Total Devastation—Along with the mass killings, the Nazis savagely destroyed the comprehensive Jewish communal life that had developed in eastern Europe. What happened to the author's ancestral home city, Vladimir Volynsk, known by the Jews as Ludmir, is typical of what happened to hundreds of cities in Russia and Poland.

Vladimir Volynsk is located in the far western Volhynia district of the Ukraine, an area ceded to Poland after World War I. It was established in about the year 1000 by Prince Vladimir who introduced Christianity to Russia. The small Jewish population increased significantly by German Jews fleeing the aftermath of the Black Death plague in the fourteenth century. The Polish leader responsible for Poland's early development, Casimir the Great, encouraged German Jews to come to Poland because of their successful economic creativity. Ludmir had become a city rich in Jewish religious life when, in the middle of the seventeenth century, the vicious Cossack Bogdan Chmielnicki essentially destroyed the city in a pogrom. By the nineteenth century, the restored Ludmir became the Jewish cultural center for the western Ukraine. In 1939, seventy-five percent of the population of 36,000 was Jewish. The city was steeped in Jewish culture, known for famous rabbis and cantors. There were synagogues of all sizes, a large yeshiva, and a couple of Jewish newspapers. Ludmir had a branch of every east-European Zionist and socialist organization.

Ludmir was taken over by Russia in 1939 as part of Stalin's pact with Hitler that gave Russia control over the eastern part of Poland. This relatively prosperous industrial/commercial city suffered badly during the

Sovietization process. For two years after the Russians took control, the people lived off the sale of used clothing that their American relatives sent. The Russian censors took any money sent by mail. After the area's takeover by the Russians in 1939 many of the young Ludmir Jews were sent to Soviet concentration camps in Siberia.

Being close to the part of Poland occupied by the Germans, Ludmir was quickly overrun by the Nazi army when they attacked the Soviet Union in the summer of 1941. A ghetto was set up, run by Germans but policed mostly by Ukrainians. About 10,000 Jews from neighboring villages were forced into the ghetto. The killings began almost immediately. Several hundred at a time were periodically rounded up and shot. Sometimes hundreds were buried alive in their homes. On one occasion, the Germans announced they were recruiting 1,000 for a work detail. When the large group assembled in the square, they were machine-gunned.

In January 1942, there was a twelve-day pogrom of burning houses and Jewish community buildings and a mass killing that took 10,000 lives. Another pogrom in December of 1942 took 5,000 lives. People survived these actions by hiding quietly in bunkers for days. The last killing spree was in December 1943. Out of the 1,800 that remained alive in the destroyed Ludmir ghetto, only five hundred survived through the summer of 1944. Then, after learning about the German intent to eradicate the ghetto before the Russians army reached Ludmir, many decided to flee the ghetto at any cost. The situation was desperate. They were reluctant to try earlier, knowing the Germans would take reprisal on those left behind. A few succeeded in getting out through the sewer and canal system at night. One group of forty joined the partisans, but only one survived the fighting. Another small group of escapees survived masquerading as Poles as they went through the neighboring town. The Russian liberators found thirty Jews alive in the ghetto rubble. After the war ended, the 140 survivors of the 27,000 that lived there in 1939 tried to reestablish Jewish life in Ludmir. With their family members killed, their homes destroyed and bitter memories of the treatment by the Ukrainians on behalf of the Nazis, this effort failed. They left Ludmir, reaching Israel and the United States by way of the Displaced Persons camps. One thousand years of Jewish life in Ludmir ended. Out of the author's thirty-three aunts, uncles, and cousins who lived in Ludmir in 1941, not one survived.

Places of Refuge—From 1942 until the liberation, the number of Jews looking for places of refuge reduced to a trickle. Individuals and only small groups numbering less than a hundred occasionally found their way to the temporary sanctuary in neutral countries of southern Europe. These efforts were risky. Swiss and Spanish border guards generally turned over to the Vichy French border guards those they caught. The Vichy France government handed them over to the Gestapo, who sent them to the death camps. The successful escapees expected to quickly move on to permanent places of refuge, but there were few haven opportunities offered by the western governments. Quotas to the United States were closed. Britain argued that the precedent of allowing some refugees in would encourage Hitler to flood the country with refugees, imposing an economic crisis on England, an insupportable, callous argument that was slow to go away.

The escapees, under pressure to leave the host countries, were ready to accept any place of asylum. Camps for displaced persons that already existed in North Africa were proposed, but the British government and the U.S. Army rejected the recommendations. They viewed sending Jewish refugees to these areas even on a temporary basis as being too hostile to the Arab population. Although Palestine was still formally closed to Jews, some Jews from the Balkan countries who escaped from the Nazis were secreted into Palestine, which was their first choice, and into neutral Turkey. In 1943 after protesting the German incarceration of their citizens in France, Turkey convinced the Nazis to allow the Turkish Jews to return to Turkey along with the other Turks. They safely took Turkish train caravans that followed the route of the Orient Express train through the heart of Europe.

After the Allied armies made military progress in Italy and landed in France, more Jews surfaced in France and Italy looking for repatriation. In July 1944, perhaps partially to encourage the British to open Palestine to Jews, President Roosevelt opened an internment camp in Oswego, New York, for 1,000 Jewish refugees who had been assembled in internment camps in Italy. He did this by presidential order because he knew Congress would not have gone along. It was an act opposed by the anti-Jewish restrictionist faction in the United States who feared it would set a precedent for bypassing the restrictive immigration quotas. The Jewish community commended Roosevelt for the action that addressed only helping Jews. (As it turned out, a year and a half later, the 1,000 Jews in the camp were offered permanent entry outside of the quota system.) However, this action did not influence the British. Later that year, Foreign Secretary Eden turned down refuge-in-Palestine as part of a deal that was being negotiated between Admiral Horthy of Hungary and the Germans that would have saved 40,000 Hungarian Jews from being sent to the death camps.

The Swedes made two outstanding efforts of providing refuge to Jews during this period that saved many lives. In 1943, they conducted a massive evacuation effort using small boats to transport over 5,000 Danish Jews to the safety of Sweden just before their arrest by the Germans. In 1944, the Swedish government sent Raoul Wallenberg to run the Swedish legation in Hungary. He used Swedish passports to save many Jewish lives by allowing the Jews to remain in Budapest under the protection of Sweden. Wallenberg also persuaded the Hungarian authorities not to send 70,000 Jews to the Budapest ghetto from where they would have wound up in the extermination camps.

The War Refugee Board—In January 1944, President Roosevelt established the War Refugee Board (WRB) under the control of the Treasury Department. The WRB charter was to act to rescue the victims of oppression who were in imminent danger of death. It was given broad powers to "specifically forestall Nazi plans to exterminate all the Jews." It was directed by John Pehle, Jr., who previously was involved in governmental rescue operations.

The authority granted to the WRB enabled it to take unorthodox rescue measures. The WRB enlisted Raoul Wallenberg to undertake his Hungarian rescue mission. The WRB got involved in several small-scale rescue missions, arranging for neutral country support of the missions through diplomatic channels, and financing the missions. These operations included financing the Hechalutz (Zionist pioneer) organization to smuggle refugees from Hungary to Slovakia, leasing boats in Sweden to smuggle refugees out of the Balkans to Turkey, and providing food for the concentration camp inmates to be distributed by the International Red Cross. The WRB was also involved in the unfulfilled Brand mission to trade 10,000 trucks for the Germans halting further Auschwitz killings, and the Kastner ransom negotiation with Eichmann that saved the lives of 1,500 Hungarian Jews.

The weakness of the WRB organization was that it received only the funding to support the WRB staff. The Jewish communal organizations stepped in to provide the money required for the WRB rescue operations. The WRB ceased operations after the war ended in Europe. Its last act was to arrange for a large shipment of food to be sent from Sweden to feed the German concentration camp inmates after the camps were liberated.

5
Jewish Resistance

People question why there was so little armed Jewish resistance to the Nazi terror. Actually, there was more resistance than is generally known. In France and Poland, Jewish underground fighters were active throughout the war, whereas the nationalist fighters in these countries mostly became active near the end of the war when it appeared the Germans were about to be defeated. In Russia, Jewish partisans fought as separate Jewish units and alongside Russian partisans. It is estimated that approximately 30,000 Jews fought as partisans in eastern Europe. Armed Jewish resistance took place in five major ghettos, forty-five small ghettos, five major concentration and extermination camps, and eighteen forced labor camps. The largest rebellion was in the Treblinka concentration camp in August 1943. One thousand revolted, six hundred escaped to fight in the surrounding woods, only forty survived after one year. In addition, there were many acts of unarmed resistance in the ghettos and camps. The Warsaw ghetto act of resistance that defied the powerful German army for twenty-eight days won the admiration of the entire free world. The Warsaw ghetto uprising was the major act of Jewish resistance that startled and confounded the Germans. It amazed the free world.

Warsaw Ghetto Uprising—In 1942, two Jews escaped from Chelmno and reported the gas chamber killing process to the Warsaw ghetto, but the people found it hard to believe. It was only after escapees from the Belzec death camp confirmed the killings in that gas chamber that the Warsaw ghetto populous accepted what happened to the earlier deportees from the ghetto and realized what was in store for them. Several small underground organizations of defiant Jews had already formed when the ghetto was established. After 300,000 had been shipped to the death camps, and the news of the gas chambers became accepted, the activists in the Warsaw ghetto decided to put up resistance to further shipment to the death camps. The underground organizations united to form the Jewish Fighting Organization (ZOB) led by twenty-three-year-old Mordechai

Anielewicz. In January 1943, the ZOB surprised the Germans who came to take away 8,000 Jews. They shot at the German troops, forcing the Germans to retreat from the ghetto and stop the liquidation process.

Learning that the Nazis were planning to destroy the ghetto, the ZOB radioed the world that they needed help to avert the imminent final liquidation of the ghetto. No help came, but the ZOB managed to acquire more arms through the Warsaw underground. Armed with heavy weapons, the Nazi liquidation process began on April 19, 1943. Armed with a few machine guns, rifles, pistols, hand grenades and homemade Molotov cocktails, 1,000 Jewish fighters fought the battle-hardened German troops house-by-house for twenty-eight days.

They fought from cellars, bunkers, and rooftops. It required day and night relentless battles and burning the ghetto block-by-block for the Germans to capture the ghetto. Of the half-million Jews in the ghetto when it was created, only 100,000 were in the ghetto at the start of the rebellion and 56,000 were captured when it ended, of which 7,000 were shot immediately. Many, including Anielewicz, committed suicide rather than be captured. A couple of hundred managed to escape through the sewer system to continue the resistance effort; they brought the news of the rebellion to the world.

Bielski Partisans—The Bielski partisans, led by Tuvia Bielski, was the most outstanding Jewish partisan resistance activity. It combined rescue with resistance. Starting with forty partisans in early 1942, it grew to 1,200 by rescuing Jews from the ghettos and collecting older Jews from the forests that were not accepted by the non-Jewish partisans. He set up a camp, which was virtually a fully functional city in the western Belorussia forest. At the same time, these partisan fighters were disrupting German supply lines. When the Nazis went into the forest to destroy the Bielski partisans, the Soviet army commander in the region suggested Bielski abandon the elderly, women, and children because they would be a hindrance to the partisan's safety. Bielski refused to accept the suggestion. He moved everyone deeper into the forest where they found safety. Over 1,200 men, women, and children emerged from the forest in the summer of 1944 when the war ended in Belorussia. (Tuvia Bielski married in the forest, immigrated to Palestine to fight in the 1948 Israeli War of Independence, and then immigrated to the United States in 1956.)

Why the Reluctance to Resist the Germans?—There were several compelling reasons why the rebellions and the attempts to escape the ghettos and concentration camps occurred so late. The German tactic of "collective responsibility" was a strong deterrent. They viciously killed many community and family members in response to individual acts of armed and unarmed resistance. Many individuals voluntarily identified themselves to the Germans as being responsible for acts of defiance in order to spare the life of others threatened in reprisal by the Germans. **The German warning that ten would be killed for every one who disobeyed their orders ended many thoughts of defiance.**

The younger people felt a responsibility for their parents. They did not want to leave them under the horrible conditions of the ghetto. They did not want to expose their families to the harm that was inevitable when the Germans learned of their escape. **They could not trade their personal freedom for the death of their parents.**

The German army and their collaborators who policed the ghettos and concentration camps were well armed. **With practically no arms available to the Jews, fighting the Germans was essentially impossible and a hopeless proposition.**

The neighboring towns were not hospitable to Jews; the townspeople frequently identified the escapees to the Germans. Many of the partisan groups did not accept Jews. Some anti-Semitic partisan groups actually killed Jewish partisans that they encountered. **After escape from the camps, there was little hope for survival.**

Starting in 1943, the resistance did get stronger out of desperation after the ability to survive the German extermination effort appeared hopeless. Unfortunately, with the Germans being so strong militarily and determined to prevent escapes, very few survived the rebellions.

6
Countries That Resisted Hitler's "Final Solution"

There were several countries in Europe that managed to resist the German effort to eradicate their Jewish citizens in spite of the German pressure to cooperate with them in implementing the Final Solution. The most outstanding was Bulgaria, who steadfastly refused to send their Jewish population to the death camps, saving all of the 50,000 Bulgarian Jews. However, Bulgaria did deport 11,000 non-Bulgarian Jews from the areas of Greece that they annexed in 1941, who wound up in Treblinka. A remarkable story is that of the Danes under the leadership of King Christian X. Although occupied by Germany, Denmark did not apply the oppressive anti-Jewish laws required by Hitler. When word came that the Germans intended to round up the Jews and send them to concentration camps, there was a massive Danish effort that successfully smuggled all the Jews (over 5,000) out of Denmark to the neutral country Sweden. Finland, although allied with Germany, avoided sending its 1,000 Jews to the death camps.

Italy was unusual. Although as Hitler's original ally, Italy instituted anti-Jewish laws, the Italian people and particularly the army opposed sending Italian Jews to the concentration camps. Mussolini, the Fascist dictator, was not particularly anti-Semitic and shielded the Italian Jews from Hitler's extermination plans. However, after the Allied invasion of Italy in 1943, the Germans took over Italy and started sending Italian Jews to the death camps.

The behavior of General Francisco Franco towards the Jews during the Holocaust period was helpful. With no Jews living in Spain, his attitude toward Jews was unknown. He may have harbored resentment towards Jews because of the many Jews who fought against him as volunteers for his opponents in the Civil War; they were independent secular Jews who did not represent the Jewish people. Nevertheless, this Spanish dictator, sympathetic to the Germans who aided him in the Spanish

Civil War, did allow Jews with transit visas to enter from France and continue on to their place of refuge. Although the Spanish border guards generally turned back Jews caught trying to enter Spain without a visa, Franco permitted about 4,000 Jews to escape from France.

7
Vatican's Attitude Toward the Holocaust

During the war, the Vatican through its church network had rather detailed information about the German concentration and death camps, but chose to suppress it. On March 9, the day after V-E Day, Pope Pius XII addressed the world community, offering his comments on the war's devastation and providing his guidance on achieving peace. In his lengthy speech, the Pope did not include the Jewish people among the list of people that were persecuted by the Nazis, disregarding his knowledge that several million Jews were slaughtered by the Germans only because they were Jews. Pope Pius XII remained silent on the genocide of the Jewish people during his lifetime. Quoting Prophet Ezekiel, Pope Pius looked for "God to put a new spirit into all people and to remove their stony heart, especially those responsible for establishing the future peace." Europe and the rest of the world were heartless by not offering relief or refuge to the half-million Jews who languished in the Displaced Persons camps for three years, until the State of Israel was established and took them in.

The "stone-hearted world community" did not hear from the Vatican during those three years. The Pope offered these closing remarks. "Then and only then will the reborn world avoid the return of the thunderous scourge of war and there will reign a true, stable, and universal brotherhood, and that peace guaranteed by Christ even on earth to those who are willing to believe and trust in His law of love." These remarks were not particularly helpful to the Jews who returned to Poland from the concentration camps and from Russia and were trying to renew life in Poland. Within one year, violent anti-Semitism erupted throughout Catholic Poland and Jews were again killed in pogroms. Many Poles very well could have taken the Pope's remarks to mean that the nonbelieving Jews did not meet the Pope's requisite for being the beneficiaries of the brotherhood and peace that he called for.

8
Gentiles Who Saved Jews During the Holocaust

There were many courageous Gentiles in all the European countries who saved the lives of Jewish people during the Holocaust at the risk of their own lives. The Yad Vashem Holocaust Memorial Foundation in Israel continues to identify and honor these "Righteous Gentiles." Some hid individuals and entire Jewish families for long periods, while others took Jewish children into their household where they safely masqueraded as Christians until the Holocaust ended. It was not unusual for a member of the benefactor family not to know that the stranger staying with the family was Jewish. It is estimated that about twenty-five thousand Polish Jews survived this way, fifteen thousand in Warsaw alone. Based on these estimates, ten to fifteen thousand Polish families in Warsaw hid Jews.

These courageous people came from all walks of life, including members of the Christian clergy. Although the Vatican itself neither condemned Hitler's policy of exterminating the Jews nor participated in the relief efforts that developed in the late stages of the war, many Catholic officials at the local level were instrumental in saving Jewish lives. The most notable one was Cardinal Angelo Roncalli who later became Pope John XXIII. He gave thousands of baptismal papers to a cooperating Hungarian official for the use of Jewish children, saving them from being sent to Auschwitz.

Many diplomats took courageous steps at the risk of their own lives to save many Jews. The most notable was Raul Wallenberg, who was truly a hero because of his moral conviction to foil Adolph Eichmann's plan to exterminate all the Jews in Hungary towards the end of World War II. His bold actions, defying the Nazi orders of extermination, saved over 100,000 Jews. Other examples include Dr. Aristedes de Sousa Mendes of Portugal and Chiune Sugihara of Japan. Dr. de Sousa, Portuguese consul in Bordeaux, France, issued exit visas to 30,000 Jews in Vichy France desperately seeking to avoid the roundup of Jews by the Vichy government—which would have meant deportation to the death camps.

When his government learned of his deeds, they removed him as consul and he became a broken man. Chiune Sugihara, the Japanese Consul in Kovno, Lithuania, granted over 6,000 exit visas to Jews enabling them to escape the impending Nazi plan to exterminate the Kovno Jews. Sugihara saved the entire 300-student body of a yeshiva by allowing Jews to hurriedly write the large number of visas that he personally could not handle. Although they were all in the name of Rabinovitz, the visas were mysteriously accepted by the Russian and Japanese border guards.

Civilians were responsible for saving many Jewish lives through their personal bold actions while ostensibly supporting the German army in Russia. The most widely known savior was Oskar Schindler, made famous by the movie, *Schindler's List*. Although he was not a noble person, to say the least, this German civilian businessman nevertheless saved the lives of 900 Jews. Another example is Uri Lichter, a Jewish engineer from Lvov, Poland. With a perfect command of the German language, he avoided the Nazi roundup of Jews in Lvov by masquerading as a Polish laborer. Elevated to chief engineer for a German construction company supporting the German army march into Russia, Lichter forged many travel passports that saved several family members and other Jews by enabling them to move with the construction company until the Russians liberated them.

Raoul Wallenberg—Under pressure from the Jewish community for doing so little to aid Jews being massacred by the Nazis, in 1944 President Roosevelt assigned Henry Morgenthau to head the War Refugee Board. The board's mission was to develop steps to counteract Hitler's "Final Solution of the Jews," which was about to happen to the Hungarian Jews. Up until that year, although he was an ally of Germany, the Hungarian leader Admiral Horthy had protected Hungarian Jews from the Nazi extermination process. That protection ended in 1944, putting the Hungarian Jews in jeopardy.

Thirty-two-year-old Raoul Wallenberg, from an aristocratic family in neutral Sweden, answered the call from the War Refugee Board to aid in the Jewish relief effort. Without any instructions on how to accomplish his mission, he went to Hungary as the first secretary of the Swedish legation. In this low-level position, he used the full diplomatic weight of a neutral country to save many Jewish lives.

When he arrived, almost a half-million Jews in eastern Hungary had already been transported to the Auschwitz extermination camp. The remaining Hungarian Jews were being forced into a Budapest ghetto from where they were being sent to Auschwitz. His first action was to pull Jews out of the death marches from the ghetto and give them Swedish visas, immediately saving many lives. He then assisted the International Red Cross effort to keep thousands of Hungarian Jewish children, orphaned by the genocide, out of the Nazi hands—he provided money, food, and shelter. He persuaded the Hungarian authorities not to send another 70,000 Jews to the Budapest ghetto from where they would be shipped to the extermination camps. His final salvation act occurred in January 1945, just before the entry of the Russians into Budapest. He frightened the German general into countermanding the order to shoot all the Jews in the ghetto; Wallenberg had suggested that the general would be brought up on charges of genocide before the War Crimes Tribunal.

Shortly after the Russians entered Budapest, Wallenberg disappeared—Russia was suspected of taking him prisoner. The Russians never did reveal the truth of what happened to Raoul Wallenberg. When Sweden investigated what happened to him, the Russians denied Wallenberg was a Russian prisoner. Despite the many reports of seeing him in the gulag prison system as late as 1967, the Russians still denied to the world that he was ever a Russian prisoner. Later, Russia finally reported that he had died in their prison of a heart attack in 1947.

Wallenberg apparently was the victim of Russian suspicions regarding his American connections and his family's involvement in efforts with Germans to end the war. Stalin took these to be plots against the Soviet Union and took some unknown action against him.

Oskar Schindler—Oskar Schindler was an aggressive German who bribed German army officials to allow him to select almost 1,000 Jews from the concentration camps to work in his factories. With the help of one of his Jewish aids, he always kept a list of the Jews working for him. Some suspect it was kept to protect him from criminal charges if the Germans lost the war.

His first factory was near the Crakow concentration camp. Contrary to the almost pleasant conditions depicted in the film, *Schindler's List,* conditions in the concentration camp where his workers lived were as awful as in every other concentration camp. In October 1944, after he was forced to close his Polish operations, he moved to a new plant in Brinnlitz, Czechoslovakia, which was near his hometown. During the transition, seven hundred of his original male Jewish workers were sent to a death camp, so he picked new replacements. Three hundred women that he planned to move to the new plant spent some harrowing days in the Auschwitz death camp before he managed to get them out. When the Russians liberated the Brinnlitz concentration camp, in appreciation for having saved their lives, several Jews shielded Schindler from being captured by the Russians and then by the Americans. In later years, several Jews who had been saved by Oskar Schindler tried to repay him; they contributed to his support when he became destitute while living in New York. They still contribute to his wife's support.

9
Grim Statistics

The Holocaust killings took place in twenty European countries. As seen from the statistics in the accompanying table, in several countries Hitler almost achieved his goal of eradicating Jews from Europe, with ninety percent of the 1939 Jewish population having been annihilated. In total, 65 percent of the 1939 European Jewish population perished in the Holocaust.

Country	1939 Jewish Population	Annihilated in Holocaust	% Annihilated
Poland	3,300,000	3,025,000	92
Germany	300,000	270,000	90
Lithuania	145,000	130,000	90
Austria	90,000	80,000	89
Greece	75,000	65,000	87
Czechoslovakia	315,000	260,000	83
Yugoslavia	75,000	60,000	80
Netherlands	140,000	110,000	79
Latvia	95,000	70,000	74
Belgium	90,000	68,000	74
Hungary	650,000	450,000	69
Romania	800,000	400,000	50
Italy	60,000	30,000	50
Estonia	4,500	2,000	44
France	300,000	100,000	33
Soviet Union	2,800,000	900,000	32
	9,229,500	**6,020,000**	**65**

10
Liberation

The liberating Allied armies found about 100,000 Jews still alive in the concentration camps. They were physically worn down by the ordeal in the camps and depressed over losing their loved ones. They had no desire to go back to their native lands that would have brought back painful memories of the hardships they suffered there—their communities were destroyed and their families gone. Thousands of camp inmates were in bad physical condition, on the verge of death due to malnutrition and could not be saved. In Bergen-Belsen alone, 12,000, mostly Jewish inmates died in spite of the British efforts to save them by bringing in many physicians.

After the Dachau camp was liberated, a document was discovered expressing Gestapo Chief Himmler's order for Dachau to be evacuated and all inmates executed. That there were any survivors in the German concentration camps is likely due to the German camp guards fleeing for their lives rather than taking the time to obey Himmler's orders to execute the inmates.

After suffering through years of Nazi horror, liberation should have been an exhilarating experience for the survivors. It did not turn out that way. The end to the German threat to their lives was indeed an immediate relief, but their physically debilitated condition when they were liberated restrained their reaction. The uncertainty of the future, clouded by the initial callous treatment of the liberating armies, added to their depression.

The world had expressed disbelief, dismay, and sorrow when learning of the terrible Nazi cruelty to the Jews during the Holocaust. Based on these sentiments, it was natural for the survivors to expect considerate treatment and assistance after their liberation. That was not the case. The first year after liberation was particularly hard for the Jewish survivors; it took several years for their lot to improve.

Liberation by the Russians—The first camps to be liberated were in Poland. What happened in Auschwitz is typical of what happened in other camps in Poland. The German camp masters and supporting soldiers and collaborators fled when they thought the Russian army was nearby. The healthier inmates had been moved earlier to camps closer to Germany. Those left behind were terribly sick and of no use to the Germans. The camp inmates left the unguarded cold camps in search of food and clothing. They found some food in the adjacent German barracks and clothing in a British prisoner of war camp six miles away. However, their main salvation was finding fields full of potatoes buried under the soil for winter storage, as was common in Poland.

Freedom, however, was slow in coming. The Russians did not come to Auschwitz as quickly as the Germans expected. After running away and out of uniform to avoid being taken prisoner, some German soldiers came back temporarily. They tracked down the Jews who had left the camps. They shot the Jews in the fields where they were collecting potatoes or in the neighboring towns where the Jews were trying to find food and shelter on their brief journey to freedom. Some were forced back to the concentration camps by the Germans; others returned to Auschwitz voluntarily because they had nowhere else to go. Such was the case in the first days after the Germans left Auschwitz on January 18, 1945.

Ten days after the Germans departed, the Russians did enter Auschwitz. They provided medical help to save many of the terribly sick survivors. In that ten-day period of isolation, the inmates were trying to help each other survive. They shared food and clothing at the risk of contaminating themselves with the diseases prevalent in the camp, such as dysentery, typhus, and scarlet fever. After being liberated by the Russians, the Auschwitz survivors left the camp as soon as they were healthy enough to travel.

The largest numbers of Jewish survivors who were liberated by the Russians at the war's end were in the concentration camps located in Poland further west of Auschwitz. Most of the survivors were Polish Jews. They went back to their homes in Poland hoping to find other members of their families; since they had survived, they hoped that possibly other family members also survived. That thought gave them the strength to walk for days, begging for food and covering hundreds of miles to get home. The Russian soldiers cooperated by giving them rides on army trucks. As they were soon to find out, very few family members survived—no parents, and only some children hidden by caring Christians. After this disappointment, very few Jews remained in Poland. Individually or in small groups, they worked their way west hoping to find a way to get to Palestine through the

Jewish underground movement, or to get into the new American Displaced Persons camps in Germany.

Liberation by the Americans—Buchenwald was the first concentration camp liberated by the Americans; it occurred six weeks before V-E Day. The American soldiers were not prepared for the camp scenes. Seeing living conditions unfit for human beings shocked them. There were survivors suffering from disease and malnutrition on the verge of death; some were skeletons, barely alive. These former prisoners were so hardened to living with death around them that they disposed of corpses like they were handling logs of wood. They were immune to the smell of the dead. There were mounds of emaciated dead bodies alongside the camps. The soldiers were not prepared to cope with the horrible physical and medical conditions of the inmates. Some survivors could not be saved under any treatment. Some survivors died because they were unwittingly fed food too rich for their deprived digestive systems.

Newsreels taken by correspondents traveling with the American armed forces who entered the Buchenwald, Dachau, and Bergen-Belsen concentration camps graphically revealed the horrors of the camps to the world. Unfortunately, it did not bring much relief to the survivors, who after the generally kind treatment they received initially at liberation, were not treated very well. The American soldiers had no behavioral instructions. Except for the Jewish soldiers, they could not develop a friendship with this tattered group of people who did not speak their language, had strange customs, and wanted what the soldiers could not give them. About seventy percent wanted to go to Palestine and thirty percent wanted to go to the United States or other countries to be with their relatives.

Jewish U.S. Army chaplains who witnessed the conditions first hand issued negative reports about the conditions in the camps. Reacting to these reports, Secretary Henry Morgenthau, Jr. convinced President Truman to dispatch Earl G. Harrison to investigate. Dean Harrison of the University of Pennsylvania Law School had displayed a compassionate, humanitarian disposition while involved in an earlier government committee on refugees. He turned out to be the right person for this most important task that affected the welfare of the concentration camp survivors languishing in the former concentration camps. In August, he reported that three months after V-E Day, Jews and other nonrepatriables were still living under guard, and were wearing prisoner garb in crowded and unsanitary conditions that resembled the slave labor concentration camps. He stressed the problems that the Jewish inmates in particular were suffering and indicated that the army personnel were not equipped to address them.

A major problem was the psychological stress on the Jewish inmates who were living in the same barracks as the non-Jewish east-European nationals; the same people who before the war's end helped the Germans oppress the Jews in the camps and ghettos. Another concern was that there was no opportunity for the inmates to communicate with the outside world in search of relatives. The Jewish inmates were completely idle and had no idea of what was in store for them. Dean Harrison indicated that they longed for words of encouragement and for some actions on their behalf. General Eisenhower, responsible for the American army in Germany, initially took issue with the report and denied bad conditions existed. After Harrison defended his report, President Truman reacted with a vital decision affecting the welfare of the concentration camp survivors. He instructed Eisenhower to correct the camp conditions, emphasizing the need to get the Jews out of the camps and into decent housing. That step was to bring physical and psychological relief to the survivors.

After President Truman's directive, General Eisenhower went to Dachau to personally see the situation. Witnessing the camp conditions that still bore evidence of the German brutal treatment, Eisenhower gave instructions for many improvements. Comfortable Displaced Persons (DP) camps were to be set up outside the concentration camps, replacing the concentration camps as the living quarters. The inmates were to be fed better and clothed adequately. Private volunteers, anxious to assist the displaced persons, were to be allowed into the camps. General Eisenhower made two decisions most important to the emotional health of the Jews.

Firstly, they were now to be housed separately from the non-Jewish displaced persons; previously, Eisenhower had ordered that no racial separation be made in the camps, believing that to do so would be copying Hitler's racial discrimination policy against the Jews. This earlier policy resulted in Jews being housed with the three times larger number of non-Jewish displaced people from eastern Europe who had political reasons for not wanting to be repatriated. They were the same people who had collaborated with the Germans or were anti-Communists and feared going back to Communist countries. These people exhibited their strong anti-Jewish feelings in the camps, making the Jews feel very uncomfortable emotionally, and occasionally, physically. Secondly, Jews would not be forced to accept repatriation to their former homelands—none wanted repatriation. They feared repatriation to their former homelands that supported Hitler's oppression of the Jews and that still had anti-Semitic prejudices.

As the American DP camp conditions improved, the camps swelled with Jews who left Poland and some that fled from the British camps, which they bitterly disliked. An amazing grapevine communication network advised Jews dispersed in Poland about the camp conditions in the different German occupation zones. The American camps were favored because the Americans accepted into their camps all Jews who had no home and considered themselves displaced persons. Before coming to the DP camps, these Jews were in Poland because Stalin took a step that was inconsistent with his normally intolerant attitude towards Jews. He permitted 150,000 Polish Jews who had taken refuge in the Soviet Union at the start of the war to return to Poland after the war ended. It may have been in gratitude to the Soviet Jews who fought so well in the Soviet army, although they were previously treated harshly as civilians.

These Jews did not stay in Poland long. In July 1946, a pogrom erupted in Kielce in which forty-two Jews were killed in a riot incited by a false ritual-murder accusation. This followed two earlier smaller pogroms. These and other brutal events that followed brought back memories of earlier Polish anti-Semitism. These incidents, which took almost a thousand lives, coupled with the Polish Communist officials' hostility towards Jews and the hostile attitude of the Polish people in general, convinced most of these Jews to leave Poland and enter the American DP camps.

Liberation by the British—The British applied the same policy as Genaral Eisenhower's initial policy of not separating Jews from the non-Jews in their camps. However, their motive was different. They did not want to give the Jews the opportunity to claim themselves as a separate people who would be entitled to a separate Jewish homeland in Palestine. In July of 1945, because of the British nonseparation policy, Jews in British camps had to suffer the mental agony of living with the same Poles, Lithuanians, and Ukrainians who had been German collaborators in the Nazi process to eliminate the Jews.

The Labour party took over the government in England, with Clement Attlee as prime minister, replacing Winston Churchill. Before the election, Attlee endorsed the policy of not standing in the way of any Jews wanting to enter Palestine. After the election, his foreign minister, Ernest Bevin, abrogated both Attlee's position and the British Balfour Declaration, which pledged a national home in Palestine for the Jewish people. Bevin wanted to gain favor with the Arab countries for their oil. The British offered little hope for the Jews in their camps. In 1946, they actually prohibited Jews who left Poland from entering their camps. Bevin kept in force the White Paper of 1939, which prohibited Jewish entry to Palestine after 1944 without Arab permission.

Liberation of the Hidden Jews—After each area was liberated, the Jews hidden in that area by noble Gentiles surfaced. They mostly elected to sorrowfully leave their benefactors and returned to their homes, only to be disappointed and shocked not to find their families there. For the "hidden" children, it frequently turned into a trauma. It took a long time for surviving parents to track down the location of their children. Some children, having lived several of their formative years as Catholics, did not want to give up their adopted religion. Many of the stand-in parents became very attached to the children they had taken care of for several years and fought legal battles with the natural parents to retain custody.

Liberation by the Bricha Organization—In 1944, an organization called Bricha (Hebrew, *"flight," "escape"*) was established by a small group of Zionist survivors of the ghettos in Lithuania and Poland. Their objective was to smuggle Jewish stragglers in the liberated Russian areas into Palestine. After V-E Day, their route through Romania closed when the Russians clamped down on this underground activity. Bricha shifted its activity to helping survivors get out of Germany and into Palestine. The Mossad le Aliyah Bet that was active in smuggling Jews out of Europe before 1942 then sponsored the Bricha organization, strengthening its capability and enlarging its role. Bricha recruited demobilized soldiers of a Palestinian Jewish Brigade who had been recruited by the British to undertake hazardous military actions in Italy. This group of tough former soldiers, dedicated to helping the downtrodden Jews, remained in Europe several years working to accomplish the Bricha objective. Using bribery and false papers to cross borders, they took every means imaginable, including mountain trails, to route the survivors from all sections of Europe to boats that left for Palestine from ports in Italy and France. The British, whose occupation zone was on the Italian border, presented every obstacle they could to prevent these transits. The French occupation zone authorities quietly cooperated.

After waiting two years for the British to change their policy and open the door to Palestine, the Jewish inmates in the American DP camps started to get restless. With no hope for a change in British policy being indicated, the DPs began to change their objective. More than half now expressed their desire to go to the United States. Because of this new agitation, the troubled American authorities got into the unusual position of actually encouraging this illegal organization to continue its efforts in order to lessen the DP interest in immigrating to the Uniated States.

Bricha was successful in moving 70,000 Jews from Europe to Palestine between 1945 and 1948. The British caught most of them trying to enter Palestine and detained them in Cyprus before they were ultimately allowed to enter Palestine. While in Cyprus, they received cultural training from Palestinian Jews that prepared them for living in Palestine. They also got military training by members of the Haganah that was hidden from the British authorities. This training turned out to be very valuable. These illegal immigrants were able to help defend the new State of Israel in the 1948 War of Independence.

The Ship *Exodus*—The last major Bricha operation involved the ship *Exodus 1947* that became the subject of the very popular movie, *Exodus*. The former elegant Chesapeake Bay steamer *President Garfield* had been converted to a British troop carrier and then to the USS *President Garfield* that ferried troops to the Normandy beaches during the Allied invasion of Europe. The *Garfield* came back to the United States ready to be junked, therefore it was affordable to be bought by the Mossad. Repaired and named *Exodus 1947,* it was the largest ship in the Bricha operation. The Bricha organization in Germany managed to transport 4,500 Jewish Holocaust survivors by train and motorcades across borders to the French port of Marseilles, where they boarded the *Exodus* for the trip to Palestine. British destroyers shot at the *Exodus* off the coast of Palestine near Tel Aviv, where the illegal entry was planned. The British then forced the *Exodus* to go to Haifa, where they rammed it.

After a brief battle on the deck that subdued the essentially unarmed Jews, the British forced the protesting passengers to disembark and immediately reboard other ships. These ships bypassed Cyprus, the usual destination for intercepted illegal immigrants, and took them to Hamburg, Germany. British sailors beat resistant passengers to force them to leave the ship, a sight that delighted Nazi sympathizers who were there to protest the return of Jews to Germany. The disappointed refugees, having waited two years to get to Palestine, wound up back in British DP camps. The brutal actions against these Holocaust survivors antagonized the world against the British.

11
Survival

Historians have interviewed many Jewish concentration camp survivors to learn what it took to survive and what type of person survived. Being lucky and having mental strength were the two major factors. Courage and physical strength were two secondary factors. How the survivors viewed the role of God in their survival varied widely. Their attitude was generally a function of their religious disposition before their incarceration. Many survivors were left with a sense of guilt and pain—they survived but their family loved ones were snatched from their side and killed.

Luck—The single and almost universal answer was that only the lucky survived. Frequently, it was only because of luck that a survivor was chosen for a work camp and not a death camp. Two Jews are in front of a German soldier anxious to kill a Jew—it was only luck that the German shot the individual next to the survivor. Luck was attributed as the reason that some escaped alive from the mass executions by the Germans or escaped detection in their hiding places. Those that recovered from deathly diseases without receiving medical attention in the ghettos and camps said they were lucky. Those who managed not to contract diseases from other close inmates ill with contagious diseases considered themselves extremely lucky.

Mental Strength—The most important personal characteristic that increased the chances of survival was mental strength. Without mental strength, the survivors could not have coped with the unimaginable agonies they suffered in the camps. They had to endure family members killed before their eyes, personal beatings and rapes, personal sickness, and sick and dying all around them. They barely had enough food to survive and had to keep up with hard physical labor under the most trying conditions. They knew that if they could not cope with any one of these traumas, they would die or killed by the Germans. Some survived because they had the mental strength to cope with the hideous task of disposing of the dead bodies, some the painful task of deciding for the Nazis which Jews would live and which would die. The mentally strong frequently contributed to the survival of others by encouraging those on the verge of giving up to continue fighting for their lives—the will to live was a key ingredient. For many, this strength did not endure after they won their freedom, the remembrance of the traumas they experienced caused mental breakdowns.

Viktor Frankl, the famous Jewish psychiatrist and author who survived imprisonment from 1941 to 1945 in four concentration camps, including the death camp Auschwitz, attributed survival to "the individual finding a meaning to their lives." In his words, "I also bear witness to the unexpected extent to which man is capable of defying and braving even the worst conditions conceivable. We must never forget that we may also find meaning in life even when confronted with a hopeless situation."

Courage—A small number of Jews survived the five years of the Final Solution due to their personal acts of courage. They took a variety of bold steps that kept them alive. In Germany, some slipped out of the Gestapo net and remained alive by constantly running and hiding. In Poland, some managed to masquerade as Poles, frequently having to run for their safety after betrayal by informers. A few managed to escape from the concentration camps.

Perhaps 30,000 Jews took the bold step of fighting as partisans behind the German lines under very trying conditions. Food and arms were hard to come by. Frequently they had to defend themselves against attacks from other ethnic partisans, such as the Poles and the Ukrainians.

Many Jews survived through the courage of others, Jew and non-Jew. Several thousand Jews survived in Hungary due to the courageous steps taken Joel Brand and Rudolf Kastner. These Jews were bold enough to personally confront Nazi officials, including Eichmann and Himmler, to negotiate for the freedom of this large group of Jews. A later attempt by Brand to barter 10,000 trucks for ending the death camp killings never materialized because Great Britain vetoed this plan; ostensibly they did not believe the sincerity of the German offer. The boldness of Swedish Raoul Wallenberg saved 100,000 Hungarian Jews. The audacity of German businessman Oskar Schindler saved 900 Jews. Thousands of young Jewish children survived because of the courage of many Gentiles who took them into their households and churches at the risk of their own safety.

Physical Strength—Physical strength directly contributed to survivability, but it was not an assurance of survival. Those with apparent physical strength were generally selected for the slave-labor quotas rather than the death camp quotas. However, when the work task ended, the Germans gave an individual's previous hard work no consideration—they were liable to be picked to meet new death-camp quotas. The hard work and inadequate food quickly wore down concentration camp inmates. To stay alive, they needed the will to survive. Without this will to survive, they could not muster up the physical strength to continue doing brutal physical work—to stop was generally fatal. The German guards were quick to shoot anyone who fell by the wayside due to exhaustion, sickness, or the loss of the will to live.

Role of God—Jews with weak religious ties felt that the God of the Jews abandoned them. Some Jews did not believe in God, while others turned atheist. To them, a God would not have allowed the Holocaust to happen. Those with religious ties to Judaism generally had two different views of the role of God in the Holocaust tragedy, neither one crediting God with their survival. Each view was based on their personal religious convictions. One view was that God had no hand in the German behavior; God gives people the ability to choose right from wrong and so the Nazi evil was a free choice, not influenced by God. The other prevalent view was that of a Jewish principle of faith that enabled Jews to cope with Jewish community disasters throughout the ages. God has strange ways. It is not for Jews to question, but to accept.

Some survivors had a strong faith in God that they never lost. They attributed their personal survival to God watching over them. Others wondered why God picked them to survive.

Religion in the Concentration Camps—God's role may have been fundamentally unclear to the religious Jews while in the concentration camps. Nevertheless, many religious Jews in the camps still practiced Orthodox rituals as best as they could under the almost impossible conditions. According to the nonreligious author Victor Frankl, who spent four years in four concentration camps, the religious interest of the prisoners was the most sincere imaginable. They read prayers in the most unlikely places where they would not be seen by the guards. They surreptitiously shared hidden *tefillin* (phylacteries—small boxes with scriptural passages, worn on the left arm and head for morning prayers), read from secreted Torahs, and missed meals on Passover in lieu of not eating *chometz* (food not prepared properly or acceptable for consumption during Passover).

A survey of 1,000 survivors taken in Israel thirty years after the end of the Holocaust indicated that about forty percent considered themselves observant religiously in the camps, but the observant number increased to sixty percent in the years after liberation. It dwindled to fifty percent at the time of the survey.

12
Rehabilitation

By 1946 there were 250,000 Jews in the DP camps in Germany and Austria, 10,000 Jewish refugees in France and other countries in Western Europe, and 32,000 refugees outside of the DP camps in Germany, Austria, and Italy. They were getting minimum sustenance from the Allied governments operating the camps and controlling the German occupation zones. President Truman was shocked at hearing of the terrible conditions in the camps and instructed General Eisenhower to provide for the Jewish inmates' physical and emotional needs. However, no funding for these efforts was requested from Congress; he was convinced Congress would not go along.

There were also almost a half-million Jews in the countries of the Soviet sphere of eastern Europe who had difficulty reestablishing a livelihood after having been uprooted from their homes. They were getting no help from their respective home countries and facing violent anti-Semitism in some countries such as Poland and Romania.

Up until 1945, the American Jewish community's awareness of the horrors of the Holocaust aroused much grief and sympathy but there was very little planning on how to help the survivors. After it became obvious that the Allied governments were not going to relieve the plight of the DP camp survivors, the American Jewish community responded to this urgent need. The major organizations involved were the Joint Distribution Committee, which administered the aid, and the United Jewish Appeal, which financed the aid. The relief was planned in 1945 and executed in 1946.

Joint Distribution Committee—In July 1945, Dr. Joseph Schwartz, European director of the Joint Distribution Committee, accompanied Dean Earl Harrison on his investigation of conditions in the DP camps. He came back with a complete understanding of the scope of the problems and needs of the Jewish people in the camps. Dr. Schwartz presented a comprehensive plan to the Jewish community, which would bring massive help to the Jews of Europe. It was structured to provide relief and rehabilitation.

Under Schwartz's direction, by the end of 1947 the JDC staff operated one hundred fourteen schools and kindergartens, seventy-four religious schools, and twenty-four clinics, hospitals, and orphanages in the DP camps of Germany and Austria. Meals were provided for 250,000 camp inmates and clothing was furnished them. Similar facilities and services were provided to the Jewish refugees in camps in other western European countries and to the large number of Jews who elected to remain in the eastern European countries. By the summer of 1947, the JDC was supporting three quarters of a million impoverished Jews in Europe.

United Jewish Appeal—Up until the need to aid the Holocaust survivors arose, large United Jewish Appeal campaigns were in the ten- million-dollar range. Based on Dr. Schwartz's report and relief plan, the UJA goal increased ten fold. A 100-million-dollar UJA campaign was targeted for 1946, the bulk going to the JDC relief and rehabilitation effort. Thanks to the fund-raising skills of Henry Montor, the extremely large UJA campaign was very successful. His themes of Jewish survival and heroism rather than pity and sorrow were very motivating, resulting in large contributions from many prominent, wealthy Jews who previously had no association with Jewish issues.

In 1947, the UJA raised $158 million, with over seventy-five percent going to the JDC. In 1948, with the creation of the State of Israel anticipated, the goal was again raised significantly. Almost $200 million was raised, with $178 million allocated for Israel. Henry Morgenthau, Jr., Henry Montor, and financier Edward Warburg spearheaded this large drive. Thirty-five philanthropists were recruited to spur the local drives. Golda Meir, who was brought in from Israel, was the leading UJA speaker. She brought tears to the audiences with tales of her personal experiences in Palestine, her expressions of concern for the future there, and her pleas for financial aid.

13
Resettlement

The quarter-million Jews in the DP camps and the thirty thousand outside the camps looking to leave Europe to start a new life away from the scene of the Holocaust had few legal opportunities for immigration. Due to the restrictive immigration laws, only 2,500 Jewish displaced persons had entered the United States through the end of 1946. Other Western countries were encouraged by restrictionist Americans to retain their respective restrictive immigration laws.

Great Britain had its 1939 White Paper still in effect so that illegal immigration to Palestine was the only recourse to the Holocaust survivors, who predominately wanted to resettle there. A World Security Conference was held as the European war was winding down. An umbrella organization of major Jewish communal organizations, the American Jewish Conference, was established to urge this conference to take no actions to prejudice the Jewish rights to establish a Jewish state in Palestine or to prejudice the rights of Jews to immigrate to Palestine. The Jewish Labor Committee, representing 500,000 members of the AF of L, the CIO, and the ILGWU, backed this action.

Immigration to the United States—Palestine was still closed to Jews by the British, and anti-immigration sentiment still prevailed in the U.S. The American Jewish community and others sympathetic to the plight of the Jewish DPs concluded that changing the U.S. quota regulations for all nationalities represented the only practical approach to increasing the Jewish immigration quota. The American Jewish community finally united on this objective. Even the anti-Zionist American Council for Judaism, which previously opposed Jewish refugee immigration into the United States, joined the quota liberalization movement. However, the congressional action to change the quotas took several years to complete. Anti-Semitic congressmen did their best to delay the action to lower the total number allowed in, and to allow in only Jews who reported to DP camps by December 22, 1945. The latter would have denied immigration opportunities to 75,000 Jews who entered the camps after that date.

In October 1946, President Truman requested congressional legislation that would have allowed in 400,000 immigrants over the next four years. The restrictionist and anti-Semitic legislators submitted a substitute bill. It limited the number to 200,000 over a two-year period and included the December 1945 cutoff date. The Jewish leaders agreed not to object to this bill, although it contained provisos that were clearly unfavorable for Jewish immigration, and to work to amend the law. An objection would have strengthened the hand of the restrictionists and would have resulted in the defeat of this breakthrough bill, which increased immigration quotas for the first time since 1924. This Displaced Persons Act passed in June 1948. The strategy for achieving favorable changes was to involve the Polish Catholic lobby, who also favored changing the cutoff date. The approach was successful. In June 1950, a revised bill was passed that allowed in 341,000 immigrants, advanced the cutoff date to January 1, 1949, and deleted some provisions that discriminated against Jews. By the end of 1952, when the new Immigration Act active period ended, 393,000 immigrants entered the U.S., of which twenty-one percent were Jews totaling 83,000.

Immigration to Palestine—From early surveys taken by representatives of the Jewish communal organizations that visited the DP camps, it was evident that most of the Jewish displaced persons preferred to go to Palestine. This was in spite of the hostile attitude to Jewish immigration by the Palestinian Arabs and the British. The DPs, who had a horrific experience during the Holocaust period, did not know which western country they could trust. They were fearful of the growing anti-Semitism in Europe that reminded them of Nazism and would not consider returning to their former homes in eastern Europe. Palestine, the Jewish "Promised Land" of their ancient forefathers, was their hope for being able to reestablish their lives in a place where they would not be considered aliens as they were in Europe.

By 1946, the American Jewish community recognized that immigration to the United States was not the answer to the Jewish DP problem. Changing the U.S. quotas would be difficult to achieve, and at best, the increased quotas would not accommodate all the Jewish DPs. Besides, their own surveys indicated that Palestine was preferred by the DP Jews. These conditions caused a change in the Jewish community's political emphasis. They now directed their efforts to open Palestine to Jewish immigration through the United Nations process. On November 29, 1947, the UN voted to partition Palestine into a Jewish and an Arab state, to be effective in August 1948. After the vote, while the State Department worked to withdraw the partition plan, the Arab States rejected the partition plan. Fighting between the Arabs and Jews erupted, which led to the Jewish Agency in Jerusalem declaring the existence of the State of Israel to be effective on May 15, 1948. That was the day that the British Palestinian mandate was to end and the British troops were to leave Palestine.

Between 1945 and 1948, 70,000 displaced Jews who were willing to face the dangers associated with the illegal entry process had entered Palestine with the assistance of the Jewish underground movement. After 1948, most of the 200,000 Jewish DPs that remained in Europe emigrated to the new State of Israel, which had an open-door policy to Jews from any part of the world. The Jewish immigrants were welcomed as "Hebrews" in their "National Home."

With most of the survivors out of Europe by the end of 1951, all the displaced person camps were closed down.

14
Nazis Brought to Justice: Nuremberg Trial

In October 1942, President Roosevelt and Prime Minister Churchill agreed that the Nazi ringleaders should be punished for their vicious crimes against humanity. In their opinion, the crimes merited the death penalty without a trial. Ironically, when they raised this with Soviet Premier Stalin, the dictator who killed so many of his countrymen without trials in the purges of the 1930s, Stalin pushed for a trial before an international tribunal as the only honorable way that would be acceptable to world opinion. The three leaders agreed. President Roosevelt later initiated the action to prepare for the trial to be held by the Big Four countries: the United States, Great Britain, France, and the Soviet Union.

Nuremberg, Germany, was selected as the site for the trial. It was considered appropriate for two main reasons. It was the city where the massive Nazi rallies were held. In this city, the laws that removed the civil rights of the German Jews were created. It was felt that war crime justice doled out in this city where loyalty to Hitler was frequently demonstrated so fervently would give the Germans a lesson in their mistake of blindly accepting the Nazi leaders and their harsh treatment of the German Jews. Allied bombing during the last days of the war had flattened three-fourths of the Nuremberg central district. All that remained essentially undamaged was the Palace of Justice complex where the trial was to be held. This devastated scene surrounding the trial area would be symbolic to the Germans of all the destruction they caused Europe.

Rather than accuse individuals of specific crimes, the Big Four representatives agreed to bring three conspiracy charges against the Nazi leadership: (1) "Crimes against Peace," including the launching of an aggressive war; (2) "War Crimes" that violated Hague and Geneva conventions; (3) "Crimes against Humanity," which included all the atrocities the Nazi regime committed.

The trial started in November 1945 and ended in October 1946. The four countries involved in the tribunal each had a prosecution team, a judge, and an alternate judge. The chief prosecutor and leader of the American team was Supreme Court Justice Robert Jackson, a former attorney general. He played a significant role in defining the charges and organizing the complicated and unusual prosecution effort, which was supported mostly by a large American staff. The American judge was Francis Biddle, the alternate John Parker. They had contrasting judicial views about the accused crimes and exerted different influences on the tribunal rulings.

The tribunal decided against including Adolf Hitler in the conspiracy charge for fear of making him a martyr. Almost for the same reason, they concluded it was unwise to include dead Nazi leaders Heinrich Himmler and Josef Goebbels, who had committed suicide before the war's end. Also dropped from consideration was Robert Ley, head of the German Labor Movement and responsible for many crimes, who committed suicide in the Nuremberg prison before the trial started. Twenty-two leaders of the Nazi regime were selected for prosecution. Prosecutor Jackson persuaded the Tribunal to include German military leaders. Martin Bormann, who was second in command to Hitler, was never found and therefore not brought to trial.

During the course of the trial, it was learned that Adolf Eichmann was directly involved in executing the Final Solution, but he was never brought to trial. One witness testified to Eichmann's bragging of being responsible for the death of five million Jews. On hearing of this testimony, Eichmann managed to escape from the POW camp for SS officers where he was held. He remained in Germany three years, then lived in Argentina for ten years before being discovered by Israeli intelligence. He was secreted out of Argentina, brought to Israel for trial that was witnessed by the world, found guilty, and executed.

Many German political and military witnesses were brought to the trial to support the accusations and to assist in the defense. Thousands of the German regime's documents describing the involvement of the defendants were used in the trial. The testimonies described many horrors inflicted on the Jews and non-Jewish victims that were not previously told by Jewish witnesses to the Holocaust—often because no one remained alive to tell the tale except the German perpetrators. For six weeks, the court heard evidence of how a quarter-million people were killed in a euthanasia program, which turned into the Final Solution extermination of millions of Jews. They were told of the various sadistic medical experiments conducted under the auspices of Himmler and Goering by German physicians in the concentration camps. As a result of this information, there were follow-up trials for approximately two hundred people who were identified as having committed war crimes. This included twenty-three who committed the euthanasia killings and conducted the medical experiments in the concentration camps.

Defense Arguments—The primary defense argument of the Nazi political leaders was that they were not involved in creating the Nazi policies towards the Jews or in instigating the brutal crimes against the rest of Europe. Therefore, they could not be accused of being a part of the conspiracy, which was the main accusation against the group. The only exception was Hermann Goering. He bragged about being the main advisor to Hitler, but claimed innocence of being a conspirator. He had an odd reason; he argued that he could not have been a party to the conspiracy because the other Hitler aides in the conspiracy despised him. They would not conspire with someone they disliked and distrusted.

The defendants also claimed that their accused actions were taken only out of intense loyalty to Hitler—they were merely following his wishes. They maintained that performing crimes strictly out of dedication to a revered leader absolved them of personal responsibility for the crimes.

Goering was the most difficult defendant the prosecutors had to contend with during the trial proceedings. He skillfully dodged most of the interrogations, but the evidence against him was overwhelming. Despite all the evidence presented that documented his involvement in planning and directing anti-Jewish directives, Goering denied organizing the Final Solution. Although German records presented at the trial documented the killing of five million Jews, Goering maintained it was a policy of emigration of the Jews and not a policy of liquidation of the Jews.

The primary defense of the military leaders was that they were only obeying Hitler's orders, not setting policies that violated international law—for instance, invading and devastating neutral countries, and killing prisoners of war. Field Marshal Wilhelm Keitel, Wehrmacht chief of staff, claimed innocence of committing the accused war crimes based on an unusual posture for a country's highest military officer. He asserted that the chief of each arm of the military made their own policies and decisions, and that he as chief of staff exerted no policy-making authority over them. Therefore, the others were responsible and not he. The Judges did not accept this argument.

Before the trial began, the judges ruled out another defense approach. They did not allow the defendants to argue their innocence of war crimes "because the rest of the world was guilty of the same crimes they were being accused of."

Tribunal Judgments—Before the trial started, many lawyers suggested that the international laws that were in place at the start of the trial would not support the charges being considered. The judicial tribunal therefore decided to make an independent assessment of Nazi Germany's actions during World War II. They evaluated the severity of the German government's actions and its impact, and considered whether individuals had any responsibility. The tribunal reached these three major judgments:

The initiation of a war of aggression is an international crime. Those who had participated in the planning and prosecution of aggressive war were guilty of the crime.

War crimes and crimes against humanity were committed on a vast scale, never before seen in the history of war. They were perpetrated in all the countries occupied by Germany and were attended by every conceivable circumstance of cruelty and horror.

The military were guilty as individuals, being responsible for the miseries and sufferings that have fallen on millions of men, women, and children. Without their military help, Hitler's ambitions would have gotten nowhere. It was not a matter of obeying orders; they actively participated in all these crimes.

The Verdict—Eleven defendants were found guilty without mitigating circumstances. This group included the highest Nazi officials, administrators of occupied countries, and top military officers. Sentenced to die by hanging were:

Hermann Goering—Second in command to Hitler, chief of the air force
Joachim von Ribbentrop—Foreign minister
Julius Streicher—Nazi governor, most notorious of the Nazi Jew-baiters
Wilhelm Frick—Interior minister
Ernst Kaltenbrunner—Security office head, Himmler's second in command
Alfred Rosenberg—Head of the occupied eastern Europe areas
Hans Frank—Governor of Poland under German occupation
Fritz Sauckel—Recruiter of east European slave-labor workers
Arthur Seyss-Inquart—German administrator of the occupied Netherlands
General Alfred Jodl—Commander of the German armies in western Europe
Field Marshall Wilhelm Keitel—Chief of staff of the German military

Seven of the defendants were found guilty with mitigating circumstances. They were sentenced to various prison terms, to be served in the German Spandau prison. They were Rudolf Hess who was Hitler's right-hand man until he parachuted into Scotland in 1941, Economics Minister Walther Funk, War Production Minister Albert Speer, Baron Constantin von Neurath who was the administrator of occupied central European countries, Admiral Erich Raeder (Navy commander of the submarine fleet), Admiral Karl Doenitz (Head of the Navy), and Hitler Youth Leader Baldur von Schirach.

Three defendants were acquitted of all charges. They were Franz von Papen (early-on cabinet member), Deputy Propaganda Minister Hans Fritzsche, and Hjalmar Schacht (early-on finance Minister).

The eleven Germans given the death penalty, who were heartless when they caused millions to suffer brutally and be slaughtered, became psychologically tormented and anguished while facing their own execution in fifteen days. Hermann Goering took his own life in his prison cell, swallowing a cyanide capsule hidden in the meerschaum pipe which he always had with him during the trial. On the gallows, the vicious, outspoken anti-Semite Julius Streicher, who always gloated about his knowledge of Judaism, called the day "Purim Festival 1946." He was referring to the day when the ancient Persian Jews were saved from the execution advocated by the Persian Prime Minister Haman, and when Haman and his family were hanged instead.

Other War Crime Trials—Trials were held by war crime commissions in several countries. Poland convicted and executed Rudolf Hess, the former Auschwitz commandant, Jurgen Stroop, who had suppressed the Warsaw ghetto uprising, and several others. Leaders of several countries who collaborated with the Nazis in killing their countrymen in addition to their Jewish population were tried and executed. The list includes Pierre Laval (leader of Vichy France), Joseph Tizo (Slovakian German puppet ruler), Ion Antonescu (Romanian puppet ruler), and Ferenc Szalasi (Hungarian chief, responsible for sending the Hungarian Jews to Auschwitz).

German war crime commissions that followed the Nuremberg Tribunal tried many lesser German officials and German industrialists who used slave labor. Most of these Germans brought to trial either received mild sentences or were acquitted. Those receiving longer sentences were generally reprieved after serving only short periods.

15

The American Response

The nation's isolationism, the State Department's anti-Jewish bias, and the will to win the war dominated the American response to issues that would have brought relief to the Holocaust survivors. These conditions influenced the few political options and actions President Roosevelt had available.

President Roosevelt's Attitude—President Roosevelt was moved by the injustices suffered by the Jews under the Nazis. He quickly condemned the Kristallnacht devastation of Jewish property, expressed horror and grief when he learned of the cruel details of the Final Solution, and voiced his objection to the British White Paper that cut off Jewish immigration to Palestine. He told King Ibn Saud of Saudi Arabia that he felt a personal responsibility for the victims of Nazism with the hope that it would encourage the king to endorse a policy allowing Jews to enter Palestine.

Treasury Secretary Henry Morgenthau presented President Roosevelt with a report outlining the State Department's obstructionist attitude with respect to trying to prevent the complete extermination of the Jews in German-controlled Europe. Roosevelt quickly accepted the report's recommendation to take the refugee policy away from the State Department and give it to a new War Refugee Board. Late in the war, in an attempt to protect the Hungarian Jews from being deported to the death camps by the Germans, he issued a strong warning to the Germans and Hungarians that they would be responsible for the fate of the Hungarian Jews. It had the intended effect—preventing the deportations.

There were many high officials in the Roosevelt State Department who had negative views towards the plight of the European Jews. President Roosevelt seldom interceded to oppose their actions of opposing relief to Jewish refugees from the Nazi persecutions before the Holocaust began and to survivors of the Holocaust.

Domestic Politics Stymies the Jewish Cause— Strong isolationist views prevailed in the country before our entry into the war. As indicated in public opinion polls, about eighty percent of Americans opposed increased immigration as a means of saving Jewish refugees from Hitler. Both the American Legion and the Veterans of Foreign Wars lobbied for a complete halt to immigration. Two other influential organizations, the Daughters of the American Revolution and the American Coalition of Patriotic Societies exerted pressure on Congress to restrict immigration. These factors influenced Roosevelt in 1944 when he was running for his fourth term. He rejected proposals to aid Jewish refugees to avoid giving his political opponents the arguments that he curried to the Jews or was under their influence.

Before the start of World War II, the political atmosphere in the United States was tinged with anti-Semitism coupled with anti-Communism. Anti-Semitism actually accelerated after the United States entered the war. The anti-Semites that included several influential congressmen used the argument that Jewish refugees from eastern Europe were Communists to oppose considerations for allowing homeless Jewish refugees into this country.

State Department Obstructionism—President Roosevelt had many Jews on his staff providing advice on domestic and political matters. However, foreign policy matters were left to the State Department which historically (before and long after Roosevelt) had an anti-Jewish bias. Secretary of State Cordell Hull was not a friend of the Jews (although he had a Jewish wife). Hull placed the handling of Jewish refugee issues in the hands of the bigoted Breckinridge Long, who had a strong dislike of Jews. Long made many decisions that adversely affected the Jewish refugees. He initially made it more difficult for Jews to get entry visas and later was influential in convincing Congress not to open the immigration quota to Jews.

In early 1943, after the details of the Holocaust became known, many influential people in the United States and Great Britain expressed their concern that not enough was being done to relieve the plight of the Jews under Hitler's control. In response to this agitation, in April 1943, Breckinridge Long set up a two-week Bermuda Conference with the British. Its purpose, presumably, was to discuss means of saving the two million remaining European Jews who faced imminent death. The conference was a farce. The only meaningful subject Long allowed to be discussed was the disposition of 5,000 Jewish refugees who had found their way to neutral Spain.

Disappointed with the results of the Bermuda Conference, the Emergency Conference to Save the Jewish People of Europe was convened in July to discuss the subject. Diverse political and civic leaders, such as Mayor LaGuardia of New York, writer Dorothy Parker, Ex-President Herbert Hoover, and journalist William Randolph Hearst supported this conference. The conference concluded that the United States had to take bold actions if the Jews were to be saved, and that a committee should be formed to develop a plan of action. The Emergency Committee to Save the Jewish People was established for this purpose. The committee proposed a Jewish army be formed and a U.S. government agency be established to undertake Jewish refugee relief. Peter Bergson, who was allied with the Jewish Palestinian Irgun terrorist group, led the Emergency Committee. The American Zionists opposed this committee for refusing to call for Palestine to be opened to the Jewish refugees, and because of its relationship to the fringe Zionist organization. Breckinridge Long gave the government's formal reply to the Emergency Committee's requests: "The U.S. is doing everything possible, therefore, a new rescue agency was not necessary." He then helped to kill congressional actions being considered in response to the Emergency Committee's recommendations by presenting exaggerated accomplishments. Long's later handling of several opportunities to save small groups of Jews seeking asylum was so bad, President Roosevelt removed him from the refugee management role. Other actions revealed the State Department's insensitivity to Jewish hardships:

In October 1943, the State Department refused to see a group of 400 Orthodox rabbis who came to Washington to persuade the government to set up a rescue agency and to drop the immigration barriers that prevented Jewish refugees seeking asylum from Hitler from entering the United States. The rabbis wanted to speak to Roosevelt directly, but he considered the subject a State Department matter. This was a very unusual affront to members of the clergy.

The State Department issued a news release covering the results of the October 1943 Moscow conference of foreign ministers from the United States, Great Britain, the Soviet Union, and China. It quoted the group as condemning Hitler for the mass killings of various nationalities in eastern Europe. The release included a long list of the nationalities affected, but it callously failed to include Jews in the list. Jews were the greatest victims—the State Department already had its own estimate that two million Jews had already been slaughtered.

In November 1943, the Emergency Committee's rescue plan received significant congressional support and President Roosevelt's backing. However, while Roosevelt was away attending conferences in Cairo and Tehran and without his knowledge, the State Department succeeded in killing the congressional action on the rescue plan.

Foreign Politics Blocks Jewish Relief—The United States was allied with Great Britain and the Soviet Union in the effort to defeat Germany. However, President Roosevelt and British Prime Minister Churchill distrusted the Soviet leader, Joseph Stalin. They were concerned over the Communist goals after the war ended. Because of this, the alliance with Great Britain became paramount with President Roosevelt and the State Department. They rejected any proposals that jeopardized this alliance, to the detriment of Jewish causes.

British Foreign Secretary Anthony Eden vetoed efforts to rescue Bulgarian Jews for fear that similar efforts would be required later to save Polish Jews. His concern about the burden that it would put on the free world overrode humanitarian considerations. Roosevelt appeared inclined to help the Bulgarian Jews, but he did not want to quarrel with Britain over this issue. There were other similar instances of acquiescing to British policies to the detriment of the Jewish refugees.

Middle East politics also interfered with Roosevelt's actions with respect to aiding the Holocaust survivors. Because of the interest in Arabian oil, and with State Department encouragement, President Roosevelt did not contest King Saud's refusal to allow Palestine as a place of refuge for Jews who might have been able to escape the Holocaust had Palestine been available to them.

Suppression of Holocaust News—The initial news about Nazi atrocities came out of Vichy France in 1941. It described the deaths of many Jews in the process of their being rounded up to be sent to labor camps. The news of the Nazi deliberate plan to exterminate European Jews and how it was being accomplished in the death camps was revealed in August 1942. Dr. Gerhart Riegner, the representative of the World Jewish Congress in Geneva, got the news from a prominent German industrialist who had the credentials to be a reliable source. Riegner passed it on to the State Department and to Rabbi Stephen S. Wise, who was the most prominent Jew at that time. The State Department initially bought the German propaganda that the Jews were being shipped to labor camps and not to death camps, and therefore did not consider it to be accurate or important. Rabbi Wise went to Sumner Wells, who convinced him to sit on the information until there was confirmation of the details. In November, after there was so much corroboration of the Final Solution, Wells told Wise to release the information to the Jewish public. The source of the new information came mostly from the Polish National Council in England, considered reliable by the State Department.

The Final Solution details released by Rabbi Wise in November 1942 made only some of the major U.S. newspapers, generally in an inside section. The initial news of mass killings by the Germans was downplayed. The American newspapers did a very poor job of reporting subsequent Holocaust news. This included the *New York Times* and the *Washington Post,* both owned by Jews.

The Vatican also had much information about the Holocaust details, but suppressed it. This was in line with the unsympathetic attitude of Pope Pius XII towards the plight of the European Jews under Hitler and his unwillingness to express moral outrage over the un-Christian behavior of Nazi Germany.

Winning the War Syndrome—The initial U.S. war objective was to protect the world's democracies from Hitler's domination. As the once seemingly invincible German armies were defeated in Russia and North Africa, the objective turned to liberating Europe. Aiding the European Jews was not a factor in the U.S. military strategy. After the severity of the Final Solution became known, Roosevelt was of the opinion that "winning the war" was the only effective means of ending the Final Solution. This attitude dominated his strategy in dealing with Jewish issues that arose as the war progressed. Most Jewish leaders came around to sharing this view—it dominated their political strategy. It was a policy shared by the Jews in Palestine who gave up their underground battle to wrest Palestine from Britain and joined the British armed forces to battle Germany in North Africa, Italy, and France.

The War Refugee Board—President Roosevelt did take a significant step that bypassed the State Departement when he established the War Refugee Board (WRB) under the control of the Treasury Department in 1944. Its charter was to act to rescue the victims of oppression who were in imminent danger of death. It was given broad powers to specifically forestall Nazi plans to exterminate all the Jews.

The WRB's major accomplishment was enlisting Raoul Wallenberg to undertake his Hungarian rescue mission. The WRB also got involved in several small-scale rescue missions, arranging for neutral country support of the missions through diplomatic channels, and financing the missions.

These operations included financing the Hechalutz (Zionist pioneer) organization to smuggle refugees from Hungary to Slovakia, leasing boats in Sweden to smuggle refugees out of the Balkans to Turkey, and providing food for the concentration camp inmates to be distributed by the International Red Cross. The WRB was also involved in the unfulfilled Brand mission to trade 10,000 trucks in exchange for the Germans halting further Auschwitz killings, and the Kastner ransom negotiation with Eichmann that saved the lives of 1,500 Hungarian Jews.

Ben Hecht: a Shining Star—The Emergency Committee to Save the Jewish People, organized in 1943, received enormous public relations support from the noted playwright and movie writer/producer Ben Hecht, who was moved by the plight of the Jews. Hecht, an assimilated Jew, spent the next seven years dedicated to the Jewish-survival cause. For these efforts, he was ostracized by the entertainment industry at a considerable personal financial loss, which did not deter him. He berated his successful Jewish Hollywood compatriots for their disinterest and silence regarding Jewish survival issues.

Eleanor Roosevelt's Attitude—Eleanor Roosevelt, a compassionate humanitarian, constantly expressed outrage over Hitler's treatment of the Jews. She lent her support to most efforts to bring relief to the Jewish refugees from Hitler and was influential in allowing several thousand Jewish children to enter this country from Vichy France. She did, however, offer only lukewarm support to the 1943 movement to establish an American relief agency, essentially endorsing the State Department's view that the U.S. government was doing everything possible until Germany was defeated. After liberation, Mrs. Roosevelt was deeply concerned for the Holocaust survivors. She contributed to the effort to improve the deplorable conditions of the Displaced Persons camps that existed right after the war's end. As a member of the U.S. delegation to the United Nations, Mrs. Roosevelt offered strong support to the establishment of the State of Israel so that the Jews could leave the DP camps and legally enter Palestine, which was their primary choice.

A Divided Jewish Community—After the defeat of Hitler, more than a quarter-million Jews were languishing in the displaced persons camps with nowhere to go. Because of how terribly they were treated in their countries of origin during the Holocaust, the Jews in the camps refused to go back there. The overwhelming majority preferred to go to Palestine and secondarily to the United States.

With the unsuccessful attempt in Congress to open U.S. immigration to Jews, opening up Palestine to Jews became a critical issue. During the two-year period when this issue was being resolved, the American Jewish community leaders took diverse positions and split into Zionists and anti-Zionists. The Zionists had three camps. The two largest differed as to whether Palestine should be a Jewish country or a binational country, both settling for a small area for Jews that was under consideration by the world leaders. The more militant third Zionist group argued for an independent large Jewish state that included present day Jordan (biblical Israel). The anti-Zionist American Council for Judaism did not want American Jews to be linked to Palestine as a Jewish political homeland—they opposed the Zionist's Palestine initiatives. They fought strongly against increasing the U.S. immigration quota for Jews, expressing concern about an anti-Jewish reaction they feared this step might cause.

16
Criticism of the American Response

Fifty years after the end of the Holocaust, there are voices within the Jewish community expressing disappointment bordering on anger at the American Jewish leaders for their inaction to help the European Jews caught up in the Holocaust. President Roosevelt receives similar criticism—he was sympathetic to the plight of the Jewish people but frequently refused to take a stance to counter political decisions made by his aides and international allies that prevented relief from going to Holocaust survivors. Are these criticisms valid?

One can look back in history and identify actions that the American Jewish leaders might have taken to possibly aid the Jewish victims of Nazism. Whether some of these actions would have been effective in achieving the intended results is problematic in view of the political climate that existed in the United States and the unsympathetic, if not hostile, world community.

An example of such a complaint is why the leaders did not apply more pressure on President Roosevelt to work with Congress to increase the extremely low entry quotas for Jews. Congress, reflecting the anti-immigration attitude that was predominant throughout the country, would have not responded favorably. Putting undue pressure on Roosevelt to pursue this important objective in the face of a sure defeat in Congress appeared counterproductive to most political analysts. Already being attacked by his political opponents and other Jew-haters for being "under the thumb" of the Jews, President Roosevelt would have likely turned bitter towards the Jews for what would have turned into a political defeat.

President Roosevelt's Unsympathetic Attitude—The actions of President Roosevelt with respect to Palestine as a haven for Jewish refugees from Nazism has received strong criticism. Jewish leadership is criticized for not being sufficiently forceful with respect to the Palestine issue. From the start of Hitler's oppression of European Jewry, no country offered a viable haven to the Jews who were managing to escape from the countries controlled by Hitler. Palestine represented the best solution from the Jewish perspective but the British adamantly kept to their policy announced in the 1939 White Paper, which essentially shut out Jews from immigrating into Palestine.

The Jewish leaders did protest against the White Paper and persuaded Roosevelt to publicly express the logic of opening Palestine to the Jews. President Roosevelt told the British government that he considered the White Paper to be an abrogation of the Balfour Declaration and asked that it be rescinded. However, when the British held to their position, President Roosevelt gave up the political battle, refusing to make this an issue that would break apart the Anglo-American relationship.

Criticism of Rabbi Wise—Harsh criticism has been directed towards Rabbi Stephen S. Wise, the most influential and respected Jewish leader of that period. For three months, he withheld from the public the news that he received which revealed the first details of the Nazi extermination process and the death camps. He did this to honor the request of Undersecretary of State Sumner Wells, one of the few State Department officials without an anti-Jewish bias and with whom Wise had a good working relationship in trying to aid the Jews. Rabbi Wise also felt he was responding to the wishes of President Roosevelt, whom he admired and respected for the greater good he did for the American people in general and for the Jewish people. With Hitler being as strong as he was at the time, no immediate American counteraction seemed possible.

Members of the Jewish community expressed anger at Rabbi Wise's loyalty to Roosevelt, which caused him to suppress the news of the Holocaust. He was pained by these attacks. In reality, after the Holocaust news came out, the reaction of the Jewish community at large was rather mild and controlled. He had revealed this information to about twenty prominent Jews and respected non-Jews; any one of them could have broken the information to the public. If anyone should be faulted, it is perhaps the members of the British government. They had received and withheld corroborated information much earlier than Rabbi Wise on the German plans to exterminate the Jews.

Rabbi Wise had a record of being a very forceful spokesman for Jewish rights in America and of continual outspoken condemnation of Hitler's treatment of the Jews. Taking this into consideration and the unlikelihood that an earlier release of the news would have saved lives, today's criticism of Rabbi Wise which faults him strictly for his judgment on when to release the news appears unjustified.

Whether To Bomb Auschwitz—The American Jewish leaders became fully aware of the Nazi plan to complete the Final Solution in advance of their retreat from the Russian army as it entered Poland. The Emergency Committee to Save the Jewish People urged President Roosevelt to act. First they requested that the railroad lines taking people to the death camps in Poland be bombed to slow the Final Solution process. When it was apparent that the Germans were planning to kill all the camp inmates as the Russians were approaching the camps, the committee requested that the death camps be bombed to give the doomed inmates an opportunity to escape. This request and its denial remain a contentious issue still being debated.

The American military turned down these requests. The formal reason given was that these bombings were too difficult to manage. This seems disingenuous, since large city targets not far from Auschwitz were being bombed at that time and Auschwitz was being overflown on missions to supply the Polish underground army near Warsaw. The American and British military commanders' disinterest in the purpose for these undertakings probably had more to do with why these requests were turned down. Ostensibly they did not want to waste any resources on a target strictly of Jewish interest and that took away from their prime objective of defeating Hitler.

Was the bombing of Auschwitz a sensible request? We have no way of knowing if the bombings of the camps would have led to some prisoner escape and freedom or if those who ultimately survived would have been killed in the bombings. Would bombing of the railroad leading to Auschwitz have saved some people from being transported to die in its gas chambers or would the Germans have applied their usual retaliatory tactics and killed those already in Auschwitz who actually survived? There are no answers.

The Goldberg Commission—In the early 1980s, a commission headed by former Supreme Court Justice Arthur Goldberg recruited several young scholars to study the behavior of the Jewish leadership during the war. The commission's report was critical of the leaders for not being sufficiently active in trying to arrange relief for the Holocaust victims. The Jewish community essentially rejected this report as not reflecting the wartime period conditions under which the Jewish leaders had to operate.

17

Holocaust Deniers

General Dwight D. Eisenhower's statement at the Ohrdruf concentration camp in central Germany on April 15, 1945.

> The things I saw beggar description. The evidence and verbal testimony of starvation, cruelty, and bestiality were overpowering. I made this visit deliberately in order to be in position to give first hand evidence of these things if ever in the future there develops a tendency to charge these allegations merely to propaganda.

There is an unusually large collection of pictorial evidence of all aspects of the Holocaust. European countries' records show millions of people disappeared. Official Nazi documents, generated as the events were happening, confirm that millions of Jews were killed in the death camps. Survivors, with concentration camp numbers tattooed on their arms to confirm their incarceration, have provided personal testimony of the camp horrors. With all this evidence, highly educated people around the world claim and write that the Holocaust is a hoax and a fabrication. It is difficult to fathom why they cannot see the truth to the Holocaust descriptions and evidence, unless it is because anti-Semitism blinds them. These "deniers" should not be given a public audience to debate their opinion because there is no honest substance to their views. Indeed, several countries have made it a crime to promote Holocaust denial in schools and in other public forums.

Denial of the Holocaust goes back to the time of the Nuremberg trials of 1946–48. Reactionary and anti-Semitic political figures could not accept Germans being guilty of the World War II atrocities. The McCarthyites called the trials a Communist plot against America. Senator William Langer of North Dakota connected the trial to the Communist purpose of destroying the Western world, accusing the Communists of using the trial as a means of taking over German property. In a speech on the floor of Congress, Representative John Rankin of Mississippi accused a racial minority of hanging German soldiers and trying German businessmen in the name of the United States.

Part V

A History of the State of Israel

Two Thousand Years of Prayer Answered

Preface to Part V

As described in the Bible, God's role in his Covenant with Abraham was to ensure that Abraham's family would multiply and become a great nation. God promised the land of Canaan as an everlasting possession to Abraham and his descendants. The Bible continues with the story of how God led the Israelites out of bondage in Egypt and guided Joshua to conquer Canaan and establish the Land of Israel as the homeland for the Twelve Tribes of Israel.

Canaan (later called Palestine) became the national home of the Jewish people: The United Jewish Kingdom under Kings David and Solomon. This kingdom then split into two. The two kingdoms, Judah and Israel, lasted several hundred years before both were conquered and the Israelites were exiled from the land. Normally these circumstances would have ended their existence as a "people" with a national culture—this happened to "*The Ten Lost Tribes of Israel.*" Almost uniquely, the Jews of the kingdom of Judah, exiled to Babylonia, remained a people, but without a national home. The national home was restored for a brief period when the Maccabees established the second Jewish Commonwealth. The Jews were again exiled from Palestine in 135 C.E. After that event, there was no political agitation for restoration of the Land of Israel for almost two millennia. However, the Jewish people never gave up hope. The return to Jerusalem became embedded in Jewish prayer and the return of the Messiah was awaited for the Land of Israel to be restored.

At the turn of the twentieth century, an unexpected change took place regarding returning to the Jewish homeland. Zionism, the political force championing the restoration of Palestine as the Land of Israel, blossomed among secular Jews rather than with the Jewish religious community. Fifty years later the modern State of Israel was indeed established.

The development of the State of Israel has been remarkable and fascinating to Jews and non-Jews alike. A land turned brown and desolate after many centuries of neglect has been converted into a productive land of greenery. A previously backward, poor, agricultural country, rampant with disease, has been converted to a modern high-tech country, with a very high standard of living, and is one of the healthiest societies in the world. The ability to overcome the Arab nations bent on destroying Israel in six wars has won the admiration of the Jews and non-Jews everywhere. The State of Israel, the only democracy in the Middle East, is anxious to have real peace with its Arab neighbors and be a creative force in improving the economies of the entire Middle East, which will improve the standard of living of all the peoples in the area.

Beyond this admiration, the Jewish people worldwide have a strong bond with the State of Israel. Israel is the place where Jews can freely go to escape intolerance anywhere in the world. Since its brief existence, Israel has absorbed over two million Jews, starting with the Holocaust survivors, then the mass expulsion from Arab lands after the Israeli War of Independence, and finally the mass exit from the Soviet Union to escape the anti-Semitism under the Communist regime. This lesson of the Holocaust (i.e., the need for a Jewish state) must not be forgotten.

The goal of this volume is to tell the remarkable story of the State of Israel in a brief, interesting manner that will appeal to those interested in a straightforward approach to this important subject. It starts with the pioneers who came to Palestine in the first half of the twentieth century to pursue the dream of building a land for Jews and run by Jews, *Eretz Israel*. It ends with highlights of the first fifty years of the State of Israel. This history coupled with the discussions regarding the Jerusalem Temple Mount in Part I will enable the reader to understand the historical context of the negotiations going on between the State of Israel and the Palestinians that is striving to arrive at an independent Palestinian entity while preserving Israeli security.

Historical narratives tend to be biased by the writer's personal outlook on the historical subject. This makes describing the history of the State of Israel a special challenge—to avoid presenting a narrow viewpoint. I am grateful to Mr. Yehuda Lev for his aid in covering the history of Israel. While serving in the U.S. Army at the end of World War II, Mr. Lev was so motivated by the Breira organization helping Holocaust survivors get to Israel that he volunteered to fight in the War of Independence in 1948. He stayed on in Israel for eighteen years, living in a kibbutz a few years and later becoming a journalist. This experience gave him direct knowledge of Israeli history, an appreciation of the diverse views of the Israelis and Arabs living in the area, and a sound understanding of the issues standing in the way of peace between them. Mr. Lev reviewed my draft and contributed many constructive recommendations for presenting a complete story and a balanced view.

Introduction

In Honor of the State of Israel

> We greet you, Country small in size
> but big and brave in enterprise—
> where liberty and learning rule
> on farm, in factory and school;
>
> —Ernest Hopwood

In biblical times, the Jewish people lived in Palestine initially under a loose federation of the twelve tribes of Israel, followed by a single kingdom, then under two kingdoms, Judah and Israel. Assyria in 722 B.C.E destroyed the kingdom of Israel. Its people, the *"Ten Lost Tribes of Israel,"* vanished from history. The kingdom of Judah lasted another one hundred thirty-six years before it was destroyed by the Babylonians. After returning to Judah from the Babylonian exile, the Judeans lived under foreign domination until they received their independence from Syria in 142 B.C.E. and established the Second Jewish Commonwealth under the Maccabees. This lasted a brief period; the Romans became the new rulers of Palestine. A failed revolt in 135 C.E. against the brutal Roman domination resulted in the almost complete banishment of Jews from Palestine.

Within one hundred years after the Jewish exile from Palestine, the peak Jewish population of 4.5 million during the Second Jewish Commonwealth dwindled to 1.5 million due to the many massacres under Roman domination and to mass conversions after Christianity became the dominant religion in the Mediterranean area. Jews were dispersed throughout the area's developed countries ranging from Persia to Spain. Regardless of the differences in religious prayers, spoken language, customs, and cultures that the Jewish people developed during their widespread Diaspora, they all had a common goal—to return to the Land of Israel (which got to be known as Palestine in the Roman days). The importance of Jerusalem to the Jewish people and their longing to return to Jerusalem has been embedded in the Jewish people's ritual prayers since their exile from Palestine—**"Next year in Jerusalem"** has been a fervent Hebrew prayer at the close of the Day of Atonement prayers.

For seventeen hundred years, there was no organized Jewish movement to return to Palestine. Some pious Jews, wealthy enough to afford the expensive hazardous trip, managed to make the trip to Palestine. Frequently, the objective was to die there and be buried in their Jewish ancestral Holy Land. The lack of an effort to return to Israel is understandable under the circumstances that prevailed during that long period. The Jewish people in Europe were subjugated everywhere they lived and had no political influence. They were powerless to prevent the periodic massacres of Jewish people or prevent the repeated expulsions from European country to country. Palestine had become a desolate country that made living there an ordeal. The Jewish people lacked the political influence and the required financial resources to make a return to Palestine realistic.

The end of the nineteenth century saw a change in the Jewish psyche that fostered the newfound interest in a return to Palestine. Oddly, it was not driven by religious motivation. The Zionist movement (return to Palestine, called Zion in Hebrew prayers) was initiated by secular European Jewish leaders who saw Jews returning to Palestine as the only solution to the civil and economic oppression that the Jews in Russia were suffering. Zionism then got its major boost from another secular source. Theodor Herzl, an assimilated Jew from Austria-Hungary, was aroused by the anti-Semitic fervor in France during the Dreyfus trial to become Zionism's driving force. He saw the need for a Jewish state as the only place where Jews would not be exposed to anti-Semitism. He envisioned the Jewish state to be a model to the world. Herzl defined the need for a strong, politically oriented organization, backed by Jewish contributions, as a prerequisite for accomplishing this Jewish state.

The Zionist fervor grew at the start of the twentieth century. Jewish pioneers increasingly went to Palestine, mostly as farmers and land developers. This movement developed the foundation for the Jewish political and military structure that later established the State of Israel, but in itself did not have the strength and influence to accomplish the Zionist goal.

In the midst of World War I, Great Britain issued its Balfour Declaration, which committed Great Britain to supporting a national home for the Jewish people in Palestine. The Balfour Declaration was written into the terms of the World War I peace treaty with Turkey, completed in 1920.

Britain was then given the mandate authority over Palestine by the League of Nations. This ended four hundred years of Turkish Ottoman rule over Palestine. Moslem countries, including Turkey, ruled Palestine since 638 C.E. except briefly during the Crusades. British officials in the 1920s ignored the Balfour Declaration to curry favor with the new oil-rich Arab countries; no steps were taken by Britain to establish a Jewish homeland as a follow-up to their Balfour Declaration.

Hitler's rise in power in Germany troubled the Jewish world and resulted in a rapid growth of the World Zionist organization. However, the Zionist movement never achieved the political influence to aid the European Jews suffering persecution and economic deprivation in the 1930s, let alone achieve its aim of establishing a Jewish homeland in Palestine. The American Zionist movement could not overcome the isolationism in the United States that stood in the way of aiding Jewish refugees from Nazi persecution. In 1939, Britain issued a White Paper that effectively closed Palestine to Jews. With all other doors closed to them, this step denied the desperate European Jews a haven that the Palestinian Jews were prepared to offer.

World War II ended, leaving more than 250,000 Jewish displaced persons in Europe with no place to go to. Although conditions in Palestine were turbulent because of friction between the Arabs and Jews, most of the Holocaust survivors preferred to go to Palestine because they felt they would be more comfortable there among the Jewish community than anywhere else. Britain, however, kept the terms of the 1939 White Paper in place, essentially ruling out legal Jewish immigration to Palestine. Finally, in November 1947, the doors to Jewish immigration were to be opened by the United Nations with their plan to partition Palestine into separate Arab and Jewish states to be effective on May 15, 1948.

Strongly different political objectives and attitudes, compounded by religious differences, did not allow the Muslim world to accept the proposed Jewish state as a part of the partition plan. The Arab governments in the area rejected the partition plan and declared their intention of removing all Jews from Palestine—"driving them into the sea." Fighting between the Arabs and Jewish settlers began. On May 14, 1948, the day the British Mandate ended, David Ben-Gurion, the leader of the Palestinian Jews, declared the establishment of the independent Jewish State of Israel. This action was followed by the invasion of the Jewish areas in Palestine by the armies of six Arab nations. Despite being outnumbered and poorly equipped militarily, the Palestinian Jews were victorious after almost a year of fighting and the new State of Israel survived.

In the three years following independence, this financially strapped, underdeveloped country absorbed 800,000 immigrants, doubling its population—a remarkable, unequaled achievement.

After six wars between the State of Israel and its Arab neighbors, the historical differences between the Arabs and the Jews are still interfering with achieving permanent peace in the area. Anwar el-Sadat of Egypt and, later, Yitzhak Rabin of Israel, two brave leaders, had overcome these historical differences to offer their previous enemies the opportunity for peaceful relations. These great leaders who had visions of peace between the previous adversaries were assassinated by Arab and Jewish extremists before they could see their goals fully accomplished.

There are currently ongoing internal Israeli conflicts regarding how to proceed with the peace process negotiations with the Palestinians that will satisfy the Palestinian objective for a Palestinian State and other associated objectives without jeopardizing Israel's security. The history of Arab terrorism and the hostility of several neighboring Muslim countries complicate the resolution of the issues. Consideration for Jewish religious pluralism in Israel has become another internal Israeli issue that is also threatening the solidarity of the diaspora Jewish community with Israel. The Orthodox community, exerting its political influence, refuses to allow Conservative and Reform rabbis to conduct conversions, marriages, and divorce, and to participate in the large-city religious councils. Israel's diverse society with different political, social, and religious views had to face many internal problems during Israel's fifty-year history. They found a way to resolve them pragmatically.

The current problems should not overshadow the remarkable and admirable achievements the Israelis have accomplished in the past one hundred years. Palestinian Arab landowners had sold the worst lands to the Jews. They were farmlands eroded by lack of trees and water. They were valleys that were swamps infected with malaria. With almost a minimum of resources, the early Jewish pioneers who came to Palestine transformed the parched, sandy soil of Palestine to the green landscape of Israel laden with trees and farmland, and they converted malaria-ridden swampland into habitable farmland. Palestine, a land that for almost two millennium was barren of people, commerce, and culture is now a thriving highly-populated community complete with libraries, universities, orchestras, and is a world leader in medicine, technology, and agriculture.

Introduction

In this area of the world, where democracy is unknown and revolutions have been commonplace, the Jewish people established the State of Israel with a democratic form of government that has been maintained throughout all crises these past fifty years. The fledgling financially strapped State of Israel, with initially less than a million Jews, was able to absorb 2.6 million Jews who needed a haven from intolerance in their homelands. No other country made similar sacrifices for their brethren. Jews of different cultures and colors who have immigrated from Muslim Mediterranean and Middle East countries, Ethiopia, Romania, Russia, India, and elsewhere were integrated into society in a relatively short period—a model for the countries with integration problems.

The Jewish people now have a *"National Home."* In 1998 the population of the State of Israel was 5.9 million, of which 4.7 million (80%) were Jews and 1.2 million (20%) were Muslim and Christian Arabs or other ethnic minorities.

1
Early History

Although the Jewish people were forced to live in the Diaspora since the failed revolt against the Romans in 135 C.E., a small number of Jews have lived continuously in Palestine. After the revolt, the Romans and, later, the Christians did not allow Jews to live in Jerusalem. The small remnant Jewish community concentrated in the holy cities of Safed, Tiberias, and Hebron. When the Ottoman Empire (premodern Turkey) took over the rule of Palestine in the sixteenth century, Jews were again allowed to live in Jerusalem. Although very small in number, Jews living in Palestine nevertheless made lasting contributions to Judaic religious and cultural life. Foremost accomplishments are the Jerusalem Talmud, the *Shulhan Aruk* (Code of Jewish Law) by Joseph Caro, and the Cabbalist teachings of Isaac Luria.

Early Jewish Pioneers in Palestine

After Jerusalem became a holy place and political center to the Muslims in the seventh century, Arabs replaced the exiled Jews who had farmed the land while they lived there. Palestine remained a flourishing country until the Crusade period. The wars between the Christians and Muslims started the degradation of Palestine. It lost its commercial value as a trade route between the West and the East. With a destroyed economy, the irrigation system decayed, Palestine became a devastated, disease-ridden land. From the lack of farming, swamps developed in the northern part of Palestine, while in the southern part, the soil eroded to become almost a desert. In 1800, there were approximately 6,000 Jews living Palestine. The very small Jewish population was mostly pious Jews wanting to live and die in the land of their forefathers, living off charitable contributions from the Diaspora Jews. The Arab population was also small and extremely poor, working for the few wealthy landowners, or living as nomadic Bedouins.

Starting in 1830 and sponsored by the British Sir Moses Montefiore, there was an effort to develop productive Jewish settlements in Palestine. Later, this activity was supported by the Alliance Israélite Universelle, founded by the respected Jewish-French lawyer, political leader, and statesman Adolphe Crémieux, who fought for Jewish and other minority rights and for religious freedom in the Mediterranean countries. In 1870, this organization established Mikveh Israel, the first Jewish agricultural school in Palestine. This expansion of the Jewish population had to be arranged with the approval of the Turks who ruled Palestine. By 1881, 300,000 Arabs and 25,000 Jews lived in Palestine.

Starting in the late nineteenth century, even before the birth of the modern Zionist movement, Jews started to come to Palestine in larger numbers from eastern Europe for other than religious reasons. They came not for personal gain but to establish Jewish communities that would establish a base for future pioneers having the same motivation. Their aim was to have Jews live as farmers as did Jews of old and do all the work in the community, which is why Arabs were not employed on a kibbutz. They were young, idealistic Jews who were willing to take on the challenge that life in Palestine represented, forsaking the opportunity to go to the United States. These pioneers established the Jewish *Yishuv* (Hebrew for settlement, the name for Palestine's Jewish community), laying the foundation for the State of Israel. Baron Edmond de Rothschild became the benefactor of these Zionist colonies that developed in Palestine. Ironically, the progressive economic improvements in Palestine that resulted from each new burst of Jewish immigration contributed to a large increase in the Palestinian Arab population. Poor Arabs from the neighboring Arab states came to Palestine in large numbers to take advantage of the new working opportunities.

The growing worldwide Zionist movement that was promoting enlarging the Jewish colonization effort in Palestine that would lead to a Jewish national home met with opposition within the broad Jewish community. The Reform Jews in the United States were vehemently opposed. The biblical "Promised Land" offered no motivation to them, and they feared that a Jewish State would lead to political problems that would threaten all Jews. The large, strong Jewish socialist organization in eastern Europe, the Bund, was anti-Zionist. This secular organization was motivated only to improving social and economic conditions in the European country they lived in. Most practicing Orthodox Jews could not support the largely irreligious Zionist movement. The Jews living in Palestine were also opposed to Zionism; the early Zionist movement was introducing a religious and economic lifestyle that clashed with their own outlook and lifestyle.

Aliyahs—The wave of Jewish immigrants that periodically came to Palestine was called *aliyah* (Hebrew for ascent—a term normally used when an individual goes up to the *bimah* [platform] in the synagogue to participate in the Sabbath Torah reading). Out of love for Zion, these Jews gave up the opportunity to emigrate to the United States or Great Britain that would have been less risky and challenging. They went to Palestine, knowing it would require great personal sacrifices and acceptance of the harsh living conditions. The first Aliyah started in 1882, and the fifth Aliyah ended in 1939 with the start of the Holocaust. At the start of the First Aliyah, there were only 24,000 Jews in Palestine, mostly living off charity.

The Youth Aliyah movement, which was part of the fifth Aliyah, has been reactivated. There are five Aliyah centers in Israel today where children are oriented to living in Israel. These children have decided to live in Israel without their parents, hoping their parents will join them in later years.

The ***First Aliyah***, aided financially by Baron Edmond de Rothschild (called the father of the Yishuv), came from Russia in 1882. These pioneers were intent in defining a new image for the Jewish people. They were to be farmers as were the ancient Jews of Israel. In fifteen years, they established twenty farming communities distributed throughout Palestine. Unable to get Turkish permission to buy the land, they proceeded with their objectives illegally.

The ***Second Aliyah***, also from Russia, came from 1904 until 1914. This group, influenced by the social reformers in Russia before the Russian Revolution, established the idealist *kibbutz* (collective village) concept of working together and living together in a democratic egalitarian community. Located in the northern Galilee, it was called Degania (cornflower). They were very difficult years for most. It took a long time before the inhospitable Palestinian land was tamed, essentially by hand, and before their agricultural efforts were productive to the point of profitability. A. D. Gordon, the "Sage of Deganya," led these *Halutzim* (pioneers) to believe in the dignity of hard work, approaching it as a holy effort to reestablish Jewish roots on its own soil. David Ben-Gurion and Izhak Ben-Zvi (second president of the State of Israel) were the most prominent members of this Aliyah. In 1909, a group of these pioneers founded the city of Tel Aviv on the sandy soil off the Mediterranean coastline next to the Arab city of Jaffa. The Jewish population of Palestine grew from 25,000 at the beginning of the Aliyah movement to 50,000 prior to World War I. In the mid-1920s, this He-Halutz (the pioneer) movement took hold in many countries around the world, bringing thousands of enthusiastic young pioneers to Palestine.

The ***Third Aliyah*** started after World War I ended. It brought dedicated pioneers from throughout the diaspora who gave impetus to establishing the Jewish national home. They undertook to make Palestine a more hospitable place to live in. Risking their lives, they had to fight off the prevalent malaria while removing the swamps. They built roads to interconnect the Jewish communities and to improve the commercial traffic, planted trees to improve the environment, and toiled by hand in the hot sun as farmers.

The ***Fourth Aliyah*** that came in 1925 brought new challenges. Thousands of middle-class Jews who came from Poland to escape the persecution that developed there were unable to adjust to the agricultural lifestyle that the Yishuv offered. With little employment opportunities, many more left the country than immigrated. After a couple of years of disappointment, this group of pioneers established small businesses and applied themselves as laborers in the new factories and power plants that were established to support the growing agricultural community. In the first year of this Aliyah, Tel Aviv, the first all-Jewish city in Palestine doubled in population to 50,000.

The ***Fifth Aliyah*** wave began slowly in 1929. It accelerated after Hitler came into power. From 1932 to 1939, over 100,000 German Jews escaped the growing Nazi terror by emigrating to Palestine. This group, more highly assimilated and cultured than the earlier pioneers, but with little Zionistic enthusiasm, was expected to have a difficult time adjusting to the hard life in Palestine, which was made dangerous by the rise in Arab nationalism that resulted in frequent attacks against Jewish settlements. That was not the case. These sophisticated immigrants adjusted quickly to the rugged lifestyle and contributed a vital element to the Yishuv. The German authorities allowed these early Jewish émigrés to trade their money for German machinery, which they were able to bring to Palestine. This helped expand Palestinian industry and strengthened the Yishuv in advance of the War of Independence.

The ***Youth Aliyah***—It did not take long for the Jews in Germany to sense the dangers of Hitler. Many parents were anxious to have their children escape the horrors of living under Nazism even if they could not leave themselves. The call to manage the emigration of German-Jewish youth to Palestine was answered by Henrietta Szold. She had already devoted her life to Zionist and humanitarian causes, which was capped by her founding Hadassah (the large woman's Zionist organization) in 1912. In 1933, at age seventy-three, she came out of retirement to establish the Youth Aliyah movement, which over the next four years rescued more than fifty thousand youths from Germany and other counties. It was a well-organized study-work-play program that prepared these youths to be productive contributors to the development of the Yishuv. Housed in children's villages (Kibbutz Ein Harod and Kfar Giladi) and with little chance of seeing their parents again, these children required special care to keep them physically and emotionally healthy. This program was a major success thanks to Henrietta Szold's warm, personal interaction with the new arrivals and her devotion to the childrens' needs as they adjusted to the drastic change in their lives.

The *Aliyah from Arab Countries*—Zionism was barred in most Arab countries and Turkey, and was actually opposed by the Jewish leaders in these countries for fear of reprisal. Nevertheless, Zionism did continue among the young and the educated Jews; 50,000 Jews from these Muslim countries made Aliyah to Palestine between the two World Wars.

Hebrew Language: The Unifying Force—There was a slow-growing movement to adopt Hebrew as the language for the future Jewish homeland as the Zionist movement progressed at the end of the nineteenth century. Pushed by Chaim Weizmann, an early Zionist activist, Hebrew became the official language at the World Zionist Congress meetings at the turn of the century. However, there were too many forces standing in the way for Hebrew to be accepted as the common language in Palestine. The pious Jews insisted that Hebrew remain the language of prayer and religious study. The older inhabitants from eastern Europe spoke Yiddish (a Judeo version of German); Jews of Sephardic ancestry spoke Ladino (a Judeo version of Spanish). French and German Jewish organizations that were involved in charity work preferred to use their native language. A new European language was essentially brought in with each Aliyah. The newer immigrants, imbued with Zionism, were anxious to adopt Hebrew, but the mechanism for changeover from their native languages needed to be developed.

The conflicts over which language to use ultimately got resolved as part of the process to provide educational facilities for the new youngsters in Palestine. Good education for their children became a requisite for every new Jewish community that was established—good education is a Judaic tradition. The major problem in providing the education was training the increasing number of teachers required. Multi-language teacher training would have been a heavy burden on a poor society and was impractical to prepare for without knowing which new languages would be required with future Aliyahs. From the teacher standpoint, teachers wanted the security of being able to move from one school to another without having to learn a new language and develop new teaching tools. The teachers' union wrestled with this problem. The Hebraists won out, and Hebrew became the common language in the school system. The parents learned Hebrew from their children who brought Hebrew into the home, and in time, it became the common language for the Jewish people in Palestine. Both Zionists and non-Zionists at the 15th World Zionist Congress finally accepted Hebrew as the language of the country in 1927.

Eliezer ben Yehuda: Father of the Modern Hebrew Language—The World Zionist Congress of 1905 declared that Hebrew would be the language of the Jewish State whenever it was to be founded. The Hebrew language was hardly suitable for that purpose. At the turn of the twentieth century, the Hebrew language was still archaic, being used only as the religious language of the Jewish people. It was not suited for modern everyday life. It lacked the terminology for business, science, technology, and medicine. The language was essentially modernized by the heroic efforts of one individual, Eliezer ben Yehuda, a Russian Jew who believed that Hebrew must be the bond that linked all the Jews of Palestine together. He created the modern Hebrew dictionary during the period when the concept of Hebrew as the spoken language was still being belittled. He did so in an extraordinary but effective manner. He insisted that he, his wife, and two daughters speak only Hebrew in their home in Russia. When a word did not exist, he created one based on a root Hebrew word. Thanks to ben Yehudah, a modern Hebrew language dictionary was in place when Hebrew was adopted as the common language in the State of Israel.

Histadrut—The Jewish labor movement became a powerful voice in Palestine after they organized the *Histadrut* (General Federation of Labor) in 1920. Its aim was "to form an organization of Jewish settlers who live by their own labor without exploiting others and who aim to establish a Jewish Commonwealth in Palestine." It called for equal rights for women and between Jews and Arabs—the equal labor rights for women materialized somewhat, those for the Arabs, barely.

Histadrut operated like a business for its members. It regulated working conditions, trained and placed workers in settlements, handled wholesale buying and selling for all settlements, built cooperative housing complexes, and even developed industries. It did much more for its members; it provided medical care, established schools for children, sponsored social activities, published its own newspaper, and founded a theater and a sports organization. Histadrut also took over failing companies to preserve jobs. Histadrut became the largest employer in Palestine.

The Jewish National Fund Charity Box: The Miracle Blue Pushke Box—*"Put a penny in this box and out would come land."* Starting in 1901, this Blue Box was in the homes of millions of Jews throughout the world in the days when the typical Jew was poor. Nevertheless, they literally contributed pennies at a time to this Jewish National Fund (in Hebrew, *Keren Kayemet*) fund-raising charity box; they also contributed to other pushke boxes supporting many charities and religious organizations in Palestine. The Jewish National Fund (JNF) was the prime source of funds to buy land for the Aliyah pioneers. In 1920, the World Zionist Organization established the *Keren Hayesod* (The Foundation Fund) to provide financial support to the development of the Yishuv other than the purchase of land, which was left to the JNF.

2
Israeli Political Scene

The current political situation in Israel is rather unusual when compared to the United States. There are so many political parties that it is difficult for one party to obtain a majority in the *Knesset* (Parliament). This multiplicity of parties has its heritage from the many factions of Zionism that existed when Palestinian Zionists were first pursuing their goal of creating a Jewish national home. The diversity of views was very broad from the very beginning. The differences covered political and economic convictions from the right to the left, religious orthodoxy versus secular lifestyle, a Jewish state versus a binational state, a smaller Israel versus the greater Israel of biblical times, Zionist movement leadership styles, how to approach Israeli security, and how to accommodate Palestinian aspirations.

The children of the Zionist immigrants and those of the Youth Aliyah became involved with Zionist politics through Zionist youth organizations, whose views reflected the diversity of the sponsoring adult organizations; there were periodic clashes between these youth groups. These Palestinian youth movements became popular among Jewish youth in the United States in the 1930s—leading to some minor emigration to Palestine, but they mostly served as youthful supporters of the American Zionist program.

General Zionists—These Zionists were middle-of-the-road politically and had no specific religious agenda. They believed that in view of the hostile world attitude, it would be impossible to obtain a Jewish state that included all of Palestine. They essentially were willing to compromise their desire for obtaining all of Palestine and accept whatever size was offered, as long as it was a Jewish state. It was a party of small businessmen who were strong advocates of a free enterprise economy.

Poale Zion—Poale Zion, the Workers of Zion, stemmed from the Second Aliyah of pioneers. They were dedicated to developing a Jewish farming society and were advocates of an independent Jewish state with a socialist structure. In their ideal society, there would be no private possession of land; there would be Jewish farmer and worker communities free of wealthy or extremely poor people. Political factions developed as the party matured; the more conservative socialist element won out. The Communists dropped out and formed the Palestinian Communist party with Jewish and Arab membership and became an advocate of a binational state.

Ahdut Ha'avoda—The socialists of the Poale Zion formed the influential labor union, Ahdut Ha'avoda, that associated with the Histadrut Federation of Labor. The goal was to make it a confederation of several Zionist labor groups, but the more radical groups decided not to join. It later became the Mapai party under the leadership of David Ben-Gurion and Moshe Shertok (later called Moshe Sharett) who played a major role in the creation and early leadership of the State of Israel.

Hapoel Hatzair—This and Poale Zion were the first political labor parties formed in Palestine. It was a labor union mostly of farm workers. It avoided associations with international socialist organizations but advocated building the Jewish homeland based on social justice.

Mizrachi—This organization represented the religious Zionists. They advocated adhering to the laws of the Torah within the current Zionist organizational activity as well as in the future homeland. They required strict observance of the Sabbath, adherence to the dietary laws, and compliance with other Orthodox rules for social behavior. There were several factions of the Mizrachi movement, split by political ideology.

Hashomer Hatzair (Young Watchman)—This Young Workers party stemmed from the youth movement promoted by A. D. Gordon during the second Aliyah. It was left wing politically and was an advocate of a binational state for Palestine. It was strong in the kibbutz movement where their members abolished the traditional family social unit; children lived apart from their parents.

Revisionists—Revisionists were so labeled because they called for the "revision" of many Zionist policies. They demanded a Jewish state on both sides of the Jordan consisting of a Jewish majority. They opposed the inclusion of non-Zionists on the Jewish Agency Board that was being promoted by Chaim Weizmann and fought his leadership of the Zionist movement. The revisionists also wanted the Zionist movement to accept the establishment of a Jewish Legion within the British army. The leader of the Revisionists was Vladimir Jabotinsky, who was supported by Joseph Trumpeldor, another prominent military man. A paramilitary youth group called Betar (Brith Trumpeldor) had been formed in Europe after World War II ended to prepare youth for life in Palestine. Betar advocated taking maximum steps to achieve a national home for the Jews. Jabotinsky took on Betar as the Revisionist Youth Group. Betar's militancy, dressed in uniforms patterned after Italian Dictator Mussolini's youth movement, contributed to some of Jabotinsky's opponents calling him fascist; they objected to his ultra-rightist militarism.

Vladimir Jabotinsky—This former Russian army officer was expelled from Palestine to Alexandria, Egypt, at the start of World War I. There he recruited other Jewish volunteers to join the Zion Mule Corps in support of the British army in the battle of Gallipoli, Turkey. Set up only as a supply unit, hence its name, it won distinction as a full fighting unit. Jabotinsky had hoped for the defeat of Turkey by the British, which he envisioned to be the quickest way for the Zionists to achieve their goal of a Jewish state in Palestine. The British lost the battle and the Mule Corps was dissolved. Jabotinsky then went to England to press for the formation of a Jewish army. In 1917, he was partially successful, the Jewish Legion was formed. Consisting of volunteers from around the world, the Jewish Legion fought under the British army in Palestine, receiving high praise for their combat effectiveness. These two military efforts in support of the British army contributed to the British government extending to the Jewish people the Balfour Declaration promise of a Jewish national home in Palestine.

Jabotinsky, the soldier and politician, was also a writer and a fiery orator who fought hard within the Zionist movement for his revisionist goals. Ultimately his movement withdrew from the World Zionist Organization and established the New Zionist Organization. The Revisionist party advocated a Jewish State on both sides of the Jordan (including Transjordan). It believed that its goals could not be achieved by concessions. Jabotinsky claimed accepting concessions was the reason why the Zionist movement was not achieving progress towards a Jewish State in dealing with the British. Aggressive action was the only way. Large-scale immigration was required for the Jews to be a majority in the Greater Jewish homeland; Palestinian objection to Jewish goals was considered to have no validity.

Joseph Trumpeldor—Trumpeldor received his first recognition when fighting with the Russian army against the Japanese in Port Arthur, Korea. He lost an arm but kept fighting. While in prison as a Japanese prisoner of war, he lectured his fellow Jewish prisoners on Zionism. Received as a war hero by the empress of Russia, Trumpeldor turned down the opportunity to remain in the Russian army and decided to go to Palestine with some friends to start a settlement. When that effort failed, he joined up with Jabotinsky to organize the Zion Mule Corps and the Jewish Legion. Trumpeldor had a grand scheme to raise a Jewish army of 100,000 in Russia that would fight its way to Palestine and claim it for the Jewish people. The Communist revolution ended his plans. He then went to Palestine. In 1920, Trumpeldor commanded a small Jewish force defending three Jewish settlements against Arab attacks from across the Syrian border. During a battle at Tel Hai, the Arabs sent a "peace mission" into the Jewish compound, then treacherously turned their guns on the settlers, mortally wounding Trumpeldor. His dying words, **"Never mind! It is good to die for our country!"** became an inspiration and motto for the fighters of the Yishuv. He died a hero honored by the Yishuv.

Brit Shalom—The Jewish Peace Alliance group, led by the president of the Hebrew University, Judah Magnes, and philosopher Martin Buber advocated a binational Jewish-Arab state in Palestine. The Zionists viewed the binational solution as one that would end all hope for Jewish nationhood; the Arabs would be a large majority that would continue the bitterness and hostility towards the Jews that prevailed.

Also supporting a binational state was Henrietta Szold. Having worked with the Arabs and Jews on health and education issues, she respected the national aspirations for both and longed for a solution that would end the animosity between these two peoples. With no such solution in sight, she settled for the binational state as the best solution. Regardless of her position on statehood, Henrietta Szold remained respected by the Zionist leaders for all her efforts on behalf of the Yishuv.

Jewish Agency for Palestine: Yishuv Connection with World Jewry—After the League of Nations awarded the Palestine Mandate to Great Britain, it encouraged the Jewish community representing all Jews to set up the Jewish Agency. The agency would assist in the establishment of a Jewish national home by representing the Jewish interests in dealing with the mandate authority. The League's requirement to include non-Zionists in the Jewish Agency was a contentious issue among Zionists for several years. President Weizmann presented a plan that achieved agreement between the Zionist and non-Zionist members at the 15th World Jewish Congress in 1927. The Plan called for:

- Equal membership of both factions on the Jewish Agency Executive Council
- Agreement to increase immigration
- The purchase of land as public property of the Jewish people

- Adopting the kibbutz system for settlements
- Recognizing Hebrew as the language of the country

After the agreement, the Agency membership was half Zionist and half non-Zionist, and periodically had non-Zionist leadership. However, it failed to raise the funds targeted to support its goals—the Great Depression of the nineteen-thirties was a major factor.

After the end of World War II, the Jewish Agency took an active role in developing the State of Israel. The role of the Agency was diminished after the Yishuv became independent. It was relegated to nongovernmental humanitarian tasks associated with bringing in immigrants and providing them relief. This enabled the Jewish Agency to retain tax-exempt status for fund raising purposes.

Vaad Leumi: Yishuv Executive Council—Consistent with their pioneering spirit, the Zionist community established an autonomous organization for managing the affairs of the Yishuv shortly after the British took on the responsibility for the Palestine Mandate. Remarkably, this was done independently of the British mandate authority's colonial rule over them. The Palestinian Jews elected members to a House of Delegates through democratic elections. Top members of the Zionist parties were appointed to the Vaad Leumi (National Committee) in proportion to their House representation.

Religious Authority—The British mandatory authorities assigned the responsibility for matrimonial law and other religious matters to the Chief Rabbinate and to the religious courts. The whole system of religious control of family law and the independence of religious authorities, which the British and later the Israelis adopted, was patterned after the Turkish "Millet" system. In 1921 the first two chief rabbis were elected, Rabbi Abraham Kook for the Ashkenazi Jews, and Rabbi Jacob Meir for the Sephardic Jews.

3
How They Lived

The immigrants to Palestine who came from many countries with diverse cultures had two characteristics that shaped their behavior in Palestine. They were embittered by the anti-Semitism that was shattering the lives of their fellow Jews whom they left behind, and they saw Zionism as the only solution that would enable Jews to live in dignity and without religious and political oppression. The reality of a Jewish state was still uncertain, and the behavior of the British mandate authority in the twenties and thirties darkened the prospects of its creation. Nevertheless, these Zionist immigrants were willing to accept the personal hardships that the bleak Palestine conditions imposed on them in the pursuit of their quest. The socialist background of those from the second and third Aliyahs coming from eastern Europe strongly influenced the kibbutz living and working style, which was extraordinary by any standard. Many of these immigrants saw this immigration of Jews from many lands in the diaspora as the fulfillment of the Jewish messianic theme. This ingathering of the Jewish people in their ancient homeland strengthened their motivation to lay the foundations that would enable other Jews to come back to the ancient land of Zion.

Kibbutz—The *kibbutz* is a farming community collective-living arrangement that was first organized in 1909 in Degania by the Second Aliyah pioneers. In accordance with their socialist and Zionist ideals, it required equal treatment for everyone and only permitted Jewish laborers. Property, clothing, food, and recreational opportunities were shared and distributed equally. The family unit was de-emphasized. Children lived and slept in communal quarters away from their parents and were raised by kibbutz members assigned to the children's area and by teachers. Parents only had time with their children after work and before bedtime, and on Saturday. Everyone had a physical chore associated with the kibbutz production, which initially was only agricultural products but in later years included industrial products. The members shared the kibbutz management responsibilities. The farmland they owned had to be developed and farmed through brute physical labor compounded by the hot Palestinian climate. For decades, the kibbutz financial success was marginal. Consequently, the members were given a minimum of basic clothing and ate what their farm produced—a chicken meal was a treat. It was a Spartan life, acceptable only to idealists.

Starting a new kibbutz was a challenge. The members had to live in temporary shacks for long periods until they could afford to build permanent houses. Developing the land to be arable was generally an ordeal, especially if it was formerly marshland. Younger members of mature kibbutzim were recruited to be trainers of new kibbutzim.

Moshav—This was a cooperative form of agricultural settlement. It appealed to those who objected to the socialist lifestyle of the kibbutzim. Every member owned and worked their own part of the settlement, but the marketing of the products and the purchasing of supplies were done cooperatively. It started out very slowly, but became more popular with the immigrants who came after 1935 without the socialist ideals of the earlier immigrants. Being more conventional than the exciting kibbutz concept, the Moshav got little international recognition.

Histadrut/Labor Socialists—Histadrut, the Jewish labor union organization, was organized and operated under the socialistic ideals. This organization struggled along with the rest of the Yishuv in its formative years. Initially, everyone working for Histadrut enterprises received the same salary that varied only with family size. The labor movement lost its influence during the terrible economic times in Palestine that occurred in the mid-1920s. There was labor movement unrest against the Histadrut for not having solutions to these economic problems. For several years, the high unemployment rate caused more Jews to emigrate from Palestine than immigrate to it. The economic situation improved with the business creativity of the Jews from Germany who came with the fifth Aliyah. Many of this large number of immigrants had socialistic backgrounds and eagerly joined the labor unions. With this membership influx, Histadrut, led by the socialist element, regained its political power in the early 1930s. However, labor unrest of a different kind persisted. There were clashes with the revisionist labor groups over the future direction of Zionism in Palestine that sometimes bordered on civil war. Issues included: the extent of the future national home; was it to be independent or associated with Britain; what steps were required to achieve it; and the nature of the Jewish relationship with the Palestinian Arabs.

Culture—The newcomers to Palestine indulged in all forms of culture. This pattern of interest in culture was an oddity from the rest of the world—it was not limited to the highly educated class of society. The common people devoured the Hebrew literature and poetry written by accomplished immigrants such as Chaim Bialik, Saul Tchernichovsky, Ahad Ha'am, Samuel Agnon, and Chaim Brenner. They went to the theaters, such as Habima, which produced international and native-written plays. Concerts on the radio by the Palestine Symphony Orchestra had a huge listening audience. Many from the distant kibbutzim struggled to attend these concerts. There were many talented musicians among the later immigrants. They organized local orchestras in the kibbutzim that were also popular. Sports organizations blossomed everywhere. Sports activity became an effective way to relieve tension for many Israelis.

Education—The educational needs of the youngsters was of paramount importance to the Zionists since they first started coming to Palestine. Quality education for everyone was the goal. Although it did actually take many years to accomplish, it was achieved in a relatively short time, considering the absence of any governmental organization to support its creation and the shortage of funds. The determined pioneers, with the help of Henrietta Szold, overcame these obstacles. Living in Palestine the last twenty years of her life, she was devoted to improving the Yishuv educational system as well as its medical needs. In time, hundreds of excellent schools were established to provide education from kindergarten through high school, even in the smallest village. An excellent teacher-training program buttressed the high quality of education. Hebrew became the common language in all schools, and English was taught in most schools as the secondary language.

Evolution of the School System—Palestine at the turn of the century had a dismal educational system in place that did not go beyond elementary school level. There was no compulsory education requirement, and free schools were seldom available. Schools for Jewish children were created as quickly as new immigrants settled down, but their educational methods and orientation were aligned to the three major Zionist elements, Labor, Mizrachi, and general Zionist. This made it difficult to have efficient classroom sizes to make full use of the limited resources available for education, and it prevented the school system from having the flexibility to accommodate the dynamics of the Yishuv population.

In the early 1920s, the British mandatory authorities took on the responsibility for educating the Palestinian Arab children and the Yishuv

Executive Council was given the responsibility for educating the Jewish children. As the member of this council, responsible for education, health, and social welfare, Henrietta Szold fought a long battle for the consolidation of the Jewish school system and the elimination of religious education from the public school system. The battle was won in 1927 when the General School system was consolidated. Free compulsory education up to age fourteen became law when the State of Israel was created. However, there were four independent Jewish school systems in place. The General School system was used in the cities and towns and had no ideological bias. The Socialist system was primarily for the kibbutzim and left wing party members in the cities. There were two Orthodox systems, one moderate and the other ultra-Orthodox. All of these systems have remained intact, although the state now funds them and they have to follow a certain curriculum. In 1978, compulsory education was extended to age sixteen and free education became available to age eighteen.

Creating institutions of higher education was an objective of the early pioneer leaders. The Yishuv was notably successful. First the Technion (Jewish Technical Institute) was founded in Haifa in 1910—it became the leading engineering institute in the Middle East. The Bezalel School for Arts and Crafts opened in Jerusalem. The Daniel Sieff Research Institute (later named the Weizmann Institute) opened in Rehoboth. It was where Weizmann conducted his chemical experiments so helpful to the British war effort and where, more recently, significant medical research has been conducted.

The crowning accomplishment was the Hebrew University in Jerusalem, which became the preeminent university in the Middle East. World-renowned German-Jewish educators who managed to leave Germany in the 1930s joined the university faculty to help make it the great learning institution. The Hebrew University foundation was laid in 1918, based on the Jewish community's optimism that the Balfour Declaration would lead to a Jewish state; it was formally opened in 1925. After the State of Israel came into existence, two universities were established in 1956. Bar Ilan University was sponsored in Ramat Gan by the Mizrachi organization in the United States and Canada. The Tel Aviv University was established to serve the large population in that city. By the 1970s, two other institutions reached university status, the Ben-Gurion University of the Negev in Beersheba for agricultural and medical research, and the Haifa University.

Health Care—The Yishuv health and welfare accomplishments made a dramatic improvement in the quality of life for both the Jews and the Arabs in Palestine. A country rampant with cholera, typhus, malaria, trachoma, and tuberculosis was transformed into a country with one of the lowest death rates in the world; these diseases were virtually eradicated.

At the turn of the century, there were only a few hospitals in Palestine, which were run by Jewish charitable organizations and by Christian missionary organizations. The bad quality of medical services combined with poor sanitary conditions resulted in a high infant mortality rate. The advancement in health care started when Henrietta Szold responded to a call for help to remedy the serious epidemics that plagued Palestine in 1916. She organized a large group of American doctors and nurses that went to Palestine with medical supplies to arrest the problem. The next improvement in health care came with the Histadrut policy of providing health care to its members.

With those starting points, over the next twenty years Henrietta Szold used the resources of Hadassah to improve the medical services of the Histadrut medical care system and to establish Hadassah health care systems throughout Palestine that provided equal medical care to Jews and Arabs alike. Arab mothers and children learned child health care from Arab-speaking Hadassah nurses. Several Hadassah hospitals and a medical school were opened, including the Hadassah Hospital on Mount Scopus in Jerusalem, which opened in 1938. It became the premier health care center in the Middle East. Bolstered by German immigrant doctors, Hadassah Hospital treated patients from all over the Third World, including many Arab countries. Israel achieved the esteemed position of having the world's highest number of doctors per capita.

Where They Lived—In keeping with the Zionist goal of establishing a Jewish national home, in 1909, a group of sixty Jewish professionals living in Jaffa decided to start a Jewish suburb on the sand dunes next to Jaffa. Named Tel Aviv, it became the first all Jewish city, with all municipal services performed by Jews, where everything shut down on the Sabbath, and all Jewish holidays were publicly celebrated. Tel Aviv grew rapidly; it became the Jewish commercial center in Palestine. The population in two other cities grew with each Aliyah. Jerusalem, the Jewish holy city, drew many to the outskirts of the Old City. Haifa became the main seaport and industrial city, expanding on its function as the oil refinery and pipeline depot for Iraqi oil. However, the majority of the urban dwellers preferred to live in small towns along the seacoast or in villages near Tel Aviv and Haifa.

The pioneer farmers opened settlements throughout Palestine. They even developed farms in the Negev, using irrigation techniques to overcome the sandy soil. After the Huleh Swamp District in the upper Galilee was purchased and drained, it became a popular location for new settlements.

Hashomer (Watchman)—The Poale Zion settlements established in the early 1900s were harassed by the neighboring Arab Bedouins and neighboring workers. Initial attempts to provide protection by employing Arab guards failed—these Arabs got embroiled in controversy with other Arabs because of their cooperative relationship with Jews. Poale Zion members took on this protection role in 1907. In 1909, the *Hashomer* organization was established to take on the responsibility of guarding all Jewish settlements, including land purchased and not yet occupied. This organization protected the living conditions of the watchmen, which gave the organization stability and made it effective.

4
Two Decades of Disappointments (1920–1939)

The 1920s started with high hopes for the Palestinian Jewish people. Great Britain appointed a British Zionist Jew, Sir Herbert Samuel, to be the high commissioner responsible for implementing the Palestine Mandate which was to take the necessary steps leading to a Jewish national home—the Balfour Declaration was to be fulfilled. The British and French worked out the Palestine Mandate with the support of the World Zionist Organization. There was little international opposition to the plan.

Within the year, the situation that appeared so positive turned around drastically. The neighboring Arab countries became hostile towards the idea of a future Jewish homeland in Palestine, and the Arabs in Palestine rebelled against the idea, attacking Jewish settlers. Sir Samuel's reaction to the Arab uprisings was to appease the Arabs. He offered little protection to the Jewish settlers. It was the start of Britain reneging on the Balfour Declaration—a policy that continued over the next twenty years. The British Foreign Office policy turned to appeasing the Arabs after every Arab riot and protest action in order to curry favor with the Arabian Gulf rulers—protection of the British oil supply dominated their policy.

In 1921, Colonial Secretary Winston Churchill reached an agreement with the Arabs that land east of the Jordan River was no longer considered covered by the Palestine Mandate. Although Churchill reiterated his support for a Jewish state, he recognized Emir Abdulla as *Emir* (ruler) of Transjordan. Abdulla was granted autonomous control of Transjordan but had to accept a remaining British army presence.

There were periodic minor clashes between Arabs and Jews over the next eight years. The Jewish and Arab nationalist interests grew more irreconcilable politically. In 1929, an Arab rebellion erupted in Jerusalem and spread throughout Palestine based on a false Arab extremist report that Jews were going to desecrate the Dome of the Rock. The British did not intervene to stop the attacks on Jewish communities. The riots, which lasted several days, resulted in over 100 Jewish men, women, and children being massacred in Hebron and Safed. With the British mandatory forces on the sidelines, the Jewish defense forces clashed with the Arabs to end the riots. There were over 150 deaths on both sides. Widespread Arab riots next occurred in 1936. It caused Britain to search for a political solution that would end the animosity between the Arabs and the Jews. Having no success, Britain issued a White Paper in 1937 that restricted Jewish immigration to 12,000 per year. The terms of the next British White Paper on Palestine issued in 1939 shocked and tormented the Jewish world; strong protests by the Jewish leaders were to no avail. The White Paper prohibited the further sale of land to Jews and restricted Jewish immigration to 75,000 over the next five years. This was at a time when European Jews were still managing to flee from the Nazis and Palestine was the most desirable haven. After May 1944, further Jewish immigration required Arab approval. To all intents and purposes, this effectively would end Jewish immigration to Palestine. It called for the establishment of a single Palestinian state, which would have a two-to-one Arab to Jewish population that essentially ended all hope for a Jewish state—**it nullified the Balfour Declaration.**

Despite the political setbacks, the Yishuv grew in many respects over the two decades ending in 1939. The population grew ninefold to 450,000, agricultural settlements expanded from 50 to 233, and there were now almost 6,000 industrial enterprises with 30,000 workers. A major industrial development was the Dead Sea potash plant, which supplied agricultural fertilizer to the world community in peacetime and vital war materials to Britain during World War II. Health, education, and cultural facilities expanded, and there was a transportation infrastructure for the cities and communities inhabited by the Jewish population. A citizen militia had been created to protect against Arab attacks. There was a political structure under the capable and internationally respected leadership of men like Weizmann, Ben-Gurion, and Sharett that was prepared to address the Yishuv's future political challenges.

Seeds of Turmoil—Until 1908 when the "Young Turks" started to modernize and liberalize the country, Turkey, a non-Arab Muslim country, did not permit any nationalistic movements in Palestine, which it ruled for hundreds of years. Even after this political freedom was granted, there was no significant Palestinian nationalist movement for an Arab state in Palestine until 1920.

In 1918 there was a dialogue between Chaim Weizmann and Emir Feisal. Feisal, the son of the Arab king of Hejaz (future Saudi Arabia), was the key Arab leader. Weizmann assured the Arabs that their sensitivities would be respected by a Jewish state and that the Zionists would support Arab political aspirations. In return, Feisal endorsed a small Jewish state. The Zionists reluctantly agreed to his offer, which was predicated on the Arab state getting its own independence from Britain.

Concurrent with Feisal's planned cooperation with the Zionists, other Arab nationalists were competing for dominance of the Arab masses. At that time, they were vying for the Arab part of Palestine becoming part of Greater Syria or joining the Pan-Arab movement that envisioned a revitalized Muslim Ottoman Empire. An independent Palestine state was not a consideration. The pact with Feisal came apart when the French refused to grant Syria its freedom. Weizmann's reluctance to interfere with the French plans for Syria caused the Arab leaders to cancel Feisal's agreement. Feisal dropped out of the political picture and his brother Emir Abdullah replaced him as the Arab leader representing Hejaz.

Evolution of Palestinian Nationalism—Palestinian Arabs accepted the Jewish immigrants without any exceptional antagonism until the influx of Jews into Palestine started to become farmers. The city-dwelling Jews were viewed as nonpolitical and nonthreatening to the Arab lifestyle. Jews had lived there under Arab/Muslim domination for over a thousand years. When Jews started buying land and living and working as farmers, the nationalists, who were mostly the younger element, viewed this as a threat to the "Arab nation's culture and lifestyle." They resented the land being sold to Jews. They objected to Jewish farmers not permitting Bedouin livestock to graze on their land. Later, as the Jewish population increased in Jerusalem, the nationalists added false threats to the Muslim religion to their expressed concerns, including "Jews were going to destroy Arab mosques."

The elder Arab leaders' attitude towards the Jews was based mostly on political considerations—they were Pan-Arab nationalists rather than Palestinian nationalists. Up until the end of World War I, these leaders did not consider opposing the Turks by asking for an autonomous Palestinian state. Zionist aspirations for a Jewish state seemed unreal, so there were no nationalistic objection to Jews at the Arab leadership level. After the war ended, the Arabs, Jews, French, and British maneuvered in the political arena, changing alliances with the hope of achieving their respective goals. First, the Palestinian Arab goal of belonging to the Muslim Ottoman Empire vanished when the British and French agreed to strip Turkey of the Middle East countries. Then the British and French dashed hopes for the Palestinians joining an independent Greater Syria by taking control of the three Middle East countries. Pan-Arab nationalism almost vanished while Palestinian nationalism grew.

In the early 1930s, both Italian and German propaganda, guns, and money fed Arab nationalism in order to develop an anti-British element in the Middle East. Their main Palestinian ally was the Grand Mufti of Jerusalem, the Muslim religious leader in Palestine. Jewish Sir Herbert Samuel, who was the first High Commissioner of Palestine for the mandate, appointed the Mufti in 1921. This appointment was part of Samuel's effort to be impartial, despite the Mufti's role in promoting anti-Jewish riots in 1920. The Mufti openly encouraged the killing of Jews. He issued false alarms about Jewish intentions to destroy Muslim holy places, which stirred up violence against Jews. During the war years, he continued his provocation from his exile in Germany.

Economic-based Arab Antagonism—Ironically, another source of the antagonism of the Palestinian Arabs towards the Jews was a consequence of improved working conditions of the Arabs in Palestine.

About 250 large Palestinian families owned ninety percent of the land in Palestine; they were the influential people. Except for the Bedouins, the Arab masses worked for these landowners, and many were indebted to them. The wealthy Arab landowners were concerned that their workers, who were paid low wages, would clamor for higher wages to match the higher wages paid to Arabs working for Jews. The Arab businessmen and farm owners could not pay higher wages to their Arab laborers because their operations were not as efficient as those owned by Jews. Out of selfish economic interest, these wealthy landowners became hostile to the Jews and started promoting nationalism. They persuaded the poor Arab workers who were still living in squalor in their villages that the Jews were ruining the country by changing the Arab lifestyle, stealing their land, and taking their jobs. The Jewish argument that life for the Arabs improved in every respect since the Jewish immigration started was ignored.

The Jewish leaders in the 1920s thought that the increased economic opportunities for the Arabs would restrain Arab nationalism. They did not adequately address the reasons for the growing challenge of Arab nationalism. During periods when there was an economic boom in Palestine, about 100,000 Arabs came from other Arab countries to work for Jews in Palestine because they earned so much more than they did in their home country. The Arab population growth was in the cities adjacent to the largest Jewish population/work areas, giving evidence to the relationship of Palestinian Arab economic growth to Jewish economic growth. These events failed to impress the poor Palestinian masses, and the forces of nationalism prevailed. Although Arab living conditions improved, they remained below those of the Jews. These conditions made the Palestinian masses responsive to the extremists.

Jewish Policy of Self-Restraint—Arabs attacked Jewish settlements throughout Palestine in 1929. The Hashomer guards were able to defend the Jewish settlements but the elderly Jews in Hebron and Safed were unable to defend themselves. Many were slaughtered wantonly. These attacks led to the creation of the self-defense "*Haganah*" organization. The Haganah became a well-trained, well-armed defense force. In the absence of the British restraining the Arab riots of 1936, the Haganah very capably defended the Jewish settlements and protected factories and transportation. In spite of the aggressive action of the Arabs, the Jewish community refused to take revenge on the Arab people, who they had no quarrel with—they blamed the Arab leaders. The Yishuv policy was *Havlagah* (self-restraint).

Arab Violence Leads to Partition Recommendation—In 1937, a British commission was established to determine how to avoid the terrible clashes that occurred the year before between the Arabs and the Jews. Provoked by Germany, who was helping to finance Arab nationalists, the Arabs had attacked many Jewish villages, the riots reaching the rebellion stage. The British, still trying to appease the Arab world, issued the Peel Report that recommended partition. It was easier on the British than condemning the Palestinians for their unwarranted bloodshed of Jews and illegal rebellion. The Zionist Congress of 1937 reluctantly gave their approval to negotiate the partition with the British. The Grand Mufti, leading spokesman for the Arabs, rejected partition. After the Mufti demanded control of all of Palestine, including the exclusively Jewish sections, the partition consideration ended.

5
World War II Years

The decade of the 1940s started with the most horrible catastrophe to befall the Jewish people. During the Holocaust period that followed, the Palestinian Jewish underground organization spirited Jews out of Europe and into Palestine against the objections and resistance of the British. The British were fighting Hitler, but at the same time, they were also fighting to keep Jewish refugees from illegally entering Palestine. The British White Paper of 1939 effectively shut out legal immigration and prohibited the purchase of land, but the Jewish underground managed to smuggle in over 75,000 escapees from the Nazi terror. This illegal immigration support continued after the Holocaust ended, with refugees wanting to go to Palestine and the British forcefully refusing their entry.

Towards the end of the Allied armies' war with Germany, the Yishuv leaders concluded that defeating the Nazis overrode any bitterness they had towards the British for their Palestinian policy. In 1944 the Yishuv leaders responded to a British call for support and established the Jewish Brigade that fought in Italy. After the war ended, members of the Brigade became recruits for the underground that rescued Holocaust survivors and organized their illegal entry into Palestine.

Jewish Volunteers—In spite of the negative British attitude towards Jewish immigration, the Yishuv concluded that it was more important to aid the British in their fight against the Nazis. After the war started, Jews in Palestine registered for national service. The Jewish Agency offered a Jewish army of forty thousand to fight for the British, but Britain rejected the offer for fear of antagonizing the Arab world leaders. They did accept about 20,000 Jewish volunteers who fought as individuals in the British Army in North Africa, Italy, and France.

Palmach Operations in Syria—In 1941, after the German defeat of France, the Germans under General Rommel in North Africa were on the march towards Cairo and beyond. With the Arabs in Palestine sympathetic to Germany, Britain relied on the Palestinian Jews to prevent the Germans from invading Palestine from Vichy-controlled Syria. The newly established Haganah strike force, the Palmach, was trained by the British to conduct sabotage operations in Syria in order to deter any German attack. The Haganah and its Palmach unit, working with the British army, was successful at destroying bridges, roads, and military installations. Moshe Dayan, who showed exceptional bravery, lost one eye while fighting the Syrians as a Palmach officer. In 1942, after the British General Montgomery forced Rommel to retreat from Egypt and Libya and the threat to Palestine ended, the British army in Palestine canceled their military cooperation with the Jewish defense forces. The Haganah and Palmach were forced into being illegal underground organizations.

The Jewish Brigade—In 1944, British Prime Minister Churchill, who had previously voiced his support of a Jewish Palestinian state after the war ended, issued a decree establishing a Jewish brigade in the British army. It was in response to Zionist urging to allow Jews to fight against Hitler under their own blue and white Zionist flag. The Jewish Brigade of 3,400 Palestinian Jews fought with distinction in Italy. This military experience proved invaluable during the War of Independence.

Jewish Parachutists: Heroine Hannah Senesh—Two hundred forty Palestinian Jews performed extraordinary acts of heroism in 1944 in the service of the British army. Selected because of their ability to speak the language of the country they were planning to enter, they were trained by the British to parachute behind the German lines throughout central and eastern Europe. Their primary mission was to arrange escape routes for downed British airmen by coordinating arrangements between the British and the partisan underground movements through the use of their coded radio transmitters. After accomplishing these objectives, the parachutists were to aid Jews who were seeking to get to Palestine by coordinating their escape with the Jewish underground. Thirty-two parachutists were dropped in the Balkans. One of these parachutists was a twenty-three year old girl, Hannah Senesh, who had already become an accomplished poetess.

Hannah Senesh came from an assimilated Jewish family living in Budapest. At seventeen, she was disheartened by the growing anti-Semitism in Hungary and became a Zionist. She came to believe that a Jewish homeland in Palestine was the only answer to anti-Semitism. She was anxious to help build it. In 1939, at eighteen, she emigrated to Palestine, leaving behind her mother who was convinced that conditions would not get too bad for the Jews in Hungary, where Jews had achieved a high level of societal integration. Hannah Senesh volunteered for the British mission because it gave her an opportunity to help Jewish children to escape from Hungary and to rescue her mother. After completing her assignment in Yugoslavia, which involved some heroic actions with the partisans, she continued through the Yugoslavian forests on foot to secretly cross into Hungary and conduct her mission there. She was captured at the border by the Hungarian authorities and accused of being a spy because of the radio transmitter she was carrying. Incarcerated for four months and tortured repeatedly in a German military prison in Budapest, Hannah Senesh was executed by a firing squad after refusing to reveal any secrets about her radio code, the underground operation, or her connection with the British army. Shortly afterwards, her mother was sent to Auschwitz.

Hannah Senesh became a heroine to the people in Israel, a symbol of heroism and martyrdom. In 1950, she was buried in Israel with full military honors. The Israelis were particularly inspired by the poem she wrote in the Balkans on her way to Hungary. It was a testament to her heroism. It was a poem cherished by all Israelis. The first stanza read:

Blessed Is the Match

> Blessed is the match consumed in kindling flame,
> Blessed is the flame that burns in the secret fastness of the heart,
> Blessed is the heart with the strength to stop its beating for
>   honor's sake,
> Blessed is the match consumed in kindling flame.

Her last poem, "One-Two-Three," was written in the Hungarian prison just before she was executed. The last stanza read:

> I could have been twenty-three next July,
> I gambled on what mattered the most,
> The dice were cast,
> I lost.

6
Birth of the State of Israel

After Germany was defeated, there were over 250,000 Jewish concentration camp survivors who moved into Displaced Person (DP) camps in the U.S., British, and French occupation zones in Germany and Austria. They would not go back to their respective home country because of their frightful experience there during the Holocaust and their sense that they would not be welcomed back to these countries that previously displayed hostility to Jews. In addition to this group, there was an influx of many thousands more from camps liberated by the Russians who did not want to stay in Poland. Many other Jews came out of hiding from the Nazis. The rebirth of anti-Semitism in the central European countries that came under Communist rule also increased the influx of refugees from the east to the west over the next three-year period. This included many Jews who came under Soviet control after Stalin's pact with Hitler in 1939 and were evacuated to the Soviet interior.

The countries of the world generally sympathized with the Holocaust survivors who suffered so badly, but they were not ready to offer them asylum. With nowhere to go, these displaced persons developed a preference to emigrate to Palestine. They knew their Palestinian Jewish brethren would welcome them. Representatives of the Yishuv, including David Ben-Gurion, had visited the DP camps to encourage them to choose to emigrate to Palestine and to alert them as to what to expect there. The DP camp inmates hoped and expected to leave quickly for Palestine. Many started to train themselves for living in Palestine. Unfortunately, the British government, who controlled access to Palestine as the League of Nations mandatory power, prevented their legal immigration for several years. In the summer of 1945, the Labor party took control of Great Britain. Under the new Foreign Minister Ernest Bevin, the British continued the policy instituted in 1939, which was to severely restrict Jewish immigration to Palestine. Immigration was limited to between two hundred and fifteen hundred monthly over the next two years. This was shamefully trivial considering how many Holocaust survivors were determined to get to Palestine since they had no other haven. It was particularly disappointing because for many years until he came into power, Bevin had been a friend of Zionism.

With immigration essentially closed, many of the Holocaust survivors, out of desperation, attempted to enter Palestine illegally. This activity was aided by Bricha, the organization established by Palestinian Jews to facilitate the illegal immigration into Palestine. The British fought these efforts in every way. They prevented the refugee's departure from Europe and harassed them at sea. Many Jews died in the attempt to enter Palestine illegally; several barely seaworthy ships sank in storms on the way to Palestine. Many others were captured and sent to detention camps in Cypress. Several boats were turned back from the shores of Palestine, including the *Exodus 1947*. Carrying 4,500 refugees, the *Exodus* was intercepted by the British off the coast of Palestine. After British destroyers damaged the *Exodus,* the refugees were forced to disembark and board other ships that took them back to British-zone Displaced Persons camps in Germany. The picture of Holocaust survivors being sent back to DP camps in Germany was a major propaganda victory for the Zionists in their struggle for world public opinion. Approximately 70,000 Holocaust survivors did manage to enter Palestine illegally between 1945 and 1948.

With over a quarter-million Jews stuck in Europe's Displaced Persons camps, the Palestinian Jews became more determined to establish a Jewish state that would have the authority to grant the Holocaust survivors a haven.

The Rocky Road to Independence—There were many challenges to the creation of the independent Jewish State that was achieved in 1948. The Arab world was against it. Aligned with the Arabs were the influential British government and other countries with little sympathy with the Jewish people. Internal Yishuv politics represented another set of obstacles—essentially all the Palestinian Jews favored independence, but the approach and political, social, and religious arrangements to be pursued varied widely. The Zionist group led by Chaim Weizmann advocated negotiating with Great Britain. The more activist Zionists, led by David Ben-Gurion, urged a militant approach of battling the Arabs and the British rather than a political approach. The Yishuv was divided between settling for a divided Palestine or a binational state or demanding the boundaries of the greater biblical Israel. Another major issue was whether the new state should be a socialist, communist, or free enterprise economic society. The mostly secular pioneers of Israel opposed the smaller religious community who argued that a Jewish state without the sanctity of the Judaic religion was not a true Jewish state.

David Ben-Gurion: Yishuv Leader—The individual that guided the Yishuv through the many challenges on the way to independence was David Ben-Gurion. This leader and statesman devoted sixty-five years to Zionist and Israeli politics, helping to achieve Israel's independence and to shape Israel's economic, social, and religious structure.

Ben-Gurion, who became a Zionist in his youth, left Russia for Palestine in 1906. In the 1920s, he advocated finding a way to the heart of the Arab people through a genuine alliance between Jewish and Arab workers. In the early 1930s, Ben-Gurion recognized that the Jewish people in Europe were approaching trouble and became determined that a Jewish state was the only place that could offer them a home and refuge before being eradicated by Hitler. He became a member of the executive committee of the Jewish Agency that ran the affairs of the Jewish people in Palestine under the British mandatory authority. Ben-Gurion frequently visited the United States during the war years to promote plans for the creation of a Jewish homeland. After the Holocaust, he led the determined Palestinian-Jewish effort to achieve a Jewish state.

Ben-Gurion undertook to establish a single secular authority to close the ranks among the disparate political, social, and religious views of the Jewish people. He envisioned this strong secular authority to be capable of guiding the Palestinian Jews through a course that would move ahead with the establishment of the State of Israel with laws that accommodated the religious community. He envisioned a return to the lifestyle of the ancient land of Israel, complete with its biblical mission to be a light to the nations of the world.

Ben-Gurion was determined to expedite the departure of the British from Palestine. He had little faith in the future of the diaspora Jewish community and believed a national home in Israel was the only future for the Jewish people. As the head of the Jewish Agency in Israel, he shaped the course to independence in 1948. His objective was to establish a sovereign state that could open the door to Jewish immigration. Asserting his strong leadership, he contained the influence of the two Jewish extremist militant organizations, which helped assure that the new State of Israel would be a democratic society.

David Ben-Gurion, as the leader of the Yishuv, had the honor to declare the independence of the State of Israel in 1948. He became its first prime minister, leading the country during the War of Independence and serving until 1953, when he stepped down. In retirement, he lived as he preached. He returned to the biblical lifestyle as a farmer, having moved to the small pioneer settlement of Side Boker, located in the Negev desert.

Jewish Extremist Organizations—The actions of the new British Foreign Secretary Bevin sowed the growth of extremist Jewish organizations. Bevin showed his intent on killing any chances of an independent Jewish state and took militant steps to prevent Holocaust refugees from entering Palestine. Comprised mostly of young members of the revisionist political Zionists, these extremist organizations believed that only through violent acts could they counter Bevin's policies.

The larger extremist group was the Irgun Zvai Leumi (National Military Organization). One of its leaders was Menachem Begin, the future prime minister who signed the Camp David Peace Treaty with Egyptian President Anwar Sadat in 1979. The Irgun's aim was to drive the British out of Palestine.

The smaller extremist group was the Fighters for the Freedom of Israel. It was known as the Sternists after their leader, Abraham Stern, a Hebrew University student who had been killed by the British. Their aim was to take revenge on the British.

These two groups conducted violent guerilla warfare. They attacked government buildings and police stations and raided military depots. They resorted to killings of policemen and soldiers and to assassinations of high British officials. The Yishuv leaders and the Jewish people in general viewed their violent actions as extreme and not fitting for the Jewish people.

Haganah Actions—The policy of the Yishuv and its Haganah military organization had been one of self-restraint. This changed as a result of the British actions against the Haganah, which had been building a defensive strength to counter the expected Arab hostility when the mandate ended. The British, seeking to disarm the Haganah, made extensive searches of Jewish settlements looking for arms. Possession of arms was made a criminal offense, with severe penalties. Although the law against arms applied equally to the Arabs and Jews, the British were invariably lenient with the Arabs and severe with the Jewish offenders. The British also tried to prevent new Jewish settlements from being established, but the determined Jews continued to build new settlements throughout Palestine. Because of the hostile British actions, the Haganah abandoned its policy of self-restraint and actually took offensive actions against the British as a means of defending the Yishuv.

Palestine Partition Plan—In 1947, the United Nations deliberated what to do when the British mandate over Palestine ended. A partition plan was finally approved. Although the portion of Palestine allocated to the Israeli State had so many shortcomings, the Zionists immediately accepted the proposed partition plan as the fulfillment of the Balfour Declaration. Palestinian Jews danced in the streets with joy. American Jews were ecstatic. The Palestinian Arab leadership, however, immediately rejected partition, declaring their intention of taking over all of Palestine as an Arab state.

Undeclared War of Arabs Against Jews—The Arab Palestinians started an undeclared war against the Jews immediately after the Muslim nations rejected the UN Partition Plan. Their aim was to destroy or starve into submission the isolated Jewish settlements. In the four months between December 1947 and April 1948, almost one thousand Jews died as result of Arab violence. It was a constant challenge for the Yishuv forces to protect the isolated settlements. There was the concern that if the Arabs succeeded in destroying some small communities, others would flee for their safety to the few larger, heavily populated areas and the Yishuv would be demoralized. Fighting took place throughout Palestine. A major battle took place in northern Palestine near the Syrian border, where the Haganah outlasted the Syrian and Druze Arab forces. The Palmach, Haganah's shock troops under the command of twenty-nine-year-old Yigal Allon, outfought the Syrians to free Safed in the Galilee, where 10,000 Arabs surrounded 1,400 Jews. After these losses, the Syrians were content to just harassing the Jews, avoiding any military confrontation until the mandate ended and the British forces left. The large cities of Haifa and Jaffa were taken over by the Jews essentially without a battle; the Arab soldiers and most of the Arab civilians fled.

Jerusalem with its Jewish population of one hundred thousand represented the major challenge for the Jewish forces. For weeks, convoys of trucks carrying food and supplies had to fight their way through ambushes on the road connecting Tel Aviv to Jerusalem. Food and water became perilously low. The situation had become critical when the Palmach destroyed the fortress at Castel, the center from which most of the Arab guerrillas operated, lifting the blockade of Jerusalem for a short period to enable supplies to be sent in.

Deir Yassin: a Massacre of Arabs—A major goal of the Yishuv was the lifting of the Arab siege of Jerusalem. The villages on the outskirts of Jerusalem became the targets in this struggle. A provocative battle took place in the village of Deir Yassin on April 10, 1948. It had a significant lasting impact on Jewish-Arab relations.

The two Jewish extremist organizations, the Irgun and the Stern Gang, collaborated to attack Deir Yassin in order to free up the approach to Jerusalem. After warning the civilians to leave before the attack was to start, they expected the Arabs to give up the village without a fight; this frequently happened when an Arab village was surrounded. (There has been a claim that the loudspeaker truck broke down, and so, the warning was not effective.) Instead, the Jewish fighters were surprised to meet with heavy resistance and found that the civilians had not been evacuated. Taking heavy losses themselves (40% killed), the Jewish forces killed many Arabs in house-to-house fighting. Women and children were killed; some found slaughtered in brutal fashion. Two hundred deaths were reported in Arab radio reports. An analysis of Arab documentation revealed that the Arabs at that time knew that the death toll, including those killed in the house-to-house fighting, was closer to one hundred. There were false reports of rape. The exaggeration was part of the Arab leadership strategy to incite the Arabs against the Israelis and to encourage them to leave the areas with large Jewish populations. It resulted in the immediate mass exodus of three-quarter million Arabs from cities and villages.

Ben-Gurion and the Haganah leadership immediately recognized this incident to be an unfortunate improper attack on civilians that violated the Yishuv's military code of avoiding attacks on civilians. They quickly denounced the extremist behavior at Deir Yassin and arrested the leaders of the attack.

Mount Scopus: a Massacre of Jews—Adding to the Arab pain caused by the Deir Yassin incident was the loss of many other Arab towns to the Jewish forces. The Palestinian Arab leaders decided to do something dramatic to lift the morale of the Palestinians. Four days after the Deir Yassin attack, Arabs attacked a Jewish supply convoy passing through an Arab area on the way to the Hadassah hospital and the Hebrew University on Mount Scopus. They mercilessly burned alive seventy-six passengers in two buses. The dead included several leading physicians and nurses of Hadassah University who prided themselves in their Jewish humanitarian efforts that served both Arabs and Jews. Also killed were several Hebrew University world-renowned educators. The Arabs considered this massacre as revenge for the Deir Yassin massacre. British peace-keeping forces watched the attack on the buses and did nothing to stop it.

The Flight of the Arabs—The Arab strategists were convinced that there was going to be a short war with the Jews because they outnumbered the Jewish Defense forces and had significantly more arms, including airplanes and tanks. They undertook a campaign by radio, newspaper, and word of mouth to encourage the Arab civilians living close to the heavily populated Jewish areas to voluntarily flee before the fighting began. This would make it easier to fight the Jews without exposing the Arab civilians to casualties. They encouraged the Arab populace to believe that they would be able to return after the Jews were driven out of Palestine and get their pick of the Jewish homes and property. After the Deir Yassin incident, the Palestinian Arabs broadcast exaggerated descriptions of the attack and suggested the Jews planned more such violent attacks. They spread false atrocity stories and fabricated tales of butchery, rape, and theft. These warnings had the effect of frightening the Palestinian Arabs into fleeing, particularly from the neighboring Arab villages. It accelerated the mass exodus of the Arabs from Palestine that had already started after being told that the Jews were on the verge of being defeated.

In the desperate hope for a peaceful accommodation, Yishuv leader Ben-Gurion pleaded with the Palestinians to stay where they lived because they had nothing to fear from living in a Jewish state. His pleas were ignored. The Arab public officials, political leaders, and wealthy landowners disregarded Ben-Gurion's encouragement to stay and were the first to flee. The Arab masses quickly followed this leadership—70,000 left Jaffa and 60,000 left Haifa alone. The Haifa Jews wanted the Arabs to stay and run the port city. The Arab leaders wanted the Arab population to flee, denying the Jews the important workforce. Many Arabs fled just to protect their families from harm in the war zones. Some Arabs were driven out by the Israeli soldiers in some hotly contested areas, such as Lydda and Ramle, in the battle for Jerusalem. By war's end, approximately 800,000 Arabs fled from the areas populated by the Jews. They mostly went to the Gaza Strip, which was under Egypt's control, the West Bank that seemed safely under Jordan's control, and to Jordan on the east bank of the Jordan River.

Israeli Declaration of Independence—After receiving assurances that the United States would recognize the new state, the leaders of the Yishuv decided to move ahead with the partition and proclaimed its independence on May 15, 1948. Ben-Gurion, the leader of the Yishuv, had this to say in his speech announcing Israel's independence:

- "Formal recognition of Israel will not solve Israel's problems."
- "The country was being invaded from all directions by regular armies of neighboring states. The Security Council will not stop the attacks."
- "The Jewish people must prepare defenses and build up military forces capable of repulsing and destroying the enemy."
- "The new State of Israel must prepare to receive their brethren from the far-flung corners of the earth."

Ben-Gurion appealed to the Palestinian Arabs to preserve the peace and join in building the new state, based on full and equal citizenship to all and to share in the advancement of the entire Middle East. He extended his hand to all the neighboring states in an offer of peace and promised Israel would do its share in a common effort for the advancement of the entire Middle East.

7
The War of Independence (May 15, 1948–July 20, 1949)

The Arab countries openly expressed their intention to invade Palestine after the British ended their Palestine Mandate. Led by David Ben-Gurion, the Yishuv prepared for this attack. The odds were awesome. A Jewish defense force of 45,000 loosely organized troops, consisting of fifty percent each of men and women, was committed to both defending their own settlements and opposing the advances of the somewhat larger, formally trained Arab armies from Syria, Egypt, Lebanon, Iraq, Saudi Arabia, and Transjordan (now known as Jordan). The Transjordanian army consisted of 10,000 British trained troops led by the famous British general known as Glubb Pasha and was backed by 50,000 Palestinian Arab irregulars. The arms situation was generally one-sided. The Arab armies had modern weapons including tanks, armored vehicles, artillery pieces, fighter planes and bombers. The Jewish defense forces had none of this equipment except for small size mortars, a few old-vintage howitzers, and several Piper Cub airplanes.

The Arab attacks came on schedule, May 15, 1948. Only three Arab armies effectively participated in the war, Jordan, Syria, and Egypt. Iraq sent a small contingent to fight with the Jordanian and Syrian armies. Lebanon, with its mixed Christian and Muslim forces, avoided alliances with the Arab rulers, who were clashing to lead the Arab forces, and essentially stayed out of the fighting. Saudi Arabia's contribution was mainly the financing of the Arab military effort.

The fighting was brutal and costly on both sides in terms of the number of soldiers killed. Each side fought well but made strategic blunders that contributed to lengthening the duration of the war. The lack of coordination between the Arab armies was their major weakness. The flexibility of the Israeli military commanders, their capitalizing on nighttime fighting, and their brave leadership by participating in the front-line fighting gave the Israeli army a large edge that overcame the military imbalance. The difference in the psychological attitude between the Jews and the Arabs was undoubtedly a significant factor. The Jews were fighting for survival—the Arabs kept vowing to drive all Jews into the sea when the State of Israel was destroyed. **With this threat, Jews had *ein breira* (no choice) but to fight and die if necessary to protect other Jews and save the Yishuv.** The Arabs had no such motivation. The desire to flee for their personal safety frequently overcame their determination to continue fighting, in concert with the Arab leaders' advice to flee from the Jewish areas because the superior Arab armies would soon be victorious and they would be returning home to take over Jewish property.

Fighting for Survival—The challenge to meet the Arab invasion was enormous. Well-equipped, professionally trained Arab armies simultaneously attacked all the Jewish-held areas. The Syrians attacked the settlements in the northern Jordan Valley with a large tank force that attempted to cut in two the northern Jewish-held area of Palestine, isolating Haifa. This was prevented by a small number of village defenders. Outnumbered and with minimal arms, through desperate battles that wiped out most of the defenders and a series of ruses by the survivors that deceived the Syrians into believing they were still a significant fighting force, the Israelis held back the Syrians until reinforcements arrived. The large Egyptian army aimed at cutting off the Negev and capturing Tel Aviv. The Egyptian advance along the coast towards Tel Aviv was held up by the heroic efforts of the defenders of Kibbutz Yad Mordechai (named after the heroic young leader of the 1943 Warsaw ghetto uprising, Mordechai Anielewicz), which held out for five days. The Egyptian advance near the Beersheba-Jerusalem Road was turned back by the 140 defenders of Kibbutz Negba who fought 1,000 Egyptians. The Iraqis and Jordanians attacked the central area where the strongest of the Israeli forces opposed them and succeeded in halting the Arab advance.

When the war started, only the poorly equipped and not-well-organized half-civilian army was available to defend the widely distributed and isolated Jewish communities. The Yishuv's first decision was not to abandon any of the isolated villages and kibbutzim to avoid demoralizing the general population. This plan was rewarding. The reports of the heroic actions of the citizen army at kibbutzim, such as Yad Mordechai and Negba, that repulsed the Arab armies bolstered the spirit of the Jewish people.

The fighting was fierce, with many casualties on both sides. Military blunders were made on both sides. The occupancy of some towns frequently changed hands several times. The Israelis fought many defensive battles: some were heroic against overwhelming numerical forces. They also captured large areas of Palestine. The Israelis fought for time to develop an organized army with a command structure, military strategies, and improved military communications. They waited for the arrival of much-needed military equipment and airplanes that they quickly made plans to obtain.

The Battle for Jerusalem—Jerusalem, the heart of the Yishuv, was in a difficult position. It was essentially isolated from the main Jewish population in the coastal area, connected by a road that went through a heavily populated Arab area and over mountainous terrain. The Arab Legion under General Glubb Pasha immediately attacked the Old City of Jerusalem. The Jewish defenders stubbornly fought off the Arab armored cars with Molotov cocktails and light antitank weapons. However, after two weeks of fighting and unsuccessful attempts to reinforce the defenders, the commander of the few fighting forces surrendered, and the Arabs allowed a procession of 1,200 civilians led by old rabbis carrying Torahs to evacuate the Old City. The Arab mobs proceeded to loot and burn the Jewish section of the Old City. Fifty-eight synagogues including the 700-year old Hurva Synagogue were desecrated and destroyed. The Old City, including the Western Wall, was closed to Jews for the next nineteen years, until retaken by the Jews in the Six-Day War. Even Israeli Muslims were denied access to the mosques in the Old City.

The Arab strategy was to starve the Jews in the New City of Jerusalem into surrender. With the resupply road blocked, food, water, and munitions started to run out. The Israelis fought hard to free the road to Jerusalem but could not bridge a several-mile gap of mountainous terrain between their forces. The Israeli forces under the command of the respected commander Yigal Allon could not overcome the Arab forces at Latrun after several days of fighting that caused severe Israeli losses. The Israelis took an alternative course of action. For a two-week period, at night under cover of darkness, they undertook to build a "Burma Road" over the mountain, bypassing Latrun. They completed the road and brought in supplies just before the United Nations truce went into effect, which would have prevented any resupply of Jerusalem without the new road.

Retired U.S. Colonel David Marcus was involved in this battle to free Jerusalem. Known as Mickey Stone to avoid complications with the

United States army, Marcus volunteered to help train the Israeli Army. He was highly respected and appreciated by the Israelis for the intensity of his involvement. Due to take charge of the Jerusalem military operations, Marcus was killed by an Israeli sentry when he went off base at night and didn't respond to the sentry in Hebrew and was mistaken for the enemy.

The First Truce Period: June 11 to July 9—The Israelis and Arabs accepted a twenty-eight-day truce period sponsored by the United Nations; both sides were weary from the fighting. The United Nations mediator, Count Bernadotte of Sweden, proposed a political solution that was quickly rejected by both sides. The Arabs would not accept the State of Israel; the Israeli's objected to the diminished sovereignty proposed.

Ben-Gurion took advantage of the month of no fighting to organize the Yishuv fighting forces into a disciplined military organization so they could improve their fighting ability. The Israelis, who previously fought a defensive war, planned to take the battle initiative with the aid of the military equipment they were expecting.

It was during this truce period when Jews fought against Jews. It happened when the Irgun, one of the two Jewish extremist underground organizations during the British Mandate, brought in a landing ship, named *Altalena,* loaded with arms and 900 recruits from Europe. Prime Minister Ben-Gurion demanded that the arms and the recruits be turned over to the newly established Israel Defense Forces (IDF). After the Irgun refused, the IDF attacked the ship. After fifteen were killed and the ship was sunk in the gunfire, the Irgun gave in and ceased to be an independent fighting force.

Military Aid Comes to Israel from Many Quarters—In June 1945, Ben-Gurion started planning for the day when the Jews would be fighting to establish their own state. During a visit to New York City for establishing a source of military equipment, he was connected with Rudolf Sonneborn, a wealthy industrialist from an affluent German-Jewish family. In response to Ben-Gurion's pleading for help, Sonneborn set up a network of sixteen Zionists (later expanded to include many others) who would raise funds and procure and smuggle munitions to the Haganah. They also bought most of the ships used in the underground transport of Holocaust survivors from Europe to Palestine. The most famous was the *Exodus 1947.* The munitions supply effort intensified after the State of Israel was established. This organization took the lead in purchasing surplus U.S. military equipment and arms from Mexico. The United States had an arms embargo in place, but the Sonneborn network found ways to get around it. Sonneborn set up the Sonneborn Institute as a business front for the Haganah support. The equipment, including fighter planes and bombers, were obtained by devious means to circumvent the American embargo, including the transfer of ownership through several Latin American countries before shipment to Israel.

Israel also received military aid from a most unexpected source. The anti-Semitic Soviet Premier Stalin, in the midst of repressing Russian Jews, not only recognized the new State of Israel but he instructed the Czech government to sell Israel vitally needed arms, including fighter planes, tanks, and artillery. In addition to the direct shipment of Soviet arms, planes from the United States would land in Czechoslovakia and load up with arms, tanks and artillery pieces before continuing on to Israel. Stalin thought he would undermine the position of the British in the Middle East by supporting the Israelis and not the Arabs. Stalin mistakenly anticipated that the socialistic Israeli leaders would shift to Communism in appreciation of the aid that he provided. He envisioned a Jewish State in the Middle East causing problems and giving the Soviets an entré to the Middle East.

In addition to the armament support, thirty-four hundred Jews and non-Jews from around the world volunteered for the Israeli army. They represented seven percent of the Israeli armed forces. About a thousand were from the United States; the volunteers from English speaking countries were especially helpful as the crews of the World War II military planes that the Israelis obtained and were not trained to fly.

The Second Truce Period—Ten days after the fighting resumed, the Arabs suffered severe military defeats by the Israelis who used their newly acquired arms and airplanes to good advantage. Britain pushed another cease-fire through the Security Council to prevent the impending collapse of the Arab forces that were becoming demoralized.

Count Bernadotte Assassinated—Count Bernadotte continued his mediation efforts after the second truce ended without peace. Count Bernadotte was in the process of proposing radical changes in the geographic areas allotted to Israel, including the loss of the Negev, when on September 17, his car was ambushed while driving through Jerusalem and he was killed. The extremist Stern Gang (or Lehi), which operated independently only in the Jerusalem area, was assumed to be responsible. Although many of the Stern Gang members were retained in prison until the war ended, the actual perpetrators of the assassination were never apprehended.

Victory Without Peace: July 20, 1949—The War of Independence ended in a victory for the Jewish people nine months after it began. After the Israeli forces managed to wrest control of the Negev away from the Egyptian forces and actually penetrated into the Egyptian Sinai, Egypt agreed to discuss a United Nations armistice arrangement in early January 1949. The United Nations new mediator, American Dr. Ralph Bunch brokered the talks on the island of Rhodes in the Mediterranean. It started as hostile discussions, with the Egyptian delegates refusing to talk directly with the Israeli delegation. It ended in harmonious, direct talk discussions and an agreement signed on February 24, 1949. Both sides anticipated that a permanent peace treaty in the near future would replace the armistice.

Other armistice agreements with the Arab adversaries followed quickly, except the one with Syria, which took three months to negotiate. The armistice with Syria was concluded on July 20, 1949, thirteen months after the war began. Iraq belligerently continued its state of war with Israel. Peace envisioned at the time to come within six months after the armistices were concluded did not happen—the Arab world would not accept the right of the State of Israel to exist. Peace with an Arab state had to wait until November 1977, when Egyptian President Anwar Sadat made history by being the first Arab country to recognize Israel and sign a peace accord.

The price of the Israeli victory was high. Six thousand of its youngest, most vibrant population were killed—a high percentage for this small country. The Israelis attributed their military victory to the valor of their soldiers and civilians who frequently fought and held off overwhelming forces.

The boundaries of the State of Israel established within the armistice agreements were essentially those occupied by the Israeli forces at the time of the armistice. The area of Israel expanded to almost twice the partition size, with the elimination of the narrow one mile corridor that connected the southern coastal area to the Negev. The coastal area remained approximately ten miles wide at places, representing a serious security hazard. There was now a corridor to Jerusalem, but the Jerusalem Old City, including the Wailing Wall, remained in the hands of Jordan.

The Refugee Aftermath Problem—Two large refugee problems emerged from this conflict. Approximately 800,000 Arabs fled the areas held by Israel. An equal number of Jewish refugees fled from several Arab countries after the war ended.

The Arab states to which the Palestinian refugees fled dealt with them as suited the needs of the host states rather than that of the refugees. Syria and Jordan, both in need of farmers, offered the refugees citizenship only if they would settle as farmers; the Arab refugees refused, since most were not farmers and many viewed acceptance of citizenship as giving up of their right to return home. The Palestinian West Bank was now part of Arab Jordan but the West Bank Palestinians were not given any autonomy by Jordan. However, a large segment of Palestinians with commercial capability did get absorbed into Jordan proper. Overpopulated Egypt did not want the Arab refugees under any conditions and kept them bottled up in the Gaza Strip. With an equal Muslim-Christian split in Lebanon's population, the ruling Lebanese Christians did not want to add a quarter of a million Palestinian Muslims that would tip the political balance in favor of the Muslims and kept the Palestinians in refugee camps. The other wealthy Arab states did little to aid the Palestinians and offered no refuge.

The Palestinian refugees were essentially confined to refugee camps in the Gaza Strip, the West Bank, and Lebanon, where they lived for many years in squalor, supported primarily by international relief aid. The Palestinian refugees had expected to return to the Israeli-held territory after the fighting ended with an Arab victory, taking back their homes and Israeli homes and property. They were disappointed as the war did not end as they anticipated. Israel did not permit their return. Since there was no peace with the Arab adversaries who remained belligerent towards Israel, the Palestinian refugees could not be expected to return as citizens loyal to the State of Israel. Although Jordan and Egypt essentially did nothing to aid the refugees economically, as the Israeli economy grew, upwards of 150,000 Palestinians from the Gaza Strip and the West Bank were employed in Israel.

Although it was a fledgling country struggling to get established, and with little financial resources, the State of Israel had a positive attitude towards the Jewish refugee problem. The Israeli people were anxious to take in the Holocaust survivors still languishing in the European Displaced Persons camps and other European Jews who wanted to escape from the postwar anti-Semitism of eastern Europe. Israel also became the refuge for the large number of Jews who were forced to flee from the Arab countries in the aftermath of the War of Independence. The State of Israel transported them to Israel and absorbed these refugees into Israeli society. These efforts were struggles for many reasons. Many Holocaust survivors were old or ill and could not make a livelihood for themselves. Jewish refugees from the Arab countries were backward socially and economically. The immigrants did not speak Hebrew. There was no housing available for the large influx of immigrants. In spite of these many challenges and obstacles, the Israeli refugee absorption effort was eminently successful.

As opposed to how the Arab world reacted to the Arab refugee problem, the world Jewish community had a positive attitude towards the Jewish refugee problem. Jews around the world supported this massive immigration effort. The American United Jewish Appeal started raising millions of dollars to support the Joint Distribution Committee's aid to the Holocaust survivors in the DP camps in 1946. After the State of Israel was established, the UJA solicited approximately $200 million annually to support Israel's refugee effort.

Revisionist History—During the month before the start of the War of Independence, the Arabs used revenge against the Deir Yassin atrocity to justify their atrocities against Jews and to encourage the Arab population to flee the areas that were to be the battleground. Fifty years later, the Palestinian nationalists and their American supporters are still using the Deir Yassin tragedy as their rallying cry. They cite exaggerated descriptions of the Deir Yassin incident such as the "Zionist militia massacre of thousands of Palestinian civilians at Deir Yassin and other villages" to support their claim that the Jews drove the Arabs out of Palestine and are therefore entitled to a full return to Israel. They disregard many historical facts to rewrite this description of events.

The Arab leadership encouragement of the Arab masses to voluntarily flee from Palestine is well-documented in the Arab press. The revisionists ignore the Arab radio broadcasts that boasted that the Jews were about to collapse and victory will come in a matter of days, allowing the departing Palestinians to return and take over Jewish property. These critics discount as propaganda Ben-Gurion's plea to the Palestinians not to leave because they had nothing to fear from living in a Jewish state, ignoring the actual fate of the Israeli Arabs who remained behind during the War of Independence.

Ben-Gurion, the Yishuv leader and spokesman, had appealed to the Palestinian Arabs to preserve the peace and join in the building of the new state based on full and equal citizenship. He extended his hand to all the neighboring countries to share in the advancement of the entire Middle East; promising Israel would do its share in the common effort. Turmoil in Arab-Jewish relations has persisted over the past fifty years because of the Muslim world's refusal to make peace with Israel. Despite this hostility, the Palestinian Arabs who remained in Israel during the War of Independence were safe. The quality of life of those who now live in the State of Israel approaches that of the Jews. The Arabs enjoy every civil right and have the same status under the Israeli law as the Jewish citizens.

Present-day critics of Israel also fail to take into account the impact of the continuing Arab world's animosity towards Israel when citing Israel's shortcomings with respect to the Palestinian Arab community. Their unwillingness to accept the existence of the State of Israel has strengthened Israel's concern for its security, affecting the implementation of the peace process. Their almost unified stance against developing commercial relations with Israel has inhibited any Israeli effort to improve the economic conditions throughout the entire Middle East.

8
Highlights of the First Fifty Years

1948: War of Independence—Six Arab neighbors attacked Israel after it declared independence. Israel overcame the larger, better-equipped Arab armies. The fighting essentially ended at the close of the year, but the armistice agreements weren't signed until the following year. The State of Israel ended up with almost twice the territory originally allocated to Israel by the United Nations. The Jewish section of the Old Jerusalem City, including the Wailing Wall, remained outside of the State of Israel and inaccessible to Jews. (The War of Independence is discussed in the previous section.)

1948: Refuge Opens to Holocaust Survivors—The first act of the new State of Israel was to cancel the 1939 British White Paper, which restricted Jewish immigration. The Holocaust survivors started pouring in from the DP camps in Europe and from Cyprus, where the British had detained those caught attempting to enter Palestine illegally.

1949: Israel Becomes a Nation—The first Jewish parliament in two thousand years was convened in March with the 120-member Knesset that was selected by a general election—fifty-two years after Herzl held the first World Zionist Congress. David Ben-Gurion was elected as the first prime minister by a coalition of four political parties, a pattern of coalition governments that existed for most of Israel's existence. The two largest parties were the labor and socialist parties. The General Zionist party that favored the free enterprise system had little influence at the beginning; its strength increased with the newcomers. Arabs voted freely in the Knesset elections, winning three seats; Arab women voting was a first for the Arab world.

The Knesset elected Chaim Weizmann to the mostly ceremonial position of president of the State of Israel, honoring him for his contributions to Zionism and the creation of the State of Israel.

1949: Armistice with Arab Adversaries—The four major adversaries, Egypt, Jordan, Lebanon, and Syria individually signed armistice agreements with Israel. The first was signed with Egypt on February 24; the last was signed with Syria on July 20. Iraq continued its state of war with Israel. The Arab nations refused to sign peace treaties with Israel or recognize it as nation. Subsequent attempts in later years by Foreign Minister Moshe Sharett to arrange for peace terms with Egypt and Jordan failed.

1949: Herzl Is Buried in Israel—Before he died in 1904, Theodor Herzl, the founder of the World Zionist movement that provided the major stimulus for the creation of a Jewish state expressed his wish that he be buried in Palestine when the Jewish people could arrange it. In 1949, his remains were transferred from the Vienna, Austria, cemetery to Mount Herzl outside of Jerusalem where there is now a Herzl Museum.

1950: Operation Magic Carpet—In a round-the-clock airlift campaign, 47,000 Yemenite Jews and 3,000 Jews from Aden, many of whom never saw an airplane before, were flown to Israel to escape their repression that was the aftermath of the Arab defeat in Palestine. The major challenge for the Yemenite immigrants was their integration into the modern world that Israel represented. They had to transform from living in a primitive, backward society without modern amenities to the lifestyle and the different family culture of Western society. The absorption of the Yemenite Jews represented a major financial and administrative burden to the young State of Israel. Housing had to be provided and Hebrew taught to the mostly illiterate Yemenites. The Yemenites needed aid in applying their old-world craftsman skills to making a livelihood in the modern Israeli commercial environment.

1950: The Law of Return—The Knesset passed the Law of Return, which gave Jews from anywhere in the world the right to settle in Israel and which granted Jews automatic citizenship. Prime Minister Ben-Gurion declared that this was a fundamental reason for establishing the State of Israel—Jews would have a haven in times of trouble. In the first three years of its existence, Jews from fifty-two countries immigrated to Israel. The majority of the Holocaust survivors remaining in Europe came. Several hundred thousand came to escape the new intolerance towards Jews in the Muslim world after the War of Independence ended. Many fled from the hostility that reemerged in eastern Europe.

1951: King Abdullah Assassinated—King Abdullah of Jordan had been considering breaking with the Arab anti-Israel coalition and coming to peace with Israel; he secretly initialed an agreement to this effect. Angered by this prospect, the mufti of Jerusalem, who was a violently hostile foe of Israel, arranged for Abdullah's assassination outside the El Aqsa Mosque on the Temple Mount in Jerusalem. Abdullah's grandson Hussein became king of Jordan the following year. The anti-Israel Pan-Arabists dissuaded Hussein from following his grandfather's interest in coming to peace with Israel.

1952: German Reparations—The Knesset overcame the pain and bitterness towards Germany that the Israelis and Jews around the world had because of the Holocaust and accepted the Reparations Agreement offered by German Prime Minister Konrad Adenhauer. Dealing with Germany under any circumstances was a very emotional issue because almost every Jewish family suffered a loss in the Holocaust. Adenhauer considered the payment, $300 per month to be a measure of atonement. This pension was paid to other survivors living in Western countries. Later, in 1998, under pressure from the American Jewish Committee and other Jewish organizations, Germany agreed to pay $150 per month to Holocaust survivors living in former Soviet-bloc countries.

1956: Sinai War—There were several events in the few years before 1956 that contributed to the Sinai War developing. Gamal Abd al Nasser came to power in Egypt after King Farouk was overthrown and courted the Soviet Union. Egypt obtained a massive amount of modern weapons from Czechoslovakia, which emboldened Nasser to make threats against Israel. Nasser violated the 1949 armistice agreement and international law by blocking Israeli shipping in the Straits of Tiran. Encouraged by Nasser's pan-Arabism and his anti-Israel activism, *Fedayeen* (Arabic for commandos or suicide squads) made organized incursions into Israel from Jordan. Nasser's nationalization of the Suez Canal and the closure of the canal to Israeli shipping in July 1956 brought the situation to a climax. The canal takeover induced Britain and France to conspire to take military action against Nasser to protect their oil shipping interests. They initiated a secret arrangement with Israel to support any action that Israel would take against Egypt.

With Nasser's military threats increasing and Fedayeen raids now coming from the Gaza Strip causing mounting casualties and losing the economic war through the blockades, Israel decided to take preemptive action to end these three problem areas. It initiated the war with a parachute incursion into the Sinai on October 29. By the sixth of November, the Israeli army, through a series of daring military actions and severe large tank battles, succeeded in conquering the entire Sinai, freeing up the Straits of Tiran. The British and French governments succumbed to international pressure and canceled their planned military actions shortly after they invaded the Suez Canal Zone. Israel won ten years of relative peace with passage through the Straits of Tiran guaranteed by United Nations forces.

1960: Adolf Eichmann Captured—Adolf Eichmann, the German SS officer who organized and supervised Hitler's Final Solution that resulted in the murder of six million Jews, was found living in disguise in Buenos Aires, Argentina. Israeli agents captured Eichmann and smuggled him out of the country. After a lengthy trial in Jerusalem that had the world's attention, he was convicted and hanged in 1962. The Israeli law that prohibited the death penalty was waived because of the enormity of his crime against the Jewish people.

The trial was important to the Jewish people in Israel in particular. It demonstrated the country's capability to win a fair legal battle against an enemy of the Jewish people. The trial had a broader accomplishment. The many Holocaust survivors and German witnesses against Eichmann exposed the horror of the Nazi actions. Their testimony also exposed the Christian community's silence and indifference to the Nazi cruel treatment of the Jews during the Holocaust period.

1967: The Six Day War—There was relative peace between Israel and its Arab neighbors for the first five years after the Sinai War. As the leadership of Syria changed, Syria, Jordan, and Egypt started minor hostile actions towards Israel. The Arab countries held a summit meeting in 1964 at which they planned further hostile actions and created the Palestine Liberation Organization. The PLO was formalized in the following year with the Palestine Covenant that calls for the destruction of the State of Israel.

In May of 1967, the Israeli government was predicting a long period of peace ahead. Egyptian President Nasser had other, militant plans. He mobilized a large army equipped with modern Soviet weapons at Israel's southern border. Nasser told the Arab world that he intended to destroy Israel. Troops, tanks, and airplanes from other Arab countries joined his ring around Israel. France, who until then was the one ally of Israel, became hostile towards Israel as part of de Gaulle's effort to gain favor in the Arab world. The climax came later in May. The United Nations succumbed to Nasser's demand that the UN remove the Emergency Force that was supposed to guarantee the peace along Israel's southern borders. Then Nasser closed the Straits of Tiran to Israeli shipping. Nasser was convinced these provocative actions would draw Israel into a war, which he was confident the Arabs would win because of the superiority of the Arab forces. The Israeli's had concluded that a preemptive attack was necessary.

On the morning of June 5, Israel's air force launched a surprise attack on the Egyptian air force, catching and destroying most of Egypt's three hundred military planes on the ground in a three-hour period. Misled by Egypt's erroneous claims of victory against Israel, Iraqi, and Syrian planes started to bomb cities in Israel. Having eliminated the Egyptian air force, the Israeli air force turned to repulsing the Arab aircraft. By the end of the day, almost all of the Jordanian, Iraqi, and Syrian planes were destroyed. Fifty-eight Arab planes were destroyed in aerial dogfights. The Israeli air force lost twenty-six aircraft.

The Israeli tank forces launched a three-pronged attack against the Egyptian forces in the Sinai that consisted of thousands of tanks in well-fortified positions. In a series of well-planned, strategic attacks that involved massive tank battles and supported by the air force that had control of the skies, the Israeli army devastated the Egyptian army and reached the Suez Canal on the fifth day. The Egyptian forces in the Gaza Strip were overwhelmed by the third day of fighting. Egypt lost over 10,000 soldiers, with another 5,000 captured, and had 800 tanks and thousands of other vehicles destroyed or captured. Israel lost 300 soldiers in the Sinai campaign.

Jordan was advised on June 5 that if they kept out of the war, Israel would not initiate a fight with Jordan. King Hussein had been under pressure by the Arab world to join the Arab attack on Israel that the Arab neighbors of Israel were planning just before the Israeli attack on Egypt. Hussein was suspicious of Nasser because of his attempt in 1960 to topple the Jordanian kingdom through assassinations and his sponsoring of a Syrian invasion of Jordan, which the Israelis thwarted with a show of force against Syria. Nevertheless, because of the political pressure, King Hussein was taken in by Egypt's false military victory claims and reluctantly entered the war with an attack against Israeli forces near Jerusalem. After some initial fierce fighting, the Israeli forces overcame the well-armed Jordanian forces near Jerusalem and occupied the entire West Bank by the end of the third day of fighting. Because the Israeli air force refrained from joining the fighting in the Jerusalem area, the battle for Jerusalem involved brutal house-to-house fighting that ended when the Israelis surrounded the Jordanian forces. The Old City was taken, putting Jews in control of their holy shrine, the Temple Western Wall, for the first time in almost two thousand years.

Before the war, Syria had been provoking Israel with its shelling of Israeli settlements from the Golan Heights. However, when the war started, Syria was reluctant to attack Israel because Syria felt its forces were inferior to the Israelis. After the battle against the Jordanians was essentially over, the Israeli forces initiated an aggressive attack. It was marked by a remarkable assault of the heavily-defended steep approach to the Golan Heights, using bulldozers and tanks under withering fire, and with a high rate of Israeli casualties and loss of equipment. This successful action was followed by heavy air attacks and paratrooper actions that succeeded in conquering the Golan Heights on the second day of fighting before a UN cease-fire went into effect.

The Six Day War left the West Bank in the hands of Israel, significantly lessening the threat to Israel by effectively increasing the narrow neck of Israel from ten to forty miles. The threat from the Egyptians was lessened with the Israeli occupation of the Sinai and the Gaza Strip—the Sinai desert and the Suez Canal became important buffers. The occupation of the Golan Heights eliminated the shelling of the Israeli border settlements. Israel assumed control of East Jerusalem, including the Old City, and declared Jerusalem a unified city.

Unfortunately, the war ended without a formal peace between Israel and their Arab adversaries. King Hussein of Jordan, who lost the West Bank and East Jerusalem, and suffered the most economically from the results of the war, indicated a desire to negotiate peace with Israel—it was not to happen until 1994. Spearheaded by Egyptian President Nasser, the Arab world, encouraged by the Soviet Union who offered to rearm the defeated Arab armies, refused to negotiate peace with Israel. Thanks to the United States and many other countries whose sympathies were with Israel, the United Nations turned back an Arab-Soviet Union attempt to roll back the borders to the pre-war boundaries. President Lyndon Johnson expressed the view that restoring the conditions that prevailed before the war was a prescription for the renewal of hostilities. Arthur Goldberg, the United States UN ambassador, laid down the United States position, accepted later by the United Nations. "Israel should not be forced to return to the old boundaries, nor should the cease-fire lines be the final boundaries. They are to be determined in the context of a negotiated settlement that provides security to Israel and recognized boundaries." This remains the United States' policy today.

After determining that the Arab countries were determined not to seek peace with Israel, the following year Prime Minister Levi Eshkol announced plans to establish Jewish settlements in the West Bank and Golan Heights, and a tourist facility at Sharm el-Sheik, at the southern end of the Sinai Peninsula.

The astonishing victory against overwhelming odds had a profound effect on Jews throughout the world. Jews who previously were ambivalent about being Jewish became proud of their Jewish heritage. The non-Jewish world was also affected by this remarkable Israeli victory; they admired the State of Israel and showed a new respect for Jews everywhere.

1967–1970: War of Attrition—Egyptian President Nasser initiated a war of attrition against Israel shortly after the Six Day War ended. The objective was to wear down Israel by slowly killing Israeli soldiers and civilians and by forcing Israel to spend scarce financial resources on military defense. It involved periodic air attacks and dogfights, military incursions into Israeli-held territory, and actions against Israeli shipping in the Gulf of Aqaba. Jordan and the PLO joined this "quiet war" by making terrorist attacks in Israel. The war intensified in 1969 when the Egyptians started using new Soviet SAM-2 guided missiles and Sam-3 missiles, which were effective against low flying aircraft. In 1970, after the Israeli air force adjusted to the new fighting techniques, Israel got the upper hand in the battles, convincing Nasser to accept U.S. Secretary of State William Rogers's three-month cease-fire plan.

Nasser used the cease-fire period to surreptitiously move the newly acquired Soviet anti-aircraft missiles close to the Egyptian side of the canal, intending them to support an attack on the Israeli forces by crossing the Canal. He was quietly preparing his army for this attack. However, when President Nasser died suddenly of a heart attack in September 1970, Egyptian plans to attack Israel were put on hold for three years.

1969: Golda Meir Becomes Prime Minister—Golda Meir was selected as the fourth prime minister of Israel, replacing Levi Eshkol, who died of a heart attack. She became the first woman to head a nation in the modern era. This former American schoolteacher, an elderly grandmother, came out of retirement to keep the Labor Party government together. She later won a full term as prime minister, serving during the Yom Kippur war.

Meir, formerly Meyerson, came to Israel as part of the third Aliyah. She was active in the Israeli labor movement and was a signatory of the Declaration of the State of Israel in 1948. Golda Meir met secretly with Jordanian King Abdullah in an attempt to persuade him to accept the new State of Israel. She was an effective fundraiser in the United States. Golda Meir's theme was solidarity of Israel with the Soviet Jews who were struggling for the right to emigrate to Israel. She was instrumental in convincing

President Nixon to grant U.S. aid in the form of military and economic assistance.

1972: Israeli Athletes Killed by Palestinian Terrorists at the Olympics—During the Olympic Games in Munich, Germany, the world watched in horror as nine Israeli athletes were held hostage by Arab terrorists. Two Israeli coaches had been killed by the terrorists as they tried to warn the other athletes. The Arabs demanded the release of two hundred Arab commandos imprisoned in Israel, which the Israelis refused to consider. Because the German authorities assumed that the hostages would be killed once the plane, made available by the Germans for the terrorist escape, arrived at the Cairo destination, German sharpshooters stormed the plane at the airport. The four Arab terrorists killed the nine Israeli hostages before the Germans killed them.

International Olympic Committee President Brundage, showing insensitivity to the Israelis, initially refused to suspend the Olympic games. (He showed a similar insensitivity to American Jews during the 1936 Olympic Games in Berlin regarding Hitler's prohibition against Jewish participation in the games.) Under world pressure, Brundage suspended the games until after a memorial service attended by 80,000 was held for the slain athletes. Fourteen other Israeli athletes who escaped becoming hostages left for home after the service.

1973: The Yom Kippur War—The Israeli military strategists felt secure that the Bar Lev system of trench fortifications along the Suez Canal, which was completed in 1969, would adequately defend against any Egyptian attack. The absence of any Egyptian attacks after Nasser died lulled the Israeli's into complacency. In the early 1970s, the Bar Lev line resources were actually weakened to save money, and the Israeli army's sharp military discipline started to deteriorate among the troops defending the Bar Lev fortifications.

Anwar el Sadat took over as Egyptian president and resumed Nasser's plan to attack Israel. He expelled the Soviet advisors to give him more freedom of action. The Israeli leaders misinterpreted this move to mean Sadat had no aggressive intent against Israel. Sadat had actually secretly strengthened his alliance with the Soviets who agreed to supply Egypt and Syria with their most advanced missile systems, aircraft, and tanks. The Egyptian army laid careful plans for the attack, spending several years practicing how to effectively cross the Suez Canal. Israeli intelligence viewed all the Egyptian military preparations, but incorrectly concluded they were bluffs.

In August, Israeli Defense Minister General Dayan, expressed the opinion that war was not imminent because the Egyptians were not adequately prepared for the war they were planning. The intelligence organizations of other countries including the United States shared this view. Early in October, the Israelis observed a massive troop buildup near the Suez Canal, and the Soviet Union started to pull out its personnel and ships from the area. The indications that war was imminent still did not arouse the Israeli high command to hurry up preparations to defend against an Egyptian attack. On the morning of October 6, Yom Kippur Day, Sadat shocked the Israelis by the Egyptian attack on Israeli forces. That day was selected for two reasons. Sadat reasoned that the Israeli army would be at its weakest when many of the troops were home for the religious holiday. Although this was true, the holiday made it easier to call up the large Israeli reserve forces, which were mostly in the synagogues that morning. It was also the day when the Suez Canal was expected to have high tide, helpful for the military crossing.

Sadat employed the same strategy that the Israelis used successfully in the Six Day War. Strike first, hit the enemy with large forces, take out the enemy's air support, and plan the military action thoroughly. **Sadat was notably successful; his attack almost resulted in the destruction of the State of Israel.**

Two hundred and fifty Egyptian planes struck the Israel airfields in the Sinai, taking out the Israeli antiaircraft defenses and giving Egypt control of the sky in the area. Thousands of Egyptian forces quickly crossed the canal, suffering surprisingly few casualties; the Egyptian military planners expected thousands of casualties. The new Egyptian antiaircraft missile defenses deployed in the canal area protected the Egyptian army from the Israeli air force. In three days, the army, supported by thousands of tanks, effective antitank weapons, and massive artillery power, overwhelmed the small Israeli forces. Almost all of the 250 Israeli tanks defending the Sinai were destroyed. Few of the five hundred Israeli forces along the canal survived. The Egyptian forces reached their planned objective, which was to conquer the central Sinai Peninsula. Had the Egyptians continued their attack, they could have easily gone further and probably penetrated into Israeli territory—the Israeli forces were so thoroughly weakened.

The Israel reserves were brought into the battle over the next ten days and counterattacked. The Israeli forces were successful in the massive tank battles that took place in the central Sinai, involving a thousand tanks on each side. The desert was littered with destroyed Egyptian vehicles and equipment. By that time, the Israeli air force had become a vital element, contributing to the defeat of the Egyptians. They had learned how to counter the Egyptian air-to-air missiles, and the battles were out of range of the Egyptian ground-to-air missile defense system that was deployed on the east side of the Suez Canal. Earlier, the Israeli air force had lost one hundred planes to Egyptian antiaircraft missiles.

The Israeli strategy for defeating the Egyptians, promoted and led by General Ariel Sharon, was to cross to the eastern side of the Suez Canal. (Most Israelis credit Sharon for turning the tide with the crossing and for the victory over Egypt. His superiors and some other generals accused him of not following direction and taking reckless actions.) This was initially accomplished on October 18 in daring crossings of the canal over portable bridges through a heavily defended area. By October 20, the crossing was expanded, cutting off the thousands of the Egyptian troops on the east side of the canal. By October 24, the Egyptian Third Army Corps had been decimated in a failed counterattack against the Israeli forces and was isolated from Egypt without food and military supplies. This desperate situation forced Sadat to accept a cease-fire sponsored by the U.S. Secretary of State Henry Kissinger. Israel was encouraged to accept the cease-fire by the Soviet Union threat to enter the war on the side of the Egyptians if the fighting continued.

Hafez el Assad, the new president of Syria was Sadat's partner in the planned Yom Kippur attack. In the first three days of the war, the Syrian forces decimated the small Israeli forces on the Golan Heights. These troops, which received little support from the main Israeli army and air force that was concentrating on stemming the Egyptian steamroller in the Sinai, heroically fought desperate battles, with heavy casualties, to slow the Syrian advance. On October 11, the Israeli army launched a counterattack that was sufficient to prevent the imminent Syrian advance into Israel proper. Over the next ten days, the Israeli reinforcements that were diverted from the Sinai won massive tank battles with the Syrians, resulting in the Syrians accepting a United Nations sponsored cease-fire on October 22. The Syrians lost 3,500 troops, 1,200 tanks, and 200 aircraft, two-thirds in aerial combat. The Israelis lost 800 troops and 250 tanks fighting the Syrians.

Israel suffered devastating losses to its military equipment and ammunition during the initial Arab surprise attack and more as the war progressed. They were practically out of munitions. Following a strategy devised by Secretary of State Kissinger, President Nixon authorized an emergency airlift of ammunition, tanks, and fighter planes to Israel, enabling Israel to recover militarily and take the offensive. The U.S. aim was two-fold, to help their ally Israel, and to give the Soviets the message that their resupply of the Egyptians would not go unanswered—this strategy succeeded in keeping the Soviets from entering the war in support of the Egyptians.

Israel did not win any peace immediately with the war's end, but it did lead to Egypt's peace with Israel in 1979. Ironically, Sadat did not look at this war as a defeat for Egypt, but saw it as a victory for Egyptian honor because this time Egyptian forces did fight well—therefore he had no further need to battle Israel militarily. The United States offer to annually provide a billion or more dollars in commercial and humanitarian aid to Egypt helped turn Sadat from military adventurism to bolstering the weak Egyptian economy. (That year, Egypt received 2.6 billion in economic aid. Israel received 2.6 billion of economic and military aid in the form of credits and grants.) It also persuaded Sadat to drop any ties to the Soviet Union—the major U.S. foreign policy objective of getting the Soviet Union out of the Suez Canal area was accomplished.

As opposed to the euphoria during the Six Day War, the world Jewish community was shocked and horrified when it learned during Yom Kippur synagogue services of the defeats suffered by the Israeli army on the first day of the war. It brought on togetherness; all factions of U.S. Jews united in rallies urging the American government to provide the aid needed for Israel's survival. Their slogan was *Am Yisrael Chai* **(The Nation of Israel Shall Live.)** They were driven by the Biblical expression *I Am My Brother's Keeper,* which throughout the ages has provided solidarity among the Jewish people in troubled times.

1974: Golda Meir Resigns—Under attack for not recognizing the Egyptian military buildup and planning of the Yom Kippur War, and for her slowness to react once the war started, Prime Minister Golda Meir had difficulty holding her coalition government together and resigned. The Labor party that barely controlled the Knesset nominated Yitzhak Rabin as the new prime minister. Rabin first achieved fame as the Palmach commander in the battle for Jerusalem during the War of Independence. He rose in the ranks to become the chief of staff during the Six Day War, leading Israel to victory.

General Dayan, the defense minister during the Yom Kippur War, was accused of gross negligence and responsibility for the many Israeli deaths during the first days of the Yom Kippur War. He was accused of failing to recognize and react to the obvious Egyptian military preparations for an imminent attack across the Suez Canal. In 1975, he was acquitted of these charges by a high-level investigative commission led by the president of the Israeli Supreme Court.

1976: Raid On Entebbe—Palestinian and German terrorists hijacked a French passenger plane that left Israel for Paris with a stopover in Athens. The hijackers wanted the release of Arab prisoners in Israel in exchange for the release of the ninety-eight Israelis held hostage and taken to the airport in Entebbe, Uganda. The Israeli government decided against negotiating with the terrorists and Prime Minister Yitzhak Rabin approved a rescue plan. With the cooperation of the Kenyan government, which gave the Israeli rescue planes landing rights in the event of an emergency (and actually allowed an unplanned refueling stop on the way home), the rescue of the hostages was accomplished.

Taking advantage of Ugandan Dictator Idi Amin being out of the country, four Israeli planes, including a large Hercules rescue plane loaded with crack commandos and military vehicles and one with field hospital equipment, landed in the dark at Entebbe. In an operation led by Brigadier-General Dan Shomron, the commandos quietly stormed the airport terminal and killed the thirteen terrorists. After fighting off several hundred Ugandan soldiers, they quickly rescued all the passengers (with only one casualty) and left with the hostages aboard the rescue plane. The only Israeli casualty was the commando leader, Lieutenant Colonel "Joni" Netanyahu (the Israeli prime minister's older brother).

The success of this daring raid, which took painstaking preparation, won the admiration and appreciation of the Israeli public and became a source of pride for all Jews. The world-at-large respected Israel for its refusal to succumb to terrorism and for the daring plan and effectiveness of the rescue mission, which became a standard for judging future rescue missions and for not negotiating with terrorists.

There was an unsuccessful attempt at the United Nations by the anti-Zionist countries to condemn Israel for the raid. The Israeli ambassador urged the countries of the world to use this event to unite in a war on international terrorism.

1977: Likud Comes to Power—In May 1977, after almost thirty years of the Labor party's domination over the Knesset, in a stunning election defeat, the Likud party, with the support of the Oriental Jews (Sephardic Jews from the Arab lands), came to power in the Knesset. The

Likud selected Menachem Begin as prime minister. Begin, who was a leader of the Irgun underground terrorist organization during the British Mandate period, had been an opposition leader in the Knesset for many years. The Likud party advocated less of a socialistic, labor-driven economy and took a hard line at any concessions to the Palestinians in any future discussions regarding peace terms.

Begin indicated that he was more interested in retaining Judea and Samaria than the Sinai Peninsula that was always part of Egypt. Begin surprised everyone when he chose as his foreign minister the ex-General Moshe Dayan, who had been a leading Labor party official. It was part of Begin's strategy to trade the Sinai for peace with Egypt and to retain the West Bank. He initiated an aggressive settlement plan for the West Bank and curtailed the funding of facilities and services for West Bank Palestinians.

1977: Sadat Visits Jerusalem—Anwar Sadat had concluded that a major change in Egyptian foreign relationships was vital for Egypt to improve its desperate economic situation. He took the bold step of indicating his willingness to discuss peace with Israel—a move intended to bring Egypt closer to receiving American aid. Despite his party's hostile attitude towards the Arab world, Prime Minister Begin extended an olive branch to Sadat, inviting him to visit Jerusalem and speak to the Knesset. In November 1997, Sadat responded with a dramatic visit to Jerusalem; thousands of Israelis lined the streets to greet the first Arab leader to visit Israel since its founding. Sadat addressed the Knesset with the hope for peace between Egypt and Israel. Begin praised Sadat for his courage in making the trip for peace, which was opposed by all the other Arab rulers and leaders. Begin and Sadat reached an important agreement that set the stage for future peace discussions. **War was to be rejected as a way of settling their disputes, and Egyptian sovereignty was to be restored over the Sinai.**

1978: Camp David Agreement: Peace Treaty in 1979—There were several follow-up meetings to Sadat's dramatic visit to Jerusalem in 1977. Many issues divided the two parties in the discussions. Compromise could not be reached on the extent of Palestinian autonomy, the treatment of Jewish settlements in the West Bank, the status of Jerusalem, and how much of the Sinai to turn over to Egypt. The acrimony between Begin and Sadat was so great at times, it appeared that reaching any agreement was hopeless.

President Jimmy Carter had been intensely involved in the peace process. As a friend of the Jewish people, he was anxious to see Israel achieve peace with its Arab neighbor. When the peace process appeared to falter, Carter invited Begin and Sadat to join him at the Camp David presidential retreat in Maryland in September 1978. After days of continued frustration due primarily to the inflexibility of Begin and Sadat, Foreign Secretary Moshe Dayan promoted a new approach. The negotiations would concentrate on what was most important to Sadat—the restoration of Sinai sovereignty to Egypt. It worked to transform Sadat and Begin into compromisers. Begin gave into Sadat's demands regarding the Sinai. Sadat was willing to postpone making hard decisions regarding the Palestinian issues that troubled Begin. An agreement on these issues was reached, with a pledge to finalize a peace accord within three months. The spectacle of Begin and Sadat, two previous enemies, embracing during the Camp David Agreement signing ceremony on the White House lawn was witnessed on national television.

The issues that arose during the peace discussions that followed Camp David were too intense; the agreement appeared to unravel. Sadat had come under severe pressure from the other Arab rulers to reopen the Palestinian issues. Anxious to see the Israeli-Egyptian peace process succeed, President Carter visited the Middle East in March of 1979 to promote new ideas. With the enticement of billions of dollars in military and economic grants to Egypt and Israel, and Carter applying some pressure on Begin, Sadat and Begin reached many detailed agreements involving Egyptian-Israeli relationships as a prelude to the actual peace treaty. Vague approaches to settling the Palestinian issues were defined in separate letters of agreement.

The first peace treaty between the State of Israel and an Arab state was signed at the White House on March 26, 1979, thirty years after the end of the War of Independence.

Begin and Sadat shared the 1978 Nobel Peace Prize for their unlikely roles—two former militant adversaries agreeing to peace terms.

1981: Israeli Air Force Destroys Iraqi Atomic Reactor—Israeli intelligence learned that the Iraqis, under the outspoken, strongly anti-Israel dictator, Saddam Hussein, had made progress building an atomic reactor that would give Iraq an atomic bomb capability; he already had the Soviet planes capable of delivering atomic bombs. Israel took a defiant step to forestall this capability which represented an enormous threat to its security. In a carefully planned and perfectly executed attack, a dozen fighter planes with in-flight refueling capability flew 1,000 miles to completely destroy the Osiraq reactor located outside of Baghdad in a pinpoint bombing attack.

The attack was considered a legitimate act of self-defense in Israel—the Israelis admired Prime Minister Begin for this courageous act. At the time, many in the world community, including the United States, condemned this attack through a UN Security Council resolution. After the 1991 Gulf War exposed Hussein's development of unconventional weapons that were outlawed by the world community, many extended a belated debt of gratitude to Israel for having eliminated Saddam's potential nuclear weapon capability.

1981: President Sadat Assassinated—President Sadat had been under attack in Egypt from many quarters for his Camp David Accord with Israel. In October, while watching a military parade to commemorate the 1973 Egyptian army crossing of the Suez Canal at the start of the Yom Kippur War, Sadat was assassinated by an army lieutenant who belonged to a fundamentalist group opposed to any dealings with Israel. Menachem Begin attended the funeral to pay respect to **"his friend and partner in peace."**

Vice President Hosni Mubarak was sitting next to Sadat when the grenade exploded that killed Sadat. Miraculously, he was not injured. Mubarak pledged "not to budge an inch" from Sadat's commitment to peace. This reassurance encouraged Israel to continue its Sinai withdrawal schedule. Mubarak has continued as Egyptian president until today. He has contributed to Arab-Israeli peace developments, particularly asserting a positive influence over Palestinian Authority Chairman Yasser Arafat.

1982: The War In Lebanon—The 1982 period when fighting took place in Lebanon between the Israelis and the Palestinians and Syrians was the most divisive for the Jewish people inside Israel and worldwide. One side maintained that the Israeli military action was necessary to bring "Peace to the Galilee." The other side viewed the intensity of the Israeli attacks and the deaths they caused to be in violation of the Jewish moral standard. The Israeli army indifference to the Lebanese Christian slaughter of Palestinians in the two Beirut refugee camps was another contentious event that disturbed many Jews.

In the summer of 1981, PLO units under Yasser Arafat's command fired Soviet long-range 130-mm guns and Katyusha rockets into the northern Galilee, disrupting life in the villages and kibbutzim. In the preceding ten years, Arafat had organized the PLO into a capable army, equipped with massive amounts of modern weapons—many hidden in civilian buildings in an attempt to use civilians as a shield against Israeli air attacks. Prime Minister Begin and Defense Minister Ariel Sharon developed a military plan to eliminate the PLO from Lebanon and thus put an end to the Galilee population disruption due to PLO shelling. The plan involved arming and supporting the Lebanese Christian Phalangists, with the goal of establishing them as the rulers of Lebanon, free of Syrian domination. A Lebanese peace treaty with Israel was expected.

Triggered by a plot by Arab assassins against Israeli diplomats that was uncovered in London, Israel launched a well-prepared attack against the PLO in all parts of Lebanon, with the initial objective of clearing a twenty-five–mile zone at the border. The objective expanded to eliminating the PLO from Lebanon and capturing the western zone of Beirut occupied by the Palestinians and Lebanese Muslims in the process.

Compared to the previous Arab-Israeli wars, Israel had the military advantage in this war. The Syrians, with whom the Israelis had a mutual hands-off agreement stemming from the terms of the Yom Kippur War settlement, entered the war for a short period. After the Israelis shot down twenty-nine Syrian planes with no Israeli losses in a 100-plane dogfight, the Israelis had control of the sky over Lebanon. In a remarkable display of Israeli military design capability, newly designed Israeli tanks outfought the best, newest-design Soviet tanks in a large tank battle. These Israeli victories took Syria out of the fray.

The PLO in Beirut refused to give up. Sharon ordered a two-month bombardment of western Beirut, causing much destruction and killing many. After the Maronite Christian president-elect Bashir Gemayel was assassinated by pro-Syrian dissidents, the Israeli forces under General Eytan allowed the Christian Phalangists to enter the Sabra and Shatilla camps outside of Beirut, slaughtering 2,300 Palestinian men, women, and children over a three-day period. With his forces decimated, Arafat finally agreed to move his PLO to Tunisia in North Africa—most Arab countries were not anxious to receive the Palestinians.

Prime Minister Begin thought that he had eliminated Yasser Arafat, the PLO Palestinian authority chairman, as a player in the Arab-Israeli conflicts. He was mistaken. Arafat became rehabilitated and went on to be the negotiator of the Oslo Peace Accord in 1993 and the Wye River Agreement in 1998. Neither did Begin achieve his objective of peace with Lebanon. After the Israelis freed the new Lebanese President Amir Gemayel of the Syrian yoke and the PLO threat, Gemayel turned against Israel as his political partner, courting favor with the Arab world. Begin's goal of eliminating a Syrian presence in Lebanon was also not met. After the fighting with the Palestinians subsided, Syrian President Assad broke the weak accord reached with Israel that ended Syrian participation in the fighting and restored a Syrian presence in Lebanon, which Begin could not oppose for political reasons.

The war had polarized the Israeli people. Many Israeli soldiers, including seasoned officers, protested the brutal actions against the Palestinians, some refusing to fight. Peace movements and protests against Begin's government intensified in Israel. The Israeli president set up a commission headed by the president of the supreme court to investigate whether Begin, Sharon, Eytan, and other military officers had any complicity in the Sabra and Shatilla atrocities. Begin was acquitted of any involvement, but the generals were admonished for disregarding the atrocities as they were taking place. They were either demoted or removed from the army. The public criticism by so many Israelis who objected to the war that blemished the Jewish reputation and the continued military presence in Lebanon that resulted in the deaths of many young Israeli soldiers weighed heavily on Begin. Depressed by this atmosphere and the death of his wife, he resigned in July 1983 and became a political recluse until he died in 1992.

The country was so divided that in 1984 and for the next six years, it could only be ruled by a coalition government that included both the Likud and Labor parties. They alternated filling the prime minister position.

1984: Operation Moses—Discovered in the late nineteenth century, the black Jews of Ethiopia, known as the Falasha, are thought to have Jewish heritage going back to biblical times. With the Falasha having little knowledge of Judaism, efforts were made to reintroduce them to the Jewish world. The Falasha were living a perilous existence in Ethiopia after King Haile Selassie was overthrown in 1974 and the country suffered a long-term famine. The Jewish world community recognized that the Falasha were being discriminated for their ties to Judaism and collaborated to extricate them to Israel. Israeli agents took the initial action in 1981.They surreptitiously moved several thousand Falasha to the neighboring Sudan and then evacuated them by boat to Israel over a several-month period. The Muslim leader of the Sudan ended this arrangement when he became afraid of antagonizing the Muslim world by his aid to Jews. The rescue operation was resumed in November 1984 under the Israeli Mossad's "Operation Moses," which received U.S. political and financial support. Eight thousand Falasha were trucked from a refugee camp in the Sudan to the Khartoum airport, from where they were secretly flown to Israel over a several month period. This operation was terminated when the Arab world discovered the operation and protested to Sudan's President Numeiri.

1986: Sharansky Arrives in Israel—The most famous and honored refusenik, Natan Sharansky, was stripped of his citizenship and expelled from the Soviet Union in 1986. After first being denied a Soviet exit visa in 1973, Sharansky finally reached Israel, the country that he longed for. This thirty-eight-year-old fighter for Soviet dissidents received a hero's welcome in Israel and joined his wife, Avital, after a twelve-year separation. Sharansky took a couple of years to learn how to live a normal life outside of prison (He spent nine years in one of the worst Soviet prisons, mostly in solitary confinement and hounded by the KGB Secret Police.) and writing his inspiring book, *Fear No Evil*. He then entered the political arena in Israel. Sharansky became a spokesman for the large number of new Russian immigrants who faced difficult times adjusting to the economic and cultural environment in Israel. He became the Knesset representative of the Russian immigrant party, the *Movement for Israel and Immigration,* and enjoyed popularity with all factions in Israel. In 1998, Prime Minister Netanyahu appointed Sharansky trade minister, inviting him to participate in the Wye Conference that negotiated steps to be taken by Israel and the PLO under terms of the 1993 Oslo Accord.

1987: Intifada Uprising Begins—Isolated disturbances against the Israeli occupying forces in the West Bank and Gaza Strip occurred since the Israeli occupation after the Yom Kippur War. The accidental killing of four Arabs in the Gaza Strip by an Israeli truck driver on December 8, 1987 triggered a new phase of violence known as the *intifada*. They were mass uprisings of mainly youthful Palestinians who were living in the refugee camps scattered throughout the West Bank and Gaza. They wielded knives, threw stones and Molotov cocktails, occasionally fired guns, and set up roadblocks.

These spontaneous group disturbances forced the Israeli occupying forces to take strong defensive measures. Initially they shot at the protesters, killing some, and causing an international outcry. The soldiers were trained to use rubber bullets to restrain the protesters, but the total scene of soldiers fighting against civilians did not sit well in the eyes of the international community. The role of fighting civilians disturbed many Israeli soldiers.

When these uprisings developed, Hamas, the Egyptian-based fundamentalist Muslim organization that violently opposed any form of an Israeli State, replaced the PLO Fatah (Arab Liberation Movement) as the instigator of the violent uprisings. Fatah supplied the weapons for the Hamas-organized sabotage operations and killing attacks. Suicide bombings that caused multiple deaths in Israel proper became prevalent. Hamas was joined by two other terrorist organizations in the militant operations against Israel. The Islamic Jihad, connected with the Egyptian Muslim Brotherhood organization opposed to Israel, operated in Gaza and the West Bank area of Hebron. The Iran-sponsored Hezballah (the Party of God) operated out of southern Lebanon.

The intifada violence lasted over five years. During this period it caused havoc to both the Palestinian and Israeli economies because of the roadblocks, prevention of Arab workers entering Israel proper, and the terrorist destruction of property. Life for the Israelis in the West Bank settlements became precarious, requiring extra Israeli military protection. Israelis, in reaction, became violent towards the Arabs; there were isolated cases of Jewish terrorist actions killing Arabs. Foreign relationships, particularly the important one with the United States, started to deteriorate. With all Israelis affected by this turmoil, the Israeli political climate became turbulent. The results of the intifada laid the groundwork for peace discussions between the Israelis and Palestinians that started in 1991.

1989: Start of Mass Immigration of Russian Jews—As part of his Glasnost policy, Soviet Premier Mikhail Gorbachev relaxed the restrictions on exit permits for Soviet Jews wanting to emigrate to Israel. By the end of the decade, there were 900,000 immigrants to Israel from former parts of the Soviet Union. These new immigrants now represent a fifth of the Jewish population of Israel. The early years were devoted to integrating into society at a period when Israel had limited resources to support the massive immigration. They had to learn to speak Hebrew, find suitable housing, and find any employment available in those difficult economic times. Other than the elderly, most of the immigrants were well educated. They have now begun to find employment commensurate with their former skills, contributing to Israel's recent high technology and medical research growth, and to an expansion of interest in music. Although some are being indoctrinated with Jewish religious practices, many remain secular; their disregard for the Sabbath and their eating of pork products is becoming a source of tension in some areas of Israel.

1991: Scud Missiles Rain on Israel During Gulf War; Operation Solomon; UN Revokes "Zionism Is Racism" Resolution—Saddam

Hussein carried out his threat to bomb Israel if Iraq was attacked after the Gulf War started. He launched Scud missile attacks of Israeli cities. These inaccurate missiles resulted in the intended terror among the Israeli population, causing extensive damage to dwellings but few deaths. Prime Minister Yitzhak Shamir advised Washington that Israel was prepared to strike back. Shamir accepted President Bush's plea to keep out of the war because Saudi Arabia would not go along with the Israeli plan to aggressively attack Iraq in retaliation for the Scud attacks. In exchange for the Israeli cooperation, the United States provided Israel with Patriot surface-to-air missiles and promised to hunt down and attack Scuds in western Iraq from where they were launched against Israel. Neither was effective in eliminating Scud attacks.

President Bush, who was appreciative of the Israeli cooperation during the Gulf War, influenced the United Nations to vote overwhelmingly to revoke the 1975 statement describing Zionism as a form of racism. This anti-Semitic statement sponsored by the Arabs was a long-standing irritant to the Jewish community and a thorn in Israeli-UN relations.

1991: Operation Solomon—In May 1991, the civil war taking place in Ethiopia put the Falashas in serious jeopardy. As a humanitarian gesture in appreciation of the Israeli cooperation during the Gulf War, President Bush convinced the Ethiopian government to cooperate with the Israeli "Operation Solomon" that was planned to quickly evacuate the remaining Falashas. Fifteen thousand Falashas, almost all those remaining in Ethiopia, were air-lifted in Israeli military and civilian transports from Addis Ababa airport to Israel in just two days.

1991: The Madrid Peace Conference—United States Secretary of State James Baker was determined to find a way for the Israelis and Palestinians to engage in peace talks. Through Baker's shuttle diplomacy, a conference in Madrid, Spain, to be sponsored by the United States and the Soviet Union, was agreed to by Prime Minister Yitzhak Shamir. Since Shamir's policy was that talks with Palestinians were illegal, the Palestinians were represented by a Jordanian-Palestinian delegation. Representatives of other Arab states, including Syria, participated in the conference. This was an historic breakthrough. Israelis and Arabs sat face-to-face and talked to each other for the first time since the War of Independence in 1948. Bilateral discussions on many detail issues were held periodically until the 1992 elections in which Shamir was defeated.

1992: Labor Party Returns to Power—The Labor party surprisingly won the elections in June, ending fifteen years of the Likud party's political dominance. The loss was attributed to the Likud's neglect of the new Russian immigrants' needs; they became a large voting block. Yitzhak Rabin barely won out over Shimon Peres for the party chairmanship and became prime minister. Peres, having served the Yishuv for fifty years, the last fifteen as foreign minister, thought he deserved the leadership role. Bitterly disappointed, he nevertheless agreed to stay on as foreign minister, contributing to the peace accords that followed.

General Rabin, the former chief of staff general who was the architect of Israel's victory in the Six Day War and who, as defense minister, addressed the intifada with a firm hand, changed Israel's attitude towards the peace process. In his opening speech as prime minister, he pledged his government would embark on the pursuit of peace with a fresh momentum. He indicated that he expected the Palestinians would become partners and not enemies in the peace process and that Palestinian rights would be restored.

1993: Oslo Accords—Early in 1993, Prime Minister Rabin followed up on his 1992 Knesset promise to seek peace with the Palestinians and authorized his Foreign Minister Shimon Peres to arrange secret talks with the Palestinians; direct Israeli contact with Palestinians was legally forbidden. Under the auspices of the Norwegian Prime Minister Johann Holst, several secret peace talk meetings between Israeli and PLO officials were held in Oslo, Norway. In August, they reached the "Oslo Accords," which laid the framework for establishing peace between Israel and the PLO. Israel was to trade land for its security. The PLO was to take steps to improve the security of Israel. One major step was to remove the twenty-six clauses in the Palestinian National Charter that call for the destruction and elimination of the State of Israel. The parties agreed that no decisions on issues between them would be resolved unilaterally. Five years were allowed for the implementation of a peace arrangement.

The Oslo Accord was signed on September 13, 1993, at the White House under the sponsorship of President Clinton. Prime Minister Rabin offered these words:

> Let me say to you, the Palestinians, we are destined to live together on the same soil in the same land. We, the soldiers who have returned from battles stained with blood; we who have seen our relatives and friends killed before our eyes; we who have attended their funerals and cannot look into the eyes of their parents; we who have come from a land where parents bury their

children; we who have fought against you, the Palestinians, we say to you today in a loud and clear voice, enough of blood and tears. Enough!

Arafat responded positively, offering to abide by the UN Resolutions 242 and 338, pledging that Palestinian self-determination would not infringe on Israel's security. He extended his hand to Rabin who shook it with little enthusiasm; Rabin was still leery of the future relationship with Arafat.

Rabin, Arafat, and Peres, the major contributors to this accord that established a set of principles for finding peace between two previously implacable foes, were honored with the Nobel Peace Prize the following year.

1994: Peace Treaty with Jordan—Prime Minister Yitzhak Rabin and King Hussein signed a peace accord, the second between Israel and an Arab nation. It called for close economic and political cooperation.

1995: Warrior-Turned-Peacemaker Prime Minister Rabin Assassinated—Prime Minister Rabin followed up on the 1993 Oslo Accords, conducting negotiations with Chairman Arafat on the transfer West Bank land to the Palestinians and the resolution of other issues. The atmosphere in Israel became very turbulent. Palestinian terrorists continued to cause havoc. In reaction to these attacks and because of their fundamental objection to ceding any portion of biblical Israel to the Palestinians, the right wing Israelis reacted violently to the steps towards peace with the Palestinians.

Rabin was under assault by the right wing Israelis for his peace plan. They could not understand how this former general who fought the Arabs all his life and previously showed his animosity towards Arafat could now be dealing with him. His answer was **"I need to make peace with my enemies, not with my friends."**

On October 28, Benjamin Netanyahu, the leader of the Likud party opposition, was the main speaker at a Jerusalem rally that denounced Rabin as a traitor. A week later, on November 4, a counterdemonstration attended by 100,000 Israelis supporting the peace process was held in Tel Aviv. Rabin made a speech explaining why as a military man he was pursuing peace and the importance of peace to the State of Israel and to all young people of the area. After joining in the singing of the "Song of Peace," Rabin was shot and killed by an assassin as he went to his car. Rabin's murderer was a young Jew, Yigal Amir. He was a religious law student at Bar-Ilan University who was opposed to the principle of trading land for peace and considered Rabin a traitor. American President Clinton, President Mubarak of Egypt, King Hussein of Jordan, and representatives of several Arab and European countries attended the funeral. King Hussein, Shimon Peres, and President Clinton offered stirring remarks and praised Rabin's courage to pursue peace. Rabin's eighteen-year-old daughter offered tearful comments. President Clinton's closing words *"shalom haver"* ("goodbye comrade") had a profound effect on the Israelis.

1996: Netanyahu Elected Prime Minister—With the backing of several small religious parties, Benjamin Netanyahu of the right wing Likud party narrowly defeated Shimon Peres of the Labor party to become the new prime minister. He reopened the expansion of Jewish settlements in the West Bank, which was opposed by the United States as a source of friction that would interfere with the peace negotiations with the Palestinians. Netanyahu took the position that further peace negotiations with Arafat required positive steps on the part of the Palestinians to reduce Palestinian terrorism.

May 14, 1998: The Fiftieth Anniversary of the State of Israel—The State of Israel stands as a model for the developing countries of the world. Of the more than one hundred new independent countries that have come into existence in the past fifty years, only Israel represents a miracle of accomplishments. The democratic form of government endured through six wars against overwhelming odds. It is the only country in the Middle East where men and women, Arabs and Jews, are equal citizens. The land has been transformed from a poor agricultural society into a high-technology country, with one of the highest standards of living in the world. White, black, and brown Jews from sixty countries and with different cultures have been integrated. Over three million immigrants have been absorbed. During the past fifty years, Israel has been the only haven for persecuted Jews throughout the world. In 1950, David Ben-Gurion had given the reason for the creation of the State of Israel: *"The State of Israel has served as one nation for all Jews."*

October 1998: Wye River Accord Between Netanyahu and Arafat—Under Prime Minister Yitzhak Rabin and his successor Shimon Peres, Israel kept its agreement under the 1993 Oslo Accord. Israel transferred to the PLO the civil administration of the Gaza Strip and twenty-seven percent of the West Bank land. This included all the major West Bank Arab cities and ninety-eight percent of the West Bank Palestinian population. After Benjamin Netanyahu became prime minister in

1996, peace negotiations between Israel and the PLO stalled. Palestinian failure to complete their promises, Israeli right wing pressure on Netanyahu to end the negotiations, and the Israeli reaction to Arab terrorist acts against Israel were the main reasons. According to the Oslo Accord, the negotiations of all issues were to be completed by May 4, 1999. With time running out and little progress being made in the negotiations that took place all summer, President Clinton invited Prime Minister Benjamin Netanyahu and Chairman Yasser Arafat to continue the negotiations at the Wye River Plantation in Maryland on October 15.

After nine days of negotiations, which at times were on the verge of a breakdown, a breakthrough was achieved with the help of the personal intervention of President Clinton and the inspiring dramatic visit of the ailing Jordanian King Hussein. Hussein, who already had the respect of both Netanyahu and Arafat, won everyone's admiration for interrupting his cancer treatment to make his plea for peace and for his fine words.

Bitter rivals, Netanyahu, who was a previous critic of the Oslo Accords, and Arafat arrived at a Memorandum of Understanding to be completed according to a twelve-week timetable. Israel would pull back from 13% of the West Bank, giving the Palestinians control of 40%, and would release 750 Palestinian prisoners. The Palestinians would delete the twenty-six clauses in the PLO Charter calling for the destruction of Israel, which they previously promised as part of the Oslo Accord and failed to fulfill. Arafat would also take several steps to fight terrorism stemming from the West Bank and Gaza. In addition, several economic measures would be taken to improve the well being of the Palestinians, particularly in the crowded, impoverished Gaza Strip. Israel was to permit the opening of the Gaza airport, which was also previously agreed to under the Oslo Accord. Two transportation corridors between Gaza and the West Bank were to be created and an industrial zone between Israel and Gaza was to be developed.

The conference deferred until after the Wye River Accord was implemented to resolve the remaining difficult issues between the Israelis and the Palestinians. They include the nature of a future Palestinian State, any Arab role in Jerusalem, Israeli water rights in the area, and the conditions for any return of Palestinians who fled from the Israeli areas during the War of Independence. Also deferred was the consideration by President Clinton as to whether to grant clemency to Jonathan Pollard, who was an American Central Intelligence Agency employee convicted in 1985 and sentenced to life imprisonment for spying for Israel. Pollard, who now wants to live in Israel and has been granted Israeli citizenship, is a hero in Israel for the important information he supplied that benefited Israel's security. His release was discussed in an effort to help sell the Wye River Accord to Israeli hard-liners in the Knesset.

Many high-ranking U.S. officials were given credit for their respective roles in the Wye River Accord. However, U.S. Middle East Special Envoy Dennis Ross was the individual who truly made the maximum contribution to this new relationship between the Palestinians and Israelis, which focuses on ending the animosity that existed for centuries and arriving at a peaceful coexistence. Several times when apparently insurmountable issues threatened to end the peace process, Ross shuttled repeatedly to Israel and to other countries in the area, speaking to Israeli, Palestinian, and other area diplomats and leaders in order to keep alive the talks between the two adversaries. (Ross was also the U.S. Middle East coordinator during the Oslo Accord discussions and the follow-up discussions in 1984.) Dennis Ross asserted his diplomatic talent at the Wye Conference, providing the American delegation with the strategy that avoided antagonizing Netanyahu, keeping him from abandoning the conference. What is remarkable is that Ross is a practicing Jew who is a member of a Conservative synagogue and shares the Jewish concern for the welfare of Israel. He earned the respect of both sides by maintaining his objectivity; he facilitated the ongoing discussions without imposing any solutions. As evidence of his evenhandedness, both Israeli and Muslim radicals accused Ross of favoring the other side.

December 1998: Early Elections Called—Israel's Knesset approved the Wye River Accord in November by a seventy-five-to-nineteen vote. Israel proceeded to turn over West Bank land, released prisoners, and allowed the Gaza airport to open according to the terms of the Accord. Since then, broad Palestinian violence erupted protesting against the Israeli release of criminals rather than terrorists. Netanyahu maintained that he did not agree to release terrorists and protested that Arafat did not take sufficient measures to control the violence. Arafat made a statement that he was prepared to unilaterally declare an independent Palestinian State, which Israel maintained violated the Oslo Accord. These provocative actions caused a lack of confidence in the Netanyahu government. The right wing accused Netanyahu of giving too much to the Palestinians without obtaining security and true peace. The left wing accused Netanyahu of backing off from the Oslo and Wye Accords. New elections were scheduled for 1999.

9
Gentile Friends of Israel

Three Gentiles stand out as significant friends of Israel for their outstanding contributions to the State of Israel during the early days of its development. Orde Wingate was a Scottish officer in the British army sent to Palestine in 1936 to help enforce the British Mandate. He immediately developed a strong admiration for the Jews there, teaching them aggressive tactics of self-defense against the Arabs attacking the Jewish pioneering settlers. This training was invaluable during the 1948 War of Independence, when the outnumbered and ill-equipped Jewish home-defense forces held off the combined Arab forces until weapons were brought in. Pierre van Paassen and Robert St. John, were distinguished correspondents who became life-long Zionists. As such, they wrote and lectured vigorously about the importance of the Jewish State in Palestine, effectively persuading Jews and non-Jews alike to support Israel.

Although they were not particularly admirers of the Jewish people, two American presidents, Truman and Nixon, stand out as friends of Israel for the singular events vital to the State of Israel that they were responsible for. President Truman took a vital step for the relief of the Holocaust survivors when the war ended, and his recognition of the newly declared State of Israel gave it a leg to stand on. President Nixon's resupply of munitions to the Israeli army when the Israeli war materiel practically ran out in the early days of the Yom Kippur War averted an Israeli military defeat. His financial aid to Israel was crucial to their military security.

In addition to these individuals, there were many Christian organizations and individuals in the United States and around the world who contributed to the development and well being of the State of Israel through their political and economic support. They were motivated by their religious convictions of God's endorsement to the Jewish right to Palestine. This important support continues today.

Orde Wingate—Scottish Christian Orde Wingate became an ardent Zionist three months after being assigned in 1936 as an officer in the British army sent to enforce the British Mandate in Palestine. He sympathized with the Jews in Palestine, who were outcasts in the eyes of the Christian world. In his words, "I felt I belonged to such a people." Because of his loyalties to the Jews in Palestine, when World War II started, rather than allowing him to fight the German forces advancing in the Middle East, the British transferred Wingate to fight with their forces in Asia. This move was a political attempt to please the Arabs who were starting to show support for the Germans. The strategy failed. The Arabs remained loyal to Hitler. Unfortunately, Wingate did not live to see the creation of the State of Israel that he longed for. He was killed in battle in Asia.

Wingate convinced the Jewish settlers to change from their passive self-defense posture to an aggressive approach of attacking the infiltrators. This tactic contributed enormously to the safety of the country and proved invaluable to the development of the future Jewish military strength. His tactical training enabled the Haganah to be so successful against the larger Arab armies during the War of Independence. Wingate's disciples Generals Gavish, Tal, and Sharon applied his tactics to take the fighting into Egyptian territory at the start of the Six Day War, leading to the startling victory.

Wingate was called *"The Friend"* by the appreciative and admiring Israelis. The sports training and military rehabilitation center in Netanya, Israel, was named *The Wingate Institute* in his honor. The institute now houses the International Jewish Sports Hall of Fame.

Pierre van Paassen—This Dutch foreign correspondent, having seen the rise of Hitler first hand, started warning the world in the early 1930s about Hitler's dangers. In the late 1930s, he witnessed the three million Polish Jews turned from middle class citizens into paupers by the deliberate policy of the Polish government, many of whom lived off doles from their American relatives. His reaction was to decry this bigoted policy to the world community. He denounced the lack of British and American interest in the frightful uninterrupted killing of the Jews by the Nazis, and he expressed concern for the lack of interest in providing Jews a means of escape or a ray of hope for their survival. Van Paassen constantly spoke forcefully for Britain to honor the Balfour Declaration. In his 1943 book, *The Forgotten Ally,* he argued that the Jews deserved their homeland in Palestine for their war efforts in Africa and the Middle East in support of the British armies. Van Paassen continued to be an avid, outspoken supporter of the State of Israel during his lifetime.

Robert St. John—As a correspondent in Palestine watching the creation of the State of Israel, Robert St. John became an admirer of how Israel was the haven for the Holocaust survivors. He was impressed by how much Israel accomplished in their trying times and under difficult circumstances. As a non-Jew describing Israel's accomplishments and pleading their case for financial aid, he was a very forceful and successful spokesman for the State of Israel bond campaigns. It was in the early years of this very important financial support for Israel, a time when American Jews had not yet learned the full importance of the State of Israel to them, and needed encouragement to buy these bonds.

Robert St. John wrote several books of Jewish interest. His book, *Jews, Justice and Judaism,* describes the role played by Jews in shaping American history. It defines the influence of Judaic values on American history and provides detailed narratives of many lesser-known Jewish personalities involved in this history. Robert St. John continued to be a friend of the Jewish people through his more recent writings.

Harry Truman—Jewish U.S. Army chaplains who witnessed conditions in the American controlled concentration camps in Germany after they were liberated from the Nazis issued very negative reports about the conditions in the camps. Reacting to these reports, Secretary Henry Morgenthau, Jr. convinced President Truman to send University of Pennsylvania Dean Earl Harrison to investigate. In August, Dean Harrison reported that three months after V-E Day, Jews and other nonrepatriables were still living under guard, and were wearing prisoner garb in crowded and unsanitary conditions that resembled the slave labor concentration camps. He stressed the problems that the Jewish inmates in particular were suffering, indicating that the army personnel were not equipped to address them. General Eisenhower, responsible for the American army in Germany, initially took issue with the report and denied bad conditions existed. After Harrison defended his report, President Truman reacted with a vital decision that brought relief to the concentration camp survivors. He instructed Eisenhower to correct the camp conditions, emphasizing the need to get the Jews out of the camps and into decent housing.

Three years later, President Truman made a major decision affecting the Jewish community. The basis for this decision started when President Truman interacted with the American Zionist community as the United Nations started to address the handling of Palestine after the British mandate of control was to end. His attitude towards Jews vacillated between being friendly and antagonistic; Jews were lobbying vigorously in 1945 for some form of a Jewish homeland. Two years later, he became firmly responsive to Jewish aspirations when he overruled his State Department advisors who favored the Arab position on two occasions. In the fall of 1947, Truman accepted the United Nations resolution to partition Palestine into two states, which the Jewish leaders supported. After the Arabs rejected the partition plan and fighting broke out, the Palestinian Jews unilaterally announced the creation of the State of Israel in May 1948. Truman again ignored the Arabist state department, rejecting Secretary of State Marshall's objection to a Jewish state. Truman said he was pained by the Jewish people's suffering under Hitler. He expressed the view that Jews needed a place to go to and quickly gave the new State of Israel diplomatic recognition. Truman's prompt action set the pace for the non-Muslim world to recognize the State of Israel.

Richard Nixon—President Nixon had not been pro-Israel, and as the secret White House tapes he recorded reveal, he bordered on being anti-Semitic. Nevertheless, Nixon authorized the emergency airlift of ammunition, tanks, and fighter planes to Israel during the Yom Kippur war in 1973. This undoubtedly saved the State of Israel from destruction. Israel had suffered devastating losses to its air force and army equipment and was practically out of all munitions. Equally important was the political message that the U.S. resupply effort sent to Egypt and Soviet Union. It convinced the Soviet Union that their resupply of Egypt's arms would not result in an Egyptian victory. They in turn forced Egypt to accept the proposed cease fire, which Israel desperately wanted. Nixon followed up by recommending a 2.3 billion-dollar appropriation to rebuild Israel's defense forces, which passed through Congress.

Part VI

Survival of the Jewish People

Jewish Survival Is Stranger Than Fiction

Preface to Part VI

The 4,000-year history of the Jewish people is an unusual story. It lasted so very long in spite of the many perils to the continued existence of the Jews as a people. What were the threats to their survival? How did they manage to survive the many challenges to their survival when other peoples failed to survive similar challenges? Who kept the flames of Judaism going when the total population of Jews was down to 200,000, of which possibly only 50,000 remained loyal to Judaism?

The answers to these questions will provide the reader with a deeper appreciation of the history of the Jewish people. It is a story of threats to survival that stemmed from internal as well as external sources. It is a story of strong leaders who faced these threats that could easily have caused the end of the Jewish people and who took the initiatives that led to the Jewish people's survival.

Old threats to survival were overcome but new ones keep surfacing. What are the Jewish people doing to continue their survival in the future? Is there hope for the future of the Jewish people?

The answers to these questions provide a source of optimism about the future of the Jewish people.

1
Historical Challenges to Survival

When the challenges to survival during the long history of the Jewish people are examined, it is remarkable, if not supernatural, that Jews have survived as a people for almost 4,000 years.

Comparison with Other Peoples: *Unique History*

The Jewish Nation lost its independence in 74 C.E. and the Jewish people were expelled from Palestine in 135 C.E. Dispersed throughout Europe, Asia, and Africa, with no central religious organization to help bind them together, the Diaspora Jews somehow maintained their ties to Judaism. There was no real hope of regaining their country. Nevertheless, Jews remained as a people with a distinctive set of religious practices and lifestyle.

In world history, there is no similar case of a group of people retaining their identity after losing control of their country and having been exiled to foreign lands for centuries. Biblical period countries such as Sumeria and Babylon (which were very advanced), Philistines (which was very powerful), Phoenicia (which was already conducting trade across the Mediterranean) all disappeared. In modern times, the American Indians lost control of their land and were dispersed, but they never regained control of their land. The Polish and Ukrainian peoples lost control of their land for centuries, but they were never dispersed from their homeland. With the birth of the State of Israel in 1948, the Jewish people have the distinction of a people experiencing a national rebirth after being without a national home for two thousand years.

First 2,000 Years: *Flirting with Disaster Internally and Externally*

When the first two thousand years of Jewish history is examined, the survival of the Jews is remarkable, almost unbelievable. The events of the early biblical history were natural conditions for failure.

It started with a relatively good life in Egypt, which turned into slavery. That was followed by the exodus from Egypt with its two-year Sinai wilderness sojourn that required Divine support for survival in this extremely inhospitable area that barely supports life. The Hebrew religious continuity was threatened with rebellions against Moses and God during the next thirty-eight-year wandering in the Palestine wilderness. To get control of the Promised Land, the Hebrews audaciously battled with the larger and more powerful Canaanite armies. Either of these turbulent events logically should have ended Jewish history.

The history that followed was almost stranger. There were two centuries of anarchy, internal strife, and battles with much stronger neighboring kingdoms. Ultimately, a United Jewish Kingdom was established, but it lasted just one hundred years. It split into two Jewish kingdoms, Israel and Judah, that fought constantly with their neighbors. When they had peace with their neighbors, the two kingdoms fought and almost destroyed each other. Most of the kings of Israel behaved like the typical tyrannical kings of ancient times. There were constant battles over religious principles between the rulers of these two countries and the religious leaders, who were the biblical Prophets. The Prophets strove to have the masses retain Judaic religious, ethical, and moral values—the kings provided bad examples in thus regard. After 200 years of this troubled existence, the kingdom of Israel was defeated by Assyria and was eliminated as a country. The large number of Israelite Jews were absorbed into the conquering nation. Almost all of the Israelite Jews ended their relationship with Judaism and the Jewish people. This was the fate of the "Ten Lost Tribes of Israel."

Under the leadership of several evil kings, most Jews that remained in the small kingdom of Judah periodically abandoned the Hebrew concept of monotheism and reverted to idol worship and immoral behavior. The Hebrew religion required the passion of the Prophets for the Judeans to survive these digressions from Judaism.

The kingdom of Judah was able to avoid foreign entanglements while the kingdom of Israel existed. After Israel was vanquished, this isolation ended and Judah was periodically invaded by several of its larger neighbors who ravaged the country. Finally, one hundred and fifty years after Israel was destroyed, the kingdom of Judah was conquered by the Babylonians and totally devastated. The Holy Temple in Jerusalem, the central factor in the religious life of the Jews, was destroyed and the mass of the Jewish population exiled to Babylon. Most of the exiled Jews, who were impoverished when they lived in Palestine, succumbed to the grandeur and wealth of opportunities that was available to them in the highly advanced Babylon. They assimilated into Babylonian society and abandoned Judaism, while life for the small number of Jews remaining behind in Judah was severely oppressive. These events should have set the stage for the end of the Jewish people, but did not. Judaism then changed its focus from the temple-centered sacrificial system of worship to God to synagogue-centered moral and ethical behavior according to the Torah laws; the Jewish people survived and grew in number.

A new type of threat to the survival of the Jews arose after the conquest of Europe and Asia by Alexander the Great. A 200-year period of Greek domination of the Middle East, including Judea (the area known as Palestine) followed. Hellenistic pagan altars and temples, gymnasiums with uninhibited sexual practices, and art, literature and theaters saturated with Greek philosophical culture had a strong appeal to many Jews, as it did to the rest of the Mediterranean world. This Hellenistic activity split families and divided the community and priesthood into two camps, Hellenists versus anti-Hellenists. It appeared that Judaism was on the verge of collapse in Judea when a despotic Hellenistic-oriented Syrian king's attempt to eliminate Jewish religious practices in Judah led to the Maccabean rebellion. This resulted in an independent Jewish State and a very significant strengthening of the Jewish people. The Maccabean dynasty that ruled for one hundred years unfortunately turned the freedom they won for the people into tyrannical treatment of the people—some Jewish rulers never learned to apply the Judaic code of ethical and moral behavior.

This two-millennium period of Jewish history ended with another major challenge to survival. The brutal domination by the Greeks was followed by two hundred years of Roman tyrannical rule and ended with Jewish rebellions. During that period, possibly a million Jews were killed. The Temple was destroyed again and Jews were forbidden to live or worship in Jerusalem. It ended with the formal exile of the Jewish people from Palestine, which lasted close to two-millennium.

Second 2,000 Years: *Centuries of Intolerance, Conversions, and Repeated Genocide*

For the past two thousand years, Jews survived as a people in spite of the tremendous forces of intolerance, mass exterminations, expulsions from country after country, economic depravity, and powerful Christian and Islamic conversion pressures.

This period started with a revolt in 70 C.E. against the Romans in which possibly 500,000 Jews were killed. The second Holy Temple was destroyed, many were exiled, and hope for political independence vanished. The Romans replaced the country's name Judea with Palestine. A hopeless second revolt, the Bar Kochba rebellion in 132–135 C.E., was a crushing defeat by the Romans. Consequently, Jewish existence in the Holy Land essentially ended. Following this tragedy, the rising Christian movement exerted its influence, decimating the Jewish population in the Diaspora. The early Christian leaders had a warm attitude towards Jews as they attempted to convert Jews to Christianity. The initial impact was the conversion to Christianity of many Jews who lived in the Roman dominated countries. When their emphasis changed from converting Jews to converting pagans, the Christian leadership's attitude turned antagonistic and intolerant towards the Jewish people.

In 400 C.E., after Christianity became the official religion in the southern European countries, a long period of severe intolerance towards the Jews set in. It was particularly bad during the 400-year period between 1100 C.E. and 1500 C.E. During these oppressive years, many Jews could not resist the intolerable pressures they were exposed to. There were mass suicides and conversions to Christianity. It started with the First Crusade when the Crusaders killed thousands of Jews as they marched through Europe on their way to Palestine. The aftermath of the First Crusade was a widespread religious and political anti-Jewish fervor, frequently sponsored and instigated by the ruling political and religious authorities. It continued for centuries. Jews were tortured and killed. They were forced to live in crowded ghettos and were prevented from engaging in most occupations/trades that served the Christian community.

To break their spirit and encourage conversion to Christianity, Jews were required to wear badges of shame. The money-lending trade, considered irreligious and ignored by Christians, was essentially forced upon Jews because the rulers saw the necessity of money-lending for running their country. *Jewish moneylenders were encouraged to serve a useful societal function but were condemned for engaging in it.*

The Black Death plague, which occurred in the fourteenth century, devastated Europe. This period was cruel for the Jewish people. In addition to the deaths caused by the epidemic, false blood libel claims against Jews caused many massacres that killed thousands of Jews at a time. Jews were accused of ritual murder and the use of human blood in religious practices—whereas the opposite was true. Mosaic Code clearly forbids human sacrifice and even forbids the consumption of an animal's blood—blood must be drained in the animal slaughtering process so that it is not mingled with the meat.

There were no meaningful health statistics kept at that time to verify the apparent lower death rate among Jews, but this perception may have been behind another false hoax that the Jews started the epidemic and were shielded from its consequences. The apparent lower death rate may have been due to two factors, superior hygienic conditions in the ghettos compared to the small towns where the Christians lived and the Jewish practices regarding the handling of the dead reduced the spread of the disease.

This horrible 400-year period for the Jews ended with the notorious Spanish Inquisition. Thousands of Jews were massacred and many burned at the stake. Thousands converted, of which many became Marranos (secret Jews). Hundreds of thousands who retained their Judaism were finally expelled in the year 1492—on the day Columbus sailed on his first voyage to America. Many Jews went to Portugal, only to be expelled from Portugal a few years later.

At various times, Jews were also expelled from England, France, Austria, and several German states. They became the *"Wandering Jews,"* going from country to country to find a place that would allow them to live and continue to practice Judaism. They settled largely in the eastern European countries (Poland, Hungary, Lithuania, Russia, and Ukraine) and the countries under Turkish rule (Greece and Turkey). In Poland and Russia, what started out to be a haven turned into a nightmare in the year 1650. Rising anti-Semitism was capped by the Cossack uprising against the Polish rulers of the Ukraine led by the savage Bogdan Chmielnicki. Poles and Jews suffered together but entire Jewish villages were destroyed; it is estimated that almost 500,000 Jews were massacred.

Somehow, in spite of all this suffering, the survivors retained their faith in God and their belief in Judaism.

Current Threats to Survival

Present-day deterioration of traditional Jewish lifestyles represents a potential long-term threat to Judaism's survival.

Intermarriage—Jewish intermarriage is increasing throughout the world. It is estimated that over fifty percent of new marriages involving Jews are interfaith, and the large majority of these marriages do not adhere to the Jewish faith or raise their children Jewish.

High Divorce Rate—The significant increase in the Jewish divorce rate indicates a weakening of the long Judaic tradition of stable, strong family relationships.

Decrease in Religious Organization Affiliations—Affiliation with Jewish religious organizations and adherence to Judaic religious practices of the larger, non-Orthodox Jewish community is decreasing rapidly. This curtails the ability of non-Orthodox rabbis to influence Judaism's survival.

Low Birth Rate—Except for Orthodox Jewish families, the family size is getting smaller than it was fifty years ago. If the current rate of 1.6 children per family continues, the Jewish population will shrink with time without consideration of the other factors that contribute to a reduced Jewish population.

Conversion—Christian and cult proselytizing is on the increase. The Jews for Jesus movement has become more effective in recent years, attracting young Jews who are looking to fill a void in their personal religious needs. Counterbalancing this trend is a growing number of mostly young intellectual Christians who have converted to Judaism. Some rabbinic leaders are promoting more active proselytizing by rabbis.

Secular Judaism—Intolerance towards the Jewish people lessened considerably worldwide, particularly in the United States, in the second half of the twentieth century. This change was a most welcome development for Jews since it brought on improved economic opportunities along with less hostile working and living environments. However, from Judaism's standpoint, this lessened intolerance caused some negative results. The increased Jewish assimilation into the general society led to a greater emphasis on secular values over Judaic values, and a loosening of the bonds to Judaism. Even in the State of Israel, secular Jews outnumber those who practice religious Judaism.

2
Road to Survival

With all the challenges to survival, how did the Jews survive as a people for 4000 years?

Great Leaders: *A Leader Emerges to Face Every Challenge*

Throughout every stage of Jewish history, strong personalities emerged to lead the Jewish people out of the latest danger to their survival. The threats to survival varied considerably over the 4,000-year history and different types of leaders answered the call.

Moses—God chose the reluctant Moses to negotiate with Pharaoh to let the Hebrews leave Egypt. The Bible, the foundation of Judaism, is a legacy from Moses. During the forty-year wandering in the wilderness, Moses, the greatest Jewish Prophet, kept rebellious Hebrews from destroying the Jewish faith just as it was being established.

Joshua—The Hebrew wanderers in the desert who fled Egypt during the Exodus were reluctant to accept the challenge of fighting the established Canaanites in order to fulfill God's Covenant with Abraham that promised Canaan as the everlasting home of Abraham's descendants. Joshua took on the challenge to lead the reluctant Hebrews into invading and conquering Canaan. Joshua, a modest man, did not seek power after the successful Hebrew entry to Canaan.

The Judges—The post-Exodus 200 years was a period of strife, unrest, and attacks from the surrounding nations. Strong individuals called *Judges* emerged at various times to lead the Hebrews in defending themselves from attacks and to maintain civil rule. The Judges, who came from all lifestyles, prevented the disintegration of the disorganized Hebrews, who had no traditional king to lead them.

The Prophets—For several hundred years after the reign of King Solomon, the life of the Hebrews deteriorated religiously, socially, and politically. The great religious Prophets, Amos, Hosea, Isaiah, Mica, Zephaniah, and Jeremiah took turns at rescuing the Judean Hebrews from moral and religious decay. During the exile to Babylon, the Prophets Ezekial, Isaiah, and Malachi gave hope to the Jews that the Temple would be rebuilt and Zion restored. Their messages encouraged resistance to the growing Hebrew assimilation into Babylonian society. The Prophets conveyed God's message to the Hebrews—they would know right from wrong and have hope for a good future.

King Josiah—Over a several hundred-year period, capped by the fifty-five-year reign of King Manasseh, the major offender of Judaic principles, the kings of Judah instituted idolatrous practices in the Holy Temple in Jerusalem and other local places of worship that violated the Judaic biblical religious practices. His youthful grandson, Josiah, who succeeded him, apparently inspired by the Judaic religious education he received under the influence of the Prophet Jeremiah, instituted a complete religious reformation in the kingdom of Judah, saving Judaism from destruction. It is a sparkling example of Jewish youth becoming more religious than their elders, which frequently happens today when youth are taught the value of Judaism.

Ezra and Nehemiah—After the exile to Babylon, the Scribe Ezra waged a forceful battle against the lack of observance of the Judaic religious practices. This behavior was on the verge of destroying the Hebrews as a people and the Judaic faith as a unique religion that recognized one God over all the people of the world. Ezra created rabbinical Judaism, which replaced the temple-oriented sacrificial system that resembled the pagan religions of the powerful countries in the area. His form of ethical Judaism that pays honor to God through proper personal behavior and prayer is essentially practiced today by all Jewish denominations.

Ezra, supported by the political leader Nehemiah, who enforced his program, had Jerusalem rebuilt and established the Mosaic laws of the Torah as the foundation of Jewish religious and civil life. Ezra instituted the Sabbath Torah reading practice—the beginning of Judaism's emphasis on education. Ezra and Nehemiah's reformation efforts preserved solidarity among the dwindling Hebrew population, of which approximately only 50,000 remained loyal to Judaism. The religious lifestyle changes Ezra instituted provided the strength that the Jewish people required to cope with the many crises they faced later.

Hillel, Shammai, and Johanan ben Zakkai—During the height of Roman tyranny, teachers like Hillel, Shammai, and Johanan ben Zakkai established learning academies and formalized the tradition of Jewish learning. Education became a Jewish strength and the asset that kept the Jews as a distinctive people without a country during the two thousand years of exile. Their lenient interpretation of the Torah commandments documented in the Mishnah (part of the Talmud) allowed the Jewish people to adapt to the circumstances of the times without violating their religion.

Johanan ben Zakkai—After the Jerusalem Temple was destroyed for the second time, in 70 C.E., Johanan ben Zakkai instituted the synagogue as the new religious center for the Jewish people in Palestine. The synagogue became the mainstay of Judaism in the Diaspora, where personal and communal prayers were offered, giving the Jewish people strength to cope with the oppressive conditions they faced over the next 2,000 years.

Johanan ben Zakkai established the rabbinic Bet Din to rule on religious matters. It provided a process for the Jewish people to obtain official guidance on how to respond to other conflicting rabbinical opinions that otherwise might have split the Jewish community. Today, the Orthodox community uses this arrangement of three highly trained rabbis for ruling on religious issues, qualifying converts, and granting divorces.

Rashi—Eleventh-century scholar, Rabbi Solomon ben Isaac, known as Rashi from the Hebrew initials of his name, generated a complete set of commentaries on the Bible and Talmud. After his commentaries were added to the Talmud, the average Jewish student became capable of understanding the Talmud; it was previously manageable only by the most intellectual Jews. The version of the Talmud that included Rashi's study technique became an integral part of the Jewish learning process. Learning by the Jewish masses became their pillar of strength during the dark days of the Middle Ages and into the twentieth century.

Maimonides—Twelfth-century philosopher and expounder of Judaism, Moses Maimonides, became a leader of the dispersed Jewish world as a result of the many religious and philosophical works he published and his efforts to encourage remote Jewish communities to retain their Judaism. His *Mishnah-Torah* was a codification of all biblical and rabbinic law that eliminated the confusion and nonessentials of the Talmud. It allowed the young and old to understand the Oral Law without having to cope with the difficult Talmud. His *The Guide for the Perplexed* provided a rational interpretation of biblical precepts, reconciling religious revelation with the truths of science. Maimonides helped modern-thinking Jews retain their Judaism.

Moses Mendelssohn—In the eighteenth century, the German Jews followed Mendelssohn's path to religious and cultural enlightenment. They escaped from the "protective" ghetto mentality and drifted towards assimilation and conversion to Christianity. Strong leaders emerged who created versions of Judaism that enabled the western European Jews to retain their Judaism and still be part of the enlightened European community.

Rabbi Abraham Geiger—In Germany, in the mid-nineteenth century, Rabbi Geiger established a version of today's Reform Judaism that discarded most of the Orthodox rituals and customs, succeeding to stem the conversion to Christianity by the large number of intellectual, cultured German Jews.

Rabbi Zechariah Frankel: Leopold Zunz—Rabbi Frankel followed by Leopold Zunz established the *Historical Judaism* movement in Germany, which was the forerunner of Conservative Judaism in the United States. They opposed the Reform movement with their policy to "adjust" the Jewish religious practices but not "reform" the religion.

Rabbi Raphael Hirsch—Traditionalist Rabbi Hirsch fought the Reform movement in Germany through a policy of strengthening Orthodox Judaism by combining Talmudic study and the study of the literature, philosophy, and the social values of the non-Jewish world, creating the earliest version of the modern Orthodoxy movement.

Bal Shem Tov and Goan of Vilna—The poor, uneducated Jews in east central Europe centering in southern Poland were taken in by several false Messiahs over a two-hundred year period. In the eighteenth century, the Baal Shem Tov created the Chasidic movement that enabled these downtrodden Jews to overcome their gloom through the mystic form of Judaism he preached. The Vilna Goan emerged in the same period, promoting modernized Talmudic study and changes in the prayers that were more appealing to the masses. His approach served to counter the Chasidic movement and to strengthen traditional Orthodoxy. Both forms of Judaism survived because of the efforts of these two diametrically opposite leaders.

Rabbi Isaac Mayer Wise—Rabbi Wise preserved the Judaic affiliation of the German immigrants to the United States in the nineteenth century through the changes he promoted in the Reform movement religious practices and the Reform movement organization that he established.

Rabbi Solomon Schechter—In the early twentieth century, Rabbi

Schechter's creative adjustments to the Reform movement's religious practices was the basis for the growth and vitality of the Conservative movement that enabled Jews unhappy with the Reform and Orthodox movements to embrace Judaism.

Rabbi Joseph Schneerson—His energetic outreach to modern-age dropouts to Judaism won many youth back to Judaism. His inspiration strengthened the large Lubovitch Chasidic movement.

Rabbi Mordechi Kaplan—Rabbi Kaplan's philosophical view regarding the practice of Judaism was the basis of the Reconstructionist movement he founded that enabled Jews less interested in religious doctrines and more interested in social values to embrace Judaism.

Theodor Herzl—Herzl, a secular Jew with a background of no interest in Jewish affairs, was aroused by the anti-Semitic fervor in France during the Dreyfus trial. Herzl worked strenuously to found modern political Zionism. His vision of the need for a Jewish homeland where abuse of the Jewish people would not happen and where Jews controlled their own living arrangements ultimately led to the creation of the State of Israel.

Russian Refuseniks—Over a fifty-year period after World War I, the Soviet Communist government suppressed the practice of Judaism such that several million Russian Jews essentially lost their Judaic identity. Jewish refuseniks such as Vladimir Slepak, Iosef Begun, Ida Nudel, and Natan Sharansky resisted the authorities by promoting the study of Hebrew and Judaism, and fighting for the right of Jews to emigrate to Israel. As a result of the efforts of this small band of heroic, militant Jews, several millions of Russian Jews reconnected with Judaism and a million Russian Jews were able to emigrate to Israel.

Strong Belief in Judaic Values: *A Resilient and Enduring Strength*

The belief in Abraham's Covenant legacy and the acceptance of Moses's Torah legacy gave the individual Jew strength to cope with the religious and secular forces that threatened Jewish survival throughout the ages. This bond to Judaic values was weak during the period of the two Jewish kingdoms, Judah and Israel. The ancient words of the Prophets gave Jews of that period hope that life would improve despite everything that happened to them.

The kingdom of Israel was destroyed, its people vanished as Jews. One hundred and fifty years later, the kingdom of Judah was vanquished, its people banished to Babylon, and the Holy Temple was destroyed. Exiled, with the Holy Temple in Jerusalem destroyed, the surviving Judeans did not turn to the god of their victors just as the northern kingdom Israelites and other cultures did when they were overwhelmed and their countries were terminated.

The Judeans did not blame God for the disasters they experienced. They blamed their hardships on themselves for sinning against God, an attitude that enabled Jews to accept the many other tragedies the Jewish people suffered in later years. They turned to the Torah as the focal point of their religion, giving them strength to cope with the oppression that followed them wherever they went throughout the ages. The Jewish people adopted the view that the laws of God (Torah laws) must be observed strictly, and that **Israel must remain a separate people to carry out God's message to all the peoples of the world.** This new set of religious principles, enhanced by the Oral Law that was formulated in the Mishnah, unified the Jews who were exiled from Palestine and scattered throughout many countries. It strengthened the Jewish people to resist the powerful influences of the Greco-Roman civilization, which overwhelmed the rest of Europe and North Africa. The Babylonian Talmud became the primary document of post-biblical Jewish law that governed the life of Jews from the early Middle Ages on. The Talmud lifted the spirit of the Jewish people and served as the core of the Jewish resistance to conversion efforts by Christians and Muslims.

Hope, belief, and prayers that the Messiah will come to bring universal peace to all earthly creatures and everlasting life to the dead. This Judaic concept was first formulated by the Prophets at the time when the United Jewish Kingdom was split in two and revived at the time of the Greek and Roman occupation of Israel. This Judaic view of the Messiah's role is the prime reason why the Jewish people rejected Christianity—the world did not experience the peace that the Messiah was to bring—that was certainly the case for the Jewish people.

Defensive Reaction to Intolerance: *Oppression Generates a Will to Survive as Jews*

From the Middle Ages until the nineteenth century, attempts by the European Christian religious and political leaders to destroy Judaism through the many oppressive religious, economic, and social laws imposed exclusively on the Jews had an opposite effect. The Jewish people found an inner strength and resisted these forces even in the face of death. They were severely demoralized, but not destroyed. The Jewish emphasis on family and Jewish-style community living and their determination to keep the Judaic faith enabled the Jewish people to cope with the almost endless pressures.

Strong family values, high moral standards, and Jewish-sponsored and oriented universal education became the fundamental bulwark against the oppressive social measures and the prohibitions against practicing Judaism.

The ghettos in central Europe and the *shtetles* (small Jewish villages) of eastern Europe became enclaves where Jewish religious and social functions could be conducted, compensating for the pain intended by the ghettos, the forced wearing of shame badges, and the denigration of the Jewish religion by many church authorities. Jews actually learned to function as autonomous civic organizations in areas that were limited only to Jews, establishing a democratic pattern well before the local population achieved such liberty.

During the Middle Ages, many rabbis took to martyrdom rather than accepting conversion to Christianity. They disallowed their followers to pay ransoms for their release, serving as examples of strength and avoiding the spread of this vile hostage practice. Jews in countries where they were not oppressed (such as Holland, Poland, Lithuania, Greece, and Turkey) aided their fellow Jews to escape the tyranny that developed in country after country during this dark period for Jews in Europe.

Current Survival Efforts at the Religious Level

With all the negative forces threatening its survival, Judaism today is still relatively strong. There are many religious and secular organizations involved in strengthening Judaism. The Conservative movement is strengthening their educational techniques and working at getting their members more involved in Judaic practices. Their acceptance of egalitarian religious practices has also broadened the role of women in the conduct of synagogue management, adding vitality to synagogue activity. The Orthodox element is still particularly vibrant; its membership is growing. Attendance at Hebrew day schools is increasing. The large Agudath Israel of America promotes Talmud study for all their members. The Lubavitcher movement works at bringing disenchanted Jewish youth back to religious Judaism. The Reform movement leadership has embraced a plan for strengthening their membership's ties to Judaism through the adoption of traditional rituals and customs in their religious services, and enlarging the "Jewish umbrella" by recognizing the children of Jewish fathers and non-Jewish mothers to be considered Jewish without the need for formal conversion. They also advocate more active proselytizing of individuals who have indicated an appreciation of Judaic values. They have undertaken the challenge to instill an understanding of the profound roots to Judaism—"its ancient wisdom, Jewish values, the strengths of the Jewish people, and the connection to God."

Rabbis, other than the Orthodox, are trying to address the serious interfaith marriage situation that exists today. The rabbis are encouraging these interfaith couples to raise their children Jewish through a variety of activities and courses that educates them about the values of Judaism to the family and that helps them make an active connection to the Jewish community. Jewish Community Centers in the large cities have similar programs. About thirty percent of the non-Jewish spouses have chosen to convert to Judaism. Those who become Jews by choice are accepted as full members of the larger Jewish community except for the Orthodox community, which only recognizes conversions conducted according to Orthodox *halachah* procedures.

Current Survival Efforts at the Secular Level

There are many organizations involved at the secular level to strengthen Judaism. The World Jewish Congress works to coordinate activities between Jewish organizations in countries throughout the world. They also work with the leaders of international countries to improve the conditions of Jews within their respective country. The B'nai B'rith's Hillel organization works at the college campus level to encourage college students to retain and reinforce their ties to Judaism. Hadassah's high level goal is to meet the challenge of continuing Jewish identity among the Jewish women of the world. Many Jewish organizations sponsor efforts in Russia and in the United States to help Russian Jews return to Judaism. In Israel, similar efforts are going on with the more recent Russian and African immigrants. Organizations like Kulanu in the United States search out lost Jewish communities throughout the world, and assist their return to full Judaic practices. Organizations like "Jews for Judaism" work at protecting and rescuing Jews from deceptive Christian missionary and cult recruiters. Jewish philanthropists support many charities aimed at promoting and strengthening Judaism through educational efforts and trips to Israel for Jewish youth.

Factors for Retaining Judaism

A recent survey conducted by the Conservative movement identified the three most important factors that influence Jewish children to retain their Judaism when they grow up to raise their own families.

- Jewish values were an integral aspect of their parents' lifestyle.
- Both parents took their children to synagogue periodically.
- Their parents had an affiliation with a synagogue.

3
Interdenominational Conflict Challenges

The control of religious practices in Israel is an issue that is currently threatening the solidarity of the two major non-Orthodox Jewish religious denominations with the State of Israel. Since the State of Israel was established, only Orthodox *halachah*-based rules for marriage, conversion, and divorce have been acceptable in Israel. The tradition of separate-sex prayer intervals at the Temple Wall (*Kotel*) in Jerusalem has been observed.

The American Conservative and Reform movements are now fighting for religious pluralism and legitimacy in Israel (e.g., the right to conduct marriages, divorce, and conversions in Israel under non-Orthodox procedures). The recent move to egalitarianism within the Conservative movement has also made the inability to conduct mixed-sex prayer at the Kotel another fiery issue. These movements for religious diversity that will also permit non-Orthodox religious leader participation in large-city religious councils are political issues being waged in the Israeli Knesset and in the courts. Although Israelis who practice Orthodoxy are a minority, the Orthodox political parties exert a strong influence on the resolution of these issues because they maintain the balance of power in the Knesset. The Orthodox want to maintain their exclusive rights to religious functions granted to them soon after the State of Israel was established.

A solution that is accommodative of both sides and that is not disrespectful to either side has been difficult to define. The traditionalist Orthodox rabbis tend to be inflexible because traditional Orthodoxy is bound by rigid customs. Recently, leading Orthodox (traditional and modern Orthodox), Conservative, and Reform rabbis have expressed a consolidated view that a compromise solution acceptable to all sides is necessary for the sake of Jewish solidarity—***"differences in religious views should not tear the small Jewish people apart."***

4
State of Israel: Vital Haven

After 2,000 years of Jewish prayers, a Jewish country with Jerusalem as its capital was reestablished in 1948 with the formation of the State of Israel. It quickly became the haven for most of the survivors of the Holocaust—the rest of the world accepted only a token amount of Jewish refugees from Europe. Since then, Israel has taken in Jews escaping intolerance from Russia, Ethiopia, and several Muslim countries. It remains the only reliable haven open for Jews who want to escape from intolerance and persecution.

Israel has earned worldwide respect because of its major accomplishments and its ability to defend itself. The signing of peace accords with Egypt and Jordan presented a basis for reduced hostilities between Israel and other Muslim countries. Because of these factors, normal relations between Israel and several of the previously hostile Arab and other Islamic countries had slowly been on the increase. The recent slow pace of negotiations between Israel and the Palestinians over how to complete the Wye Accord, compounded by the recent new Intifada uprising in the fall of the year 2000, has interrupted the normalization process. Not all Arab countries are ready to accept a Jewish state. Israel still has intransigent Arabic enemies, such as Iraq, Iran and Libya, who are still bent on Israel's destruction. Many other Arab and non-Arab Muslim countries remain hostile.

In the past, when the State of Israel was in jeopardy, world Jewry stepped up to support it politically and financially. Before the new intifada began, decreased tension in the area and interdenominational issues within Israel tended to weaken emotional ties to Israel by many American Jews, although Jewish organizational support remained strong. The new intifada's impact on life in Israel and on Israel's stability and security has rekindled the strong ties between American Jews and Israel. Jewish prayers still connect with Jerusalem and Zion as they have for the past 2,000 years.

Finding true and lasting peace for the State of Israel is the vital challenge affecting the survival of Jews everywhere.

5
Recent Survivability Evidence

There has been startling new evidence of the survivability of the Jewish people. Ethiopians and, more recently, Ugandans have been discovered, who, without the benefit of prayer books or religious leaders, have been clinging to aspects of traditional Judaic practices. They possibly go back to the days of the famous Egyptian Queen Cleopatra who invited mercenary Jewish seamen with their flotilla of Nile riverboats to help her expand south into the Sudan and Ethiopia. Because they were pious, the Hebrews converted their native wives and servants to Judaism, raising their children in the Jewish faith. The majority of these Ethiopian Jews known as Falashas (black Jews) has been absorbed in Israel and are in the process of adapting to full Judaism. The more recently discovered Ugandans have indicated their desire to be restored to full Judaic status.

Several unrelated groups that have been isolated from the Jewish community and that still practice some form of Judaism have been discovered in India; the largest are the Bene Israel and Cochin Jews. They too have made a commitment to live as full Jews; some have already emigrated to Israel. Their origin is unclear, but they appear to date back to 600 C.E. when Middle Eastern Jews were active merchants trading in Asia. Other speculation traces them back to the Ten Lost Tribes of Israel dispersed throughout Asia by the conquering Assyrians. The legend of the Chinese Jews having lived in Kaifeng is appearing to be realistic, with more evidence surfacing of Jews being in China since the eighth century. They probably arrived there under the same commercial impetus that brought Jews to India. There is speculation that they actually trace back to 200 B.C.E., when Jews were active traders on the Silk Road between the Middle East and China.

The return to Judaism is surfacing among descendants of the crypto-Jews (*Marranos*) of Sephardic Jewish origin living in Spain, Portugal, Mexico, Brazil, Peru, and the southwestern United States. Their secret practice of aspects of Judaism, which continued for centuries, is coming out into the open. Their Jewish roots are being rediscovered and many are eager to return to full Judaism. There is also a return to Judaism by other descendants of the Jews affected by the Spanish inquisition. In the seventeenth to eighteenth century, many *Conversos* (new Christians who abandoned Judaism completely) left Portugal to join Jewish communities in Amsterdam and in several Mediterranean cities. Some of these Conversos whose ancestors abandoned Judaism have recently identified themselves as Jews and are returning to Judaic practices.

After almost seventy years of Jewish spiritual and cultural darkness in the former Communist world of the Soviet Union, Russian Jews are increasingly recognizing their Jewish heritage and returning to Judaic religious practices and customs. Second and third generation families who never knew of Judaism are becoming fervent Jews.

There is no stronger testimony to the survivability of Judaism than the behavior of the Jews caught in the Holocaust. First in the ghettos and then in the concentration camps, Jews continued to practice their Judaism under the most difficult conditions. ***Although exposed to unbearably vile physical and mental conditions in the concentration camps, very few survivors abandoned Judaism.***

6
Jewish Population History

Until the modern era, population counts were not very accurate and historians had to develop their estimates of Jewish population based on references to Jews found in the sparse historical documents of each period. In many cases, these documents were written by authors with an anti-Jewish bias, so the numbers may have had been distorted to suit their agenda. As an example, the notorious anti-Semite Apion likely exaggerated the number of Jews in Alexandria, Egypt, to support his posture that there were too many influential Jews living there. At best, population counts documented in history books can only be rough estimates. The population history presented in this section represents the conservative estimates found in other books covering Jewish history. The 4.5 million figure for the year 100 C.E. assumes one million in Babylon, one and a half million in Palestine, a half-million each in Syria, Egypt, and the Roman Empire, and a half-million in the Grecian lands.

The size of the Jewish population varied throughout the ages in relation to the threats to their survival. The low point of 200,000 occurred after the exile to Babylon in 500 B.C.E. It rose significantly during the time of general population growth in the Middle East and Mediterranean areas and when the Hebrew religion represented an attractive alternative to paganism. The insurrections against the Romans in Palestine and Egypt, followed by the rise of Christianity with its powerful politically backed conversion effort caused a rapid decline in the Jewish population. It dropped from 4.5 million in 50 C.E. to 1.5 million in 250 C.E. For the next 1,500 years, it went up and down between 0.9 to 1.5 million. The low points were during the First Crusade, the conversions during the Inquisition period in Spain and Portugal, and the eastern Europe massacres in 1648–49. As soon as the political climate became less brutal in eastern Europe, there was a rapid population growth. It reached a peak of 16.5 million in 1940. The terrible Holocaust took 6 million Jewish lives. The population recovered slowly, only reaching 13 million in 1985 before it started to shrink due to the lower birth rate trend among non-Orthodox Jewish families and the increasing intermarriage rate.

The percentage of Jews is constantly shrinking as a percentage of the total world population. It was estimated to be 2% in the early peak population years of 1000 B.C.E. and 50 C.E. It shrunk to 0.7% in 1940 and is now 0.2%. The percentage of Jews in the United States has dropped from a post-World War II high of 4% to 2% in 1998.

The World Jewish Congress estimates that in 1998 there were 5.6 million Jews in the United States, representing the largest Jewish community in the world. Israel, with its increasing Jewish population aided by immigration and a modest birth rate, was at 4.8 million compared to 4.7 million in 1998. Seven other countries have a Jewish population more than 100,000; France (600,000), Russia (450,000), Canada (360,000), Ukraine (310,000), United Kingdom (300,000), Argentina (230,000), and Brazil (130,0000). A study conducted by the Institute of the World Jewish Congress indicates that if the worldwide assimilation trend continues, the Jewish Diaspora population will be halved within thirty years—from the estimated 8.4 million in 1998 to about 4.4 million. The study determined the breakdown of the religious affiliation of Jews living outside of Israel. It estimated that out of the 8.4 million total Jewish population, there are approximately 3.5 million affiliated with Reform or Conservative Judaism, and there are 1 million Orthodox Jews, of which 350,000 are ultra-Orthodox.

Jewish Population History

Year	Population (million)	Comments
1200 B.C.E.	0.7	Small increase after Joshua's capture of Canaan
1000 B.C.E.	2.0	Due to King David's victories and the impact of the United Kingdom's growth
500 B.C.E.	0.2	Low point after the end of the Kingdom of Israel, the destruction of Judah, and the defections from Judaism during the Babylonian exile
200 B.C.E.	0.5	Previous 300 years were turbulent and nonproductive
100 C.E.	4.5	Dramatic rise due to the effect of Hasmonean Dynasty (Maccabees) rule over Israel, and widespread conversions to Judaism in the Diaspora before the rise of Christianity
300 C.E.	1.5	After the two major rebellions against the Romans and the mass conversions to Christianity
500–1750 C.E.	0.9–1.5	Minimum population occurred during the First Crusade, the Inquisition in Spain, the eastern Europe massacres
1940 C.E.	16.6	Peak Jewish population; dramatic rise from 1750 due to healthier political climate and high birth rates; prior to start of the Holocaust killings
1945 C.E.	11.0	Reflects the six million Jews killed in the Holocaust
1985 C.E.	13.0	Small recovery from low caused by Holocaust
1998 C.E.	13.0	Assimilation and low birth rate nullifies normal population growth

7
Hope for the Future

There is reason to believe that Judaism will endure. Just as Judaism has overcome the many challenges to its survival over the past 4,000 years so too it will overcome the many challenges to its survival in the future. Some changes in Judaism's religious and organizational structure will likely materialize in the future in response to new challenges as has happened over the past two thousand years. For example, polygamy was banished, fathers are no longer able to arbitrarily betroth their infant daughter, and women were granted the right to study Talmud. New leaders will step up to strengthen the religious and cultural bonds that keep the Jewish people together.

Changes are already taking place. Many Conservative congregations have adopted egalitarian religious practices, which has strengthened these congregations. The return to traditional religious practices by many Reform and Reconstructionist temples has resulted in increased religious vitality of their memberships. The Orthodox movement has increased its membership, finding ways to conform to Orthodox religious requirements while enabling its members to live and engage in the modern commercial world. There is a progressive movement developing among the Orthodox community, particularly among well-educated Orthodox women, to find a way for women learned in Judaism and Torah to take a more active role in religious rituals within *halachah* (Jewish laws). Their voice is beginning to be respected in the currently exclusively male Orthodox religious society.

Index

A.D. Gordon, 344, 350
Aaron, 25, 28, 32
Abdullah, King, 362, 386, 391
Abraham, 10–17; legacy to western civilization,16; legacy to Judaism, 17; legacy of Sarah's burial, 17
Adam and Eve, 8
Adenhauer, Konrad, 387
Agudath Israel of America, 221, 237
Ahab, King, 55
Akeda (sacrifice of Isaac), 13
Akiba, Rabbi, 94, 95
Al-Aqsa Mosque, 15, 16, 387
Aliyah, 344–346
Allon, Yigdal, 372, 378
American Civil Liberties Union, 212
American Council for Judaism, 231
American Federation of Labor, 204
American Jewish Committee, 221, 387
American Jewish Congress, 222
Amos, Prophet, 66
Anielewicz, Mordechai, 288, 377
Anti-Defamation League, 226, 246, 250
Anti-Semitism: at the U.S. government level, 250; Austria-Hungary, 150; Charles Lindbergh, 250; Dreyfus case in France, 151; Eastern Europe, 265; France, 151; Germany, 149, 265; Henry Ford, 248; in 1990s, 250; Klu Klux Klan, 248; Poland, 132, 303; Protocols of Elders of Zion, 249; Romania, 151; Russia, 134, 265; Soviet repression, 164; U.S. hate group, 249
Arabs: economic-based antagonism, 363; Palestinian refugees, 381; peace process problems, 434; violence, 364

Arafat, Yassir, 399, 400, 406–408
Aramaic (use), 63
Assad, Hafez el, 394
Assyria, 54, 57, 58
Auschwitz, 278–283, 299–300, 329

B'nai B'rith, 223; founding, 192
Baal Shem Tov, Rabbi, 136, 427
Babi Yar, 283
Babylonia, 60, 62
Badge of Shame, 114
Balfour Declaration, 159, 200, 338
Bar Kochba Rebellion, 94, 99
Baruch, Bernard, 199
Begin, Menachem, 371, 396–401
Begun, Iosef, 175, 428
Belzec, 281, 283
Ben-Gurion, David, 350, 368–370, 373–375, 379, 383, 385, 407
Bene Israel, 435
Benjamin, Judah, 198, 243
Bergen-Belsen, 279, 299, 301
Berger, Rabbi Elmer, 231
Bergson, Peter, 322
Bernadotte, Count, 379, 380
Bet Din, 93; canonizes Bible, 93; establishes dietary law, 98
Betar, 350
Bethlehem: Rachel's tomb, 18; Jesus nativity, 88
Bible: authorship, 41; canonized, 93; corroboration of biblical events, 22; creation story, 7; enemies in the wilderness, 33; flood, 9; Garden of Eden, 8; justice, 37; sacrificial laws, 36; slave treatment, 37
Bielski: partisans, 289; Tuvia, 289
Bigotry: against Judah Benjamin, 243;

441

against Leo Frank, 246; by General Grant, 244; in nineteenth century, 242; in twentieth century, 244
Birkenau, 282
Birobidzhan, 166
Black Death, 115, 122
Black-Jewish Relations, 211
Brand, Joel, 307
Brandeis, Louis D., 161, 203, 230
Bricha, 304, 369
Brit Shalom, 252
Bronfman, Charles, 206
Bronfman, Edgar, 228
Buber, Martin, 352
Buchenwald, 266, 279, 301
Bunch, Ralph, 381
Bund, 165, 343

Camp David, 397
Canaan, 10, 11, 21, 26, 29–33, 44; living in Canaan, 46
Cardozo, Benjamin, 203
Caro, Joseph, 342
Carter, Jimmy, 397
Cave of Machpelah, 17
Chanukah, 78
Chasidic Judaism, 219; birth, 136
Chelmno, 281, 283
Chinese Jews, 435
Chmielnicki, Bogdan, 132, 284, 422
Christianity: Christian vs. Jewish faith, 91; Jewish rejection of Christianity, 91; link to Judaism, 90; New Testament, 87; rise of Christianity, 86; spread of Christianity, 85
Clifford, Clark, 235
Clinton, William, 405, 407, 408
Cochin Jews, 435
Columbus, Christopher, 125, 187
Concentration Camps: German, 266, 277, 278; Russian, 275
Conservative Judaism, 141, 217, 430, 433, 438
Conversos, 122, 187, 189, 436
Covenant with God, 12, 13
Creation Story, 7

Crémieux, Adolphe, 147, 343
Crusades, 15, 120, 121, 421
Crypto-Jews, 122, 435
Cyrus, King, 63

D'Amato, Alfonse, 253
Dachau, 266, 279, 299, 301
David, King, 49–50; legacy, 50
Dayan, Moshe, 366, 393, 395, 397
Death Camps, 280; statistics, 283
Deborah (ancient Judge), 47
Deir Yassin, 372, 383
Diaspora, 85, 93, 421; definition, 86
Doctor's Plot, 172
Dome of the Rock, 15, 16, 360
Douglas, William, 238
Drancy, 280
Dreyfus, Alfred, 151, 154
Dubinsky, David, 205

Egypt: migration to Egypt, 21; unfavorable conditions for Hebrews, 22–23; see Exodus
Eichmann, Adolf, 272, 316, 388
Einhorn, Rabbi David, 197
Eisenhower, Dwight, 302, 302, 330
Einstein, Albert, 200–201, 264
Eizenstat, Stuart, 253
Elijah, Prophet, 44, 55, 65, 66
Elijah the Goan, Rabbi, 137
Elohim, 26, 42, 53
England, 111, 121, 124, 146, 159–161, 268–270, 303, 312, 360–365, 387
Entebbe, 396
Eretz Yisrael, 94, 336
Evian Conference, 269
Exilarch, 104–105
Exodus from Egypt, 21–23, 26; democracy during exodus, 28; enemies in the wilderness, 33–34; false spy report, 31; forty years in the wilderness, 31; golden calf, 33; rebellions in the wilderness, 32; route, 29–30; when it occurred, 27; who participated, 29
Exodus, Ship, 305, 369

Ezekial, Prophet, 62, 69
Ezra, Moses ibn, 118
Ezra, Scribe, 41, 71–73, 74, 425

Falashas, 401, 404, 435
False Messiahs, 128–130
Farrakhan, Louis, 212, 251
Fatah, 403
Fertile Crescent, 9
Feydayeen, 387
Final Solution: countries that resisted, 291; in action, 277–285; planning, 272–276
Fisher, Max, 240
Ford, Henry, 152, 222, 248
France, 112, 115, 125, 144, 147, 151, 279, 286, 387, 388
Frank, Leo, 246–247
Frankel, Rabbi Zechariah, 141, 427
Frankfurter, Felix, 203, 234
Frankl, Victor, 307, 308
Frumkin, Ester, 165, 168

Gabirol, Solomon ibn, 118
Garden of Eden, 8
Gedaliah, 61; Fast of Gedalia, 61
Geiger, Rabbi Abraham, 141, 427
Gemara, 96–98
General Zionists, 349
Geniza (Judaica storage facility), 217
Gentiles Who Saved Jews, 294–297
Germany, 112, 115, 127, 138–143, 149, 180; see Holocaust, Nazism
Gershom, Rabbi, 116
Ghetto: during Holocaust, 274, 278; life in Middle Ages, 115; origin of name, 115; Warsaw Ghetto, 288
Gideon, 47
Gilgal, 45
Goan of Vilna, 137, 427
Goering, Hermann, 272, 316–319
Goldberg, Arthur, 202, 204, 390; Goldberg Commission, 329
Golden Age in Spain, 117–119
Gompers, Samuel, 199, 204
Grand Mufti, 351, 363, 364

Grant, Ulysses, 244
Gratz Brothers, 196
Great Assembly, 74, 75, 81
Great Britain; see England

Hadassah, 224, 238, 358, 373
Haganah, 305, 364, 366, 371, 373
Halachah, 98, 101
Halevi, Judah, 118
Hamas, 402
Ha-Nasi, Rabbi Judah, 95
Harrison, Earl, 301, 302, 412
Hashomer Hatzair, 350, 359
Haskalah Movement, 147–148, 153
Hasmonean Dynasty, 77, 79–82
Havlagah (self-restraint), 364
Hebrew Immigrant Aid Society, 208
Hebrew Language, 346, 347
Hebron, 14, 17, 364
Hecht, Ben, 325
Hellenism, 75–77
Helsinki Human Rights, 174, 175
Herod, King, 83, 84
Herzl, Theodor, 153–155, 386, 428
Hezballah, 403
Hezekiah, King, 58
HIAS, 208
Hillel, 85, 89, 425; organization, 223
Hillman, Sidney, 205
Hillquit, Morris, 204
Himmler, Heinrich, 272, 276, 316
Hirsch, Rabbi Raphael, 142, 427
Histadrut, 347, 350, 355
Hitler, Adolf, 150, 262–265, 272
Holding Camps, 279
Holocaust: American response, 320; background, 261; brutal treatment, 283; criticism of American response, 327; death camps, 280; deniers, 330; introduction (overview), 259; lesson, 260; statistics, 283, 298; suppression of news, 323; survival analysis, 306; U.S. State Department obstructionism, 321
Holland, 114, 124, 189

443

Hopwood, Ernest, (poem), 337
Hosea, Prophet, 66
Hussein, King, 387, 389, 390, 408
Hyskos, 21, 22

Inquisition, Spanish, 122–123, 125
Intifada, 402
Iraqi Atomic Reactor, 398
Irgun, 371, 373, 397
Isaac, 13
Isaiah, Prophets, 67–68
Ishmael, 13, 17
Islam, 102, 104, 117
Israel ben Eliezer, Rabbi, 136
Italy, 115, 125, 144, 146

Jabotinsky, Vladimir, 160, 350, 351
Jackson-Vanik Amendment, 173
Jacob, 18, 20; becomes Israel, 19; daughter Dinah, 20; sons and grandsons, 19; wives, 18
Jacobson, Edward, 234
Jacobson, Marion, 238
Javits, Jacob, 210
Jehu Dynasty, 55
Jeremiah, Prophet, 68
Jericho, 45
Jeroboam, King, 55
Jerusalem, 14, 45, 50, 53, 56–60, 338, 372–374, 377–381, 390, 408
Jesus: birth, 88; death, 89; historical information, 87; ministry, 88
Jethro Legacy, 31
Jewish Agency, 314, 350, 352, 370
Jewish Brigade, 365–366
Jewish Legion, 351
Jewish National Fund, 348
Jewish Physicists, 200
Jewish Population History, 437–439
Jewish War Veterans (JWV), 224; founding 196
Jewish Welfare Board, 199
Jews in America: arrival, 187–190; Columbus connection, 187–189; from Eastern Europe, 193; from Germany, 191; Sephardic Jews, 189, 214
Jezebel, 55
Johanan ben Zakkai, Rabbi: establishes Bet Din, 92; saves Judaism, 92, 425
Joint Distribution Committee (JDC), 159; supports Holocaust survivors, 208, 310–311; World War I relief effort, 159
Jonah, Prophet, 68
Jonathan (Maccabee), 79
Joseph, 20–21; historical role, 21
Joseph, Rabbi Jacob, 218
Joshua, 44, 424
Josiah, King, 59, 425; religious reformation, 59
Judah the Maccabee, 79
Judaism: Ashkenazi, 112; Chasidic, 136, 219; Conservative, 141, 217; Historical, 141; Orthodox, 142, 218; Reconstructionist, 220; Reform, 140, 215; Sephardic, 189, 214; spread of Judaism, 85
Judenrat, 275
Judges (biblical), 47, 424

Ka'aba (*Black Stone in Mecca*), 102
Kabbalah, 128, 342
Kaplan, Kivi, 212
Kaplan, Rabbi Mordecai, 214, 220, 428
Kastner, Rudolf, 307
Khazars, 112
Kibbutz, 354; established, 344
Kibbutz Negba, 377
Kielce, 303
King, Martin Luther, 238
Kingdom of Israel, 54–56
Kingdom of Judah, 56–62
Kissinger, Henry, 240, 395
Klu Klux Klan, 247, 248
Klutznik, Philip, 223
Knesset, 349, 385, 386, 395, 396
Kohler, Rabbi Kaufmann, 216
Kosygin, Alexei, 173
Kotel, 14–16, 433
Kristallnacht, 266; Jewish reaction, 267

Kulanu (*all of us*), 226

Labor Party, 391, 395, 396, 404, 407
League of Nations, 15, 201, 339
Lebanon, 382, 385; war, 399–401
Lehman, Herbert, 210
Levi, Primo, 284
Levy, Commander Uriah, 197
Levy, Rabbi Richard, 216
Liberation: by Americans, 301; by Bricha, 304; by British, 303; by Russians, 299; of hidden Jews, 304
Likud Party, 396, 404, 407
Lincoln, Abraham, 198, 244
Lindbergh, Charles, 199, 250
Long, Breckinridge, 321–322
Lubovich, 219
Luria, Isaac, 342
Luther, Martin, 113

Madrid Peace Conference, 404
Magnes, Judah, 352
Maimonides, Moses, 118, 426
Majdanek, 281, 283
Malachi, Prophet, 70
Manasseh, King, 59
Mandate, 233, 352, 353, 360, 372, 376
Marranos, 122, 125, 187, 189, 435
Marshall, George, 234–235
Marshall, Louis, 164, 199, 210, 212, 221, 246
Mattathias (Maccabee), 78
Mecca, 102, 104
Medina, 103, 104
Mein Kampf, 169, 262, 264
Meir, Golda, 171, 391, 395
Mendelssohn, Moses, 138–143, 427
Mengele, Joseph, 284
Mesopotamia, 9–10
Messiahs: European false messiahs, 128–30; King David's lineage, 51; prophet references, 65–67, 70; Jesus, 88–91
Micah, Prophet, 67
Midrash, 99
Mishnah, 96

Mizrachi, 350
Monsky, Henry, 223
Montefiore, Moses, 146–147, 343
Moshav, 355
Morais, Rabbi Sabato, 197, 217
Morgenthau, Henry, 295, 301, 311
Moses, 24, 424; forbidden to enter promised land, 26; Golden Rule, 36; greatest Prophet, 26; left out of Passover Haggadah, 39; legacy, 35–38; Mosaic Code, 36; selected as liberator, 25
Moses ibn Ezra, 118
Moslems: Shiite, 103; Sunni, 103
Mount Moriah: holy to Jews, 14; holy to Muslims, 15; political issue, 16
Mount Scopus, 373
Mount Sinai, 25, 30
Mubarak, Hosni, 399, 407
Muhammad, 13, 15, 102; negative attitude towards Jews, 103
Muslim World: affect on Jewish life, 104; control of Spain, 117; rise in power, 102

NAACP (Jewish support), 211, 212
Nagdela, Samuel ibn, 118
Napoleon, 135, 144–145
Nasser, Gamal Abdal, 387–391
National Council of Women, 226
Nazareth, Jesus nativity, 88
Nazism: final solution in action, 277–287; final solution planning, 272–276; four year plan, 266; kristallnacht, 266; neo-Nazism, 180; rise, 261–263
Nebuchadnezzar, 60–61
Nehemiah, 73–74, 425
Netanyahu, Benjamin, 407–409
Netanyahu, Joni, 396
New Amsterdam, 189–190
New Testament, 87–88, 89
Niles, David, 234–235
Nixon, Richard, 239–240, 394, 413
Noah, 9
Nobel Peace Prize, 398, 406

North American Conference on
   Ethiopian Jews (NACOEJ), 226
Nudel, Ida, 175–176, 428
Nuremberg: laws, 264, 267; trial,
   315–318; verdict, 318–319

Oglethorpe, James, 190
Olympics Massacre, 392
Omri Dynasty, 54
Operation Magic Carpet, 386
Operation Moses, 401
Operation Solomon, 404
Oppenheimer, Robert, 200–201
Oral Torah, 72, 95
Organization for Rehabilitation Through
   Training (ORT), 226
Orthodox Judaism, 142, 218
Oslo Accords, 405
Oswiecim; see Auschwitz
Ottoman Empire, 339, 362

Paassen, Pierre van, 411
Pale of Settlement, 134–135
Palestine Liberation Organization
   (PLO), 388, 403
Palestinian Nationalism: evolution,
   362–363; intifada, 402–403; 1937
   violence, 364
Palmach, 365, 366, 372, 395
Paris Peace Conference, 163–164
Patriarchs, 10–21, 100
Paul (Saul of Tarses), 89–90
Peres, Shimon, 404, 405, 406, 407
Pharisees, 80, 81, 82, 85, 87, 88
Philistines, 47
Pinsker, Leo, 153
Poale Zion, 168, 349
Pogroms, 133, 149, 266, 285, 303
Poland: migration of Jews from
   Germany, 127; righteous gentiles
   aided Jews, 294; seventeenth
   century oppression, 132–133; see
   Holocaust, Pogroms
Pollard, Jonathan, 253–254, 408–409
Pontious Pilate, 84
Popes: Clement VI, 122; Clement VII,
129; Gregory, 121; Innocent III,
121; John XXIII, 294; Paul II, 179;
Pius IX, 147, 149; Pius XII, 179,
293, 324
Portugal, 126–127, 189, 294
Prophets, 64–70, 424; Moses, 26
Protocols of the Elders of Zion, 152
Provence (France), 112, 126

Rabin, Yitzhak, 395–396, 404–407
Rachel's Tomb, 18
Ramses II, 23, 27
Rashi, Rabbi, 98, 116, 426
Rathenau, Walter, 262
Reconstructionist Judaism, 220
Red Sea, 29
Reed Sea, 29
Reform Judaism: in Europe, 140–141; in
   the United States, 215–217
Refuge, 268–271, 285–287
Refusniks, 173–178, 428
Rehabilitation (Holocaust), 310–311
Religious Poets, 118
Religious Rituals: aliyah (ascent to
   Torah reading), 344; ancestral
   groupings (Kohenim, Levi, Israel),
   25; burial practices, 17; candelabra,
   40; Chanukah, 78, 99; dietary laws,
   36; egalitarian practices, 218;
   Elijah and the coming of the
   Messiah, 55; Ephraim and
   Manasseh blessing, 20; evening
   prayer, 18; Fast of Gedaliah, 61;
   koshering, 19; matzah, 28;
   mezuzah, 38; mitzvah, 38; Mosaic
   Code (commandments), 35;
   orthodox seating arrangements,
   215; Passover, 28, 40; patrilineal
   vs. matrilineal descent, 216; prayer
   for return to Jerusalem, 338; Rosh
   Hashanah, 40; Sabbath holy day,
   74; Shavuot, 40; Shema, (Hear O
   Israel prayer), 38; Sheva B'rachot
   (7 wedding blessings), 41; shiva
   (mourning period), 41; shofar, 153;
   Succoth, 40; tephillin, 38, 41; Tisha

B'Av, 60; tombstone, 18; Yom Kippur, 40
Resettlement: in Palestine, 313, 403; in the United States, 312–313
Resistance to Nazi terror, 288–290
Revelation on Mt. Sinai, 30
Revisionists (Israeli), 350–352
Reigner, Gerhart, 323
Rome, 82–84, 90, 92–94, 111
Roosevelt, Eleanor, 325
Roosevelt, Franklin, 199, 201, 315, 320–323, 327; unsympathetic attitude towards Palestine as haven, 327; winning the war syndrome, 324
Rosenwald, Julius, 207
Ross, Dennis, 409
Rothschild, Edmond, 343
Russia: czarist tyranny, 134–135; migration of Jews from Germany, 127; Pale of Settlement, 134; Russian revolution impact, 159; World War I, 158

Saadiah Goan, Rabbi, 116
Sachsenhausen, 266, 279
Sadat, Anwar el, 392–395; visits Jerusalem, 397; Camp David Peace Treaty, 397–398; assassinated, 399
Sadducees, 80, 81, 82, 87
Sage of Deganya, 344
Samaria, 55
Samaritans, 56
Samson, 47
Samuel, 48
Samuel, Sir Herbert, 360, 363
Sanhedrin, 81
San Remo Conference, 164
Sarah, 11–12, 14; legacy of burial,14
Satmar Chasidim, 219
Saul, King, 48
Schechter, Rabbi Solomon, 217–218, 427; discovers Geniza, 217
Schindler, Oskar, 296–297
Schindler, Rabbi Alexander, 216
Schneerson, Rabbi Joseph, 219, 428

Schwartz, Joseph, 225
Scud Missile Attack, 403–404
Senesh, Hannah, 366–367; poem, 367
Sephardic Jews, 189, 214
Septuagint (Bible in Greek), 76
Settlement Houses, 209
Shabbetai Zevi, 130
Shamir, Yitzhak, 403–404
Shammai, 85, 425
Shaprut, Hasdai ibn, 118
Sharansky, Natan, 175, 176–178; in Israel, 402
Sharon, Ariel, 394, 400–401
Shechem, 21, 56
Shiite Muslims, 103
Shilo, 47, 48
Shoah, 259
Shulhan Aruk, 342
Silver, Rabbi Abba Hillel, 231
Simon Wiesenthal Center, 227, 253
Sinai War, 387
Six Day War, 388–391
Slavery, Biblical Treatment, 37
Slepak, Vladimir, 174–175, 428
Sobibor, 281, 283
Sodom and Gomorrah, 12
Solomon, King, 51–52
Solomon, Haym, 196–197
Soloveichiks, Rabbis, 218
Sonnenborn, Rudolf, 379
Soviet Jews: American political support, 237–241; Communist repression, 167–168, 171–172; Jackson-Vanik Amendment, 239–240; Refusniks, 173–178; Yiddish forbidden, 165
Spain: aided Holocaust survivors, 291; expulsion, 125–126; Golden Age, 117–119; initial migration, 111; inquisition, 122–123, 187, 189; Sephardic heritage, 112
Spingarn, Arthur, Joel, 212
St. John, Robert, 411–412
St. Louis, Ship, 271
Stalin, 163, 165, 167, 173, 175
State of Israel: birth, 368–375; British disappointments, 360–361; culture,

356; early pioneers, 342; education, 356; first fifty years, 385–409; health care, 357; Hebrew language unifying force, 346; introduction (overview), 337–341; revisionist history, 383; seeds of turmoil, 361; U.S. recognition, 234–236; vital haven, 434
Stein, Jacob, 240
Stern: Abraham Stern, 371; Stern Gang, 371, 380
Stone, Mickey (David Marcus), 378
Struma, Ship, 270
Stuyvesant, Peter, 189
Sunni Muslims, 103
Supreme Court Justices: Brandeis, 203, 205; Cardozo, 203; Frankfurter, 203; Goldberg, 204
Survival: comparison with other peoples, 418; current survival efforts, 430–432; current threats to survival, 423; defensive reaction to intolerance, 430; first 2,000 years, 419; great leaders, 424; hope for the future, 440; interdenominational conflict challenges, 433; recent survivability evidence, 435; second 2,000 years, 421; strong belief in Judaic values, 428
Syria, 337, 352, 361, 362, 377, 385, 388–390, 394, 399–401, 404
Szold, Henrietta, 224, 352, 358

Talmud, 95–98; Aggada, 99; Babylonian, 97, 429; Gemara, 96; Jerusalem, 98; Halachah, 98; Midrash, 99; Mishnah, 96; modern, 137; place in history, 100
Temple Mount; see Mount Moriah
Temple in Jerusalem: destruction, 60; initial building, 51; rebuilding, 63; second destruction, 92
Ten Commandments, 35
Ten Lost Tribes, 25, 37, 435
Ten Plagues, 28

The Golden Rule, 36
Theresienstat, 275
Tisha B'Av, 60
Torah: authorship, I–25; oral, 72
Touro, Synagogue, 190
Touro, Cantor Isaac, 190
Touro, Judah, 207
Treblinka, 281, 283, 288
Trotsky, Leon, 165
Truman, Harry, 412–413; recognizes the State of Israel, 234–236
Trumpeldor, Joseph, 350, 351, 352
Twelve Tribes of Israel, 19

United Jewish Appeal (UJA), 227, 311
United Jewish Kingdom: collapse, 51–54; King David, 49–51; King Saul, 48; King Solomon, 51–52
United Nations, 233, 234
United States: anti-Semitic State Department bias, 200, 321; civil rights, 210; Civil War, 197; great depression period, 205; labor leaders, 204; motion picture industry, 213; opening up the west, 195; philanthropy, 206; Revolutionary War, 196; social welfare organizations, 208; societal benefits and rights, 202; Supreme Court Justices, 202; Vietnam War, 201; World War I, 198; World War II, 199
Untermeyer, Samuel, 199
Uzzia, King, 58

Vaad Leumi (executive council), 353
Vatican: attitude towards Holocaust, 293; self appraisal, 179
Vespasian, Roman General, 92
Vietnam War, 201–202
Vladimir Volynsk (Ludmir), 284
Volcker Commission, 253

Wailing Wall; see Western Wall
Wallenberg, Raoul, 295–296
Wandering Jews, 422

Wannsee Conference, 273
War of Independence, 376–381
War of Attrition, 391
War Refugee Board, 287, 295, 324
Warsaw Ghetto Uprising, 288–289
Weizmann, Dr. Chaim, 160–161, 350; elected President of the State of Israel, 385; influences President Truman, 234–235
Western Wall, 14–16, 381, 389, 433
Wexner, Leslie, 206
White Paper on Palestine, 268, 270, 304, 320
Wiesel, Elie, 174
Williams, Roger, 190
Wingate, Orde, 410–411
Wise, Rabbi Isaac Mayer, 215, 427
Wise, Rabbi Stephen J., 199, 210; establishes "Free Synagogue," 210; NAACP fundraiser, 212; organizes World Jewish Congress, 228; suppresses Holocaust news, 323; Zionist advocate, 230
World Jewish Congress, 228, 253
World War I, 158–162, 198–199, 351
World War II, 169, 199–201, 365–367
Wye River Accord, 407–409

Yad Mordechi, 377
Yahweh, 38, 42, 53
Yehuda, Eliezer ben, 347
Yishuv (Jewish controlled region): in Palestine, 352; in Poland, 170
YMCA, 207
YMHA, 208
Yom Kippur War, 392–395
Young Israel Synagogue, 218
Youth Aliyah, 346

Zechariah, Prophet, 70
Zedekia, King, 60–61
Zephania, Prophet, 69
Zion Mule Corps, 160, 351, 352
Zionism: birth, 153–155; communist suppression, 168, 171; congresses, 155
Zionist Organizations: in Israel, 349–352; in the U.S., 229–232
Zunz, Leopold, 141, 427